OXFORD
UNIVERSITY PRESS

Great Clarendon Street, Oxford OX2 6DP
United Kingdom

Oxford University Press is a department of the University of Oxford.
It furthers the University's objective of excellence in research, scholarship,
and education by publishing worldwide. Oxford is a registered trade mark of
Oxford University Press in the UK and in certain other countries

First published 1984
This edition 2010
Reprinted 2012

British Library Cataloguing in Publication Data
Data available

Library of Congress Cataloging in Publication Data
Data available

ISBN 978-0-19-928339-2

Printed and bound by CPI Group (UK) Ltd, Croydon, CR0 4YY

THE POLITICS OF
THE POLICE

The University of Law, 133 Great Hampton Street, Birmingham B18 6AQ
Telephone: 01483 216041   Email: library-birmingham@law.ac.uk

Birmingham I Bristol I Chester I Guildford I London I Manchester I York

For Toby, Charlotte, Ben, and Joanna

EPIGRAPHS

He who lets himself in for politics, that is, for power and force as means, contracts with diabolical powers and for his action it is not true that good can follow only from good and evil only from evil, but that often the opposite is true. Anyone who fails to see this is, indeed, a political infant.

Max Weber, 'Politics as a Vocation'

If the Lord does not guard the city, the watchman keeps watch in vain.

Psalm 127

What is good? … Only to do justice, and to love mercy, and to walk humbly with your God.

Micah, VI, v:8

The romance of the police force is … the whole romance of man. It is based on the fact that morality is the most dark and daring of conspiracies. It reminds us that the whole noiseless and unnoticeable police management by which we are ruled and protected is only a successful knight-errantry.

G. K. Chesterton, *The Defendant*

Crime isn't a disease, it's a symptom. Cops are like a doctor that gives you aspirin for a brain tumour, except that the cop would rather cure it with a blackjack.

Raymond Chandler, *The Long Goodbye*

CONTENTS

PART III SOCIOLOGY OF POLICING

PART IV LAW AND POLITICS

PREFACE TO THE FOURTH EDITION

The politics of policing, like everything else, has been fundamentally transformed since I wrote the first edition of this book, in the last millennium, in the Orwellian year of 1984. Then the police were subject to a storm of political conflict and controversy. During the 1984–5 miners' strike they were in equal measure reviled by the left and revered by the right. Labour politicians such as Jack Straw, Paul Boateng, and Peter Hain, together with future Labour politicians such as Harriet Harman and Patricia Hewitt (then prominent in the civil liberties movement), campaigned to limit police power and autonomy, and sought to subject the police to control by democratically elected local government. This sharp polarization of political perspectives on policing was especially shocking, as it came after some decades in the middle of the twentieth century when the British police seemed to stand above politics, as consensual symbols of national pride and solidarity.

By the time I wrote the second edition, in 1992, policing had become less intensely politicized. The love affair between the Conservatives and the police cooled, as ministers began to wonder why there seemed to have been no pay-off in terms of falling crime rates for the special treatment the police had received during the 1980s relative to the rest of the public sector. On the other side, Labour, in its new realist guise under Neil Kinnock and John Smith, sought to recapture lost ground in the politics of law and order by courting the police. The then Shadow Home Secretary, Tony Blair, successfully won back public confidence for Labour when he promised to be 'tough on crime and tough on the causes of crime'. For their part, police chiefs had come to realize the urgent need to regain popular support, which had been eroded by a succession of scandals together with increasing public concern about crime and disorder. In the early 1990s there was a growing consensus between political and police elites about the need to reform policing in a community-oriented direction, aiming to ensure efficiency and quality of service.

All this changed in 1993, when Conservative Home Secretary Kenneth Clarke launched a package of police reforms, continued by his successor, Michael Howard. They were predicated on an explicit narrowing of police priorities to 'catching criminals', and a reconstruction of police organization and management on 'businesslike' lines to ensure the economic achievement of the government's performance targets.

The New Labour government elected in 1997 broadly accepted the changes in police governance of the mid-1990s, even though they were almost the obverse of the model of accountability for which many of them had campaigned during the 1980s. However, Labour placed policing in a different context with the Crime Reduction Programme and the Crime and Public Order Act of 1998. These required the police to work in partnership with local government and other social agencies to produce evidence-led analyses of local crime and disorder problems, and develop 'joined-up' strategies for their solution, regularly monitoring their success.

The problems of police discrimination, corruption, and abuse, which were at the heart of political conflict in the 1980s, had not gone away by any means, and the media continued to highlight recurring police scandals in these areas. But they had become relatively submerged by an overriding and consensual concern with security and protection from the risks of crime and disorder. As Jack Straw rightly pointed out, the fact that Stephen Lawrence's murder became the emblematic *cause célèbre* of the 1990s indicated a sharp contrast with the early 1980s. During the urban disorders of the 1980s the key complaint was discriminatory policing of young black men as suspects (which remains a potent concern, as indicated by the controversies around stop and search). However, the demand for effective and equal protection of ethnic minorities against crime, starkly symbolized by Stephen Lawrence's brutal, unsolved murder, had come to the political forefront. There was a new consensus around crime control as the priority for policing, with partisan conflict raging about which party delivered this most effectively.

In the first decade of the new millennium this fundamental cross-party consensus on the politics of tough law and order continued, but with more febrile conflict over delivery. The heat of debate about security and policing was intensified by the fears engendered by the tragic terror attacks first in the USA on 9/11/2001, and then in other countries including the London bombings of July 2005. These came on top of continuing concerns about more routine forms of crime and disorder, ratcheted up by an ever-more ferocious tabloid press. In this volatile and contradictory political maelstrom issues of police malpractice and injustice have been subordinated to the clamour for toughness, although they have certainly not disappeared. Evidence-led toughness on the causes of crime, manifest in New Labour's optimistic early years, increasingly fell victim to a parade of the publicity-seeking short-term initiatives that Tony Blair once referred to as 'tough, with immediate bite' (Newburn and Reiner 2007: 335). The centralizing, managerialist, 'businesslike' micro-management of policing initiated under the Tories continued with a vengeance under New Labour. So too has the pluralization of policing, with an increasing role for the private sector and for 'responsibilized' citizens.

What continues to be overlooked by the competitive conflict to deliver policing solutions for crime and insecurity is the wider social context. This is bracketed out as the focus narrows to what works in policing—the pursuit of magic-bullet strategies like 'zero tolerance' that hold out the deceptive promise of a technical solution to the problems of crime and disorder. The analysis of the history of policing in this book argues that, while police strategy is important, the successful legitimation of the British police in the nineteenth and early twentieth centuries depended upon the wider social process of increasing social inclusion and the spread of citizenship. The apparent decline in the effectiveness and legitimacy of the police since the late 1960s was only superficially due to failures of police policy and tactics. The key changes were in the wider social context, above all in the shift to neo-liberal, free-market economic policies, with a reversal of the general (if slow and spasmodic) trend to increasing social equality and solidarity that had prevailed since the eighteenth-century Enlightenment. Interdependent with the recent transformation of political economy and social structure, there has occurred a cultural revolution, the growth of an increasingly rugged individualism and neo-social Darwinist celebration of the survival of the fittest. Policing an ever-more fragmented and pluralistic post- or late modern world, riven by inequality and divisions engendered by neo-liberal economics, has become an increasingly fraught enterprise. The economic collapse since 2007 is likely to exacerbate this further, in the absence of the social democratic, welfarist, and Keynesian policies which provided the social security that is the necessary underpinning of public safety.

This book's review of the history, functioning, and governance of the British police suggests that there is a fundamental paradox of policing, encapsulated in the quotations in the frontispiece. Policing is about the basic antinomies of human nature and social organization. As elaborated in Chapter 1, policing is the aspect of control in any social relationship or group that is directed at the identification and emergency rectification of conflict and deviation. Its resource in accomplishing this is legitimate force, and its mode of deployment is surveillance with the threat of sanctions. Policing inherently operates with dirty hands. It uses morally dubious means to achieve the overriding imperative of preserving and reproducing social order. In divided and complex societies, however, there is unlikely to be agreement about the borderline between order and oppression. One side's reasonable and necessary force is the other's unjust tyranny. The police have developed in modern societies as the specialist organization charged with the maintenance of order, and entrusted with the capacity to deploy the legitimate force that states monopolize. This 'diabolical power' is a perpetual scandal in liberal democracies which—notwithstanding the inequalities and conflicts generated by complex market societies—purport to represent popular will and the rule of law. The concern of politics in a just society should be with minimizing the need to resort to policing, not to compete in its enhancement as the parties do today.

The paradox is that not all that is policing lies in the police, to paraphrase Durkheim on the contract. The police will appear more successful the less they are actually necessary. The sources of order lie outside the ambit of the police, in the political economy and culture of a society. To the extent that these provide most people with meaningful and rewarding lives, conflict, crime, and disorder will be relatively infrequent. Subtle, informal social controls, and policing processes embedded in other institutions, regulate most potential deviance. When these informal control processes are successful, the police will appear highly effective in crime prevention, and deal effectively and legitimately with the crime and disorder that do occur. The police stand as romantic symbols of order and morality, 'knights errant' ever ready to protect against threats.

The last three decades of the twentieth century were characterized by a set of profound transformations. Social and economic inequality and exclusion increased sharply and rapidly, reversing the post-Enlightenment slow march of solidarity and justice. The popular and political reactions to the attendant dramatic rise of crime and disorder were increasingly punitive and harsh. Policing became pressured to have zero tolerance of the socially marginal and outsiders. The war of all against all that is inherent in laissez-faire economics enjoins people to become ever-more ruthlessly assertive defenders of purely individual interest. In short, the three pillars of the good life identified by the prophet Micah, justice, mercy, and humility, have been undermined. With the conditions of civility eroded, 'the watchman keeps watch in vain'. Good policing may help preserve social order: it cannot produce it. Yet increasingly this is what is being demanded of the police. As the epigraph from Raymond Chandler puts it, policing is at best symptom relief like aspirin. It cannot substantially reduce our social tumours, let alone eradicate them. And it always leaves unwelcome secondaries.

In the earlier editions of this book, I acknowledged my intellectual debts to a host of scholars from whom I have gained what understanding of policing I have (the mis-understandings are all my own). In the quarter century since the first edition of this book the field of policing research has grown beyond the capacity of even dedicated specialists to keep abreast of. In 1979 Simon Holdaway edited a collection of papers entitled *The British Police* that could claim to include contributions from almost all the researchers then active in the field. In recent years not only has Tim Newburn published two editions of a *Handbook of Policing* challenging the bookbinder's art at nearly 1,000 pages, and including 30 chapters by specialists on a large range of aspects of polic-ing, but this is accompanied by a similar-sized volume of forty-five *Key Readings*. That these invaluable encyclopaedic ventures do not exhaust the contemporary field even in Britain is shown by the fact that there is also a burgeoning library of 'handbooks' of similar proportions on specialist aspects of the policing enterprise: *Handbook of Crimi-nal Investigation; Criminal Justice Process, Investigative Interviewing, Knowledge-Based Policing, Crime Prevention and Community Safety*—as well as many others in criminol-ogy more broadly. This means that listing the individual scholars who have inspired me in all the editions would now exhaust my word allowance. I listed eighty-five in the preface to the third edition and eager readers are referred to that; it will at least save it from decay on the shelves. I owe them and many others (especially my Ph.D. supervisor Michael Banton) very much for their inspiration and support over the years.

As with all writers, my most profound debts are highly personal. My children, Toby, Charlotte, and Ben have always stimulated me with fresh, cool ideas, encouragement, and 'when will you get there?'. I am intensely proud of their achievements, and aware that they all could—no doubt will—produce much better books than this one. My wife, Dr Joanna Benjamin, has provided constant encouragement, imagination, intellectual and ethical commitment. My sister Ann and her family have also been an unfailing source of support in good as well as hard times. Finally, our dog, Carina, who took me for refreshing walks that kept me going through the first three editions sadly passed away before this was begun, which hasn't helped my blood pressure.

I owe my original impetus and inspiration for anything I do to my late parents. As the Book of Proverbs (1:8) enjoins, I shall endeavour to hear the moral instruction of my father and not forsake the law of my mother.

August 2009

PART I

POLICING: THEORY AND RESEARCH

1

WATCHING THE WATCHERS: THEORY AND RESEARCH IN POLICING STUDIES

The academic study of policing is just about fifty years old, venerable enough to seem an ancient edifice to most of the growing numbers studying it today, but still fairly young by comparison with most disciplines. Yet it has lately been threatened with fundamental paradigm change, perhaps even extinction, by arguments that the fields of security and governance have been transformed so completely that a change in conceptualization is necessary. These claims will be considered in this chapter, which offers a broad overview of the study of policing. It begins with a discussion of the concepts of police and policing, and the long-term evolution of these processes. Following that, we will review the development of police research, and assess critically the new transformation thesis. Finally, the vexed conceptual relationship between policing and politics will be probed.

WHO ARE THE 'POLICE'? WHAT IS 'POLICING'?

Most research on the police has been concerned primarily with immediate policy matters. Researchers have assumed a taken-for-granted notion of the police and their proper functions (Cain 1979). A particular modern conception has tacitly been taken as inevitable. The police are identified primarily as a body of people patrolling public places in blue uniforms, with a broad mandate of crime control, order maintenance and some negotiable social service functions. Anyone living in a modern society has this intuitive notion of what the police are. However, to understand the nature and role of policing, especially over a broader span of space and time, requires some conceptual exploration of the taken-for-granted idea of police.

Modern societies are characterized by what can be termed 'police fetishism', the ideological assumption that the police are a functional prerequisite of social order so that without a police force chaos would ensue. In fact, many societies have existed without a formal police force of any kind, and certainly without the present model. The police contribution to the control of crime and maintenance of order is debatable, as studies of police effectiveness indicate (see Chapter 5).

It is important to distinguish between the ideas of 'police' and 'policing'. 'Police' refers to a particular kind of social institution, while 'policing' implies a set of processes with specific social functions. 'Police' are not found in every society, and police organizations and personnel can have a variety of shifting forms. 'Policing', however, is arguably a necessity in any social order, which may be carried out by a number of different processes and institutional arrangements. A state-organized specialist 'police' organization of the modern kind is only one example of policing.

SOCIAL CONTROL

The idea of policing is an aspect of the more general concept of social control. Social control is itself a complex and much-debated notion (S. Cohen and Scull 1983; S. Cohen 1985; Sumner 1997; Innes 2003c). In some sociological theories social control is seen broadly as everything that contributes to the reproduction of social order. This makes the concept all-encompassing, virtually coterminous with society. It would include all aspects of the formation of a culture and the socialization of the individuals who are its bearers.

The problem with this broad concept of social control is its amorphousness. It fails to distinguish the specificity of what are ordinarily understood to be control processes: that they are essentially reactive, intended to prevent or respond to threats to social order. As Stan Cohen acerbically expressed it, the broader usage is 'a Mickey Mouse concept', and the term should be restricted to refer to 'the organised ways in which society responds to behaviour and people it regards as deviant, problematic, worrying, threatening, troublesome or undesirable' (Cohen 1985: 1–2).

The idea of social control may be evaluated positively or negatively, according to different political interests and positions. In conservative versions of functionalist sociology, social control was seen as the necessary bulwark of the consensus that underpinned social order. Ensuring adequate control mechanisms in the face of deviance or disintegration was a functional prerequisite of any society, although it was especially hard to accomplish in rapidly changing modern societies.

The development of labelling theory and subsequent radical positions within criminology and the sociology of deviance changed the moral evaluation of social control institutions. From being seen as a necessary protection against deviance, social control came to be regarded as *producing* deviance through labelling and stigmatization (Becker 1963). Social control agents were seen as oppressors to be questioned and opposed (Becker 1967). More structuralist or Marxist versions of critical criminology saw these simple reversals of moral blame as merely making social control agents 'fall-guys' for the inexorable working of a wider structure of power and privilege (Gouldner 1968; McBarnet 1979). All radical analyses see social control at least in part as the oppressive maintenance of the privileged position of dominant groups. More complex critiques, however, see social control as inextricably intertwining the maintenance of universally beneficial order *and* social dominance and oppression: 'parking tickets' *and* 'class repression', as Marenin (1983) expresses it.

THE IDEA OF POLICING

Policing cannot usefully be analysed as coterminous with social control but must be seen as a specific aspect of it. Policing implies the set of activities aimed at preserving the security of a particular social order, or social order in general. That order may be regarded as based on a consensus of interests, or a (manifest and/or latent) conflict of interests between social groups differentially placed in a hierarchy of advantage, or a complex intertwining of the two.

Policing is *aimed* at securing social order, but its effectiveness is always debatable. Policing does not encompass all activities directed at achieving social order. What is specific to policing is the creation of systems of surveillance coupled with the threat of sanctions for discovered deviance—either immediately or by initiating penal processes. The most familiar such system is of course the one denoted by the modern sense of police as discussed above: regular uniform patrol of public space coupled with *post hoc* investigation of reported or discovered crime or disorder.

THE IDEA OF POLICE

Policing thus defined may be carried out by a diverse array of people and techniques, of which the modern idea of police is only one. Indeed the term 'police' itself originally carried a broader connotation than 'policing', let alone the narrow institutional meaning it implies today (Rawlings 1995, 2002, 2008; Zedner 2006). This was exemplified by the 'science of police' which was a broad international movement in the eighteenth and early nineteenth centuries, aimed at maintaining and promoting the 'happiness' of populations (Radzinowicz 1948–69; Reiner 1988; Pasquino 1991; McMullan 1996, 1998; Garland 1997; Neocleous 1998, 2000a, 2000b, 2006; Dubber 2005: chap. 3; Dubber and Valverde 2006).

Policing may be done by a variety of agents: professionals employed by the state in an organization with an omnibus policing mandate—the archetypal modern idea of the police—or by state agencies with primarily other purposes (such as the Atomic Energy Authority Police, parks constabularies, the British Transport Police and other 'hybrid' policing bodies; see Johnston 1992: chap. 6). Police may be professionals employed by specialist private policing firms—contract security—or security employees of an organization whose main business is something else—in-house security (Shearing and Stenning 1987; South 1988; T. Jones and Newburn 1998, 2006; Button 2002, 2006, 2008; Wakefield 2003). Patrol may be carried out by bodies without the full status, powers, equipment or training of the core state police (Hofstra and Shapland 1997; Crawford *et al.* 2005; Johnston 2007b). Policing functions may be performed by citizens in a voluntary capacity within state police organizations (such as the Special

Constabulary; see Leon 1989; M. Gill and Mawby 1990), in association with the state police (such as neighbourhood watch schemes; see Bennett 1990; McConville and Shepherd 1992), or in completely independent bodies (such as the Guardian Angels, and the many vigilante bodies which have flourished at many times and places; see Johnston 1996; Abrahams 1998). Policing functions may be carried out by state bodies with other prime functions, such as the Army, or by employees (state or private) as an adjunct of their main job (such as concierges or bus conductors). Policing may be carried out by technology, such as CCTV cameras (Norris and Armstrong 1999; Sheptycki 2000b; Goold 2004, 2009). Policing may be designed into the architecture and furniture of streets and buildings (R. Jones 2007), as epitomized by Mike Davis's celebrated example of the bum-proof bench (Davis 1990). All these policing strategies are proliferating today, even though it is only the state agency with the omnibus mandate of order maintenance that is popularly understood by the label 'the police'.

THE EVOLUTION OF POLICING

Until modern times, policing functions were carried out primarily as a by-product of other social relationships and by citizen 'volunteers' or private employees. Anthropological studies show that many pre-literate societies have existed without any formalized system of social control or policing. A cross-cultural study of the relationship between legal evolution and societal complexity in a sample of fifty-one pre-industrial societies found that 'elements of legal organisation emerge in a sequence, such that each constitutes a necessary condition for the next' (Schwartz and Miller 1964: 160). Police in the sense of a 'specialized armed force used partially or wholly for norm enforcement' were found in only twenty of the fifty-one societies in the sample (ibid.: 161). These were almost all societies that were sufficiently economically developed to have monetary systems, and with a high degree of specialization including full-time priests, teachers, and official functionaries of various kinds. Police, the study found, appear 'only in association with a substantial degree of division of labour' (ibid.: 166), and are usually preceded by other elements of a developed legal system like mediation and damages.

Specialized policing institutions emerge only in relatively complex societies, but they are not a straightforward reflex of a burgeoning division of labour. Specialist police forces develop hand in hand with social inequality and hierarchy. They are means for the emergence and protection of more centralized and dominant class and state systems.

A valuable review of the anthropological literature concluded that the development of specialized police 'is linked to economic specialization and differential access to resources that occur in the transition from a kinship- to a class-dominated society' (Robinson and Scaglion 1987: 109). During this transition communal policing forms are converted in incremental stages to state-dominated ones, which begin to function as agents of class control in addition to more general social control (Robinson, Scaglion, and Olivero 1994). The complex and contradictory function of contemporary police, as simultaneously embodying the quest for general and stratified order—'parking tickets' as well as 'class repression' (Marenin 1983)—is thus inscribed in their birth process.

British police ideology has always rested upon the myth of a fundamental distinction between their model of community-based policing and an alien, 'Continental', state-controlled system. Conventional histories of the British police attempt to trace a direct lineage between ancient tribal forms of collective self-policing and the contemporary Bobby. Such claims have been characterized aptly as 'ideology as history' (Robinson 1979). It is true that many European systems of police did develop more overtly as instruments of state control (B. Chapman 1970; R. I. Mawby 1991, 2008). Revisionist histories, however, have emphasized the relationship between modern police development and the shifting structures of class and state in Britain as well as the United States and other common law systems. The supposedly benign 'British' model was in any case for home consumption only. A more militaristic and coercive model was from the outset exported to colonial situations, including Ireland (M. Brogden 1987; S. H. Palmer 1988; D. Anderson and Killingray 1991, 1992; Brewer *et al.* 1996; Mulcahy 2008).

Although contemporary patterns of police vary considerably in detail, they have tended to converge increasingly around fundamentally similar organizational and cultural lines, without the qualitative distinctions of kind implied in traditional British police ideology (Bayley 1985; R. I. Mawby 1991, 1999, 2008). This has been facilitated by the emergence of a new international body of technocratic police experts who are responsible for the diffusion of fashions in police thinking around the globe, as witnessed by the recent spread of enthusiasm for 'community policing' strategies (Skolnick and Bayley 1988; Fielding 1995, 2002, 2009; Skogan 2003, 2006; Brogden 1999; Brogden and Nijhar 2005).

POLICE: FUNCTION OR FORCE?

It is problematic to define contemporary police mainly in terms of their supposed function (Klockars 1985). As Bittner has emphasized, the police are called upon routinely to perform a bewildering miscellany of tasks, from controlling traffic to controlling terrorism (Bittner 1970, 1974; Brodeur 2007). This has been a commonplace finding of empirical police research from the outset (as shown in Chapter 5). The uniting feature of the tasks that come to be seen as police work is not that they are aspects of a particular social function, whether it be crime control, social service, order maintenance, or political repression. Rather it is that they all involve 'something that ought not to be happening and about which someone had better do something now!' (Bittner 1974: 30). In other words, policing tasks arise in emergencies, usually with an element of at least potential social conflict. The police may invoke their legal powers to handle the situation, but more commonly they resort to a variety of ways and means to keep the peace without initiating legal proceedings. Nonetheless, underlying all their tactics for peacekeeping is their bottom-line power to wield legal sanctions, ultimately the use of legitimate force. 'A benign bobby ... still brings to the situation a uniform, a truncheon, and a battery of resource charges ... which can be employed when appeasement fails and fists start flying' (Punch 1979b: 116).

The distinctiveness of the police lies not in their performance of a specific social function, but in being the specialist repositories for the state's monopolization of legitimate force in its territory. This does not imply that all policing is about the use of force. On the contrary, 'good' policing has often been seen as the craft of handling trouble without resort to coercion, usually by skilful verbal tactics (Muir 1977; Bayley and Bittner 1984; Norris 1989; Kemp, Norris, and Fielding, 1992).

Nor are the police the only people who can use legitimate force. This remains the right (and in some circumstances the moral duty) of every citizen. There are many occupations in which the potential for the legitimate use of force may arise with a fair degree of frequency, most obviously in the case of private security officers, although their only legal police powers are those of the private citizen. Legitimate force may also regularly need to be wielded by people not exercising a primarily policing role, for example workers in the health or social services handling disturbed patients, or public transport staff dealing with disorder. However, they are not 'equipped, entitled and required to deal with every exigency in which force may have to be used' (Bittner 1974: 35). Indeed, other workers are likely to 'call the cops' at the earliest opportunity in troublesome situations, and use legitimate force themselves only as an immediate emergency measure in the interim.

To sum up, 'policing' is an aspect of social control processes which occurs universally in all social situations in which there is at least the potential for conflict, deviance, or disorder. The 'police', a specialized body of people given primary formal responsibility for legitimate force to safeguard security, is a feature only of relatively complex societies. The police have developed in particular with the rise of modern state forms. They have been 'domestic missionaries' in the historical endeavours of centralized states to propagate and protect a dominant conception of peace and propriety throughout their territories.

This is not to say, however, that they have been mere tools of the state, faithfully carrying out tasks determined from above. Whether this is regarded as legitimate or not, all police forces have been characterized by the discretion exercised by the lowest ranks in the organization, necessitated by the basic nature of police work as dispersed surveillance. The determination of police work in practice is achieved by the interplay of a variety of processes and pressures, and is problematically related to formal policies determined at the top.

Many of these features of modern police organizations are currently under great challenge, and policing is undergoing profound changes in what many commentators have interpreted as a fundamentally new stage of social development. Policing has been increasingly a focus of political controversy over the last half-century, and this has been a factor generating the development of a burgeoning body of research and theoretical analysis.

THE DEVELOPMENT OF POLICING RESEARCH

Police research only began in Britain in the early 1960s. The impetus for research on the police in Britain came from the politics of criminal justice and theoretical developments in criminology, sociology, and law. This paralleled the pressures generating the contemporaneous growth of police research in the USA (S. Walker 2004; Skogan and Frydl 2004: chap. 2; Sklansky 2005: Part II). The underlying context was the rising concern about crime and disorder, and a growing public questioning of authority. The police became increasingly visible, controversial, and politicized in response to these tensions and pressures. Many academics have been motivated primarily by the intellectual project of advancing the analysis of policing as a mode of control and governance. Nonetheless the politicization of law and order in the last thirty years has shaped the trajectory of police research (for a fuller account, see Reiner 1989b, 1992a; Reiner and Newburn 2007).

SOURCES OF POLICE RESEARCH

Police research in Britain has emanated from a variety of sources. These include: academic institutions, official government-related bodies, think-tanks and pressure groups, and journalists.

Academic research

From the 1960s to the 1980s most police research was carried out by academics, in a variety of disciplines including criminology, sociology, social policy, law, history, psychology, and economics. Policing research is a mainstay of the many centres for criminology and criminal justice that have burgeoned around the country since the late 1970s. Academic and professional research journals have proliferated. Textbooks and monographs on policing are being published at such a pace that is no longer possible for even specialists in the field to keep up.

Official police research

The greatest volume of police research today no longer emanates from academe. There has been a rapid growth of research by policy-making bodies and by the police themselves. In the last twenty five years the research of the Home Office Research, Development and Statistics Directorate (formerly the Research and Planning Unit) has become increasingly concerned with policing matters. Before 1979 hardly any of its work touched on policing, but during the 1980s police research became a prominent focus of the Unit's research.

Official government police research is not confined to the Home Office. Local government bodies have sponsored police research. During the 1980s several radical Labour local authorities established police-monitoring groups which collected information on a regular basis about police practices and policy (Jefferson *et al.* 1988), and financed outside research projects by academics. Following the Crime and Disorder Act 1998, local authorities became involved in police research in a rather different way. Earlier local government police research was primarily critical. The new model of research, conducted in conjunction with the police, is policy oriented, directed at achieving the most effective and efficient crime reduction policies through audits of local circumstances.

A number of government-established quangos also became important producers of police research in the 1990s. By far the most influential has been the Audit Commission, which produced a stream of highly influential studies of aspects of police performance aimed at enhancing the value for money of police activities (Audit Commission 1990a, 1990b, 1993, 1996).

Perhaps the most significant growth point in official police research is by the police themselves (Brown and Waters 1993; J. Brown 1996). This takes a variety of forms. Since the 1980s a large number of graduates joined the service, and many serving officers are taking degrees on a seconded or part-time basis. Many officers acquired the skills for conducting research. Occasionally research projects begun by serving police officers as students have resulted in influential publications (Holdaway 1983; M. Young 1991, 1993 are early examples). A significant number of former police officers have become academic specialists in police research (e.g. P. Waddington 1991, 1994 1999a, 1999b; Wright 2002; Williamson 2006, 2008).

As recently as the mid-1980s in-house police research departments were mainly one-or two-person operations with little research expertise. Their function was primarily to collate the statistics and information required for such routine publications as the chief constable's annual report and the design of bureaucratic forms. At best their research projects were 'foregone conclusions', evaluations of pet schemes which were designed never to show failure (Weatheritt 1986). However, an increasing proportion of force research departments produce methodologically sophisticated research on many aspects of policy and practice, sometimes coming to critical conclusions.

Think-tanks and independent research organizations

Independent research organizations, notably the Policy Studies Institute (PSI) and the Police Foundation, have made significant contributions to policing research. The PSI had a distinguished record of research on economic and social issues before its influential first venture into the policing field (1983), and subsequently conducted significant work on other policing topics.

The Police Foundation is a politically independent registered charity with no core government funding. Although it has firm establishment roots (Prince Charles is its president), it has succeeded in maintaining a quality of critical independence and objectivity in its work (Irving and McKenzie 1989; Weatheritt 1986, 1989; Wakefield 2006; Fielding 2009; Thiel 2009; Lloyd and Foster 2009). In addition to a variety of in-house research projects the Police Foundation has sponsored research by academics and by police officers (e.g. Blair 1985).

The Police Foundation and the PSI joined forces in 1994 to establish an independent inquiry entitled *The Role and Responsibilities of the Police.* This was explicitly intended to be an unofficial substitute for the Royal Commission on policing, which many commentators inside and outside the force felt was called for by the increasing controversies surrounding the police and their evident decline in public support. It resulted in a significant research-informed report, and several important publications (Police Foundation/ Policy Studies Institute 1996; Saulsbury *et al.* 1996; Morgan and Newburn 1997).

In addition to these independent research organizations, and other more recent additions such as Policy Exchange (Loveday and Reid 2003; Loveday 2006), several pressure groups and politically aligned think-tanks have generated influential research-based work on the police. They include Liberty (formerly the National Council for Civil Liberties) which, as well as producing regular reviews of new legislation and policy developments, financed work by academics through its research arm, the Civil Liberties Trust (formerly the Cobden Trust). It also commissioned an independent inquiry chaired by Professor Peter Wallington into the policing of the miners' strike in 1984 (McCabe *et al.* 1988). Other examples of police research by politically oriented think-tanks include studies of police accountability by the New Labour-oriented Institute for Public Policy Research (Reiner and Spencer 1993), and work by Conservative-leaning bodies, such as the Institute of Economic Affairs (Dennis 1998; Dennis and Erdos 2005).

Journalists

Since the beginnings of police research in this country in the early 1960s, studies by journalists have made significant contributions to analysis and debate. These include Whitaker 1964; Laurie 1970; Cox *et al.* 1977; Graef 1989; Rose 1992, 1996; Davies 1999b). The hallmark of much of the best journalistic studies has been the ability to probe aspects of police malpractice that academics have seldom dealt with.

CHANGING AGENDAS OF POLICE RESEARCH

The focal concerns of policing research have varied over time, related closely to the changing politics of criminal justice. In earlier surveys of police research in Britain I have suggested that four stages could be distinguished: consensus, controversy, conflict, and contradiction (Reiner 1989b, 1992a). The contradictory stage now seems to have resolved into a period in which research is dominated by a clear (though not unchallenged) crime control agenda (Reiner and Newburn 2007).

The first empirical research on policing by a British academic was Michael Banton's *The Policeman in the Community* (Banton 1964; for recent analyses of this see McLaughlin 2007: chap. 2, Murji 2009). Like almost all writing on the police at that time it was framed within a celebratory mode, and assumed a harmonious view of British society. Its premise that 'it can be instructive to analyse institutions that are working well in order to see if anything can be learned from their success' (Banton 1964: vii) exemplified the *consensus* stage of police research.

During the 1970s and 1980s British police research was increasingly characterized by themes reflecting the growing conflicts around policing. During the *controversy* stage of police research in the late 1960s and early 1970s policing was beset by a flurry of problems, ultimately resulting from growing divisions and declining deference in society generally (see Chapter 3).

Reflecting these tensions, an increasing number of academic researchers began working on the police in the late 1960s and early 1970s. The key theoretical influences were symbolic interactionism and the labelling perspective, which saw policing as an important process in shaping (rather than merely reacting to) the pattern of deviance through the exercise of discretion (Cain 1973; Chatterton 1976, 1979, 1983; Holdaway 1983; Manning 1979, 1997a; Punch 1979a, 1979b).

The introduction to Simon Holdaway's 1979 collection of essays on the British police, which includes examples of most of the research then being conducted, sums up accurately the focal concern: 'one of the basic themes running through this book ... is that the lower ranks of the service control their own work situation and such control may well shield highly questionable practices' (Holdaway 1979: 12).

Research tended to be critical of police practice, whatever its institutional base. While academics, journalists, and pressure groups were concerned primarily with police deviance, official government research pointed out the limitations of policing as a means of controlling crime, reflecting a more general 'nothing works' mood (R. Clarke and Hough 1980, 1984; Morris and Heal 1981; Heal *et al.* 1985. See Chapter 5).

The issues examined in the controversy stage linked directly to the key focus of the *conflict* stage of police research: accountability—who controls policing? This indicated the increasing politicization of policing in the late 1970s and early 1980s, analysed in Chapter 3. It also reflected the growth of radical criminology. Many academic studies of the police in this period were explicitly Marxist (e.g. S. Hall *et al.* 1978; Brogden 1981, 1982, 1987; Jefferson and Grimshaw 1984; Scraton 1985; Grimshaw and Jefferson 1987), and almost all the others (including some Home Office research as well as the work sponsored by radical local authorities) were critical of the police on issues such as racial discrimination. Uniting all the various causes of concern and controversy was a critique of the inadequacy of existing mechanisms for holding the police to account, whether as individuals through the complaints process or the courts, or force policy and operations as a whole through the institutions of police governance (see Chapter 7).

By the late 1980s a new stage of debate and research on policing was emerging, in which a number of *contradictory* tendencies seemed to be in competition. The key theme was the growth of an avowed 'realism', across the political spectrum. Most marked in this country was the new 'left realism' advocated by Jock Young and others (Lea and Young 1984; Kinsey, Lea, and Young 1986). This contrasted itself with what it called the 'administrative criminology' of the Home Office and other parts of the criminal justice policy-making circle, and the 'new right' realism associated most clearly with James Q. Wilson in the USA (Wilson 1975). Although clearly these variants embodied vastly different political and theoretical assumptions, they shared a similar trope of 'realism'.

The espousal of 'realism' reflected wider developments in both criminological theory and criminal justice politics. In criminology it was part of a more general turn away from grand theory. The momentum was towards research of a policy-oriented and managerialist kind. The common premise was that crime was a serious problem above all for the poorer and weaker sections of society, and research should be directed primarily at developing concrete, immediately practicable tactics for crime control.

Police research came increasingly to focus on the search for what works in effective crime control practice, monitoring, and evaluating the policing initiatives that proliferated in the search for greater effectiveness. These innovations have been credited with an important share in crime reduction during the 1990s, especially in the USA. At the harder end of crime control tactics, the much-touted 'zero tolerance' approach, rooted in the idea of 'broken windows' developed by James Q. Wilson and George Kelling (1982, has been popularly seen as the basis of the New York 'miracle' of rapidly declining violence and crime in the 1990s, although these claims are highly questionable (see Chapter 5).

This was paralleled by a new, 'second order', political consensus about law and order which emerged in the 1990s (Downes and Morgan 2007; Reiner 2007a: chap. 5). During the 1970s the political parties had become polarized over law and order. In the 1980s the police basked in a honeymoon period with the Thatcher government. They were a special case with regard to the drive for 'value for money' and cuts in public expenditure, a loyal police being seen as essential to defeat the 'enemy within' in the shape of militant trade unionism and other resistance to the economically polarizing consequences of free-market economics. Labour was successfully stigmatized as anti-law and order, because of its social democratic interpretations of crime and disorder as—at least in part—produced by economic inequality and social exclusion, and because of its civil libertarian concerns. In the later 1980s Labour struggled to regain public confidence in its criminal justice policies, and in particular to repair broken bridges with the police. This process only succeeded during Tony Blair's tenure as shadow Home Secretary in 1993, when he promulgated the famous soundbite 'tough on crime, tough on the causes of crime'.

During the 1990s there emerged a new cross-party consensus on law and order, based on a shared commitment to toughness in the war against crime. There was renewed faith in the efficacy of policing and punishment, epitomized by Michael Howard's 'prison works' mantra. The overriding priority for the police had to be crime control. This was spearheaded by Kenneth Clarke and Michael Howard, architects of the mid-1990s policy package embodied in the 1993 White Paper on Police Reform, the 1993 Sheehy Report on pay and career structures, and the 1994 Police and Magistrates' Courts Act, aimed at creating a 'business-like' police, constrained by market disciplines to achieve efficient and economic delivery of their primary objective, 'catching criminals' (as the White Paper put it). New Labour left this reform package intact, although it gave it a spin in a more sophisticated direction with the 1998 Crime and Disorder Act and its programme for crime reduction through partnership and evidence-led implementation and evaluation (discussed further in Chapters 3, 6, and 7). The promise of a research-based strategy was rapidly dashed by the relentless drive for short-term results (Maguire 2004; Hope 2004), and the proliferation of headline catching initiatives to deal with immediate crises (Newburn and Reiner 2007).

The driving paradigm for most police research now is clearly *crime control*. In the USA and Britain there is a resuscitated belief among policy-makers and some researchers that policing is a key element in crime control, not only through broader community strategies but through tougher, more directed patrol and detective work. There was explicit rejection of the earlier 'nothing works' pessimism (Sherman 1992, 1993, 2004; Bayley 1998; Nuttall *et al.* 1998; Bratton 1998; Weisburd and Eck 2004).

In this new intelligence-driven, crime control paradigm, policing research figures in an integral way. Policy-oriented research is no longer just a matter of *post hoc* evaluation of police initiatives, although the quantity and sophistication of evaluation has (debatably) grown (Bennett 1990; Pawson and Tilley 1994; Cohen 1997a; Brodeur 1998; Skogan and Frydl 2004; Skogan 2004). Detailed crime analysis and the tailoring of specific local policing responses in conjunction with other agencies were at the heart of the problem-oriented and intelligence-led approaches which the new Labour government promoted, albeit with mixed evidence of success (P. Jordan 1998; Maguire 2000, 2008; Tilley 2008; N. Cope 2008). These require an ongoing research capacity within police forces, as well as closer collaboration with policy-oriented researchers outside. The failure of public confidence in policing to rise as crime rates have fallen in the later 1990s has stimulated a particular policy concern with reducing fear as well as crime itself, focused on the 'reassurance policing' programme (Hough 2003; Millie and Herrington 2005; Innes 2006).

Critical and theoretical work certainly did not disappear, in Britain or elsewhere. As will be discussed in the next section, there has also been a growing body of theoretical work probing the impact of the major changes in political economy, culture, and society variously characterized as post or late modernity, risk society, globalization, and neo-liberalism. Nonetheless, critical and theoretical work has been eclipsed quantitatively by pragmatic policy-oriented police research on crime control.

NEW POLICING THEORIES

This section will critically review some influential attempts in recent years to develop a fundamentally new perspective on policing. It will argue that they misrepresent older perspectives and are mistaken in their characterization of current crises. They arise in part out of a commendable thirst for can-do answers to the manifest problems of order and justice in recent times. But they involve putting faith in market solutions without recognizing their fundamental perils. A lesson of policing history, this book suggests, is that democratic policing can be approximated to only in a context of social, not just liberal—and certainly not neo-liberal—democracy.

NEW POLICING THEORIES: A CRITICAL SYNTHESIS

The common theme of all the new perspectives is what a pioneering critique called the 'transformation thesis' (T. Jones and Newburn 2002). In the words of its most influential exponents: 'Modern democratic countries like the United States, Britain and Canada have reached a watershed in the evolution of their systems of crime control and law enforcement. Future generations will look back on our era as a time when one system of policing ended and another took its place' (Bayley and Shearing 1996: 585).

This has further developed into the claim that a new theoretical paradigm is needed to make sense of these developments, replacing the concepts of police and policing altogether by a framework based on 'the governance of security' (Johnston and Shearing 2003). The main exemplar of the new theoretical perspectives on policing is without doubt the celebrated work of Clifford Shearing and a number of associates, which has most explicitly argued for a complete paradigm shift, from 'policing' to 'security governance'. There is also a growing body of work advocating a 'new police science', spearheaded by Markus Dubber's acclaimed historical analysis of the 'police power' (Dubber 2005; Dubber and Valverde 2006. For an incisive, sympathetic critique, see Loader and Zedner 2007), which, although developed without reference to Shearing *et al.*, has a common inspiration in Foucault's ideas about governmentality. Richard Ericson and Kevin Haggerty's influential account of policing the 'risk society' is a third important strand of the new theoretical perspectives, largely incorporated into the wider transformation and paradigm shift theses (Ericson and Haggerty 1997; Johnston 2000). Other 'new policing' theses (McLaughlin 2007) include a variety of discussions about the impact of post or late modernity on policing (Reiner 1992; McLaughlin and Murji 1999; Waters 2007), and Pat O'Malley's claim that policing is now 'post-Keynesian' (O'Malley and Palmer 1996; O'Malley 1997).

In Bayley and Shearing's 1996 formulation the transformation thesis rests on two elements: that 'policing is no longer monopolised by the public police, that is, the police created by government', and that 'the public police are going through . . . an identity crisis' (Bayley and Shearing 1996, in Newburn 2005: 714). In recognition of the empirical changes indicated by the first of these transformations it has become normal to refer to 'policing' rather than 'the police' in the titles of books and papers. The 'new police science' explored by Dubber and others is an exception to this terminological trend, speaking of 'police' rather than policing in an explicit harking back to the eighteenth-century usage, before the advent of '*the police*' and a narrowing of the word's connotations.

Despite this terminological difference, the 'new police science' has elements in common with the security governance perspective. Above all, they share a rejection of what Johnston and Shearing call 'mainstream criminological discourse', said to be 'still preoccupied with issues relating to the administration of security and justice by states' (Johnston and Shearing 2003: 10). Similarly the 'new police science' castigates 'the trap of twentieth century criminology, which tries to think of policing in isolation from other practices of power' (Neocleous 2006: 19). In an otherwise sophisticated and scholarly analysis entitled 'Theoretical Foundations of the "New Police Science"', Neocleous starts from a caricature of research on policing, which is echoed in much of the new theoretical literature. He speaks of 'the backwater of a very narrowly conceived "police studies" . . . Reduced to the study of crime and law enforcement . . . most research on the police eschewed any attempt to make sense of the concept itself or to explore the possible diversity of police powers in terms of either their historical origins or political diversity' (ibid.: 17). The main thrust of his essay is to relocate the idea of police within a framework of political economy and broader issues of governance, harking back to the eighteenth-century 'police science' that preceded the coming of the modern police.

I am entirely in sympathy with this call for a political economy of policing—but I will suggest it is in line with the mainstream sociology of the police, *pace* Neocleous's dismissal of this as a 'backwater'. In their wholesale rejection of the importance of the empirical sociological research on policing, the new theories lose the baby with the backwater.

THEORIES OF POLICING: THE ANALYTIC DIMENSIONS

A theory of policing has to tackle a number of related questions. In characteristically crisp fashion Lenin famously reduced all political issues to 'Who? Whom?', and these certainly are core questions for policing. But elaborating on this couplet, I would suggest that theorizations of policing must include analysis of the following eight dimensions:

(1) What is policing?

(2) Who is involved in policing?

(3) What do they actually do?

(4) What are the means and powers of policing?

(5) What social functions do they achieve?

(6) How does policing impact on different groups?

(7) By whom are the police themselves policed, by what means, and to what ends?

(8) How can the developing purposes and practices of policing be understood?

The new policing theorists' answers to these questions are of course diverse, complex, and evolving. Nonetheless they can be ideal—typically represented as discussed in the following sections.

What is policing?

As indicated earlier, the main plank of the transformation thesis is the supposed end of the state monopoly of policing, i.e. its principal concern is *who* does policing. The seminal texts are surprisingly coy or bland about the prior theoretical issue of defining policing, although they are clear—but wrong!—about what policing *was* pre-transformation and in the reviled traditional police studies. It is common ground that policing (an activity) must be distinguished from the police (a specific type of institution), as argued above.

Defining the specificity of policing is more problematic, as seen earlier. Two kinds of definition can be distinguished: functional and tactical. Most common attempts to define policing are functional—what policing achieves, or rather, is supposed to achieve. This is largely true of the new theories:

We are interested in all explicit efforts to create visible agents of crime control, whether by government or by non-governmental institutions. So we are dealing with polic*ing*, not just *police*. At the same time, we say *explicit* attempts to create policing institutions so as not to extend our discussion to all the informal agencies that societies rely on to maintain order . . . So the scope of our discussion is bigger than the breadbox of the police but smaller than the elephant of social control. Our focus is on the self-conscious processes whereby societies designate and authorize people to create public safety. (Bayley and Shearing 1996, in Newburn 2005: 715–16)

Thus policing is defined by a variety of intended functions: crime control, order maintenance, public safety. The reconceptualization of policing as security governance does not change this much. 'In this book when we talk of the governance of security we will be referring, in particular, to programmes for promoting peace in the face of threats (either realized or anticipated) that arise from collective life rather than from non-human sources . . . that have their origin in human intentions and actions' (Johnston and Shearing 2003: 9).

Such functional definitions of policing are problematic because they have little fit with what police (public or private) actually do or can do. As the new theorists themselves have shown in their empirical work, police are called upon to deal with many tasks other than crime or disorder, and they can make little contribution to crime control or social peace—however effective they are (Shearing 1984; Bayley 1985: 120–7, 1994: 29–41; Johnston 2000: chap. 3; Chapter 5 in this book). It is the 'elephant' of social control rather than the 'breadbox' of policing agencies which accomplishes the functions attributed to policing (in so far as they are met at all). This is because the sources of order lie outside the ambit of the police, in the political economy and culture of a society. To the extent that these provide most people with meaningful and rewarding lives, conflict, crime, and disorder will be relatively infrequent. Subtle, informal social controls embedded in other institutions do the heavy work of policing. The 'breadbox' of overt policing agencies is important in its impact on many people's lives, but its contribution to overall social order and peace is symbolic rather than instrumental (Manning 1997a, 2003).

Functionalist definitions also sanitize a key aspect of policing—that it deals with conflict and hence has a perpetual Janus face, helping some by controlling others. Thus one party's functional policing may be another's repression. The order that the police are charged to protect always has a double aspect. *General* order, the requirements of any coordinated and complex civilization, is conceptually distinct from but inextricably intertwined with *particular* order—specific patterns of inequality and dominance. Policing deals simultaneously with 'parking tickets and class repression' (Marenin 1982), and it is this tension that bedevils attempts to regulate policing (N. Walker 2000). This is glossed over by talking, as the above definitions do, of 'societies', as opposed to dominant social powers (democratic or otherwise), authorizing policing.

A more satisfactory alternative analysis suggests that tactics or capacities rather than functions constitute the distinctive character of policing (Klockars 1985), as Egon Bittner argued some forty years ago, and was elaborated above (Bittner 1970, 1974; Brodeur 2007). The distinctiveness of the police lies not in their performance of a specific social function but in being the specialist repositories for the state's symbolic monopolization of legitimate force in its territory.

What agencies and agents are involved in policing?

As indicated earlier, many other agents and agencies apart from the police can and do perform policing tasks. Despite the pluralization of policing, it is only the state agency with the omnibus mandate of order maintenance that is still popularly understood by the label 'the police'.

The question is whether the new theories are correct in asserting that the shift away from state policing towards private, citizen, and transnational forms amounts to a fundamental and qualitative transformation. This claim has been subject to some cogent critiques. Although the personnel employed by private security have indeed grown to be more numerous than public constabularies in many countries (Button 2008: 5–6), they were already coming close during the supposed heyday of state policing in the post-war decades (Jones and Newburn 2002). Moreover, part of the increase in private security employment statistics occurred because corporations have increasingly substituted contract for in-house employees with partial security functions. More broadly, Jones and Newburn show that the growth of private security represents an increasing formalization of social control as the number of employees with *secondary* but still substantial security functions (bus and rail conductors and inspectors, park-keepers, roundsmen, etc.) has declined sharply (2002: Table 41.1). This directly contradicts the new theorists' claim that such secondary security functions have proliferated (Johnston and Shearing 2003: 126). Some forms of citizen auxiliary police such as the Special Constabulary have declined, not increased, in numbers, although the recent introduction and rapid proliferation of Police Community Support Officers (PCSOs) indicates the diversification of the 'extended policing family'. The mushrooming of private security performing an increasing array of functions, and the internal diversification of state policing, certainly are significant developments, but what is debatable is whether they amount to a qualitatively new model of policing requiring an entirely new analytic paradigm.

The state has never had a monopoly of security arrangements (Zedner 2006), even though in stable liberal democracies it has claimed control over *legitimate* force. There is no evidence, however, that this domination of *legitimacy* is under challenge. The new theorists claim that the status and image of private security has been transformed, not just their quantitative presence (Bayley and Shearing 1996, in Newburn 2005: 716–17). While they are certainly more in demand it is far from clear that they are viewed more positively by the mass of the public. It is noteworthy that until the Second World War in popular fiction and entertainment the public police hardly figured as heroic characters, and the protagonists of crime stories were private sleuths of various kinds (from the cerebral confreres of Sherlock Holmes and Poirot to the hard-boiled gumshoes depicted by Hammett and Chandler), as Chapter 6 shows. Since the Second World War, and especially since the 1960s, when the new theorists claim the public police monopoly has come under increasing challenge, public police heroes have dominated popular culture. Private police have become marginalized, scarcely appearing except as residual and unheroic characters, like the brutal security guards of *Pulp Fiction* and the comic *Paul Blart: Mall Cop*. Although for primarily economic reasons it has been government policy to develop civilianization and auxiliaries like the PCSOs, these do not threaten the hold over the mainstream 'sworn' constables in the public imagination. Indeed the popular media have regularly reviled PCSOs ('Blunkett's Bobbies') and similar initiatives. While there has undoubtedly been a pluralization of policing in recent decades, in neither substance nor symbolism does it amount to qualitative transformation.

What do police actually do?

One of the earliest findings of sociological research on policing, replicated time and time again over the last fifty years, is that—contrary to popular images—most police work does not involve crime or at any rate law enforcement (see Chapter 5). Police routinely under-enforce the law, using their discretion to deal with incidents in a variety of other 'peacekeeping' ways even if an offence may have been committed. Discretion may be operated in a variety of discriminatory or other controversial ways, although it may often be the consensually wise way to deal with troubles. But although the way discretion is exercised may often be problematic, it is inevitable and necessary, if only for pragmatic reasons of the limited capacity of the criminal justice system. Calls to the police for help only involve clear references to crime in a minority of cases, although the exact proportion varies between places, over time, and above all according to different definitions of the categories and research methodologies. Nonetheless, what is beyond dispute is that most policing does not involve any use of their law enforcement powers. The police may be the normal gateway to the criminal justice process but it is one they open relatively seldom.

Altogether the police are marginal to the control of crime and the maintenance of order, and always have been. Only a tiny fraction of crimes ever come to their attention or are recorded by them, and the overwhelming majority of these are not cleared up (apart from serious violent offences such as homicide). This does not mean that the police do not play a useful role in managing the crimes they deal with, nor that they could not boost their performance by exploring new tactics—as they have done in recent years. But seeing the police as major players in crime control is an 'impossible mandate', and their primary contribution is and remains symbolic not instrumental. The basic reason for this is the huge array of potential offences and offenders relative to any conceivable resources for policing, as shown in Chapter 5. The toughest zero-tolerance or the smartest intelligence-led approaches cannot do more than chip away at the edges of this mass of potential targets.

The marginality of crime to policing and policing to crime was a staple conclusion of the sociology of the police until the 1990s, and several new theorists themselves contributed seminal research studies confirming it (Ericson 1982; Shearing 1984; Bayley 1985, 1994). So it is somewhat disconcerting to find statements like 'The risk-communication view of policing we are advancing here obviously decenters the criminal law and criminal justice aspects of police work' (Ericson and Haggerty 2002, in Newburn 2005: 553)—as if it had formerly been central. Or 'Police are no longer the primary crime-deterrent presence in society' (Bayley and Shearing 1996, in Newburn 2005: 717)—as if they ever had been, outside media mythology and police hucksterism.

The transformation thesis juxtaposes contemporary policing forms with a depiction of the past not in terms of its reality but its mythical representation, which the theorists' earlier empirical work had done much to deconstruct. This misrepresentation of past policing as primarily concerned with crime fighting is linked to a particular account of the supposedly contrasting means and powers of policing before and after the postulated transformation.

What are the means and powers of policing?

A pivotal theme of the new policing theorists is that the alleged change in responsibility for crime, order, and security from the public police alone to the pluralized marketplace of contemporary policing is linked to a fundamental and welcome shift in style, programmes, and practices. 'It seems reasonable to conclude . . . that pluralising has made communities safer' (Bayley and Shearing 1996, in Newburn 2005: 720).

One argument adduced for this is quantitative: pluralization has been associated not only with a huge expansion of private security personnel, public police auxiliaries, and a 'responsibilised' citizenry, but a considerable (albeit proportionately slower) growth of public police officers (ibid.; Johnston 2007: 28–9; Newburn 2007: 232). This is assumed to enhance public safety in itself, despite the huge volume of research questioning the impact of increasing police numbers on crime (Bayley 1994, 1998; Chapter 5 in this book). But their main line of argument concerns alleged qualitative changes in policing resulting from pluralization. This thesis rests primarily on differences in technique and style between private and public police.

The core of the new policing perspective is that pluralization represents a qualitative and desirable shift because state policing embodies a 'punishment mentality and coercive technologies', while corporate security rests on 'the risk paradigm' (Johnston and Shearing 2003: chaps. 3, 6). They say that 'private police emphasise the logic of security, while public police emphasise the logic of justice. The major purpose of private security is to reduce the risk of crime by taking preventive actions; the major purpose of the public police is to deter crime by catching and punishing criminals' (Bayley and Shearing 1996, in Newburn 2005: 721). The supposedly more effective, efficient, and benign private corporate style is also seen as a model that is positively transforming public police, through reforms of internal governance under the influence of the 'New Public Management' (NPM) and innovative operating strategies such as community, risk, and problem-oriented policing (O'Malley 1997; Johnston 2000: chaps. 4, 5, 10; McLaughlin 2007: chap. 4). The paradox, they claim, is that Anglo-American public policing was originally established after 1829 on a Peelian model with an explicit preventive, forward-looking philosophy. Over time this is said to have degenerated into a reactive, coercive, punitive justice mentality (Johnston and Shearing 2003: 15) that would now benefit from further moves restoring the private model that Peelian policing displaced.

This analysis involves mischaracterization of the techniques, programmes, and resources of both old and new policing. As argued above, the portrayal of policing in the past as primarily concerned with crime is questioned by a host of research evidence.

Although the defining feature of state policing is the symbolic monopolization of legitimate force, the tendency of police was to minimize actual use of force, for principled and pragmatic reasons, although the *abuse* of force—particularly against those marginal and powerless groups that have aptly been called 'police property' (J. A. Lee 1981)—has been a perennial problem. Nonetheless the predominant style of policing observed in ethnographies of policing was peacekeeping and 'secret' social service (Punch 1979b). The prevailing analysis emphasized that the police were *not* themselves responsible for the effective containment of crime and disorder, indeed that this would be an 'impossible mandate' (Manning 1997a). Security, crime control, and order maintenance depended on a complex network of informal social, economic, and cultural controls of which the police were only one part, primarily important symbolically rather than instrumentally (Banton 1964; Walker 1996; Loader 1997; Loader and Mulcahy 2003). This is uncannily prescient of the image of 'nodal governance'—'that governance takes place through nodes and nodal arrangements . . . the police constitute one node amongst many nodes engaged in governance of security' (Shearing 2007: 252), postulated as a rebuttal of the old idea that 'policing belongs to the police' (ibid.). The new theorists promote this as the image of the *future* (although their notion of nodal governance is seen as a network of explicit security providers, not general processes conducive to social peace such as the maintenance of full employment or stable families and communities with cultural capital, cf. Johnston 2007a: 32–3). But the idea of the police as one aspect or 'node' of security among many was a well-trodden theme of the sociology of policing from its beginnings.

If the new theorists exaggerate the element of crime control by the public police pre-transformation, they also minimize the coercion implicit in their own accounts of the practices of private security. It is true that private police (and indeed police auxiliaries such as the PCSOs) generally lack the special police powers and the arms available to public police (Stenning 2000; Button 2007), although this is gradually changing (Crawford 2006: 114–17). But this does not mean that their capacity to control the areas they are responsible for is based on a superior mentality of risk analysis and intelligent problem solving. Certainly the individual calibre of security officers in terms of selection and training is far below the public police (Michael 2002; Button 2007, 2008: chap. 4). Against this, however, corporate security has enormous advantages stemming from the powers of private property ownership, as well as a much narrower remit. The new theorists have illuminated the recent trajectory of social control enormously by their account of the expansion of 'mass private property' (Shearing and Stenning 1983, 1987; Kempa *et al.* 2004), areas which are legally private but function as public spaces accessible to many people, such as shopping malls, 'gated' residential estates, entertainment complexes, theme parks, industrial estates. They are right to emphasize that the extent of crime and disorder in such places is generally low (although in part this may be because it is not reported to or recorded by police). But their accounts themselves indicate the extent to which such internal peace results in large measure from exclusionary tactics depending ultimately on coercion. The key point is that the owners of mass private property, and the security officers who are their agents, enjoy the power to exclude without the legal hurdle of reasonable suspicion (Crawford 2006: 124–34; T. Jones 2007: 848–9).

As a condition of entry they can and frequently do require searches and checks that are more intrusive and often discriminatory than their controversial counterparts exercised by the public police on the streets, without even the minimal accountability to law that the latter are circumscribed by. Potential sources of trouble and conflict can be swept out—possibly onto the public streets (a burgle-my-neighbour tactic that means that enhanced private security may directly reduce public safety). The nodal theorists themselves speak of such areas as 'security bubbles'. But as they depend largely on the exclusivity provided by the power of property and the purse, the bubbles vary in scope and desirability. They are positional goods, stretching from champagne bubbles through beer bubbles to toxic-waste bubbles.

Shearing and Stenning's fascinating and rightly celebrated analysis of Disney World as the exemplar of future security itself shows clearly the importance of exclusion in safeguarding the tranquillity of that hedonistic idyll. Exclusion derives from the cost of entry, its physical seclusion, a myriad of devices inscribed into its architecture and routines, and when these fail, the power of the guards in the Mickey Mouse costumes to expel the deviant (as in the anecdote about the threat to send away the researcher's young daughter unless she complied with the rule prohibiting going barefoot). The similar 'Club Med' example given by Johnston and Shearing (2003: 9) makes explicit that the security of such enclaves is a 'club good' depending on the barring of all but a privileged few (Hope 2000; Crawford 2006). The familiar cliché of the iron fist in the velvet glove applies to private security at least as much as to public policing, belying the purported sharp contrast between mentalities and practices. The apparently superior success of corporate security derives from its power to coerce compliance as a condition of being in the bubble, as well as its much narrower remit: to maximize the bottom line of profitability, not any notions of public good. The excluded are of no concern to them, unlike the way they are, at least in principle and potentially in practice, for public police.

What social functions do they achieve?

To the new theorists the bottom line is plain: 'Both quantitatively and qualitatively, then, the pluralising of policing should increase public safety' (Bayley and Shearing 1996, in Newburn 2005: 721). This takes over the popular image of policing which I have called 'police fetishism', that they are the vital functional prerequisite of social order, so that without a police force chaos would ensue. This myth has been constructed over the last two centuries by a complex of cultural processes, not least campaigning by the police themselves and the endless reproduction in the media of storylines depicting heroic police as 'the thin blue line' battling (usually successfully) to protect or restore order and justice (explored further in Chapter 6). But for reasons indicated earlier, the police are marginal to the control of crime and disorder. Public peace and security are primarily a function of deeper processes in political economy and culture.

This does not mean, however, that strategic changes in police tactics cannot have a crime-reducing effect, and there are many such claims. Most notably, the police have, of course, popularly been credited with the huge drop in crime in New York City in the

1990s, not least because they have not been shy to claim the credit. There has, however, been much debate about the precise contribution made by policing to the crime drop of the 1990s (see Chapter 5). Many analysts point out that the timing of the drop did not tally with the policing changes, that substantial (although smaller) crime reductions were achieved in many parts of the USA and the rest of the world without similar policing tactics, and that other economic, social, and criminal justice changes played a large part.

The crucial problem with traditional policing tactics ('random' uniform patrol and after-the-event investigation) is that they are spread too thinly over the multitude of potential victims and offenders to be able to achieve much preventive cover or detection. The innovative tactics that have produced some improvements in police performance are directed at remedying aspect(s) of this (see Chapter 5). 'Smart', intelligence-led analysis helps to identify and target crime hotspots and prolific offenders. 'Problem solving' may identify and remove risks. 'Community policing' may improve the flow of information and public cooperation that is crucial for investigation. 'Zero-tolerance' order maintenance blitzes can create false impressions of police omnipresence and omnipotence that may deter potential offenders and reassure others. All these are examples of the kind of risk-oriented strategies that the new policing theorists attribute to the influence of the commercial private security industry. 'Through community policing and order-maintenance policing, the public police are developing strategies for reducing disorder and the opportunities for crime that are similar to the practices readily accepted by commercial and informal communities from private police' (Bayley and Shearing 1996, in Newburn 2005: 721). But they are more plausibly interpreted as formalizations of tactics that were deeply engrained in traditional public policing. Cultivating public cooperation was central to the Peelian model from the outset, especially because of the deep and wide hostility to the creation of the new police in 1829, and many measures were adopted to secure consent, as Chapters 2 and 3 show. Community policing, spreading out from John Alderson's pioneering vision in Devon and Cornwall in the 1970s to become a worldwide vogue, was a bid to recapture the popular support that had been built up between the mid-nineteenth and twentieth centuries but was threatened by social and economic change (Brogden 1999; Brogden and Nijhar 2005; Savage 2007: 75–8, 131–5). The only sense in which it was inspired by private sector examples is that it has parallels with the heritage industry developing in the same period as a response to similar stresses. Its consumerist phase, at its height in the early 1990s as 'businesslike' management began to be the new gospel and even prisoners were rebranded as 'customers', was modelled on the private sector but has had scant positive results. The careful cultivation and use of information was a staple tool, exemplified in studies of criminal investigation before and after the creation of the new police (e.g. Styles 1982, 1983; Rock 1973; Maguire and John 1996a, 1996b; Norris and Dunnighan 2000). Appraising situations and people to assess risk and danger was a repeatedly noted trope of traditional police culture (see Chapter 4). These are not aspects of a new risk-oriented, actuarial mentality, although they are of course greatly enhanced by recent technological developments (Tilley 2008; Cope 2008; Maguire 2008).

What has undoubtedly been imported from private sector models, largely but not only at the behest of neo-liberal governments, is the NPM with its focus on central government 'ruling at a distance' by devolving responsibility to local levels of service delivery, 'steering' the local 'rowers' by target setting, performance measurement, league tables, competition, 'best value', financial, and other instrumental sanctions. The new-police theorists take over an enthusiasm for these tactics from the neo-liberal belief that private enterprise and market models work best (O'Malley 1997, in Newburn 2005: 701–10; Johnston and Shearing 2003: chap. 5; McLaughlin 2007: 96–7, 182–7). But such faith is largely a priori, with little evidence that the new managerial models have the intended benign effects on practice, except in cases where there were particular patholo-gies in unequivocally underperforming units (which may include the NYPD before the reforms of the 1990s). Indeed, even right-of-centre, market-oriented think-tanks have questioned the way NPM has been implemented, with the likelihood of perverse incen-tives that may direct police activity away from the important but hard to the trivial but achievable (Loveday et al. 2007: 16–19).

The claim that pluralization improves the achievement of policing functions is fundamentally questionable, however, not only empirically but as a category error. It pre-supposes that policing is best thought of in terms of the achievement of macro-functions such as crime control, law enforcement, maintaining public order, and security. The problems are not only the thorny practical ones of measuring the achievement of such functions and identifying the policing contribution towards this. As suggested earlier, functionalism misidentifies the bulk of policing activity which is an emergency res-ponse to a myriad of problems for which policing can at best provide only an interim solution. Tank Waddington expressed this most succinctly: 'The police are the social equivalent of the AA or RAC patrolmen, who intervene when things go unpredictably wrong and secure a provisional solution' (Waddington 1983: 34). To switch to a medi-cal metaphor, they are analogous to paramedics or A & E doctors, delivering first-aid relief but generally unable to cure the basic problems. Their contribution may well be enhanced by the kind of partnerships with other local agencies that are mandated by the Crime and Disorder Act 1998, which the new theorists celebrate rightly at least in principle as an illustration of the nodal-governance mentality (Johnston and Shearing 2003: chap. 7; McLaughlin 2007: 126–30). But even this is often unlikely to be able to tackle the root causes of problems, which lie outside the locality and require central government or even transnational support (such as unemployment, crunched credit to aid local enterprise, or public finance to develop infrastructure). This is a major lacuna of the nodal vision, indicating a necessary role for the state (Loader and Walker 2001, 2006, 2007; Goldsmith 2003; Marks and Goldsmith 2006; T. Jones 2007: 859–61; Zedner 2009: 161–7).

Policing cannot be seen primarily as satisfying grand social functions but rather as a Sisyphean labour of continuous partial emergency alleviation of recurring problems. They should be judged by the quality of interaction in their case-work interventions, rather than by the results, by the process not the product, presenting thorny problems of assessment and accountability (Reiner 1998). The statistical measures of performance that are the stock-in-trade of NPM and 'businesslike' models may be useful diagnostic tools, prompting questions about comparative results and reflexive analysis of why one sector's results are less favourable than a comparator's. But used as sanctions they are likely to lead to dissimulation of practices, distortion of statistics, and counter-productive diversion of activity to the measurable and easily achievable (Hough 2007). To think of policing as capable of achieving the grand functions of order and security is a dangerous category error, but police can bring balm to desperate suffering.

How does policing impact on different groups?

Policing is regularly blighted by inequality, injustice, and discrimination in its operation. Groups that are low in power and status, such as the poor and unemployed, ethnic minorities, young men (and underclass young women), gays, and lesbians, become 'police property' (Lee 1983), disproportionately likely to be treated as suspects at each stage of the criminal justice process: stop–search, arrest, detention, charge, prosecution (as Chapter 5 elaborates). This arises for a variety of reasons. The kinds of crime that the police in practice focus on: volume property offences, violence and disorder in public space, are more likely to be perpetrated by young, poor men (and certain ethnic minorities are disproportionately poor). These groups spend more time in public spaces, lacking the wherewithal to enter mass private property citadels of consumption. So they are more 'available' to become targets of suspicion (Waddington *et al.* 2004). They are likely to fit stereotypes of suspiciousness, and have less power to challenge successfully (and hence deter) coercive police actions. These same groups are also disproportionately likely to be victimized by crime, and tend to receive less satisfactory police treatment (Heidensohn and Gelsthorpe 2007; Phillips and Bowling 2007; Hoyle and Zedner 2007). They are also less often recruited into the police, and have often suffered discrimination internally in career terms.

Discrimination and disparity in the treatment of different groups is a perennial problem of policing. They violate the public service mandate of the police, and contradict the principle of equality before the law. The revelation of discrimination usually creates a major scandal, setting in train efforts to reform the police (Foster *et al.* 2005; Savage 2007: chap. 1; McLaughlin 2007: chaps. 6, 8).

This is in sharp contrast to private policing. Inequality of treatment is a barnacle on the boat of so-called public service policing. But it is the hull of the corporate policing vessel. Private security firms have duties to their shareholders and to those they con-tract to provide services to. The consequences of their activities to other parties—those they police, and the public at large—are not even a formal concern. As Zedner argues cogently:

Although the practice of state policing never fulfilled its collectivist pretensions, it did profess, at least, to provide a public service available to all. To the extent that it failed to fulfil this idea, as fail it did, its failing could be measured, criticised and sanctioned. Private providers make no such claim but avowedly seek to protect the partisan interests (whether individual, communal or commer-cial) of those who pay. No surprise here: it is central to the logic of market societies that goods be distributed not according to need, but to the ability of the consumer to buy. (Zedner 2006: 92)

The new policing theorists themselves have demonstrated how the growth of mass private property creates security fortresses separated sharply from the surrounding society, and dubbed this a 'new feudalism' (Shearing and Stenning 1983). This analysis of growing social division originally had sinister and critical tones, but as the transformation thesis has developed it has come to be represented positively as 'nodal governance', with the private sector and its actuarial mentality of risk prevention supposedly setting an example to the public police. But, as argued above, the peace of security bubbles is achieved through exclusionary and coercive tactics derived from the powers of property ownership, rather than any superior strategy. The new theorists recognize the problem of equity, and explore the possibilities of levelling up security provision. They recognize difficulties in increasing the provision of police to poorer areas, or communal self-help alone (Bayley and Shearing 1996, in Newburn 2005: 722–3). So their main hope is finding means 'to enable poor people to participate in markets for security' by vouchers or block grants (ibid.: 730–1). 'In effect, communities would be given security budgets that they could spend on various mixtures of public and private policing' (ibid.). This presupposes that the problems can be met by policing and that pluralization improves its efficacy—propositions that were questioned earlier. It also raises the issue of how the redistributive security budget is to gain political acceptance, as the theorists recognize. 'Distributional problems between rich and poor might still arise, of course, particularly if the rich refused to pay. All policies that have any prospect of mitigating the growing class differences in public safety depend on the affluent segments of our societies recognising that security is indivisible. The well-to-do are paying for crime now; but they have not learned that they will save more by levelling up security than by ghettoising it' (ibid.: 730). Achieving this consensus in support of redistribution presents a formidable challenge. But as safety depends on much wider social and economic justice than can be provided by security measures alone, tackling the 'root causes' of threat, the task is the even more daunting but necessary one of constructing a consensus for a broader alleviation of inequality. The new theorists offer impressive and inspirational examples of successful efforts to organize security in poor communities such as the South African township Zwelethemba (Johnston and Shearing 2003: 151–60). But these are dependent on outside financial and other support (Marks and Goldsmith 2006; T. Jones 2007: 858–60). The state remains the necessary 'anchor' for security (Loader and Walker 2006, 2007) to avert stark polarization between safe and dreadful enclosures.

By whom and how are the police themselves policed?

Who guards the guardians is of course one of the most ancient conundrums of governance. The issues of accountability remain vexed in debates about policing, as Chapter 7 shows. One of the reasons for this is the Janus face of policing discussed earlier: policing usually involves conflict control, and is simultaneously a general and a partisan good. Thus the problem of accountability has a double aspect: achieving effective and efficient service delivery, but also minimizing any abuse or injustice in the use of coercive powers.

In the last two decades, with the dominance of the politics of law and order, the issue of accountability has shifted strongly towards emphasizing effective delivery of security with much lower priority given to the control of malpractice. Crime control has been declared as the overriding objective of policing, and a 'calculative and contractual' structure of monitoring and incentives is intended to achieve this. Police powers have been expanded at an accelerating rate while the safeguards attached by the Police and Criminal Evidence Act 1984 have been diluted. The Human Rights Act 1998 and the introduction of the Independent Police Complaints Commission by the Police Reform Act 2002 are two significant countermeasures, but the dominant trend is clearly towards a relatively unregulated growth of police powers (see Chapter 7).

The transformation thesis claims that pluralization is making policing more accountable and responsive. Private security, they claim, is inherently so because of the contractual relationships between client and security firm, and between the latter and its employees, which provide sanctions for performance failures. As far as the public sector is concerned, they welcome a more businesslike structure of accountability based on NPM principles (Johnston and Shearing 2003: 26). In the endlessly cited nautical analogy of the NPM gurus Osborne and Gaebler, government should 'steer' but not 'row' public services (Osborne and Gaebler 1992). 'Rowing' must be devolved to local levels of delivery such as police Basic Command Units, whose performance is steered by target setting, performance measurement, and corresponding sanctions. This brave new world of 'rule at a distance' is contrasted with a supposed sclerotic old regime of centralized command and control of state services. The latter is necessarily inefficient because of the Hayekian problem: 'top-down government does not permit entrepreneurship because those "at the top of the pyramid" do not have "enough information to make informed decisions" [Osborne and Gaebler 1992: 15] about how to govern locally' (Shearing 2006: 23). Such problems do not apply to the corporate sector, which is supposedly kept vibrant, responsive, and efficient by market incentives.

This formulation misrepresents the past and current pattern of police governance. In Anglo-American policing it was never the case that the state 'rowed'. The British legal doctrine of constabulary independence explicitly sought to shield police officers from direct instruction by government, central or local, although the operation of this in practice has always been more problematic (see Chapter 7). In the USA until relatively recently with the politicization of law and order, the federal government role in local and state law policing was minimal. Sociological studies of policing in action have shown that decision-making is shaped largely by the rank-and-file officers on the street, who enjoy a considerable measure of discretion (Skolnick 1966; Wilson 1968; Muir 1977; Smith 1983; Mastrofski 2004).

So Anglo-American policing has traditionally been governed 'at a distance' by the state (unless it is tautologically equated with it). This has been transformed in the last twenty years by the application of new 'calculative and contractual' modes of regulating policing supplying central government with unprecedented formal and effective levers for penetrating 'constabulary independence', which is now an empty rhetorical formula (Savage 2007: chaps. 3, 5; T. Jones 2008). This creeping centralization of control over policing has been increasingly controversial, and in recent years both parties have pledged to bolster local input in a complicated and confusing variety of ways, but it is doubtful that this new localism will succeed in reversing the current central dominance (McLaughlin 2007: chap. 7; Newburn 2007).

Legal and state regulation of private security is notoriously weak and patchy, and there have long been calls for its enhancement (Button 2008: chap. 5). However, the new policing theorists see private policing as more accountable and responsive because of commercial pressures. Inadequate performance by companies is sanctioned by the threat of contract termination, and individual officers are kept on their toes by fear for their jobs. 'Private police are more responsive than public police to the "bottom line" of safety. If safety is not increased, private police can be fired' (Bayley and Shearing 1996, in Newburn 2005: 721). How effective private security is in satisfying its customers is no doubt variable, but in principle it may be acceptable to say caveat emptor. But they have no responsibilities for *public* security apart from the limited sections allowed into their 'nodes'. It is hard to see how pluralization has enhanced accountability, either in the sense of responsiveness to public concerns about safety or malpractice.

How can the developing purposes and practices of policing be understood?

The transformation thesis is primarily presented as a description of trends and an analysis of their 'progressive' potential. The main explanatory theme is what can be called 'truth will out': the new trends have emerged because they solve manifest problems with the old, supposedly state-dominated policing arrangements. This is summed up in the following passage:

Peel's aspiration to ensure prevention through the certainty of detection and punishment has remained unrealised during the two centuries since the inception of the new police. There are a number of reasons for this, some of which relate to shortcomings within policing, others to problems within the wider criminal justice system. For example, during most of the post-war period, steadily rising rates of crime have exposed the limits of the Peelian project. Added to that . . . the public's willingness to report offences cannot be taken for granted; the police's capacity to detect offences is limited; and the court's [sic] ability to secure convictions is restricted. (Johnston and Shearing 2003: 67)

These claims distort the history of policing in a number of ways. Crime rates fell steadily after the 1850s as the Peelian police were rolled out across the country (following the County and Borough Police Act 1856), remaining low until the First World War, as Chapter 3 discusses. Indeed the criminological question for conferences in the late nineteenth century to mull over was how to explain *falling* crime trends (Radzinowicz and Hood 1986), a puzzle that was not to recur until the 1990s. It is doubtful that the falling crime rates were primarily due to the policing changes, for reasons elaborated in Chapters 3 and 5. A much greater role was played by the long-term process of converting the 'dangerous classes' into the solid working class by incorporating them into the civil, political, and economic rights of citizenship. But even if the falling crime rates were a political conjuring trick to promote the Bobbies, it worked, and the myth of Scotland Yard's prowess ('always getting their man') became an international symbol of successful policing.

Although crime rates rose in the 1920s and 1930s, they declined again in the first post-war decade, and the myth of the Bobby as an important aspect of British national pride reached its zenith in the 1940s and 1950s. Recorded crime rates did begin to increase almost continuously after the mid-1950s, only falling briefly in the early 1990s and mid-2000s. The increase up to 1980 was largely a statistical illusion, as more property crime was reported to the police by victims due to the spread of household insurance. The real explosion in crime came in the 1980s and early 1990s, when the new British Crime Surveys confirmed the police-recorded trend (Reiner 2007a: chap. 3). The police certainly got some of the blame for this—but as unfairly as the credit they had received for the earlier fall. The main factor in the crime explosion was the advent of neo-liberal economic policy with its consequent effects of precipitously increasing inequality, long-term unemployment, and social exclusion, and a culture of ever expanding consumer aspirations and egoism (Reiner 2007a: chap. 4; Hall *et al.* 2008). Faced with these huge crime increases, swamping their resources, the police were able to detect only a diminishing proportion of offences, further undermining public confidence in them.

But neither the crime trends nor the changing public standing of the police were primarily due to failures of the Peelian model. The real driver of the problematic crime and criminal justice trends of recent years was the neo-liberal dominance that the new theorists see as bearing the seeds of a solution. In the new policing theories neo-liberalism is discussed almost entirely as a rational set of programmes and ideas, curiously abstracted from its material effects and origins (Harvey 2005 provides a succinct account of the economic and political sources and consequences of neo-liberalism). The rhetoric of neo-liberal advocates is presented as if they corresponded to practice (e.g. O'Malley 1997, in Newburn 2005: 701–12), ignoring the now clear disastrously deleterious effects. There is an acceptance of neo-liberal claims about the possible pathologies of state institutions but no recognition of the pathologies of the market that were understood even by neo-classical economists of earlier generations such as Alfred Marshall and Pigou.

The new theorists' critique of the state is presented as developing out of the radical criminologies that flourished in the 1960s and early 1970s.

Three decades ago cutting-edge criminological theory grappled with 'the problem of the state'.... While the state —through the law—presented itself as an independent adjudicator between competing interests and claimed to ensure that all individuals had equal access to justice, formal legal equality was, in reality, a sham ... Thirty years ago the state was considered to *be* 'the problem', its capitalist character rendering it structurally incapable of representing general 'public interests' over particular private ones. (Johnston and Shearing 2003: 33–4)

They then reflect on the 'strange paradox' that 'many of today's theorists' bemoan 'how neo-liberalism has disaggregated the state apparatus' (ibid.). There is no paradox here. The nub of the critique of the state was that it was captured by the interests of capital, and the problem was how to make it deliver on its promise to represent the public good. As Tawney put it some seventy years ago, 'The question is not merely whether the State

owns and controls the means of production. It is also who owns and controls the State'
(Tawney 1935: 165). 'The reality behind the decorous drapery of political democracy',
he argued is 'the economic power wielded by a few thousand—or . . . a few hundred
thousand—bankers, industrialists, and landowners' (ibid.: 60).

To espouse neo-liberalism, 'capitalism unleashed' (Glyn 2006) from behind the
ideological veil of the state, is jumping from the frying pan into the fire. The claim
that there are 'possibilities for disaggregating neo-liberal strategies and practices, and
rendering their often highly innovative developments available for appropriation
and development by a "progressive" postwelfare politics' overlooks the inherent
dysfunctional consequences of markets (O'Malley 1997, in Newburn 2005: 712). Markets
have many unwelcome economic consequences unless states take countervailing measures: growing inequalities of power and wealth; allocation of resources tilted towards
the desires of the rich (the democracy of the market is not one person one vote, but
one pound one vote); insecurities caused by vicissitudes of health, age, natural disas-
ters; and, as we have relearned, painfully, wild macroeconomic fluctuations. (These
points are elaborated in Reiner 2007a: 1–11.) Market-dominated societies are associated with further social, ethical, political, and cultural problems: the financialization
of all values, anomie produced by the stimulation of desires and aspirations beyond
the possibility of achievement, egoism, corruption of democracy by the best politicians
money can buy (Palast 2004; Jacobs and Skocpol 2005), authoritarianism as the 'strong
state' seeks to suppress resistance to the pathologies of the 'free market' (Polanyi 1944;
Gamble 1994).

Specifically relevant to policing, there is now a host of research evidence showing
that neo-liberalism—as contrasted with social democracy—is associated with higher
risks of serious violent crime, *and* more punitive cultures and penal practices (Hall
and Winlow 2003; Dorling 2004; Cavadino and Dignan 2006; Reiner 2007; Lacey
2008; Hall and McLean 2009; Wilkinson and Pickett 2009), as a consequence of its
economic, social, and cultural pathologies. The main explanatory deficit of the new
policing theories is a bracketing-out of the significance of political economy in shaping
the context and problems that police organizations, cultures, and officers face. Expla-
nations of changing programmes and practices, and their impacts—intended and
unintended—require a multi-layered political economy of the macro-, intermediate,
and immediate social processes and contexts that shape policing (Reiner 2007b: 343–4),
a perspective reminiscent of the eighteenth-century 'science of police' which preceded
the Peelian institution (ibid.: 345–7).

Analysing the historical roots of the recent policing transformations through the lens
of political economy suggests a very different diagnosis to the new policing theorists'.
The pluralization of policing and the application of NPM to the public police are symptoms of, not solutions to, the current predicament. As elaborated in Chapters 2 and 3,
the Peelian police were established in Britain (and the USA) in the early nineteenth
century against wide and deep hostility, especially from the then politically, socially, and
economically excluded masses. The police were established not because of technical
failures of the previous forms of citizen policing, but because these were all controlled

by the gentry, making manifest the class nature of governance and law (Silver 1967). The big job facing the early police leaders was to gain public consent, and somewhat different strategies were followed in Britain and the USA (W. Miller 1999). The British route was a set of organizational policies seeking to represent the police as disciplined, apolitical, minimally armed, 'citizens in uniform' without special powers separating them from the public, enforcing an impartial law that benefited all classes as well as providing emergency social services to those in need. These ultimately succeeded in dispelling hostility and winning a fragile legitimation of the police, but only because the policies were developed in a benign context of the general march of social, political, and economic citizenship (as classically spelled out by Marshall 1950). This reduced the extent of crime and disorder confronting the police allowing them to consolidate the image of operating with minimum force and allowing room for the service role to be emphasized.

Police legitimacy was gradually undermined after the late 1960s but not because of defects in the policing model. The ultimate source was economic neo-liberalism, initially heralded in the 'Selsdon Man' manifesto on which the Heath government was elected in 1970 but defeated by trade union opposition, reimposed on a reluctant Labour government by the International Monetary Fund (IMF) in 1976, enthusiastically espoused by the Thatcher Tories in 1979, and deeply embedded by New Labour's embrace of it in the 1990s. This set in train massive economic and social dislocation (especially large-scale long-term unemployment, inequality, and social exclusion) and an increasingly anomic and egoistic culture, which in the 1980s generated a crime explosion and public disorder on a scale not seen for a century. Mediated by the unintended reversal of the policing policies that had achieved legitimation, the result was a decline in public confidence in the police.

How to deal with this was politically controversial in the 1970s and 1980s, and there appeared sharp politicization of the issue of law and order (Downes and Morgan 2007; Reiner 2007a: chap. 5). The Tories espoused a tough new law-and-order rhetoric, while Labour clung to a social democratic analysis of the social roots of crime and disorder similar to the one suggested here. This fundamentally changed in 1992 when the then Shadow Home Secretary Tony Blair's celebrated slogan 'tough on crime, tough on the causes of crime' heralded New Labour's conversion to the law-and-order approach, the first of several 'Clause 4' moments signifying its embrace of neo-liberalism.

For the police this meant calling a bluff that had been successful for 150 years. The police had been symbolically acclaimed as the guardians of the public against threats of crime and disorder, but the real work achieving this was an array of economic, social, and cultural processes that incorporated most sections of society into a common status of citizenship and held tensions and conflicts at bay. When neo-liberalism unravelled this complex of subtle, hidden controls, the thin blue line turned out to be a Maginot line. The 'sovereign state' myth (Garland 1996) was unmasked, naked as Anderson's Emperor in his new clothes. As researchers had suggested all along, the police alone could not have much impact on crime and disorder. But the newly ascendant and unquestioned politics of law and order demanded that they do just that. The 1993

White Paper on Police Reform declared bluntly that the police task was simply 'catching criminals', vindicating a folkloric view that official statements from Peel to Scarman had been at pains to deny. This kick-started the NPM-inspired reforms of the 1990s and 2000s, from the quixotic hunt to extirpate extraneous tasks and free them for their core criminal-catching role, to the calculative and contractual businesslike management regime to keep them on their toes doing it (Savage 2007: chaps. 3, 5). Meanwhile the 'new feudalism' also gathered pace, as those with the power to do so built their exclusive bubbles of security.

The transformation of policing stems not from the inherent deficiencies of old, state policing or the technical superiority of a new corporate mentality of pluralism combining private security and an NPM-invigorated public sector. It results from the destabilizing and criminogenic effects of neo-liberalism, which is the problem not the solution.

There have been many valuable analyses of the legal, constitutional, procedural, and organizational requirements for democratic and legitimate policing (see Chapter 7). British policing history suggests that a further ingredient is needed: social democracy. The organizational elements of the legitimation of the police only succeeded because of the wider transformation of British society that culminated in the post-war Keynesian and welfare state settlement, incorporating all sections of society into a common status of citizenship. The political triumph of neo-liberalism since the 1970s and the ensuing 'death of the social' (Rose 1996) eroded these conditions of peace and security. The necessity of reversing this, of a future social democratic policing, is discussed in Chapter 8.

POLITICS AND POLICING

'The group of words, police, policy, polity, politics, politic, political, politician is a good example of delicate distinctions' (Maitland 1885: 105).

Most police officers stoutly maintain that policing and politics don't mix. Chief constables regularly declaim on the political neutrality of the police service. Sir Robert Mark, commissioner of the Metropolitan Police (the Met) in the early 1970s, wrote (1977: 12): 'We [the police] discharge the communal will, not that of any government minister, mayor or public official, or that of any political party.' As shown in Chapter 3, an important ingredient of the legitimation of the British police was non-partisanship.

This notion of the political neutrality or independence of the police cannot withstand serious consideration. It rests on an untenably narrow conception of 'the political', restricting it to partisan conflict (Armatrudo 2009: chap. 4). In a broader sense, all relationships which have a power dimension are political, so policing is inherently and inescapably political.

As argued above, their specific role in the maintenance of order is as specialists in coercion. The craft of successful policing is to be able to minimize the use of force, but it remains the specialist resource of the police, their distinctive role in the political order.

In this sense, the police are at the heart of the state's functioning, and political analysis in general tends to underplay the significance of policing as both source and symbol of the quality of a political civilization.

The control of overtly political behaviour is the task of the specifically political police, or 'high policing' (Bunyan 1977; Turk 1982; Brodeur 1983; P. Gill 1994; Mazower 1997; Huggins 1998; Sheptycki 2000a, 2007). A characteristic of the British police tradition is the attempted unification in the same organization of the 'high policing' function of regulating explicit political dissidence with the 'low policing' task of routine law enforcement and street-level order maintenance. In most other countries there is a greater degree of organizational separation, although the Special Branch developed in the late nineteenth century as a separate, specifically political, unit within the police in Britain (Porter, 1987).

What chief constables are most concerned to claim is that the police are not involved in partisan politics, but impartially enforce the law. This narrower claim is also sustainable only in small part, if at all. A distinction must be made between partisanship in intent and in impact. In a society that is divided on class, ethnic, gender, and other dimensions of inequality, the impact of laws, even if they are formulated and enforced impartially and universalistically, will reproduce those social divisions. This is the point encapsulated in Anatole France's celebrated aphorism about 'The majestic equality of the law, which forbids the rich as well as the poor to sleep under bridges, to beg in the streets, and to steal bread' (*Le Lys Rouge*, Paris, 1894). In practice, of course, the inequalities of social power are likely to have an impact on the processes of legislation and administration of justice, so that the law itself may deviate from formal impartiality. For both these reasons the impact of law and its enforcement in an unequal society will be objectively political even in the narrower sense of partisanship, favouring some groups at the expense of others. 'The rich get rich, and the poor get prison' (Reiman 2004)—and they also get more criminal victimization and the hard end of police power. Policing bears down most heavily on the most marginal and least powerful groups in our society, who are in effect denied the full status of citizenship (P. Waddington, 1999a) and are 'police property' (J. Lee, 1981), especially at times of economic or political conflict or crisis (S. Hall *et al.* 1978; Crowther 2000a, 2000b).

As I shall argue, the British police tradition has to a large measure eschewed overt partisanship. The constitutional structure within which it operates, autonomous of direct control by elected authorities, is intended to preserve this. Moreover, it must be emphasized that, while policing is inherently political and indeed partisan in reproducing social inequalities, at the same time it preserves the minimal conditions of civilized and stable social existence from which all groups benefit, albeit differentially.

However, if policing is an inherently political activity, it does not follow that it usually appears as such. Policing may be inescapably political, but it need not be politicized, that is, the centre of overt political controversy over its manner, tactics, or mode of operation and organization. Like riding a bike, policing is the sort of activity that is thought about mainly when the wheel comes off. When things are running smoothly it tends to be a socially invisible, undiscussed routine.

This book explores the de facto politics of policing in terms of its uneven social impact (Chapter 5), the political ideology of police officers and the political role of the police in popular ideology (Chapters 4 and 6), and the politicization of the police, their involvement in overt political conflict (Parts II and IV). As Chapters 2 and 3 show, the British police were established in the face of acute political opposition. To gain acceptance, the architects of the British policing tradition constructed an image, organization, and strategy which were intended to win over the various strands of political opposition. Over the first century and a quarter of its existence the police in England and Wales were largely successful in accomplishing their depoliticization, and came to be seen as legitimate by the mass of the population.

It should be stressed, however, that there are inherent limits to police legitimation in any society. Since policing is centrally concerned with the resolution of conflicts, ultimately dependent on the capacity to use force, there is in most police actions someone who is being policed against. In this sense the police are inherently dealers in and dispensers of evil and can never command universal love. For policing to be accepted as legitimate, it is not necessary that all groups or individuals in a society agree with the substantive content or direction of specific police operations. It means at minimum only that the broad mass of the population, and possibly even some of those who are policed against, accept the authority, the lawful right, of the police to act as they do, even if disagreeing with or regretting some specific actions. Of course, in conditions of relative social harmony, acceptance of judicious policing may be a lot more wholehearted. But as policing is inherently an activity concerned with the ordering of conflict, 'policing by consent' cannot imply complete and universal approval. To suggest otherwise is dangerous in that it raises expectations which can never be realized. This is the inherent limit to all the fashionable notions of 'community policing', despite this becoming the 'rhetorical giant' (Manning 1997a: 11) of police reform talk around the world. As P. Waddington (1999a: 223) sums it up trenchantly, '"community policing" is an oxymoron, for if the police could serve the *whole* community there would be little point in having a police at all'.

The politics of policing at the end of the first decade of the twentieth century, exhibits a number of paradoxes. Despite many years of criticism and loss of legitimacy the police remain pivotal—at least symbolically—to a crucial policy concern of the public: crime. There is now bipartisan consensus around a fundamentally 'law and order' definition of the issue, and of the police role. However, there is fierce partisan conflict over specific strategies and over who can deliver the best results. Policing and crime control are scarcely debated in principled ways, but are fiercely contested at a pragmatic level.

The competing arguments and strategies will be evaluated in the light of the substantial body of evidence about police culture, operations, and images that is reviewed in Part III. The nub of my conclusion is that all the reform initiatives of recent years have been vitiated by a failure to reject the 'law and order' framework, and to recognize the inherent limitations of policing. They have been fatally damaged by government policies which aggravated unemployment and exclusion, especially among the young and ethnic minorities, creating problems of policing a new and growing underclass

(Crowther 2000a, 2000b). The problems reflect broader structural changes in political economy and culture, often referred to in a broad-brush way as 'globalization', which limit the scope of action of governments. However, the divisive and unsettling consequences of neo-liberal globalization have become manifest since credit crunched in 2007 and brought economic collapse. The social, economic, and cultural transformations of the last quarter of the twentieth century multiplied the problems facing the police.

In the first half of the 1980s, the police were pigs in the middle of sharply polarized political debate. They were the darlings of the Tories and in conflict with Labour-controlled police authorities, to which the national Labour Party threatened to make them more accountable. Gone were the halcyon days of consensus, when the police stood above the party fray as beloved totems of the nation. By the early 1990s the police stood at a lower ebb in public trust and esteem than at any time since they were established in the nineteenth century. They had been rocked by scandals revealing gross miscarriages of justice. At the same time the police appeared less able to protect people from criminal victimization, which was rising at record speed, although it fell again in total after the mid-1990s—but without reassuring an ever more fearful public.

By the mid-1990s the configuration had changed again. Seeking to be 'tough on crime and tough on the causes of crime', New Labour courted the police assiduously, while the Tories sought to apply tough 'businesslike' market-based rigours to their management and accountability. There was good news and bad news for the police. The good news was the return of a degree of consensus about policing, and about their symbolic importance to a vital objective for any government. This was reflected in a stabilization of public confidence in the police, following its precipitous decline up to the early 1990s. The bad news was the new consensus view that the police were failing badly on almost every front, and in need of drastic reform. It was increasingly apparent that the police felt trapped in a time warp. They were intent on reform. However, the impact of reforms on public perceptions of the police was continuously being undercut by scandalous revelations, as well as unrealistic expectations of performance and probity built up in the bygone era when the lid was shut tight on scandals.

In response to all these problems, police and government have pursued a number of reform strategies at a bewilderingly accelerating pace, and competing ones have been on offer. Police thinking at policy-making levels is a bricolage of different themes originating at different times in response to the crisis of the moment. There remain echoes of the 1981 Scarman philosophy emphasizing peacekeeping and consensus, which were reinforced by the 1999 MacPherson report on the Stephen Lawrence case, and point towards 'community' and 'problem-solving' policing. Such Scarmanesque echoes are intertwined with facets of management theory, the 'quality of service' language of consumerism, and bytes of business speak. However, these softer tones have been threatened increasingly by a renewed enthusiasm for tough policing, embodied above all in the much-debated notion of 'zero tolerance', and vastly exacerbated by the terror attacks of the 2000s around the world, and in London in 2005.

This book analyses how the police got to their present situation, and what research on their working suggests about the prospects of success for the reforms being pursued. The verdict is far from encouraging, largely because the effects of neo-liberal, free-market economic policies have been to increase social divisions, poverty, injustice, relative deprivation—and the anger they give rise to—the bitter fruits of which the police must cope with. To seek to return to the 'golden age' of consensus about policing symbolized by the Dixon of Dock Green myth is chimerical at best. The more pragmatic but attainable target is to achieve public recognition for doing a 'dirty work' occupation as professionally, efficiently, and impartially as it can be done in an ever more fragmented and divided society. Whether even that can be achieved must be doubtful in a period of massive social transformation, generating profound dislocation and insecurity. As at the birth of modern policing in the early nineteenth century the success of their efforts depends largely on much wider questions of political economy and culture, in particular whether the malign consequences of neo-liberal hegemony can be reversed and the long march of inclusive social democratic citizenship restored.

PART II

HISTORY

2

THE BIRTH OF THE BLUES: THE ESTABLISHMENT OF PROFESSIONAL POLICING IN BRITAIN 1829–56

'I never saw any of them again—except the cops. No way has yet been invented to say good-bye to them.' Philip Marlowe's fatalistic lament, with which Raymond Chandler concluded his classic mystery *The Long Goodbye*, embodies a basic assumption shared even by those who are critical of the police. Welcome or unwelcome, protectors, pigs, or pariahs, the police are an inescapable fact of modern life. As seen in Chapter 1, while *policing* is a universal feature of social relations, specialized *police* institutions are not. Formal police organizations are associated with social complexity, inequality, and the development of modern states. There are question marks about the continuing centrality of this form of police in late or postmodern societies. In some respects current transformations of policing contain echoes of pre-modern patterns (Zedner 2006).

A consideration of the highly contested process by which modern professional policing in Britain came into being makes problematic the police fetishism that sees the police as a condition of existence of social order. The establishment of the police was a protracted and painful struggle, in the face of bitter resistance and smouldering hostility. In the late eighteenth and early nineteenth centuries the police idea was fiercely controversial.

INTERPRETATIONS OF POLICE HISTORY

Traditional accounts of the origins and development of policing in Britain reflected a framework of palpably conservative assumptions. The police were seen as an inevitable and unequivocally beneficent institution, a cornerstone of national pride, which had been developed by English pragmatic genius as a response to fearsome threats to social order and civilized existence. The initial opposition to the police was attributable to vested interests, malevolence, or blinkered obscurantism, and rapidly dissipated when the benefits of a benign police institution became apparent to all.

This view of police history as the inevitable march of progress came under challenge in the 1970s, when a new, Marxist-inspired revisionist account became dominant. In this the police were seen as a means (together with associated reforms of criminal procedure, punishment, social policy, and political representation) of maintaining the dominance of a ruling class against the interests and opposition of the various sections of the working class, who constituted the majority of the population.

This revisionist interpretation was itself challenged by later work (S. Cohen and Scull 1983). More recent research suggests that both the traditional and the early revisionist accounts embody questionable assumptions, and a more complex, post-revisionist picture of police development has emerged (Emsley 1996, 2007, 2008, 2009; D. Taylor 1998: chaps. 4, 5; Rawlings 1999, 2002, 2008; Phillips and Storch 1999; Beattie 2001; A. T. Harris 2004; Godfrey and Lawrence 2005: chap. 2). To assist the reader in following the various interpretations, a chronology of the key events in British police history is given in the Appendix (pp. 261–4).

THE COP-SIDED VIEW OF HISTORY: THE ORTHODOX STORY

The orthodox studies are all more or less informative versions of the same 'ideology as history' (Robinson 1978). There is a spectrum of sobriety and rigour running from jingoistic eulogies intended for a popular audience (Minto 1965), through the early pioneering explorations of the English police tradition (M. Lee 1901; Reith 1938, 1940, 1943, 1948, 1952, 1956), to some awesomely detailed and scholarly work (Radzinowicz 1948, 1956, 1968; Hart 1951, 1955, 1956; Critchley 1978). The orthodox interpretation still appears in local force histories, and even the occasional general history (Stead 1985). Although the different orthodox accounts vary in analytical penetration and informative detail, they share certain core assumptions. These can be distilled into the answers to ten questions about the 'new' police. The orthodox view can then be contrasted with the revisionist and post-revisionist positions on these issues.

What was the source of the need for a new police?

The orthodox view sees the need for police reform as a straightforward rational response to the twin pressures of urban and industrial revolution. These brought new problems of order which were met by the new police. 'The breakdown in law and order marched in step with the progress of the Industrial Revolution' (Critchley 1978: 21).

What was wrong with the old policing arrangements?

'The eighteenth-century system was one of very severe penalties . . . but very weak and capricious enforcement machinery' (D. Philips 1983: 54). The punitiveness of the criminal code was increasingly seen as both inhumane and counter-productive. It made victims reluctant to prosecute, and juries loath to convict. That certainty of punishment was a more effective deterrent than severity became a fundamental axiom of the late-eighteenth-century 'classical' criminology of Beccaria and others. It was closely tied in with the arguments for police reform proposed by Henry and John Fielding, Patrick Colquhoun, and Jeremy Bentham (Rawlings 2008: 65).

The key agents of the 'old' policing system, the constables, watchmen and amateur justices, were widely lampooned by eighteenth- and nineteenth-century advocates of police reform, and by the orthodox histories. The office of constable had become so onerous that it became common to hire deputies. Penny-pinching led to the use of men who were 'scarcely removed from idiotism' (Critchley 1978: 18). Many magistrates exploited their offices for fees (the so-called 'trading justices'). The London nightwatchmen, the 'Charlies' (instituted in the reign of Charles II), were said to be 'contemptible, dissolute and drunken buffoons who shuffled along the darkened streets after sunset with their long staves and dim lanterns, calling out the time and the state of the weather, and thus warned the criminal of their approach' (ibid.: 1978: 30). Those members of the old constabulary who were not ineffective were represented as corrupt, milking their offices for rewards and fees. Thief-takers became thief-makers. The prototype of both, Jonathan Wild, had subordinates who 'stole on commission, and surrendered what they had taken to Wild who then returned the goods to their erstwhile owners' (Rock 1977: 215). In short, the old system was said to be uncertain, uncoordinated, reliant on private and amateur effort, and prone to corruption.

What were the motives for police reform?

The large and rapidly growing cities were seen as breeding grounds of crime and disorder. The novelist and lawyer Henry Fielding was a Middlesex judge in the 1740s and 1750s, and an early advocate of police reform. He and his brother John established the Bow Street Runners, a pioneering body of thief-takers (Beattie 2006, 2007). Fielding compared London to 'a vast wood or forest, in which a thief may harbour with as great security as wild beasts do in the deserts of Africa or Arabia', while Horace Walpole wrote of being 'forced to travel, even at noon, as if one were going to battle' (Critchley 1978: 21). Rapid urban and industrial development brought immense social dislocation, demoralization, crime and social conflict. 'Civilisation works its miracles and civilised man is turned back almost into a savage', wrote de Tocqueville after visiting Manchester (Hobsbawm 1968: 86).

Patrick Colquhoun, a London stipendiary magistrate and leading exponent of police reform, attempted in his 1795 *Treatise on the Police of the Metropolis* to quantify the number of criminals and the amount of loss engendered by their crimes, as a contribution to the then burgeoning 'science of police'—a branch of political economy with a much broader conception of 'police' than the specific bureaucratic organization now connoted by the term (Reiner 1988, 2007: 345–7; Pasquino 1991; McMullen 1996, 1998; Neocleous 2000a, 2000b; Dubber 2005: chap. 3; Dubber and Valverde 2006). In 1810 the government began publishing annual figures of indictable committals for trial in England and Wales, which showed an apparently inexorable increase (Philips 1980: 180). Even at the time, it was debated whether these reflected a 'real' increase in offending (Emsley 2007), as opposed to such factors as increasing ease of prosecution (Hay and Snyder 1989). But the Home Secretary, Robert Peel relied heavily on these statistics in the parliamentary debate before the 1829 Metropolitan Police Act.

In addition to the fear of rising crime, the orthodox view recognized the importance of public disorder as a motive for police reform. This was a concern about disorder in the double sense of declining moral standards, and the threat of riot. Colquhoun and other police reformers waxed loquacious about moral decay, which was also seen as an economic and political threat (Dodsworth 2007).

The role of politically motivated disorder in the creation of the new police was underplayed by the orthodox view. The notorious 1819 Peterloo Massacre (the brutal—there were eleven deaths and hundreds of injuries—suppression by magistrates, cavalry, and yeomanry of a large but peaceful demonstration in St Peter's Field, Manchester, in support of parliamentary reform) does not feature in Critchley (the standard orthodox reference). It got the briefest of mentions in Reith (1956: 122), and was assimilated to the 'crime industry'. The only political disorders that featured prominently in the orthodox histories were the Gordon Riots, the reactionary anti-Catholic demonstrations that were the immediate stimulus for Pitt's abortive 1785 Police Bill, the first attempt to establish a professional police force. Concentrating on them allowed the problem to be more readily depicted as 'City [of London] gangsterdom' (Reith 1943: 29).

The overall theme of the orthodox histories, then, was that police reform was motivated mainly by fear of crime, but also by moral and mob disorder, engendered by the problems of rapid transition to an urban industrial society. The early nineteenth century was seen simply as 'gangsterdom', 'an epoch of criminality' (M. Lee 1901: 203).

Who opposed the new police?

Given this picture of the new police as unequivocally necessary to control the evil by-products of industrial growth, the orthodox view was at something of a loss in explaining the weight and power of opposition to the establishment of the police.

After Pitt's 1785 Bill a series of expedients was introduced, notably the 1792 Middlesex Justices Act, creating twenty-one paid magistrates controlling seven police offices. In 1798 a Select Committee on Finance, largely influenced by Colquhoun, favoured a new police, but no legislation was introduced. Six parliamentary committees—in 1812, 1816, two in 1817, 1818, and 1822— considered London's policing arrangements, but recommended against a new police, before Peel was eventually successful in 1829.

The orthodox historians' only explanation of this was to impugn the intelligence or integrity of the opponents of the police. The rock upon which Pitt's 1785 Bill had foundered was the City's opposition to encroachment on their corporate rights, and Peel deftly avoided this by excluding the City from his 1829 Act. Much of the resistance to the police legislation from 1785 to 1856 was couched in rhetoric drawing on the supposed traditional liberties of Englishmen, which was invoked by aristocratic Tories and working-class radicals alike. The frequently quoted passage from the 1822 Committee Report—'It is difficult to reconcile an effective system of police, with that perfect freedom of action and exemption from interference, which are the great privileges and blessings of society in this country'—is dismissed by Critchley as 'thoroughly reactionary'.

Reith saw the opposition in an even more sinister light: 'It was the efforts of gangsterdom alone, and the success of its propaganda, which frustrated for nearly a century every attempt to end the menace of crime and disorder by creating police' (Reith 1943: 12). Altogether the orthodox view had no analysis of the social location and basis of the various currents of thought concerning the police, and denied the opposition any meaning or rationality that was not venal.

How long did opposition to the police last?

After the new police took to the streets, the orthodox histories have to account for the opposition of the masses who were not directly represented in the parliamentary debates. This opposition, although clearly virulent in the early 1830s, was depicted as rapidly evaporating once the worth and virtue of the new police became apparent. At first pamphlets circulated exhorting the populace to 'Join your Brother Londoners in one heart, one hand for the ABOLITION OF THE NEW POLICE', and attacking 'Peel's bloody gang'. During the fighting between the police and a meeting of the National Political Union, a PC Culley was fatally stabbed. The inquest jury returned a verdict of 'justifiable homicide'. This clearly indicated the strength of continuing public opposition to the police, but the conventional view had it that after a parliamentary inquiry, 'public opinion . . . veered in favour of the police' (Critchley 1978: 55). In the orthodox narrative, this was the crucial turning point. 'The police, though they did not then know it had won their final and conclusive victory over the Ultras. More importantly, they had won an even greater victory in the long term—the seal of "public approval"' (Ascoli 1979: 105). Altogether, in the orthodox view, opposition to the police may have been nasty and brutish, but it was blessedly short.

What was new about the 'new police'?

The orthodox histories argued both that the 'new' police established between 1829 and 1856 was a novel creation in terms of efficiency and integrity, and that it had roots in ancient traditions of communal self-policing.

The 'newness' consisted of the institution of a bureaucratic organization of professionals, rationally administering a policy of 'preventive policing', that is, regular patrols to deter crime, suppress disorder and maintain security. Gradually with the spread of the 'new' police throughout the country, following the Metropolitan 'prototype', a more coordinated network of systematic law enforcement came into being, but without a degree of central direction that would be incompatible with traditional liberties, thus striking a balance 'nicely adjusted to the British genius' (Critchley 1978: 101).

The 'newness' of the Metropolitan Police was also emphasized by the high standards of entry and discipline established by Peel and the two commissioners he appointed, Colonel Charles Rowan (of the Light Brigade) and Richard Mayne, a barrister. This meant that only one-sixth of the original intake of nearly 3,000 men remained four years later.

On the other hand, the force's ancient origins in communal self-policing and the continuity of the office of constable (with its common-law powers theoretically unaffected by incorporation into a bureaucratic body) were also stressed. This argument was pioneered by Melville Lee (1901: xxvii): 'Our English police system ... rests on foundations designed with the full approval of the people, we know not how many hundreds of years before the Norman conquest.' It was echoed by Reith, who saw the police as 'directly traceable to the dawn of European history, and to the customs of the Aryan tribes of the Continent whom their leaders made responsible for securing the observance of tribal laws' (Reith 1943: 14. See also Rolph 1962: 1–10; Critchley 1978: 1–28; Ascoli 1979: 1, 9–16). As far back as the tenth century, however, there was already a clear-cut feudal hierarchy into which the vestigial kin structure and communal self-policing traditions had been incorporated for order maintenance by a succession of invaders (Robinson 1979: 49, n. 36).

What was the social impact of the new police?

In the orthodox account, the social impact of the police was the clearly benign one of solving the problem of order and checking the spread of lawlessness: '3000 unarmed policemen, cautiously feeling their way against a hostile public, brought peace and security to London in place of the turmoil and lawlessness of centuries' (Critchley 1978: 55–6). This not only protected individual victims but stabilized society within a liberal democratic framework. The reformers' purpose was enunciated most clearly by Colquhoun in his *Treatise on the Police of the Metropolis*: 'Everything that can heighten in any degree the respectability of the office of constable, adds to the security of the state, and the life and property of every individual.' Reith waxed loquacious on the splendid advantages brought about by Peel's creation. 'It is an unquestionable historical fact that the appearance of public orderliness in Britain, and of individual willingness to cooperate in securing and maintaining it, coincides with the successful establishment of the police institution' (Reith 1943: 3). The same sentiments were echoed by most of the orthodox histories (M. Lee 1901: xxv–xxvii; Gorer 1955: 294–8, 305–12; Critchley 1978: xvii; Ascoli 1979: 3–4, 346–9). In the orthodox view the police were not only successful in the more immediate and mundane jobs of crime control and order maintenance; through their efforts they were ultimately to transform the whole national character, and, indeed, world civilization.

Who gained from the new police?

It was a striking theme of the orthodox analysis that not only did the police benefit society as a whole but, contrary to initial fears, their major impact was on the welfare of the working class and the poor. They were the guardians of the weak against the strong. Melville Lee (1901: xxx) claimed the police were 'designed to stand between the powerful and the weak, to prevent oppression, danger and crime'. Reith took up the argument. The 1839 Royal Commission report on the setting up of a rural constabulary was said to provide 'a remarkable picture ... of the sufferings endured by the working classes as the consequences of absence of police' (Reith 1956: 203). Critchley also pursued the theme that the poor had most to gain from the police. 'The wealthy paid gamekeepers to protect their property and slept with arms near at hand, and the middle-class tradesmen formed voluntary protection societies. The poor simply managed as best as they could until the reform of rural police was at last put in hand' (Critchley 1978: 28).

While on the one hand the poor and the working class were singled out by the orthodox histories as beneficiaries of the police, they were also pinpointed as the source of most crime. This followed on from Colquhoun's contemporary analysis linking indigence to crime and the need for police (*Treatise on Indigence*, 1806). Ascoli also stressed the particular contribution of the poor to the eighteenth-century 'crime problem': 'While the upper and middle classes exploited the financial possibilities of privilege and position, the lower orders—with no such advantages—resorted to crime on an unparalleled scale' (Ascoli 1979: 28). Despite this, by 1837 the new police were 'universally accepted' (ibid.: 111).

The orthodox historians were thus unanimous in claiming the universal benefits of the police, emphasizing the special gains of the poor and working class. They not only came to be protected from criminal victimization but were prevented from sinking into crime themselves through the promotion of that 'moral improvement of the labouring classes by the exercise of supervision and restraint' which Colquhoun saw as a prime police function (Radzinowicz 1956: 233; Dodsworth 2007).

Who controlled the police?

It was a central claim of the orthodox histories that English police power was only the crystallized power of the people. This was one reason for their eagerness to stress the roots of the police in ancient traditions of communal self-policing. The police were the police not of government but of the community. 'Happily for English liberty there has never existed in this country any police force at the disposal of the central government, powerful enough to coerce the nation at large. Our national police has always been of the people and for the people' (M. Lee 1901: 61). Reith emphasized 'the historic tradition that the police are the public and that the public are the police' (Reith 1956: 287).

Critchley more soberly rejected this idea of 'a mystical fusion between the police-man and the ordinary citizen' (Critchley 1978: xviii). But both he and Ascoli claimed emphatically that the new policing arrangements were democratically accountable: 'The device which is most characteristically English has been to arm the police with prestige rather than power, thus obliging them to rely on popular support' (ibid.).

The Metropolitan Police were made accountable to the Home Secretary as their police authority, to the chagrin of the 'arrogant and inefficient' justices and parochial authorities whose status and power was thus undermined (Ascoli 1979: 93–5). The relationship between Home Secretary and Metropolitan commissioner was nego-tiated as one in which the minister 'should deem it imprudent' to interfere in the force's internal working over the head of the commissioner, or in its '*operational role*' (ibid.: 106–12). The commissioner was 'the servant of the Crown and people, answerable to Parliament, in its capacity of *vox populi* . . . He, and every member of his force, is subject to the same law of which they are the executive arm . . . He is, by definition, as impartial in his field as the judiciary' (ibid.: 11).

Mayne's victory over the attempt of Samuel Phillips, under-secretary at the Home Office, to intervene more closely in police matters was seen as a triumph over 'bureaucratic arrogance'. That it left the path clear for considerable practical autonomy for the professional police commissioner was no danger. 'Not once did Rowan and Mayne seek to abuse their power nor did they consider themselves anything other than servants of the public, with a statutory duty to preserve the King's Peace' (ibid.: 112).

A measure of central direction over provincial policing arrangements marched on steadily from the 1835 Municipal Corporations Act (which required all boroughs to institute police forces). It was opposed by a continuing strain of rhetoric, denouncing each step as a sinister French, Russian, or Venetian (but at any rate distinctly Continental) usurpation of the traditional English rights of self-government, what Birmingham MP George Muntz called 'local institutions which had been in existence since the time of King Alfred' (cited in Critchley 1978: 116–17). In the end, the 1856 Act expressed a rough balance between the continuing responsibilities of local government and justices, and a measure of central government supervision. This was exercised through the establishment of a Home Office Inspectorate of Constabulary, which had to certify a force as efficient before it could qualify for a new Exchequer grant of 25 per cent of the cost of pay and clothing. This proved to be a wedge with which the Home Office was able to introduce more central direction, and chief constables to construct a large measure of autonomy from local control. But it incorporated a balance of nominal power, so the orthodox histories could see the pattern as embodying the principle of democratic accountability.

The final ingredient in popular control of the police was the strategy governing recruitment and training. 'It was a deliberate policy to recruit men "who had not the rank, habits or station of gentlemen" . . . the police was to be a homogeneous and democratic body, in tune with the people, understanding the people, belonging to the people, and drawing its strength from the people' (Critchley 1978: 52, citing Gash 1961: 502).

Thus the orthodox analysis maintained that the 'people' control the police. Partly this was a matter of formal channels of legal and democratic accountability. But fundamentally it derived from selecting the police in a representative way, and imbuing them with a sense that their powers derived from consent not coercion.

What model of historical explanation underlies orthodox police history?

The orthodox histories operated with a model of explanation which was teleological and unilinear. By 'teleological' I mean that the underlying dynamic driving the development of the police was an assumed 'fit' between the 'new police' model and the order maintenance requirements of an industrialized, liberal–democratic society. This urged on the progressive unfolding and realization of the police idea. But police development was not just the product of impersonal forces. The structural problems of industrialism and urbanization constituted merely 'the demand for order'. The supply of appropriate ideas and institutions to provide the requirements for order without eroding traditional liberties came from a battery of 'far-sighted' reformers who were the personalization of national genius. The accomplishments of these perspicacious 'pioneers of policing', the Fieldings, Colquhoun, Peel, Rowan, and Mayne, were celebrated in the orthodox histories (Stead 1977). However, the 'correct' ideas of these great men (as well as the 'false' notions of the opposition) were essentially epiphenomenal. At most they oiled (or spoked) the wheels of development and speeded (or retarded) its progress.

The pattern of development was portrayed as 'unilinear', that is, it had one clear direction, and despite temporary spills and setbacks never departed from this trajectory. The irresistible force of industrialization and its control problems, meeting the immovable object of stubborn English commitment to liberty, could result in only one outcome: the British bobby. Critchley and Radzinowicz emphasized English empirical trial and error, and the absence of tidy logicality, grand philosophical design or 'lofty constitutional principles'. But trial and error was only the specific mechanism by which the path was charted. The implicit explanation of police development was that the model which ultimately emerged (in stages, to be sure) best met the conflicting demands of order and liberty. The implicit explanatory schema was of the mutually conditioning interaction of innovative ideas and social circumstances, a sort of idealist dialectic. Having outlined the traditional view of police history, I shall turn to a similar analysis of the 'revisionist' critique that became dominant in historical work of the 1970s, contrasting its answers to the same questions. Revisionism was an unequivocal advance, specifying concrete and precise social bases of political conflict around the police, and relating policing to a wider context. However, it embodied opposite distortions to the orthodox account—a lop-sided rebuttal of cop-sided history.

While the orthodox view has been usefully analysed as 'ideology as history' (Robinson 1979), and revisionism has undeniably exposed orthodoxy's shortfalls as history, this does not dispose of it as ideology. The Reithian Police Principles, derived from those originally formulated by Sir Robert Peel in 1829 (Reith 1956: 286–7), may not be or ever have been realized in practice. But they have undeniably been a significant reference point for British police thinking. Moreover, as an aspiration for what a police force should be like they ought not to be dismissed too readily. A police force with the Reithian ethic as an institutional ideal to which obeisance is paid is preferable to one which is not committed explicitly to the 'transmuting of crude physical force ... into the force ... of public recognition' (ibid.: 286).

A LOP-SIDED VIEW OF HISTORY? THE REVISIONIST ACCOUNT

The model I have constructed of the traditional view is clearly an ideal type. It synthesizes the essential elements of the work of a diverse group of writers, none of whom fits the pure model in every respect. The ideal type of 'revisionism' I am about to construct is even more of a 'one-sided accentuation'.

The essence of revisionism was captured in the quote from Engels that heads Storch's 1975 article, the flagship of the approach. 'Because the English Bourgeois finds himself reproduced in his law, as he does in his God, the policeman's truncheon ... has for him a wonderfully soothing power. But for the workingman quite otherwise!' How does revisionism answer the same ten questions that the orthodox view addressed?

What was the source of the need for a new police?

Revisionism stressed that industrialization and urbanization occurred within a specifically capitalist framework. Crime and disorder, those consequences of industrialism which the traditionalists identified as the basis of the demand for order, are not hard and unequivocal categories. Each was defined variously by different political viewpoints and social classes. At the root of the new problem of order was the shifting, accentuated pattern of class division and conflict associated with the rise of capitalism.

The rapid growth of large cities involved the development of much greater segregation between classes. The poor areas may have generated more crime and disorder as a consequence of anonymity, demoralization, and despair. The upper-class perception of routine crime altered, so that it came to seem symptomatic of a deeper threat to the social order as a whole, stemming from the 'dangerous classes', the rapidly growing urban poor (Silver 1967: 3).

The meaning of collective disorder also changed. Until the early nineteenth century, riotous protest was an accepted, mutually understood means by which the politically unrepresented masses communicated grievances to the ruling elite—'bargaining by riot'. But with the spread of industrial capitalism riot came to be regarded not as a form of proto-democracy but as a fundamental threat to the social and political order (Hobsbawm 1959: 116).

Capitalism also required a tighter disciplining of hitherto relatively loosely regulated aspects of social relations. 'A stable public order was a precondition of rational calculation on the part of industrial capitalists' (Spitzer and Scull 1977: 277).

The development of a formally 'free' labour market meant that the traditional practice of workers retaining some of the produce they handled had to be stopped, and replaced by the 'cash nexus' (Bunyan 1977: 61). Payment in kind was redefined as theft. This was part of a broader pattern of change whereby a 'moral economy', in which prices and relationships were seen as subject to traditional conceptions of justice, was replaced by a pure market economy, governed only by the impersonal laws of supply and demand (Thompson 1968, 1971, 1975, 1992; Neocleous 2000a, 2000b, 2006: 29–34).

The new mechanized conditions of factory production also required that the formally free labour force be subject to tighter discipline in both work and 'leisure' time to fit the rhythms and regimentation of capitalist organization. This produced 'the criminalisation of traditional street pastimes which were solely recreational' (P. Cohen 1979: 120–1). The police officer became a 'domestic missionary' (Storch 1976), 'the moral entrepreneur of public propriety' (P. Cohen 1979: 128), charged with converting the folkways and mores of savage street dwellers to respectability and decency.

Revisionists distinguished significantly between fractions of the ruling class. The industrial bourgeoisie gained in significance relative to the still dominant landed gentry. The bourgeoisie and their property were more exposed to crime and disorder, less embedded in traditional social networks of deference and paternalistic personalized authority, and more reluctant to give their time or life and limb in voluntary police bodies.

What was wrong with the old police?

The revisionists challenged the orthodox view that the main problems with the old police arrangements were corruption and inefficiency. There may have been widespread corruption among the thief-takers, but this is endemic in detective work throughout police history and continues today (Hobbs 1988; Newburn 1999; Punch 1985, 2009).

The main debate, however, was about the alleged inefficiency of the old police. Several critics discerned upper-class snobbery and condescension in the traditional knockabout humour at the expense of the old constables and Charlies (M. Brogden 1982: 53). What was represented by respectable contemporaries as inefficiency or corruption pure and simple may have been fear of the sympathy between the old police and their own communities which made them unreliable as the policing of morality, crime, and disorder became politicized. The loyalty of working-class police drawn from the local community could not be depended upon by manufacturers for controlling industrial disputes (Foster 1974: 56–61). It has been suggested that similar motives stimulated the later American establishment of state police forces and the 'professionalization' of city forces in the late nineteenth and early twentieth centuries (Robinson 1978).

In any case, the revisionists argued that social order in the eighteenth century was not dependent upon the direct effectiveness of the formal control apparatus. Contrary to the view of contemporary reformers and orthodox police historians that the eighteenth-century criminal justice and penal systems were an antiquated and irrational mess, they effectively maintained the stability of the old hierarchical social order. A combination of rules and rituals emphasized both the majesty and terror of the law, embodied above all in the 'Bloody Code', the proliferation of new capital offences in the early nineteenth century (Thompson 1975; Hay 1975; Styles 1977), and the ceremonials of death sentences and public execution (Gatrell 1994; Linebaugh 2006). This was combined with strict adherence to legality, so the system symbolized impartial and formal justice. Despite the proliferation of the death penalty for many new offences, less than half the people condemned to death were executed. This was precisely the nub of the utilitarian reformers' criticism that severe nominal punishments, which were unlikely to be carried out, were counter-productive as deterrents. Hay turned the orthodox argument on its head. The moral bonds built up between superiors and subordinates throughout the social hierarchy by the process of interceding to seek mercy, and the debts incurred when it was granted, cemented a social order of small communities based on personal ties more effectively than an efficient criminal justice system could have done. In the end the rulers gained most from their own mercy. 'The private manipulation of the law by the wealthy and powerful was in truth a ruling-class conspiracy ... [which] made it possible to govern eighteenth-century England without a police force and without a large army' (Hay 1975: 52–6).

The old institutions of suppressing riot were, claimed the revisionists, counter-productive rather than merely ineffective. The traditional means of responding to collective disorder were the Army, the militia (raised by compulsory ballot by the lord lieutenant of a county), and volunteer forces, the yeomanry, and special constables. The militia was politically unreliable, as those selected often employed deputies, who would be drawn from the same social strata as rioters. The Army was like a sledgehammer. It could only alternate 'between no intervention and the most drastic procedures—the latter representing a declaration of internal war with lingering consequences of hate and resentment' (Silver 1967: 12). The volunteer forces had been *politically* dependable. But urban bourgeois manufacturers were less ready to answer a call to arms—'the classic confrontation of an agrarian military tradition and a pacific commercial and industrial one' (ibid.: 10). Not only were the manufacturers less personally valorous than their hunting and shooting rural counterparts, but they saw that 'the use of social and economic superiors as police exacerbated rather than mollified class violence' (ibid.). As the 1839 Royal Commission on the Rural Constabulary put it: 'the animosities created or increased, and rendered permanent by arming master against servant, neighbour against neighbour, by triumph on the one side and failure on the other, were even more deplorable than the outrages actually committed'. This motivated the establishment of a 'bureaucratic police system that . . . drew attack and animosity upon itself, and seemed to separate the assertion of 'constitutional' authority from that of social and economic dominance' (ibid.: 11–12).

The new manufacturing and merchant urban bourgeoisie lacked certain protections against crime which the rural gentry enjoyed. They did not have the ecological safeguards of large estates and lack of proximity to the 'dangerous classes' (M. Brogden 1982: 49–50), nor did they enjoy the services of private retainers and guards. Their capital took the form of movable merchandise and machinery, much more vulnerable to theft or damage.

In short, the revisionist view emphasized not so much the intrinsic ineffectiveness of the old privatized policing as its growing unsuitability for the new class relations of a capitalist society.

What were the motives for police reform?

The immediate motives for establishing the new police were the same in the revisionist and the orthodox account, but with the emphasis reversed. The basic source of increasing disorder was capitalist development. This disrupted existing social networks, destroyed moral communities, replaced personal bonds by the cash nexus, and caused immense deprivation and demoralization. The official crime statistics which began to be published in the early nineteenth-century registered an upward trend (Gatrell 1980, 1988). However, the revisionists questioned how much of this was a genuine increase in criminality, and how much was due to changed sensitivities, penal reform, and the availability of police, leading to a greater propensity to prosecute offences (King 2000, 2003, 2006; Emsley 2007). What was certainly true was that many respectable and influential contemporary commentators took the figures as indicating that a new police was needed. Police reform was part of a much broader rationalization of the penal code, punishment (the use of prison as the standard mode), criminal procedure, and the prosecution process, as well as other aspects of social policy with a control element (Donajgrodski 1977; D. Philips 1980; Hay and Snyder 1989; Beattie 2001).

However, the crucial reason for the creation of the new police was seen as neither crime control, moral discipline nor riot control per se. It was the need for a force that could stabilize relations between conflicting social classes as far as possible. Therefore the police were charged with an 'omnibus mandate' of regulating all facets of working-class life (Storch 1975: 88; Neocleous 2000a, 2000b). In the revisionist view, then, the motive for formation of the new police was the maintenance of the order required by the capitalist class, with control of crime, riot, political dissidence, and public morality being separate subsidiary facets of this overall mission.

Who opposed the new police?

Opposition to the new police came partly from sections of the upper class. But this was not irrational obscurantism, as the orthodox histories implied. The source of ruling-class opposition was a distinct sector of the class, the landed gentry, and was perfectly rational in basis. The gentry did not need to support a public police out of rate-payers' money, when their own security was adequately protected by private means. They could rely on 'large numbers of personal servants to guard their plate and their wives' (Hay 1975: 59). Furthermore, their local political power bases would be undermined by a more rationalized and professional police, for they controlled the magistracy that was the focal point of the old system. This remained a strong strand of the opposition to each increment of standardization from 1829 to 1856, and accounted for the form that local police authorities ultimately took. Furthermore, it was feared that the development of a more rationalized system of crime control would rupture the delicately constructed relationships of deference and condescension that were the microscopic basis of order. The gentry could expatiate high-mindedly on the threat to traditional liberties posed by the importation of French-, Russian-, or Prussian-influenced policing schemes, and scoff at the evidence of the volume of mere larceny assembled by Colquhoun and Peel. But if initially opposition to the police came from the landed gentry, this evaporated as the threat of Chartism grew. Later upper-class opposition was over the specific form and control of the police rather than the principle itself.

The source of deepest opposition to the new police was the working class, both before and after the inception of professional policing. This was only indirectly reflected in Parliament, for the working class did not have the vote. But in places with class-conscious working-class majorities, following the 1832 Reform Act's enfranchisement of the petty bourgeoisie 'who were dependent on working-class custom', pressure could be put on MPs to achieve a measure of indirect working-class parliamentary representation (Foster 1974: 52–4). As Foster's study of Oldham shows, Oldham MPs invoked the standard libertarian rhetoric about 'tyranny', describing the police as 'an unconstitutional force so palpably for the express purpose of coercing the people' (ibid.: 69–70).

But the prime arenas for working-class opposition to the police were extra-parliamentary, expressed in collective disorder and small-scale street conflicts. Anti-police riots regularly followed the coming of the 'plague of blue locusts' to northern working-class communities (Storch 1975: 94).

How long did opposition to the police last?

Whereas in the orthodox histories initial working-class opposition to the police disappeared fairly rapidly after the advent of the new police, the revisionists traced a line of intermittent overt hostility (expressing continuous latent conflict) right down to contemporary urban disorders. Philip Cohen discerned the same 'ancient tradition of collective self-defence' against police interventions in street life in the London of the early 1900s, although overt physical conflict came to be replaced by a perennial hostility between the police and working-class male youth (P. Cohen 1979: 120–1; see also White 1986, 2008, 2009). M. Brogden documented a similar 'residue of continuing, if spasmodic conflict between the police institution and the lower orders . . . For the . . . participants in the street economy . . . attitudes to the police institution throughout the first century of policing remained essentially unchanged. They were subject to continuing, occasional, and apparently arbitrary "culls"' (M. Brogden 1982: 180–1). He traced a direct line from the nineteenth-century anti-police riots in Liverpool to Toxteth in 1981: 'The composition and objectives of the street combatants of July 1981 replicates the sentiments of those earlier anti-police demonstrations' (ibid.: 241–2). While relations between the regularly employed, respectable, and organized sections of the working class and the police were not characterized by open conflict to the same degree, approval was tentative and brittle, with many violent and bitter struggles in the first three decades of this century (ibid.: 186–9; 1991).

What was new about the 'new police'?

To the revisionists, the novelty of the 'new' police was neither efficiency nor integrity. Ineffectiveness, indiscipline, and corruption remain endemic among modern police officers. The novelty of the 'new' police was that they were a bureaucratically organized force charged with a mandate to 'prevent' crime by regular patrol and surveillance of the whole society (but especially the denizens of the 'dangerous classes'—St James's was to be guarded by watching St Giles). Intermittent and spasmodic law enforcement dependent upon private initiative was replaced by continuous state policing financed by the public purse. Control through particularistic traditions of personal deference was displaced by impersonal authority legitimated by values of legal rationality and universalism. '[T]he bureaucratization of police work placed day-to-day operations of the control system in the hands of faceless agents of the state, men who no longer operated in their own self-interest, but (presumably) in the general interest' (Spitzer and Scull 1977a: 280–1).

With this notion of a sharp break between old and new, the revisionists rebutted the orthodox 'citizen in uniform' mythology of fundamental continuity between the modern constable and antique traditions of tribal self-policing. The police were changed by becoming a large, disciplined, legally empowered, and technologically advanced organization, clearly distinct from the ordinary citizen.

What was the social impact of the new police?

In the revisionist account the advent of modern professional policing transformed the social order into a 'policed society'. This 'is unique in that central power exercises potentially violent supervision over the population by bureaucratic means widely diffused throughout civil society in small and discretionary operations that are capable of rapid concentration' (Silver 1967: 8). The net result was the penetration of society by the political and moral authority of the dominant strata, the construction of an essentially manipulated (and thus vulnerable) consensus.

The new police constituted part of a move to a more centralized social order, in which the state penetrated the depths of society, spearheaded by the police institution. But for the police to operate as the advance scouts of the state implied some integration with the policed. The consent negotiated was perennially tenuous and liable to be disrupted in times of crisis. Normally, however, the police painted a surface gloss of serenity over the volatile conflicts of capitalism.

Who gained from the new police?

Revisionism stood on its head the orthodox conception of universal benefits from policing, with special gains to the poor and weak. The beneficiaries of the new police were seen as the bourgeoisie who established them, and the police themselves, who carved out opportunities for social advancement and greater power. The bourgeoisie gained most from the new police, who protected their property, safeguarded their security, and stabilized the social order on which their power and position was based. The petty bourgeoisie, particularly shopkeepers, were also identified as benefiting especially from the new police, who protected them from depredation and economic competition from the lower strata involved in the street economy (M. Brogden 1982: 182–3). This particular view was largely shared by the orthodox historians. Finally, creation of the new police opened up an avenue of social mobility to those working-class men who were prepared to endure the hostility of their former fellows. As the police occupation gained some measure of professional stability, it began to draw in working men who were attracted by the middle-class image of respectability and a career (Steedman 1984: Part 2; P. Lawrence 2000, 2003; Shpayer-Makov 2002). The chief constables (who in the county forces often were ex-Army officers) became powerful figures with a considerable measure of autonomy over an important area of local policy (M. Brogden 1982: 70–1; Steedman 1984: 41–55; Wall 1998).

Who controlled the new police?

The one thing on which revisionists agreed was that 'the people' did *not* control the police. But there was some debate about whether or not the provincial police were controlled by the local elite (or in the case of the Metropolitan Police by the Home Secretary). As indicated earlier, the Home Secretary nominally had control over the Metropolitan Police as its police authority. But from early on the commissioners were conceded a large discretion to determine the conduct of the force. The commissioners also successfully fended off control attempts from the existing magistracy. However, the relationship between the Home Office and the commissioner continued to be ill-defined, with, for example, a prolonged argument between them in 1886–7 over the issue of the policing of demonstrations in Trafalgar Square (Bailey 1981: 94–125).

Much discussion among revisionists concerned the degree of control of police by local elites in the counties (through the magistracy) and in boroughs (through the Watch Committee). The two positions on these issues reflected wider theoretical differences between an 'instrumentalist' conception of the police as 'tools' of the dominant class and a 'structuralist' account of policing as a function of the political economy.

Foster implied an instrumentalist view in his description of the struggles over control of the police in Lancashire between the working-class movement and the manufacturers in the first three decades of the nineteenth century. When local constables were controlled by the town vestry in Oldham, or by the Police Commission following the 1826 Oldham Police Act, they were exposed to popular pressure. However, the 1839 County Police Act placed control of the police in the hands of the magistracy, and the police became a weapon of the employers. The rules of conduct for the new force laid down that policemen should be 'non-political', that is, insulated from the earlier form of popular control (Foster 1974: 56–61).

The clear import of Foster's account was that the police were under the control of the police authorities, and the question was: who dominated the authority? Storch also suggested an instrumentalist view when he attributed the 'implantation of a modern police in the industrial districts of Northern England' to 'a new consensus among the propertied classes that it was necessary to create a professional, bureaucratically organized lever of urban discipline' (Storch 1975: 86).

The structuralist account was put most clearly by M. Brogden (1982). One of the main theses of Brogden's book was that, contrary to the weight of both orthodox and radical received opinion, chief constables achieved a large measure of autonomy very early on after the establishment of the new police. This was true not only of county forces, whose chief constables had overt control over policing, but also of boroughs, where chief constables were supposed to be under the direction of the Watch Committee. (A similar position was advanced in Jefferson and Grimshaw 1984b.) In the case of Liverpool, Brogden found that the head constable began to show a measure of independence from the Watch Committee as early as 1841 (five years after the force was established), and by the end of the century had achieved 'considerable latitude of decision-making'. However, Liverpool may well have been a special case: it was one of the largest borough forces, and Brogden emphasized the peculiarities of the local political economy. Moreover, it was Brogden's thesis that the organizational autonomy constructed by the chief constable was a relative one. Neither chief constable nor local elite had much freedom of manoeuvre, as both were constrained by the exigencies of the political economy. Thus Brogden referred to the often-cited instance of the 1890 Watch Committee instruction to Head Constable Captain Nott-Bower to 'proceed against all brothels'. This order has usually been invoked to demonstrate Watch Committee control. Brogden argued that the episode meant the opposite. Not only was it an isolated occurrence, but the chief constable could within a year revert to the old approach because the strict prosecution policy had such damaging effects on trade. What Brogden illustrated was not so much the autonomy of the chief constable, as that both he and the Watch Committee were bearers of structural imperatives (M. Brogden 1982: 69).

However, while the revisionists argued about the precise relations of local elite and police chief, and of both to the political economy, they were united in denying the orthodox claim that the new police were subject to popular control.

What model of historical explanation underlies revisionism?

The revisionist account was teleological and unilinear (like the orthodox history). In the instrumentalist variant, the ruling class was induced to establish the police by the perceived 'fit' between the police and the control requirements of capitalism (as distinct from modern industrialism per se). 'The genius of the British ruling class is that they realised the need to have such a force and set about creating it' (I. MacDonald 1973, cited in Bunyan 1977: 62).

In the structuralist account the link between the exigencies of capitalism and police development was not necessarily mediated by a clear ruling-class perception of this purpose. But there was the same notion of an inexorable drive along only one possible trajectory. The working-class resistance which revisionists admiringly celebrated was nonetheless doomed to romantic failure. The ideas of the opposition (laudable) or the proponents of police reform (oppressive) were ultimately epiphenomenal. The real dynamic was the unfolding requirements of capital. To the idealist dialectic of the orthodox view, revisonism counterposed a materialist dialectic of a similarly deterministic kind.

ORTHODOXY AND REVISIONISM: CRITIQUE AND SYNTHESIS

Revisionism constituted an unequivocal advance in our understanding of the emergence of the new police. Above all, it was located in a broader analysis of the social conflicts and in particular the class and power structure of the eighteenth and nineteenth centuries. This was hardly surprising, for it was largely the work of professional historians sharing a wider concern for social, economic and political history. However, the early revisionist view was in many respects merely an inversion of the traditional approach. To the latter's uncritical consensus model it opposed an equally one-sided conflict perspective. Just as the orthodox historians, faced with evidence of hostility and opposition to the police dismissed this as malevolent or misguided, so too the revisionists, confronted with apparent periods and pockets of working-class consent to policing, regarded this as manipulated, a brittle skin over a bubbling volcano of resentment. To the revisionists, conflict between police and working class in a capitalist society had structural roots, so periods of social integration could be only an artificially constructed, temporary truce. On the other hand, in the traditionalist analysis a liberal–democratic industrial society was structurally integrated, so social conflict could only be a superficial phenomenon (and was often regarded as manipulated by agitation—a counterpart to the revisionist conception of an artificially constructed ideological consent, 'false consciousness'). I shall critically evaluate the orthodox and revisionist analyses in terms of the ten dimensions on which I compared them, suggesting a more complex picture, informed by the burgeoning historical research literature of the last three decades (for recent summaries see Rawlings 2008; Emsley 2008).

I shall start with the question: What model of historical explanation underlies revisionism?—the basic model of historical explanation, as the logically prior issue. Both the orthodox and revisionist approaches assumed a 'fit' between the type of police system and the control requirements of an industrial or capitalist society. It was those conditions, not of their own making, which called into being the actions of the men who made their own history by creating a new police force. The ultimate question is whether a complex modern industrial society could exist without some sort of police force, in the minimal sense of a body of people mandated to intervene in situations potentially requiring the exercise of legitimate force. This is an essentially metaphysical issue, dependent upon conceptions of human nature, the 'iron laws' of social inter-action and organization (if any), views of morality, justice, and even deeper matters of ultimate ends, meaning, and the nature of being—the province of religious belief. Anthropological evidence clearly documents small-scale societies without specialist police, and police institutions have complex conditions of emergence. Nonetheless it seems utopian to suppose that we could do without a police force in any conceivable large-scale and complex industrial social order, whether or not it was capitalist. Policing is Janus faced, reproducing simultaneously the conditions of existence of complex social coexistence, 'general order', *and* of specific patterns of inequality and hierarchy, 'special order', 'parking tickets and class repression' (Marenin 1983). But, even if some police force is necessary in the last analysis, it does not follow that alternative lines of development were or are impossible. Without constructing a 'counter-factual' history of the police, let us consider just one or two possibilities.

Is it conceivable that Peel might not have been able to pilot the 1829 Act so skil-fully through Parliament? After all, most histories do express surprise that, following so many decades of opposition, the Act was eventually passed as smoothly as it was. It may be granted that the metropolis would eventually have needed a new police. But by the time that eventuality materialized, perhaps the reformed Parliament would have taken a different view of making the Home Secretary the police authority? Per-haps it would have wanted to include a measure of local elected representation for the police authority—no taxation without representation.[1] Or we can contemplate a rather different counter-factual. Is it not conceivable that those contemporaries who pressed for a more militaristic response to the industrial and political disturbances during the post-Napoleonic Wars and Reform Bill crises could have carried the day?[2] Then we might not now speak of England's comparative uniqueness in not having a 'third force' explicitly specialized for suppressing riots, and of its relatively benign tra-dition in crowd control. Once it is conceded that the path of development was not predetermined, our perspective on all the other questions shifts. Above all, the ideas and arguments of contemporaries assume a new significance as independent sources of influence, not just more or less wise or misguided epiphenomena hastening or hin-dering, but not diverting, the course of history. Furthermore, while these ideas and arguments are related to class position, and broadly limited by structural constraints generated by the political economy, they are not foreordained by them. Nor are people's strategies necessarily the best for their interests.[3] It is in this light that I shall turn to the other nine questions about the emergence of the police.

What was the source of the need for a new police?

The police are needed to deal with conflicts, disorders, and problems of coordination which are necessarily generated by any complex and materially advanced social order. The orthodox histories (and undoubtedly many police officers themselves) see these as stemming from a perennial and asocial struggle between good and evil. To deny the reality of the evil deeds that big-city police confront every day would be to invite the opprobrium that practical police officers, who are in the 'tomorrow business', rightly heap on armchair academic utopians. But many of the issues they confront are rooted in structural contradictions and tensions which are inevitable in any advanced society. A fundamental difficulty in analysing policing is that the police have the inextricably dual function of handling troubles derived both from the problems of *any* industrial society *and* from its specifically capitalist form. Orthodoxy neglects the latter dimension, the role of the police in conflicts generated by inequality and privilege. But revisionism pushed aside the aspects of policing concerned with universal interests in social order, cohesion, and protection. The police cannot be written off either as 'conning bastards' or as all sweetness and light (M. Brogden 1981). Problems of interpersonal offending and political conflict are engendered by the pressures of industrialization and urbanization whatever the social framework, but in early nineteenth-century England they took the concrete form of class conflict in capitalism (although the prevalence of intra-class victimization must not be overlooked). With the decline of the influence of Marxist perspectives in the academy during the heyday of neo-liberal hegemony the significance of class inequalities in shaping policing has been sidelined. Historical research has increasingly focused on detail, bracketing off the wider social issues at the core of revisionism. In some cases they are explicitly denied. A recent paper on the eighteenth-century police reformers, for example, castigates the work of Neocleous (2000a, 2000b) for being 'based upon anachronistic neo-Marxist assumptions about the nature of capitalism and class struggle' (Dodsworth 2007: 440). However, the fact that the eighteenth-century police reformers operated with 'a discursive structure . . . entirely alien to that of Marx' (ibid.: 451) does not mean that the problems they were addressing were not shaped by the class inequalities and conflicts of emerging industrial capitalism. Although the orthodox interpretation rightly identified the control problems spawned by rapid urbanization and industrialization as shaping the demand for police reform, the revisionists are correct in their emphasis on the specific tensions and conflicts engendered by class divisions.

However, these overarching perspectives only have the propaedeutic function of pointing our attention in a certain direction. To assist our enquiries further we must proceed to the interrogation of the usual suspects.

What was wrong with the old police?

The orthodox histories depicted the old control institutions as corrupt and inefficient; the revisionists portrayed them as effective in maintaining ruling-class hegemony in the eighteenth century precisely through a lack of technical rationality. What they agreed on was that the old institutions were ineffective in a direct instrumental sense.

More recent research has cast doubt on the received certainties of both sides of the debate. Neither the old constables nor the watchmen were as ineffective or corrupt as painted by orthodoxy (Kent 1986; Paley 1989; Reynolds 1998). Some of the provincial justices had been assiduous and effective in crime detection (Styles 1982). Some of the developments in policing during the eighteenth century, such as the Bow Street Runners or the Thames River Police, achieved a degree of preventive and investigative competence that was not evidently inferior to the subsequent Peelian police (Styles 1983; Beattie 2001, 2006, 2007; A. T. Harris 2004; Rawlings 2008).

Nor were the existing forms of riot control as ineffective, either technically or politically, as the orthodox and revisionist cases suggest. In particular, both the Army and local magistrates seemed quite adept at cooling down potential disorder. In the longer term, philanthropy and poor relief were often mobilized to reduce the tensions generating disorder. Altogether it might be more appropriate to ask why in the acute economic distress and upheaval of the early nineteenth century, and with the revolutionary ideological example of France, there was not *more* political turbulence than there was. If the fear of riot and the 'dangerous classes' was as acute as both orthodox and revisionist historians suggest, the long delay in police reform remains a baffling mystery. 'A large-scale police force was not created in England before 1829 because the authorities were confident that they could maintain public order using the old system, with *ad hoc* modifications. In this they were more justified than has often been allowed' (Stevenson 1977: 47–8).

Hay's analysis of the eighteenth-century criminal justice system has been challenged by subsequent research. Styles (1977) pointed out that the proliferation of new capital statutes (especially the Black Act) which Hay, Thompson, and the other revisionists saw as the spearhead of an 'extending tyranny of exclusive property' were the least used of all capital statutes. Furthermore, Hay and his associates emphasized primarily those criminal activities 'which involved a clear conflict of interpretation between authority and local communities', such as blacking, poaching, and smuggling. They played down the routine thefts and assaults that were the bulk of prosecuted criminal offences, and over which there might have been more general consensus. Brewer and Styles's 1980 collection confirmed Hay's account of the highly discretionary character of eighteenth-century criminal law, and the ideological significance of 'the rule of law'. But they qualified the picture of it as a unilateral weapon of the ruling class. The judicial process *could* be used as a class tool, and to legitimate existing social arrangements or changes desired by the patrician class. As in any legal order, its benefits were disproportionately available to those with the greatest means. 'But this does not mean that we should regard the seventeenth- and eighteenth-century legal process as simply an instrument of an elite, or as serving only a class function' (J. Brewer and Styles 1980: 19). Even the grievances of the poor tended to be expressed in terms of authority's dereliction of legal duty, rather than a challenge to authority per se (P. King 2000, 2006).

Langbein (1983) launched the most vitriolic onslaught on Hay's 'fatal flaws'. He partly relied on his own data from mid-century Old Bailey cases, which suggested that 'we often cross a class line when we move from the offender to his victim, but not a class gulf'. The overrepresentation of the poor as defendants was an indication not of the intrinsic class character of the law or criminal justice system, but of the way that universal law impartially applied in an unequal society mirrored that inequality. 'To seize upon that as the *raison d'être* of the criminal justice system is, however, to mistake the barnacles for the boat' (Langbein 1983: 120).

In sum, then, later historical work suggested a more complex view of the 'old' policing arrangements than either orthodoxy or revisionism. The eighteenth-century criminal justice system was diverse and discretionary, but not as ineffective as earlier writers suggested. Nor was it the unilateral weapon of the ruling class portrayed by revisionism. The establishment of the new police was not due to the patent breakdown or inadequacy of the old.

What were the motives for police reform?

The motive stressed by the police reformers, notably Peel in his introduction of the 1829 Metropolitan Police Bill in Parliament, was fear of rising crime. But it was unclear whether crime *was* increasing. The statistics for committals to trial certainly registered an apparently inexorable upward trend. But there were those even in the 1829 debates who challenged the validity of these figures in the light of the greater ease of prosecution since the 1750s (D. Philips 1980: 179–80; Emsley 2007). By the time we come to the debates on the 1839 and 1856 Bills opponents were ready to jump in with the obvious argument that the police reformers were using rising crime statistics to justify the extension of a preventive police, the efficacy of which was called into question by those very figures. Police reformers were forced to abandon the numbers game (Watts-Miller 1987: 43–7).

Nor does the argument of such orthodox histories as Tobias (1967) that whatever the quantity of crime, it was of a more serious nature—the work of a growing professional criminal class—derive much sustenance from recent evidence. Outside London there is little indication that offending was the work of people exploiting crime for a livelihood, or making rich pickings out of their offences. On the other hand, the revisionist notion of 'social' crime as proto-political protest is also hard to sustain. Most offences were 'prosaic and undramatic, involving small amounts being stolen, squalid robberies, burglaries and assaults . . . nor are there visible indications of social purpose, still less of the individualistic waging of the class war, behind most "normal" criminal acts' (Philips 1977: 286–7; D. Taylor 1998: chaps. 1–3).

The 1856 County and Borough Act, which spread the new police throughout the country, was motivated partly by dread of vagrant criminality associated with the end of the Crimean War and the prospect of a footloose army of unemployed returning soldiers. There was also apprehension that the end of transportation meant that 'an organised race of criminals' released on tickets-of-leave would roam the country-side (Steedman 1984: 25). But these fears were only able to overcome concern about threats to liberty and rate-payers' purses after two abortive Police Bills had been de-feated in 1854 and 1855, and after much parliamentary shenanigans and wheeler-dealing. Evidently the threat to social order posed by crime cannot have been so clearly overwhelming as either the police reformers (or the orthodox and revisionist histories) implied.

The same qualifications must be levelled at the fear of political and social disor-der, which revisionists see as the primary motive for police reform. True, reference to riot was not (as the orthodox view has it) entirely absent from Peel's 1829 parliamen-tary presentation. (He raised it in debate, although not in his introductory speech.) The disorders associated with Chartism were certainly very much at the forefront of the debates leading to the 1839 County Police Act. But a strong current of influen-tial contemporary opinion agreed with Disraeli that expanding the police throughout the provinces amounted to a declaration of civil war against the people and would be counter-productive. Social harmony could be restored only by the privileged part of the nation once more recognizing their duties to the second nation (Watts-Miller 1987: 47–8). Fears for the survival of the social order, even at the height of Chartist agitation, were not sufficient to overcome the traditional suspicion and miserliness of over half the counties of England and Wales, who refused to utilize the possibility of establishing a rural constabulary allowed by the 1839 Act (Philips and Storch 1999). Monkkonen has made similar points about the parallel thesis that the American city police were a straightforward response to rising crime or political and class conflict: 'If each city had adopted a uniformed police only after a riot, changing crime rate, or the need for a new kind of class-control agency, many places would not today have a uniformed po-lice' (Monkkonen 1981: 57). Rather, 'growth of uniformed urban police forces should be seen simply as a part of the growth of urban service bureaucrats' (ibid.: 55). The establishment of the English and Welsh provincial police was to some extent a product of a similar process of gradual and uneven diffusion of models of rationalized urban administration (Emsley 1996: chap. 3; Jones 1996; Taylor 1998; Philips and Storch 1999). The development of the Portsmouth police, for example, was not the product of any local pressure for reform arising out of crime or disorder, but part of the national spread of Whig conceptions of rationalized local government by the 1835 Municipal Corporations Act which made all boroughs establish a Watch Committee and 'new' police force (J. Field 1981: 42–8).

In short, the police reformers certainly perceived those threats of crime and disorder that orthodox and revisionist historians pick out as the motives for police reform. But influential sections of the elite did not share this panic. The entrepreneurial activities of the reformers themselves, who became dominant in central government, and the dif-fusion of their model of rational local government administration, played a large part in the setting up of the new police throughout Britain. It was not an automatic reflex of urbanization and industrial capitalism.

Who opposed the new police?

The revisionist critique of orthodoxy's dismissal of opposition to the police as simply misguided or malicious is confirmed by subsequent research (D. Taylor 1998: chap. 4; Philips and Storch 1999). 'In the 1830s and 1840s opposition to the new police was part of a "rejectionist" front ranging from Tory to gentry to working-class radicals against an increasing number of government measures seeking to regulate and control more and more aspects of productive and social life' (Weinberger 1981: 66). Detailed analyses of the various parliamentary debates about the new police suggest, however, that the complex and diverse currents of opinion do not fall neatly into any clear-cut politics of class interests. Whereas the manufacturers had perhaps more need for a new police than the gentry (as the revisionists argue) they were more influential in local borough government than at Westminster, so had an interest in resisting centralizing measures like the 1856 Act (and *a fortiori* its two abortive predecessors). Above all, however, a close reading of the debates suggests the importance of varying political philosophies and principles which were not reducible neatly to sectional interests (Hart 1978). More-over, many contemporaries, lacking the benefits of hindsight (or perhaps even if they had them!), were genuinely unsure about the validity of conflicting arguments about the efficacy or counter-productiveness of new policing arrangements for crime control, social harmony, and political order. Fears about threats to liberty, concern about fiscal prudence, anxieties about local democratic accountability of the police, were neither irrational nor readily correlated with identifiable sectional interests. These partly inde-pendent conflicting ideological currents—misguided, laudable, or whatever—shaped not only the pace but the pattern of police reform.

How long did opposition persist?

The evidence of sustained anti-police hostility and violence that the revisionists accu-mulated was certainly sufficient to dispel the orthodox notion of early acceptance of the new police by the mass of the population. But the revisionists erred in the opposite way, neglecting the clear evidence of growing acquiescence and indeed support for the police among a broad section of the working class, as well as the middle class. In many places the police came to be accepted and used by sections of the working class quite soon after their inception. Nor can this be put down to their 'service' activities stitching a velvet glove of superficial acquiescence over the reality of the iron fist of repression (although the 'service' role of the police *was* significant (see Emsley 1983: 146–7, 158–9).

D. Philips's (1977) study of the early years of the new police in the Black Country, for example, demonstrated that in many ways the police were resented by the working class. The incursion of the new police into working-class leisure activities through enforcing public order offences, or the use of the police by industrialists to control strikes and redefine traditional popular conceptions of workers' legitimate 'perks' as pilfering, caused considerable disgruntlement. But this did not signify rejection of the legitimacy of the police. A significant proportion of prosecutions at quarter sessions was brought by unskilled working-class people. Many working-class people accepted the basic legitimacy of the laws protecting property, and the agents who enforced them, however much they may have resented specific aspects of property law (notably the Game Laws) which were clearly class biased in intent and practice (Emsley 1983: 158–60). Working-class attitudes to the law and its enforcement were clearly complex and ambivalent, and varied between different times and places. But there seems to have been in many areas as early as the 1850s a large measure of working-class assent to the basic legitimacy of the legal order, based not on ideological manipulation but on the use of its coercive aspects by working-class victims against offenders (Ignatieff 1979). Nor was the 'domestic missionary' role of the police uniformly resented by the working class. Some radical leaders, and the emerging 'respectable' working-class strata, welcomed control of 'the most dissolute and abandoned' habits of the rougher elements, seen as not only an immediate menace in everyday life, but a threat to the political and social advance of the whole class (Emsley 1983: 157–8). By the 1870s it seems that the police had attained a large measure of legitimacy in the eyes of the working class, even though this could be readily disrupted by specific actions. But the rhetoric of resentment against individual practices came to be couched in the terms of the system itself rather than a rejection of its legitimacy. 'From opposing the very idea of a policed society, radical critics had come to judge the police by those abstract standards laid down by the system's pioneers; judicious discretion mixed with firm impartiality in enforcing laws that were often blatantly biased against working people' (J. Field 1981: 59).

What was new about the new police?

Local research on provincial forces suggests that often the 'new' police were not very new. There were many transitional policing innovations which paved the way (Emsley 1996: chaps. 2–4; Philips and Storch 1999).

In the provinces some towns and counties had small constabularies established by particular statutes in the 1820s, for example the Oldham Police Act 1826. More generally the Lighting and Watching Act 1833 enabled rate-payers to set up their own police forces independently of local justices and their old constables, and several small town parishes utilized this Act. The Horncastle force, for example, apparently satisfied respectable townspeople by controlling routine crime and public disorder (Davey 1983). By the time of the debates preceding the 1856 Act which did away with these small independent forces, the argument was about the distribution of costs and control of the professional police, not the principle itself. Despite the establishment of nominally 'new' police as a result of the 1835 Municipal Corporations Act, 'in some boroughs the former watchmen were put in uniforms and now called policemen' (Emsley 2008: 76). Similar conclusions have been drawn about the Rural Constabulary Act 1839. This left it to county magistrates to determine whether or not to establish a force. Less than half the counties of England and Wales took advantage of this permissive legislation, and even where they did, this did not usually signal a drastic change in either the style, personnel, or intrusiveness of policing. Fiscal tightfistedness often vitiated the possibility that the police could be numerous enough to achieve close surveillance of any area (Emsley 2008).

Nor does the evidence imply that the 'new' police represented a sharp break towards the establishment of a professional police with a significantly higher calibre of personal efficiency and virtue than the old constables. In many places they were, at least for a short time, largely the same men (J. Field 1981: 43–7). The policy of not recruiting people with 'the rank, habits or station of gentlemen' (whether motivated by parsimony or political prudence) meant that the social status of the intake was similar to the old constabulary. Furthermore, many studies document the very high turnover rates in the first decades of the new police, both as a result of dismissals for drunkenness or other peccadilloes, and through rapid resignation due to the discipline and demanding nature of the job (D. Philips 1977: 64–75; J. Field 1981: 52; Weinberger 1981: 79–84; Emsley 1983: 71–3; Steedman 1984: chaps. 3–5; Shpayer-Makov 2002). There was not as distinct a movement towards a powerful professional system of surveillance as suggested by both orthodoxy and revisionism, whether for protection *or* oppression of the population.

What was the social impact of the new police?

The previous sections imply that, for good or ill, the 'new' police were not that new, nor was their impact as sharp as either defenders or detractors claim. The immediate effect was primarily the processing of more minor public order offences (Emsley 1996: chap. 4). An analysis of Sheffield City Police data 1845–62 shows the police arresting substantial proportions of young working-class men, overwhelmingly for minor summary offences (C. A. Williams 2000), with one-fifth of the male population acquiring a police record. In the longer term, however, the police were associated with a general increase in the orderliness and pacification of Victorian society. Gatrell shows that from the 1850s until the First World War 'the war against criminal disorder was palpably being won by the State, and contemporaries knew it' (Gatrell 1980: 240–1). The 'Watchman State' was not constructed at a stroke, but it did emerge eventually (Gatrell 1990). However, recent research has questioned the statistical evidence for falling crime in the late nineteenth century, suggesting that the figures were manipulated to suit the joint interests of police and government in creating an appearance of order and pacification (H. Taylor 1998a, 1998b, 1999; for a critical assessment of Taylor's thesis, see Morris 2001; Emsley 2007).

Other authors, while broadly concurring with Gatrell's picture of declining crime, are sceptical about the precise contribution of the police to this (Emsley 1983: chap. 7, 2007). However, it is arguable that the prime way in which the police affect law enforcement is not through their technical efficacy in apprehending criminals, which depends on many factors beyond their control, but by symbolizing the existence of a functioning legal order. In this light the effectiveness of the police depends not so much on the *proportion* of offences they clear up, as on their showing the flag by clearing up a sufficiently high absolute number (Gatrell 1980: 242–3). As Emsley crisply puts it, 'while policemen were not the ultimate answer to theft and disorder which they and many reformers claimed (and continue to claim), they became the placebo of property' (Emsley 1983: 162).

The police were also a factor in the declining extent of disorder, whether in the sense of riot or everyday standards of street conduct. Obviously riot did not disappear, and in some periods political and industrial conflict intensified, as in the 1880s or immediately before the First World War. On occasion the police not only were unsuccessful in controlling a crowd, but aggravated disorder by provocation or poor tactics (Bailey 1981: 94–125; Emsley 1996: chap. 5). But overall, the degree of collective violence tended to decline secularly, as much because of changes in crowd behaviour as police effectiveness. The everyday orderliness of the streets increased, which evoked the approval of respectable citizens whatever the impact on those reliant on the street economy.

In sum, while their initial impact on anything but the casual street economy and its marginal illegalities was small, eventually the police were implicated in a broader process of pacification or integration of Victorian society. Although the weight of their distinctive contribution to this is impossible to state precisely, it was significant.

Who gained from the new police?

The orthodox view has it that the police brought universal benefits, but especially to the weaker sections of society. The revisionists argue the reverse. The police were an agent of oppression of the majority on behalf of the ruling and middle classes. The police institution also benefited police officers themselves, providing a channel of social mobility to greater security, status, and power.

Recent research supports both views partially. While gaining in their capacity as victims of routine offences of theft and assault and from some police services, in other respects the working class were at the sharp end of many police activities (Weinberger 1981: 73–6; Williams 2000). This is especially true, of course, of the lower strata within the working class, those dependent on the street economy or irregular employment. They were the targets of the routine public-order policing which the middle class supported enthusiastically. The regularly employed workers also suffered from police actions during periods of heightened industrial conflict. It is probable also that the quality of police respect would be inversely related to the social status of a person with whom they were dealing (Emsley 1983: 152; Steedman 1984: 6).

The middle and upper classes certainly gained a sense of security, which many contemporaries gratefully expressed. Others began to take the police for granted as they became socially invisible public servants. Some took this to the cynical conclusion that the police officer was a mere 'fool in blue' who did nothing but walk about, and wondered if he was worth his weight in higher rates (Steedman 1984: 6–7, 142–5).

It is clear that at first police officers did not gain from the job in terms of social mobility and a career. They merely took advantage of it for short spells while unable to obtain other work. However, in the third quarter of the nineteenth century, the development of a notion of police work as a distinctive career, with a specific ideology of service, professional identity, and craft skills, slowly emerged (Steedman 1984: chap. 8; Klein 2001; Shpayer-Makov 2002). Police work began to hold out an opportunity for social mobility to some working-class men.

Who controlled the police?

The middle class and working class had a greater capacity to influence the old parish constables or local forces than they had after the creation of the new police. This was the source of the objections of many towns to incorporation under the Municipal Corporations Act 1835, or amalgamation with surrounding counties as proposed in 1856 (Emsley 2008). On the other hand, it was one reason why Chadwick and other reformers wanted more centralized control. To them local control smacked of corruption and inefficiency. The working class had no direct influence on Watch Committees until the slow extension of the franchise to them. It was perhaps no coincidence that by that time Watch Committees had lost much of their power over the increasingly autonomous chief constables. The middle class had some degree of influence over Watch Committees, depending on the local political balance. They had less involvement in the gentry-dominated magistracy, which completely controlled the county police until 1888.

Nominally chief constables had the authority to control police policy and administration in the counties. However, as the magistracy chose men with a social background and standing which ensured a harmony of outlook, the gentry viewpoint dominated in county policing (Wall 1998). In the boroughs the powers in theory and practice of Watch Committee over chief constable remained paramount. Even the 1856 admixture of a measure of central control through the Home Office Inspectorate and Exchequer Grant did not change this pattern at first. However, during the 1870s chief constables in both counties and boroughs began to assert a greater measure of professional independence. This was facilitated by legislative changes conferring on the police more duties directly from national government, as well as more powers and resources (Steedman 1984: 53–5, 62–3, chap. 10; Emsley 2008: 78–81).

In sum, the orthodox view has no foundation for the claim that the 'people' controlled the police. The new police signified a move away from a degree of popular control that had existed in some places over parish constables. They also emerged after the 1870s as increasingly autonomous of local government and magistracy.

CONCLUSION: A NEO-REITHIAN– REVISIONIST SYNTHESIS

All historians of the emergence of professional policing in Britain have shown that it was surrounded by acute political conflict. The orthodox historians were clearly wrong in their lack of appreciation of the rational basis of opposition to the police, rooted in different social interests and political philosophies. On the other hand, revisionists overemphasized the extent of continued working-class opposition, and the overt role of the police in class and political control. While not securing the quick and relatively painless passage into acceptance suggested by the Reithians, the police did gain increasing acquiescence from substantial sections of the working class, not only as a result of 'soft' service activities, but in their 'hard' law enforcement and order maintenance functions. This anchored consent in substantial benefits and cooperation, not mere ideological manipulation. The police succeeded in acquiring this degree of legitimacy, in which they were no longer widely seen as a politically oppressive force, by a combination of specific strategies which did give the British police a unique character, implanting them firmly in national mythology. I would claim that a neo-Reithian–revisionist synthesis is the most appropriate for understanding this.[4] This gives due weight to the success of the police reformers and the tradition they created, but also recognizes that policing is embedded in a social order that is riven by structured bases of conflict, not fundamental integration. The manner of policing such a divided social order may be more or less harmonious and consensual, or overtly oppressive. The processes by which the comparatively benign British policing tradition was constructed in the century after their controversial introduction, the manner of their legitimation and depoliticization, will be the focus of the next chapter.

NOTES

1. Watts-Miller (1987: 51) raises this intriguing possibility:

> The Metropolitan Police, Radzinowicz and others tell us, soon became an 'accepted institution'. This ignores continuing criticism and government attempts to stifle it.... Although central control kept the capital in more 'reliable' hands, it is open to question if a Bill such as Peel's could have passed after 1832, or 1835, the 'Magna Carta' of local self-government. All that is certain is Parliament's refusal to accept the 'accepted institution' outside London.

2. Wellington argued after the Reform Bill was passed:

> From henceforth we shall never be able to carry on a government without the assistance and support of a military body. If we cannot have a regular army in such a state of discipline and efficiency as that the King can rely on them, we must and we shall have a National Guard in some shape or other' (Silver 1971: 185).

3. As Watts-Miller (1987: 58) put it trenchantly: 'The executive of a modern state is also a committee to mismanage the affairs in common of the bourgeoisie.'

4. I call this neo-Reithian in order to emphasize the virtues of that ideal of pacific policing by popular consent which Reith attributes to the British police. However, as an account of history Reith requires drastic critical revision to recognize the structured conflicts which surrounded policing in a class-divided society (and continue to do so).

3

OUT OF THE BLUE: POLICE LEGITIMACY 1856–2009— CONSTRUCTION, DECONSTRUCTION, RECONSTRUCTION

Modern British police came into being as a deeply contested institution in the early nineteenth century. Yet by the middle of the twentieth century they had become a key component of national identity. The first part of this chapter analyses the initial construction of British police legitimacy. In the latter half of the twentieth century the totemic status attained by the modern British police became increasingly contested and undermined, as 'law and order' was deeply politicized (Downes and Morgan 2007; Reiner 2007a). The second section of this chapter analyses this deconstruction of police legitimacy. During the 1990s the position of the police in Britain seemed to move onto a new stage which may be characterized as 'post-legitimacy'. A new consensus developed accepting the politics of 'tough' law and order and a profound restructuring of state, society, and culture. The reconstruction of this pragmatic and precarious 'post-legitimacy' is analysed in the final section. The police are a Teflon service: they have survived all manner of scandal and controversy to remain a powerful political and cultural force, more so than any other state institution in an increasingly neo-liberal, privatized world in which the state has 'hollowed out' (Loader and Mulcahy 2003; McLaughlin 2007; Reiner 2008). However, they are now only one element in an array of competing policing services, and are subject to increasingly rigorous audit. At a tactical level policing policy has never been more fiercely controversial. But the deeper issues of legitimacy which were struggled over for more than two centuries—the contribution of the police to the shaping of the fundamental structure of power and advantage in society—have largely been bracketed out of debate.

FROM CRUSHERS TO BOBBIES:
THE DEPOLITICIZATION OF THE POLICE 1856–1959

A GOLDEN AGE OF POLICING?

The British police were established in the face of massive opposition from a wide range of political interests and philosophies. While middle- and upper-class suspicions were rapidly allayed, working class resentment lived on, expressed in sporadic physical violence and symbolized by a stream of derogatory epithets for the new police: 'Crushers', 'Peel's Bloody Gang', 'Blue Locusts', 'Jenny Darbies', 'Raw Lobsters', 'Blue Drones'. Yet by the 1950s the police had become not merely accepted but lionized by the broad spectrum of opinion. In no other country has the police force been so much a symbol of national pride (Loader and Mulcahy 2003).[1]

Many contemporary statements testify to the almost universal acceptance the police had attained. In 1955, Geoffrey Gorer claimed 'that the bulk of the population has . . . incorporated the police man or woman as an ideal and become progressively more "self-policing"' (Gorer 1955: 311).[2] Michael Banton began his pioneering sociological study of the police with the 'idea that it can be instructive to analyse institutions that are working well in order to see if anything can be learned from their success' (Banton 1964: vii). Above all, the fictional character PC George Dixon, who first appeared in the 1950 film *The Blue Lamp*, and was subsequently resurrected for a long-running TV series, embodied the quintessential beloved British bobby, and still stands as a regularly evoked ideal (Leishman and Mason 2003; McLaughlin 2005a; Reiner 2008: 320–1). The relative social harmony and consensus of the mid-twentieth century, symbolized by the Battle of Britain and the Festival of Britain, was also the finest hour of the British bobby myth.

By the end of the 1950s there were indications of increasing tension. Recorded crime was rising at a rate described by the chief inspector of constabulary as an 'upsurge', 1958 saw race riots in Notting Hill and Nottingham, and there was growing police anxiety about their relations with the 'law-abiding', but increasingly car-owning, public. In the late 1950s some relatively minor incidents led to the November 1959 announcement by the Home Secretary of a Royal Commission 'to review the constitutional position of the police' (Bottoms and Stevenson 1990). But it is significant that the Royal Commission's national opinion survey found 'an overwhelming vote of confidence in the police'. As far as police acceptance by the public is concerned, the 1950s seem a 'golden age' of tranquillity and accord, with only hesitant harbingers of coming crisis. Paradoxically, however, this may well have shrouded considerable malpractice and corruption, as is indicated by the evidence of oral histories in poor areas and some police memoirs (Mark 1978; P. Cohen 1979; White 1986; Daley 1986; Brogden 1991; Weinberger 1995).

Legitimacy and 'policing by consent'

The orthodox police historians saw the police as having already overcome any serious opposition to their presence by the early years of the twentieth century. Critchley (1978: 326), for instance, characterized the 1900s as 'the zenith' of police public relations in Britain. He cited a 1908 *Times* editorial which claimed: 'The policeman in London is not merely guardian of the peace; he is the best friend of a mass of people who have no other counsellor or protector.' This rosy portrait aroused the ire of revisionist historians for its cosy complacency. 'The "public" (meaning the middle and upper classes) ... held their "bobby" in patronizing "affection and esteem" ... but these sentiments were never shared by the undermass, nor in fact by the working class generally' (R. Roberts 1973: 100).

The Royal Commission on the Police's Final Report (1962) was criticized rightly for neglecting aspects of their own survey data which called into question the optimistic overall summary (Whitaker 1964: 151–7). However, their survey results show no evidence of variation *by social class* in attitudes to the police, indicating that middle-class veneration of the police had trickled down the social structure. While 85.2 per cent of the professional and managerial classes had 'great respect' for the police, so too did nearly 82 per cent of the skilled and unskilled working class. Of the semi and unskilled working class 24.3 per cent and 29.8 per cent of the skilled working-class respondents reported 'unsatisfactory experience' of police conduct, but even more (33.3 per cent) of the professional and managerial strata did. This confirms those contemporary opinions that stressed the widespread acceptance of the police throughout the class structure. The Shaw and Williamson (1972) survey of public attitudes to the police, one of the few to include a class dimension, has often been cited as evidence of working-class reservations about policing (for example, Brogden 1982: 204). But their data showed only tiny inter-class differences, and some results went in the opposite direction to the one predicted. For example, they found that 86 per cent of respondents in class III had 'respect' for the police, compared to only 81.7 per cent in class I.

Apart from the empirical evidence, there are conceptual ambiguities in the much-debated notion of policing by consent. Both the orthodox and revisionist approaches operate with absurdly absolutist conceptions of what consensual policing could mean. Policing is an inherently conflict-ridden enterprise. As discussed in Chapter 1, the essential function and distinctive resource of the police is the potential use of legitimate force. Police work is thus 'a tainted occupation ... ambivalently feared and admired, and no amount of public relations work can entirely abolish the sense that there is something of the dragon in the dragon-slayer' (Bittner 1970: 6–7).

If there was universal consensus about norms, values and appropriate modes of social behaviour there would be no need for a police force. In most situations there is somebody being policed against, whose assent to policing is bound to be brittle. At best they may utter a grudging 'It's a fair cop, guv' in the time-honoured tradition of British gangster movies. Those who are frequently at the receiving end of police authority are unlikely to give it much consent other than a sullen acceptance of de facto power. Realistically, the most that 'policing by consent' can mean is not universal love of the police, but that those at the sharp end of police practices do not extend their resentment at specific actions into a generalized withdrawal of legitimacy from the institution of policing per se. Contemporary research shows that legitimacy is only in small part based on perceptions or experience of actual police practice. It is more dependent on the extent to which policing is seen to be conducted in a procedurally fair way, and is asymmetrically much more sensitive to 'bad' than 'good' instances of police work (Tyler 2004, 2007; Skogan 2006). Above all, however, it is dependent on wider images of the social order (Jackson and Sunshine 2007; Hough 2007a, 2007b; Smith 2007a, 2007b; Jackson *et al.* 2009). One of the most robust findings of research on public legitimation of the police is that it is much higher among those who have no direct experience of police than those who do, whether this be as suspects, victims, witnesses, or recipients of services (D. J. Smith 2007a: 295–7).

By the 1950s 'policing by consent' had been achieved in Britain to the maximal degree it is ever attainable. The police enjoyed the wholehearted approval of the majority of the population who did not experience the coercive exercise of police powers to any significant extent, and de facto acceptance of the legitimacy of the institution by those who did. Police *power*, that is, the capacity to inflict legal sanctions including force, had been transmuted into authority, power which is accepted as at least minimally legitimate.[3] How did the police come to be accepted as legitimate authority figures rather than politically controversial bearers of power? How did their image change from 'crushers' to 'bobbies' between the early nineteenth century and the mid-twentieth?

The construction of consent

The achievement of consensus policing in Britain was mutually interdependent with a wider process of pacification of social relations. Most crucially, it was intertwined with the incorporation of the working class, the main source of initial hostility to the new police, into the political and economic institutions of British society. Many sociologists have argued that the distinctive character of British policing, its relative legality and eschewal of force, was a product of social homogeneity and tranquillity, especially as contrasted with the USA (Banton 1964: chap. 8). But the opposite is the case. Peel and the other architects of the benign and dignified English police image shaped their policies because of the strength of opposition to the very existence of the police. They encouraged a low-profile, legalistic stance precisely in the teeth of the bitter political conflict and acute social divisions of English society in the first half of the nineteenth century, not as an expression of underlying harmony.[4] In the USA by contrast, a more free-wheeling and aggressive style of policing evolved, because of the political integration of American society as something approaching a property-owning democracy (W. Miller 1999). Popular participation in government meant confidence that control of the police could be entrusted to the political process, rather than legal rules and regulations.

The policy choices made by the creators of the British police were central to the way the force was accepted. But these policy-makers acted in conditions of class resistance and political conflict not of their own making, and were informed and limited by particular ideological traditions. There were eight specific policies laid down by Peel,

Rowan, and Mayne which were crucial for the engineering of consent in the face of initial opposition.

POLICE POLICY AND LEGITIMATION

Bureaucratic organization

The basis of the 'new' police idea was the establishment of a full-time force of professional police officers, organized into a bureaucratic hierarchy. This contrasted with the previous reliance on a motley assortment of part-timers, entrepreneurial thief-takers and amateur volunteers. Entry and promotion were meritocratic not partisan or nepotistic. Rowan and Mayne set initial entrance requirements for the Met that were quite demanding and stringently applied (W. Miller 1999: 267). In many provincial forces established after the 1835 and 1839 Acts there was much more continuity between the 'old' and 'new' police. But after 1856 and the introduction of a minimal element of standardization through the Inspectorate of Constabulary, this began to change (Emsley 1996: chap. 3, 2008). Training was not taken very seriously in many forces until after the 1919–20 reports of the Desborough Committee, which introduced much stronger standardization and central direction into all aspects of administration and conditions of service. The Committee had been appointed following the 1918 and 1919 police strikes in London and Liverpool, and resulted in a major shift towards centralization (Critchley 1978: 190–4). Rowan and Mayne elaborated a strict set of rules and regulations governing dress, deportment and discipline, and the prescribed demeanour for dealing with the public (W. Miller 1999: 37–42). These were inculcated during drill and training, and enforced by sanctions for disobedience. In the early years there was a high turnover due to dismissals, mainly for drunkenness (Shpayer-Makov 2002).

A quasi-military chain of command was constructed, and at first the policy was to appoint former non-commissioned military officers to the higher ranks, because of their experience as disciplinarians. This later changed in favour of internal promotion from the ranks (Wall 1998). The promotion system became an instrument of bureaucratic control. Only those who obeyed orders 'readily and punctually' could aspire to be promoted, for 'he who has been accustomed to submit to discipline will be considered best qualified to command' (W. Miller 1999: 40).

The policy of bureaucratization was partly contradicted by low pay. This, plus the irksome discipline itself, meant that all early police forces had a massive problem of rapid resignations. But during the 1870s the notion of policing as a career offering status and security, if not high pay, began to emerge, and a more stable body of professional officers developed (Shpayer-Makov 2002).

Although never realized completely, the image of policemen as disciplined members of a bureaucratic organization of professionals was constructed by the 1850s in London. An 1856 article in the *London Quarterly Review* summed up the ever-uncertain process of conversion of human raw material into 'well-regulated machines', impersonal embodiments of bureaucratic authority: 'Amid the bustle of Piccadilly or the roar of Oxford Street, P.C.X. 59 stalks along, an institution rather than a man' (cited in W. Miller 1999: 15).

The rule of law

The way in which the police maintained order and enforced the law was itself supposed to be governed by legalistic procedures and constraints. Adherence to the rule of law was a prime requirement of the Metropolitan Police. At first the London 'police courts' were generally unsympathetic to the force, and they remained fiercely concerned to maintain their role and image as independent regulators of the legality of police conduct (J. Davis 1984: 332). On several occasions the magistrates laid down rulings which effectively halted particular law enforcement policies.

Although an impediment to the exercise of police power, the commissioners were aware that subjection to legal regulation was a major factor in the legitimation of police authority. In any case, the magistrates became less wont to question police behaviour after the mid-century, indicated by a growing tendency to dismiss charges of assault brought against the police, and a greater readiness to convict on police evidence (ibid.: 329).

The commissioners were well aware of the importance of the police maintaining an image of subjection to the rule of law as a way of alleviating opposition. They laid down strict regulations and sanctions governing the use of the wide discretionary powers conferred on constables by statutes such as the Vagrancy Act 1824 (source of the notorious 'sus' law), and the Metropolitan Police Act 1839, which gave the London police broad stop-and-search powers. While the Commissioners believed such powers were needed, they exerted strict disciplinary sanctions over abuse, and encouraged 'all respectable persons' to bring complaints to them (W. Miller 1999: 4–12, 56–66, 94).

The strategy of minimal force

All police forces claim to use as little force as necessary, but the British tradition stands out for its eschewal of arms (Waddington and Wright 2008: 466). With characteristic forthrightness, in a television interview Sir Robert Mark, commissioner of the Met, articulated the crowd control strategy of the Metropolitan Police thus: 'The real art of policing a free society or a democracy is to win by appearing to lose.' Their secret weapon was not water cannon, tear gas or rubber bullets, but public sympathy. To this end, he claimed, the Metropolitan Police had trained an especially comely horse the—'Brigitte Bardot'—of police horses to collapse, feigning death, at a word of command. This was guaranteed to win the support of the animal-loving British public. The British 'police advantage' of public support rather than lethal hardware as a means of crowd control was a carefully chosen strategy (Bowden 1978: 35, chap. 9). It was a calculated response to the fears of an oppressive *gendarmerie* which had motivated so much resistance to the force.

Rowan and Mayne limited constables' weapons to the truncheon, carried concealed until 1863. Its use was intended to be a last resort. Complaints of police violence diminished after the early 1830s, implying that the commissioner's regulations had some effect on behaviour (W. Miller 1999: 49). On specific dangerous assignments or beats, selected officers might carry a pistol or a cutlass, but each occasion of use or even drawing of such a weapon was closely scrutinized, and if not justified as self-defence would probably result in dismissal.

Some post-1839 county police forces, notably Essex, adopted a military model of policing. But the strategy that the Home Office encouraged after 1856 was prevention by 'a police force essentially civil, unarmed and acting without any assistance from a military force' (Steedman 1984: 32–8). The army was available as the ultimate backup should preventive policing fail, and was used on many occasions in the latter part of the nineteenth and early twentieth centuries. But gradually the non-lethally-armed civilian police force became the sole means of riot control (Waddington and Wright 2008: 467). Paradoxically, one of the last occasions troops acted in a public order role was in 1919 during the Liverpool police strike.

Although they have certainly never acted with kid gloves, there is no doubt that the British police developed a tradition of containing industrial disputes and political demonstrations with minimum force when contrasted with other countries. There have been periods of special anxiety and controversy about intensified political and industrial conflict, with attendant complaints of police brutality and right-wing bias. The most notable were the series of clashes between police and the organized unemployed of 'Outcast London' in the late 1880s, the bitter industrial disputes immediately before and after the First World War, and the conflicts between the police and the unemployed movement and anti-Fascist demonstrators in the 1930s (J. Morgan 1987; Weinberger 1991). But the Home Office tried to ensure that police tactics were kept within legal limits (Bailey 1981: 9–125; P. T. Smith 1985).

In the unprecedented economic and political crisis of the 1930s public order became an issue in a way it had not been since the middle of the nineteenth century. The violence surrounding Fascist meetings was the stimulus for the Public Order Act 1936. Concern about the brutality used to suppress marches of the National Unemployed Workers' Movement, led to the growth of the National Council for Civil Liberties after 1934. A detailed consideration of 1930s conflicts concludes, however, that, despite considerable evidence of bias and brutality by police officers against the NUWM and anti-Fascists, 'the police do seem to have reacted less in political terms than in response to the challenge to public order and to their own position as the custodians of law and order' (Stevenson and Cook 1977: 243). Geary (1985) documents the declining levels of violence between police and pickets in industrial conflicts between the 1890s and the 1970s, arguing that industrial conflict changed from something resembling a war to something like a sporting contest. As far as individual violence involving police is concerned, there is similar evidence of a sustained decline in the first century of policing. But from the 1860s until the First World War there was a dramatic decline both in assaults in general, and specifically in assaults against the police. From a national annual average of 67.5 per 100,000 in 1857–60, the recorded rate of assaults on the police had fallen to 24.1 per 100,000 in 1911–14, with a consistent decline in between (Gatrell 1980: 286–93). The accuracy of the recorded figures is debatable in view of the long-standing police tendency to under-record such offences (Weinberger 1995: 31–2). Whatever the totality of reasons underlying this long-run decline in violence (Eisner 2001), it is clear that the police reflected and contributed to it.

Non-partisanship

When the 'new' police force was established working-class leaders and Radicals saw it as a thoroughly political military and spy agency, 'the minion and paid servant of the Government' (*Poor Man's Guardian* 11 October 1830: 3).

Crucial to legitimating the police was an image of non-partisanship. Rowan and Mayne declared that in the middle of acute social conflict they 'endeavoured to prevent the slightest practical feeling or bias, being shown or felt by the police . . . the force should not only be, in fact, but be believed to be impartial in action, and should act on principle' (cited in W. Miller 1999: 12).

The police were insulated from direct political control, and police authorities (the Home Secretary, local watch and standing joint committees) tended to abstain from interventions in operational policy. It was not until the 1920s, though, that this discreet stance began to be transmuted explicitly into a notion of constabulary independence from policy guidance, which would have been considered 'so unconstitutional as to be absurd' in the nineteenth century (G. Marshall 1965: 31).

Peel and the Metropolitan commissioners insisted on excluding patronage in appointments and promotions at a time when this was normal civil service practice. Police officers were also denied the vote until 1887. This tradition dies hard. In an article celebrating the 150th anniversary of the Metropolitan Police, the then commissioner, Sir David McNee, wrote: 'I no longer exercise my right to vote, nor have I since I was appointed a chief officer of police. Police officers must be men and women of the middle, bound only by the rule of law' (McNee 1979: 25). The insistence on suppressing indications of overt political control or partisanship softened the initial conception of the police as a tool of government oppression (Emsley 1996: chap. 5, 2008: 81). As an 1864 article in *Chambers's Magazine* said of the police, 'they know nothing of politics; the man in blue preserves his neutral tint . . . the good old cause of order is the only side the policeman supports' (cited in W. Miller 1999: 13).

Accountability

Although the police were not formally controlled by any elected body, they were seen as accountable in two ways. First, the legality of police action was reviewable by the courts; the police were held accountable to the rule of law. Second, they were purported to be accountable through an almost mystical process of identification with the British people, not the state. Although lacking any tangible control by elected institutions, they were supposedly in tune with the popular will because of their social representativeness and lack of special powers. The ideology developed of the constable as 'citizen in uniform', doing on a paid basis what all citizens had the power and social duty to do (Royal Commission on the Police 1962). So 'the police are the public and the public are the police' (Reith 1956: 287). The recruitment policies of the police were attuned to this principle, drawing upon manual working class backgrounds representative of the mass of the people (Weinberger 1995: chaps. 1, 3; Klein 2001; Shpayer-Makov 2002). After the First World War this principle was supposed to govern even chief officer selection in all forces, and since the Second World War it has done, with all chief constables working their way up through the ranks and almost all sharing working-class origins (Wall 1998).

The service role

The notion of the friendly bobby was summed up for modern ears by the cliché: 'If you want to know the time, ask a policeman.' The meaning was rather different in the nineteenth century. 'The popular catchphrase ... reflected not so much the confidence of the Victorians in the reliability of the police, as their assumption that any policeman who did not quickly ... win ... a watch from the pockets of a drunken reveller was unnaturally honest or dull' (Rolph 1962: 52).

The nineteenth-century police reformers cultivated the service role in order to secure legitimacy for more coercive policing functions. Edwin Chadwick was the most explicit about this. He urged that it would 'exercise a beneficial influence on the labouring classes ... by showing them that they are cared for by the authorities, and are not, as they must but too commonly suppose, merely and exclusively the subjects of coercion' (Donajgrodski 1977: 67).

Certainly in the nineteenth century the police carried out a range of tasks wider than law enforcement and order maintenance. Some were formal duties, such as inspecting weights and measures or inspecting bridges, others were informal, such as knocking people up early in the morning for work (Emsley 1983: 158–9). Then as now these were often regarded by the police themselves as unwelcome 'extraneous' duties (Steedman 1984: 53–4). Many of the service tasks benefited the middle class at the expense of the working class, such as the enforcement of nuisance laws. But others did benefit the working class too. How crucial the service role was in securing consent may be questioned, and to some it was mere ideological window-dressing (Brogden 1982: 208–19). Arguably the crime-control role of the police, in particular their taking over of most prosecutions, was a more valued and useful service to the mass of the population than the 'friendly' non-coercive 'services' to which the term is usually confined. But the 'service' role played a part in securing police legitimation.

Preventive policing

The primacy of prevention over detection was emphasized in the famous opening lines of Peel's celebrated instructions to the Metropolitan Police (cited in Critchley 1978: 52–3):

It should be understood at the outset, that the object to be attained is the prevention of crime. To this great end every effort of the police is to be directed. The security of person and property ... will thus be better effected than by the detection and punishment of the offender after he has succeeded in committing crime.

The practical implementation of this principle meant the concentration of manpower on uniform patrol of regular beats. This was motivated not only by a belief in the efficacy of the police constable's 'scarecrow function', but to allay anti-police fears of the abominable French experience of undercover police spies.

Hostility to the idea of plain clothes police delayed the formation of detective branches for many years. Mayne, in particular, was concerned to minimize use of detectives because of public fears about police spying (W. Miller 1999: 33–4). In 1842 Rowan was able partly to overcome such anxieties and secured the Home Secretary's approval for a detective branch of six men. When it was proposed to expand the number of detectives in 1845, *The Times* declared: 'If it be dangerous, and perhaps unconstitutional, to maintain a few government spies, what will be the effect of impressing that character on the whole police force of this vast metropolis?' (cited in Baldwin and Kinsey 1982: 11). By 1868 when Mayne died there were still only fifteen detectives in a force of 8,000. Mayne's successor, Lieutenant-Colonel Edmund Henderson, prompted partly by a moral panic about rising crime in the late 1860s, placed more emphasis on the detective branch, creating permanent divisional detectives. Mayne's fears seemed vindicated when, in 1877, the three top Scotland Yard detectives were involved in a major bribery scandal. Paradoxically, the response to this was the establishment of a separate Criminal Investigation Department (Emsley 1996: 72–3). By the 1880s the police had become sufficiently well entrenched in public confidence for the formation of a specifically political unit, the Special Irish Branch, initially to deal with Fenian terrorism (B. Porter 1987). It subsequently acquired a wider remit than Irish terrorism, and became the Special Branch. But in the early years the primacy of the idea of prevention by uniformed patrol was a factor in the achievement of legitimation.

Police effectiveness

The final aspect of police policy contributing to legitimation was the core mandate of crime prevention and order maintenance. How effective the police actually were in crime control remains debatable (Gatrell 1980, 1990; Weinberger 1995; H. Taylor 1998a, 1998b, 1999), but certainly the appearance of success in crime-fighting was cultivated. In the 1860s there was a moral panic in the respectable classes about a new 'crime wave', and the police, especially the aged Mayne, were blamed. Fear of crime was fuelled by anxiety about a supposed epidemic of garrottings (the Victorian equivalent of mugging) and by rising official statistics of recorded indictable offences. Conservative critics campaigned for the police to be 'armed with preventive powers similar to those exercised by the Continental police'. This was precisely what working-class spokesmen feared. *Reynolds's Weekly Newspaper* claimed that 'The Government proposes converting the English Peeler into a species of continental policeman ... the mouchard, or spy, will become an established institution among us.'

Gradually, however, the bulk of the working class became reconciled to the criminal justice system. A sizeable proportion of the work of the police courts comprised prosecutions and summonses for theft and assault brought by working-class men and women. While most theft cases were brought by the 'respectable' working class, 'more surprisingly it was members of the casual poor, sometimes convicted criminals themselves, who predominated in making assault charges' (J. Davis 1984: 321). Slowly, the new police and criminal justice system were inserting themselves into working-class life not only as an intrusive controlling apparatus but also as a potential means of redress. The growth of a sense of police effectiveness was probably at least as significant as the image-building aspects of legitimation. Police success 'in securing the cooperation of the public depended less on keeping a rosy image of impartiality than on securing a near-monopoly over the market in violence and redress. Street by street, the police negotiated a complex, shifting, largely unspoken "contract"' (Ignatieff 1979: 444–5). This was threatened by heavy-handed control of industrial or political conflict, or by overzealous policing of working-class leisure pursuits. Recognizing this, the early Metropolitan Police Commissioners were discreet in their enforcement of laws which were unpopular with the working class, such as the Sabbath laws (W. Miller 1999: 129–38).

By the 1870s, then, the police had come to be seen as offering an effective law enforcement service to the middle and upper classes, who complained when its quality seemed to decline. The working class also made use of it, but the less respectable sections were predominantly at the receiving end of law and order. As long as the working class was and felt largely excluded from even minimal political and economic participation, so too their acquiescence to policing remained fragile and grudging.

THE SOCIAL CONTEXT OF POLICE LEGITIMATION

The all-important final factor which facilitated the legitimation of the police was not any aspect of police policy or practice, but the changing social, economic, and political context. The working class, the main structurally rooted source of opposition to the police, gradually, unevenly and incompletely came to be incorporated as citizens into the political, social, and economic institutions of British society (T. Marshall 1950; Bulmer and Rees 1996).

The process of incorporation had very clear limits. It enabled the bulk of the working class to share in the growth of the economy. However, class inequality remained in proportionate terms virtually unaltered, and has widened substantially since the neo-liberal resuscitation of free market economics in the late 1970s and the return of what is now called social exclusion (Levitas 2005; Reiner 2007a: 95–114).

Nonetheless, the wide gulf between Disraeli's 'two nations', which was sharply manifest to all in the mid-nineteenth century as the new police came into being, had become hedged round and blurred by the 1950s, the high point of police legitimation. In the 'affluent society' there was supposed to be an 'end of ideology', and this included controversy about the police. The accomplishment of the first century of policing transformed the police from a widely hated and feared institution to a body regarded as the embodiment of impersonal, rule-bound authority, enforcing the rule of law on behalf of the broad mass of society rather than any partisan interest.

FROM PLODS TO PIGS: THE POLITICIZATION
OF THE POLICE 1959–92

From a position of almost complete invisibility as a political issue, after 1959 policing became a babble of scandalous revelation, controversy, and competing agendas for reform. The tacit contract between police and public, so delicately drawn between the 1850s and 1950s, began to fray glaringly. Evidence mounted of an increasing haemorrhage of public confidence in the police. Fully 83 per cent of the national sample surveyed in 1959 for the Royal Commission on the Police said they had 'a great deal of respect for the police'. In 1989 a MORI poll for *Newsnight* asked the same question of a national sample. The proportion having 'a great deal of respect' for the police had slumped to 43 per cent.

The 1960 Royal Commission on the Police was the outcome of a series of *causes célèbres* which seem in retrospect pretty small beer. In 1956 and 1957 disciplinary or legal proceedings involving alleged corruption were brought against the chief constables of Cardiganshire, Brighton, and Worcester. Again in 1957, allegations were made in Parliament that a policeman had beaten a boy in Thurso (a small Scottish town), and that this complaint had not been properly investigated. In 1959 a row in Nottingham raised the fundamental constitutional issue of the respective responsibilities for law enforcement of chief constable and watch committee. Captain Popkess, the chief constable, was suspended by the Watch Committee because he refused to give it a report of an investigation into criminal allegations involving councillors. The Home Secretary told the committee to reinstate Popkess, but the case illustrated the lack of clarity about the roles of chief constable, Watch Committee, and Home Secretary (G. Marshall 1965: 13–14).

Other anxieties about policing mounted in the background. After 1955 the crime statistics began to rise inexorably each year, heralding 'a crime wave unparalleled in modern times' (Critchley 1978: 254). The teddy-boys and beatniks of the mid-1950s created new 'folk devils' and presaged perennial moral panic about the threats to law and order posed by shifting styles of youth culture (S. Cohen 1972; Pearson 1983; Loader 1996; M. Lee 1998; Newburn 2007). Future concerns about public order policing were signalled by the 1958 Notting Hill and Nottingham race riots, and the launching of CND and the Aldermaston marches in 1957.

The immediate trigger for the Royal Commission was none of these grave matters, but a Whitehall farce. In December 1958 Brian Rix the comedy star was stopped for speeding by a PC Eastmond. An obscure argument developed between Eastmond and a civil servant who intervened in the incident, resulting in mutual assault allegations, which were settled out of court. This provoked a parliamentary debate which raised all the fundamental issues of police accountability.

During the debate the Home Secretary indicated his intention to institute the Royal Commission. It considered but rejected the case for a national police force, although it was effectively argued in a highly respected memorandum of dissent by

Dr A. L. Goodhart. The majority report claimed that the advantages of rationalization, coordination, and efficiency could be achieved by a more limited programme of amalgamations and greater central control.

The commission's proposals on accountability and complaints, and their implementation in the Police Act 1964, were widely seen as vague, confused, and contradictory (G. Marshall 1965). The net effect of the Act was to strengthen the hands of the Home Office and of the chief constables at the expense of local police authorities (as Chapter 7 shows).

The continuing relevance of the problems that had led to the Royal Commission were highlighted by some scandals which occurred before the passage of the Police Act 1964, and which demonstrated the need for an effective system for complaints and accountability. One involved Challenor, a detective sergeant in the Metropolitan Police, who planted false evidence on at least two dozen suspects, apparently unnoticed by colleagues and supervisors (Grigg 1965). The Sheffield Inquiry into allegations of brutality involving a 'rhino whip' underlined the reluctance of officers to 'hear, or speak, or see any evil' about their colleagues (Whitaker 1964: 136–7). There was also concern about rough police handling of anti-nuclear protests.

Despite its inadequacies, the Police Act 1964 constituted a settlement which was generally accepted for a time. This was aided by the transformation of police organization in the mid-1960s, centring on the new, motorized Unit Beat System of patrol. The emphasis was on technology, specialization, and managerial professionalism as the keys to winning 'the fight against crime'. 'The "British Bobby" was recast as the tough, dashing, formidable (but still brave and honest) "Crime-Buster"' (Chibnall 1977: 71).

Given the now universal bad press accorded the 'fire brigade' policing style that the Unit Beat System brought into being, it is salutary to recall that its birth was greeted with general acclaim. It was intended simultaneously to bolster efficiency, improve relations with the public, and advance the policeman's lot. As originally conceived, the area constables would have the function of preserving close relations with local communities, the panda cars would provide a faster emergency service, the collator would analyse information provided by the patrol officers for use in detecting offences, and all police officers would gain enhanced status and job interest. All birds were to be killed by the same stone. In practice, the system soon frustrated these hopes, partly because of shortage of manpower to implement it properly, but primarily because of the unintended consequences of the ability of rank-and-file culture to frustrate managerial purposes. The constables' action-centred perspective on policing was accentuated by the technology of fast cars, sirens, and flashing blue lights (Holdaway 1977, 1983). At first, however, the police image may have changed from the cosy 1950s Dixon of Dock Green to the more abrasive Inspector Barlow of the 1960s TV series *Z Cars*, but neither was a politically controversial figure. The police were no longer Plods, but not yet pigs.

By the end of the 1960s the growth of the counter-culture, and police clashes with anti-Vietnam War and anti-apartheid demonstrators in 1968–9, heralded a renewed politicization of policing. In 1970, the Police Federation chairman announced to the annual conference: 'We have been eyeball to eyeball with the fanatics, the lunatics and the hooligans.' Later that year, the Federation magazine drew attention to the institution of a 'Pig of the Month' contest in *Frendz*, an underground newspaper.

Should we be upset? Not at all. The pig has made a notable contribution to our national well-being over the centuries. As such, it has a great advantage over hippy squatters . . . whose concepts of sanitation are far more primitive than its own . . . In America, they say P-I-G stands for Pride, Integrity and Guts. (*Police*, September 1970: 6)

What processes were transforming the police image from Plod to pig? All the factors that produced the earlier depoliticization of policing had question marks placed against them after 1959, as social and economic changes had the unintended effect of reversing them.

POLICING POLICIES AND DE-LEGITIMATION

Bureaucratic organization?[5]

Recruitment, training, and discipline. The first element in the undermining of police legitimacy was the erosion of the image of an efficient, disciplined bureaucracy. Partly this was a question of standards of entry and training, which (though much higher than in the nineteenth century) had not kept up with general improvements. The generous pay award recommended by the 1960 Royal Commission was intended to remedy this problem, but police earnings were rapidly outstripped by inflation. The poor educational standards of recruits—and in particular the shortage of graduates— which the Royal Commission had lamented, remained a concern. Despite increasing attention to training, which was straining the manpower capacities of forces (J. Martin and Wilson 1969: 103), there were still many complaints that it was inadequate for the complex needs of modern society. The old emphasis on drill and discipline was also being eroded as a response to a growing ideology of 'man-management', and the need to match changing social fashions in order to attract recruits (Reiner 1978: 186–94).

There have been many attempts since the 1960s to raise educational and training standards. In the 1960s various schemes were introduced to attract graduates to the service, and encourage higher education for serving police officers (Savage *et al.* 2000: chap. 4). These included the Graduate Entry Scheme, the Bramshill Scholarships, and the Special Course at Bramshill for potential high-flyers. These have played an increasing part in the careers of senior officers (Reiner 1991; Wall 1998; Savage *et al.* 2000: chap. 4; Golding and Savage 2008: 748–52). However, significant results were not achieved until the 1980s, when as a result of the 1978 Edmund-Davies pay award (and unemployment outside the service) the intake of graduates accelerated sharply. There was also increasing interest from serving officers in specialist criminal justice degrees (J. Brown 1996; Savage *et al.* 2000: chap. 4). Significant changes occurred in recruit training, as well, largely following from the 1982 Scarman Report (Fielding 1988; Savage 2007: 29–30, 111–12; Mawby and Wright 2008: 235–6). Despite the merit of these developments, they have not prevented an erosion of public confidence in police professional standards.

Corruption scandals. The main way in which the image of the police force as a dis-ciplined, impersonal bureaucracy came to be dented was the series of Scotland Yard corruption scandals that rocked it after 1969 (Cox *et al.* 1977). Since then the police have experienced a repeated cycle of scandal and reform (Sherman 1978; Punch 2003, 2009). In retrospect the establishment of the CID as a separate department in 1878, in the wake of a corruption scandal, had only aggravated the problem. The Met's own his-torian concluded that 'it is beyond argument that by the summer of 1922 the CID had become a thoroughly venal private army' (Ascoli 1979: 210). Allegations of malpractice by London detectives remained rife (Laurie 1970: chap. 10).

Nonetheless, the revelations published by *The Times* in November 1969 were a bombshell with lasting reverberations. It was not simply that *The Times* had been able to tape-record discussions between detectives and a villain, thus proving their allegations beyond the shadow of a doubt. Nor was it just that the corruption uncovered was very grave (involving deals to cover up serious crimes, setting up criminals as *agents provocateurs*, perjury, and planting of evidence). What was most shocking was the revelation of the systematic, institutionalized and widespread network of corruption, the so-called 'firm within a firm'. The Yard's initial attempt at investigation only confirmed this, with a pattern of obstruction, leaks, and disappearing documents. Eventually Frank Williamson, formerly a Manchester detective chief superintendent but in 1970 Her Maj-esty's Inspector of Constabulary (Crime), was brought in. Williamson's investigation was also frustrated, and he resigned prematurely, in disgust at his experiences.

During the mid-1970s there were two more major corruption scandals at the Met, one involving the Drug Squad, the other the Obscene Publications Squad. Both revealed systematic malpractice, and led to the imprisonment of several senior detectives. The Drug Squad under Detective Chief Inspector Kelaher was implicated in unorthodox methods, including fabrication and manipulation of evidence in order to achieve major 'busts'. The 'Porn' Squad was riddled with graft on a grand scale. Relations between crooks and criminals were warm and intimate. On one occasion a pornography dealer went into Holborn Police Station wearing a CID tie to examine seized material for 'recycling'. Confiscated blue films were shown on the squad's projector at regular Friday evening 'stag' parties (Cox *et al.* 1977: 168).

Home Secretary Reginald Maudling's answer was to appoint as commissioner an 'outsider', Robert Mark, who had been assistant commissioner since 1967 but had previously served entirely in provincial forces. Mark's appointment was seen as clearly signalling a battle against corruption: 'He had the reputation of a "Mr. Clean", the "Manchester Martinet", the "Lone Ranger from Leicester"' (ibid.: 132).

Mark introduced a dramatic strategy of associated reforms, clearly seeing the excision of the 'cancer' at the Yard as the price of its continued independence (Mark 1978: chaps. 7–10). He established a new specialist elite department, A10, to inves-tigate all complaints against police officers, put a uniformed officer in charge of the Yard CID and uniformed supervisors over all divisional detectives, abolished the 'Porn' squad, moved many detectives back into uniform, rotated detectives frequently, and cultivated more open relations with the press. As a result of this new climate some five hundred policemen left the force during Mark's period as commissioner, many voluntarily in anticipation of being investigated.

The resilience of corruption at the Yard was shown by new revelations in 1978. They alleged involvement of detectives, including some in the Robbery Squad, in major armed robberies (Ball *et al.* 1979). The allegations were an unwelcome by-product of the 1970s strategy of developing 'super-grasses'—informants induced to reveal large numbers of names in return for immunity from prosecution. (This tactic was subsequently transported to Northern Ireland, with equally dubious results: Greer 1995.) The commissioner, Sir David McNee, responded by setting up Operation Countryman under the direction of the Dorset chief constable, Arthur Hambleton. Hambleton and his team claimed on several occasions that their work was being sabotaged by corrupt Yard pressure, and by the time the operation was wound up only two convictions had been achieved. Yard officers in turn spread smears about the incompetence of the 'Swedey', as the provincial detectives came to be contemptuously called.

The Countryman investigations cast doubt on any idea that the endemic corruption in the Yard detective squads had been eliminated. Research on professional criminals suggests a perennial web of corrupt deals and police malpractice (Hobbs 1988, 1995).

Three centuries' experience of thief-taking suggests that a standard method of plain clothes criminal investigation, the cultivation of close relations with criminals as informants, operates perennially on the borderline of legality. During the 'golden age' of high public confidence, the evidence of police and underworld memoirs and oral histories suggests extensive and routinized corruption behind the façade of legitimacy (Mark 1978; Daley 1986; Weinberger 1995: chap. 10; Emsley 1996: 241–7). As Tom Tullett, a former CID detective, and *Daily Mirror* chief crime reporter, put it in his eulogistic account of the 1960s Murder Squad investigation of gangland killings: 'In this kind of "war" the police had to think like villains themselves, using every ruse, trick and disguise' (Tullett 1981: 243). The trouble is that rule-bending which may be justified initially by a sincere determination to 'crack down' on serious crime may serve as the 'invitational edge' of the kind of wholesale and predatory wrongdoing revealed in the 1970s (Manning and Redlinger 1977). The explosion of corruption scandals was the product of the dangers inherent in traditional detective methods, coupled with the novel pressures of the 1960s and 1970s. These included the rise of large-scale organized crime, and growing toleration of some illegal activities (like drug-taking or pornography) which increased their profitability and lessened the sense detectives had that conniving at them was harmful. The decline in public deference also made it much more likely that police wrongdoing would come to light and that allegations against them would be believed.

The 1970s scandals fatally damaged the image of the police as impersonal and disciplined law enforcers, which the tradition built up by Rowan and Mayne had stressed. While in the 1960 Royal Commission survey 46.9 per cent of the public did not believe bribe-taking occurred, the 1981 Policy Studies Institute study of Londoners found that only 14 per cent believed the police 'hardly ever' took bribes (Policy Studies Institute 1983, i: 249). The recent replication of the PSI study, the *Policing for London* survey found this percentage unchanged (Fitzgerald *et al.* 2002), although in some other respects the proportion of Londoners perceiving the police as corrupt had dropped by 2002 (Hough 2007a: 200–1).

During the 1980s there were fewer scandals involving personal corruption (although they revived during the 1990s: Newburn 1999). Attention switched to abuses of police powers undermining the rule of law, what Sir Paul Condon, Metropolitan Police Commissioner for most of the 1990s, dubbed 'noble cause' corruption.

The rule of law?

The issue of police adherence to legality became acutely politicized in the 1970s. On the one hand groups like the National Council for Civil Liberties publicized evidence of widespread police malpractice, while on the other the police began to lobby for greater powers to aid the 'war against crime'.

Civil libertarians had been arguing for years that the rights of suspects (encapsulated in the 'Judges' Rules', the non-statutory administrative directions laying down procedures for questioning and taking statements) were routinely violated (Whitaker 1964: chap. 7; Laurie 1970: chap. 10). Such claims were crystallized by the 1972 conviction, on charges arising out of the murder of Maxwell Confait, of three teenage boys, one of whom was mentally retarded (Baxter and Koffman 1983). One boy's parents managed to get Christopher Price (then MP for Lewisham West) to take up the case, and after a three-year struggle the verdict was quashed by the Court of Appeal. Concern about the case led to an official inquiry under Sir Henry Fisher, a high court judge, which reported in 1977.

The Fisher Report found that the boys' rights had been violated, leading to their false confessions. They were interviewed without an independent adult present; they were not informed of their rights to phone a solicitor or friend; there were several improprieties in questioning and charging, amounting to unfairness and oppressiveness. Altogether, Fisher found 'some of the Rules and Directions do not seem to be known to police officers'. He suggested that reform of the Rules should be conducted in the light of a broader inquiry—'something like a Royal Commission'. The hint was taken up shortly afterwards when the prime minister, James Callaghan, announced the Royal Commission on Criminal Procedure (RCCP), which reported in 1981.

Senior officers repeatedly claimed that police work could not be done effectively if legal procedures were properly adhered to (Mark 1978: 58). The same opinion was common among the rank and file (Reiner 1978: 77–81, 221–3). This view translated into practice, according to observational studies. Holdaway described a variety of tactics for controlling suspects which 'distance . . . officers from the constraints of legal rules and force directives' (Holdaway 1983: 101), such as 'verballing' or 'working the oracle' (fabricating statements). The PSI study also found that while 'outright fabrication of evidence is probably rare . . . departure from rules and procedure affecting evidence are far more common. . . . There will be no fundamental change as long as many police officers believe that the job cannot be done effectively within the rules' (Policy Studies Institute 1983, iv: 228–30).

Apart from violations of rules concerning collection of evidence, there was also a mounting campaign in the late 1970s against police abuse of physical force, stimulated by a number of notorious cases (Box 1983: 82; Ward 1986). The refusal of the Director of Public Prosecutions to prosecute any police officers in connection with these only fuelled critics' suspicions. The Home Affairs Select Committee reported in 1980 on the procedures for investigating deaths in police custody. It revealed a growing number of such deaths, from eight in 1970 to forty-eight in 1978, with a total of 274 in 1971–9. The proportion of these officially categorized as due to 'misadventure' or 'accident' doubled. These figures underestimate the number of deaths connected with police custody, for they exclude those which closely followed release. There is no warrant for saying that all such cases involved police misconduct, let alone abuse or brutality. Nevertheless, it was clearly an issue that provoked concern about police departure from the rule of law.

The RCCP report was eventually transmuted into the Police and Criminal Evidence Act 1984 (PACE). This purported to provide a balanced codification of police powers and safeguards over their exercise, synthesizing the concerns of the 'law and order' and the civil liberties lobbies (Chapter 7). Nonetheless, the issue of police abuse of powers increased rather than abated in the late 1980s and early 1990s. Between 1989 and 1991 police confidence in the police was shaken by a series of scandals revealing serious malpractice. In October 1989 the Court of Appeal released the 'Guildford Four', the three men and a woman sentenced to life imprisonment in 1974 for the Guildford and Woolwich pub bombings. In the words of the Lord Chief Justice, Lord Lane, new evidence gathered by the Avon and Somerset Constabulary showed that some of the Surrey officers investigating the bombings 'must have lied' at the trial of the Four. In 1990 the Court of Appeal exonerated the 'Maguire Seven', who had also been jailed in connection with the bombings. A further blow to confidence in the police was the release in March 1991 of the 'Birmingham Six', who had been convicted in 1975 of the savage Birmingham pub bombings. Other *causes célèbres* considered by the Court of Appeal in the early 1990s included the cases of Judith Ward (whose conviction for a 1974 IRA coach bombing was quashed), and the four men convicted for the 1978 murder of a newsboy, Carl Bridgewater. There was also continuing concern about a number of even older miscarriages of justice, such as the cases of Craig and Bentley, and Timothy Evans, stemming from the early 1950s (Woffinden 1990). Allegations of corrupt conspiracies to pervert the course of justice reached as high as the cabinet in the Stalker case, arising out of the removal of John Stalker from his inquiry into fatal shootings in Northern Ireland by the RUC (Stalker 1988). Although these cases profoundly shook public opinion, police representatives often argued they had occurred before recent reforms, and could not happen under the procedures now in force. This argument was itself weakened by a number of *causes célèbres* involving more recent abuses (C. Walker and Starmer 1999; Nobles and Schiff 2000, 2004; Walker 2002; Naughton 2005, 2007; Savage and Milne 2007). Some featured on-the-street violence not related to the bringing of a prosecution, and thus untouched by PACE, such as a 1986 attack on a group of black youths in Holloway. Directly calling into question police adherence to the rule of law was the scandal involving the West Midlands Serious Crimes Squad, which was disbanded in June 1989 by the then chief constable, Geoffrey Dear, after allegations of serious malpractice. Perhaps most damaging of all was the Court of Appeal decision in November 1992 to uphold the appeals of the 'Tottenham Three', who had been convicted of the brutal murder of PC Blakelock during the 1986 Broadwater Farm riot (Rose 1992), on the basis of forensic evidence that the accused's statements had not been recorded contemporaneously (as PACE requires). These investigations had supposedly taken place under PACE procedures.

The anxiety produced by these revelations of abuse was enough to make the Home Secretary announce in March 1991 (after the release of the Birmingham Six), the establishment of a Royal Commission on Criminal Justice, chaired by Lord Runciman, the first Royal Commission in twelve years. The change in public views of the police was encapsulated by a *Guardian* cartoon following the successful appeal by the Tottenham Three. A man, late for a date, offers his girlfriend the excuse 'I asked a policeman the time, and he lied!'

The strategy of minimal force?

Was the traditional policy of 'winning by appearing to lose' abandoned, perhaps replaced by one of losing while appearing to win (Squires and Kennison 2010)? That was the question raised by a clear trend to harder-line policing of political and industrial conflict. The preparedness of the police to cope with public order problems began to be expanded and refined during the 1970s. The militarization of policing proceeded apace in the 1980s in the wake of more serious disorder, although since the early 1990s police around the world have been experimenting with more sophisticated strategies (D. Waddington *et al.* 1989, 2009; Jefferson 1990; P. Waddington 1991, 1994; Vogler 1991; Critcher and D. Waddington 1996; M. King and Brearley 1996; della Porta and Reiter 1998; Bessel and Emsley 2000; M. King and D. Waddington 2004; della Porte *et al.* 2006; D. Waddington 2007; P. Waddington and Wright 2008).

Without much public debate de facto 'third forces' emerged, specifically trained and readily mobilizable to cope with riots. The Metropolitan Police Special Patrol Group, formed in 1965 as a mobile reserve, developed a paramilitary role in dealing with public order and terrorism. All forces now have similar units (under various names), trained in riot control, use of firearms and sometimes CS gas. After 1974 all forces formed Police Support Units (PSUs) to help in controlling crowds, strikes, and demonstrations. These were specially trained for public order duties, including the use of shields, but normally engaged in ordinary policing at local level. However, they were readily mobilizable to deal with problems arising outside their own force under mutual aid arrangements.

All these mutual aid arrangements were the fruits of the establishment panic in 1972, after the Saltley coke depot had to be closed during picketing by miners after a six-day struggle. While Saltley was seen as an abject defeat by many Conservatives and police officers, it was regarded by others as an example of the traditional 'winning by appearing to lose' strategy. Reginald Maudling, the then Home Secretary, believed it would have been possible for sufficient force to be used to clear the gates, but the long-run consequences for social stability would have been disastrous (Jeffery and Hennessy 1983: 236). After Saltley there was much debate about the need for a 'third force' specializing in riot control, along the line of the French CRS (Compagnies Républicaines de Sécurité). The police succeeded in scotching the idea, but in effect created 'third forces' within their own organizations, as the 1984–5 miners' strike indicated. In this strike a massive, centrally coordinated police operation was directed by the National Reporting Centre, with much criticism of 'police-state' tactics in a controversy that still rages (Reiner 1984, 1991: chap. 8; Fine and Millar 1985; McCabe *et al.* 1988; Green 1991; Milne 2004; Beckett and Hencke 2009; Granville Williams 2009). It is hard to remember the shock that greeted the bringing out of police riot shields at Lewisham and Notting Hill in 1977, replacing the traditional protection of dustbin lids. But shields, strengthened helmets and other protective equipment became regular sights. After the police failure to contain the 1980 Bristol riots and their lack of success in preventing widespread damage and police injuries in the 1981 Brixton, Toxteth, and other disorders, police preparation for riot control redoubled, with Home Office support. During the riots themselves, of course, there was an evident intensification of police tactics, notably the first use of CS gas in riot control in mainland Britain, and high-speed driving of police vehicles to disperse crowds. Altogether in the 1981 riots levels of injury unknown for nearly fifty years in English disorders were inflicted on both police and civilians by boot, brick, fist, truncheon, and petrol bomb.

The immediate response of Conservative politicians and police was to call for tougher tactics, equipment, and legal powers for the police.[6] Mrs Thatcher told Parliament that the government agreed to the use of water cannon, CS gas, and plastic bullets if chief constables wanted them. A deputation of senior English police officers visited Northern Ireland to discuss riot control with the RUC and see what lessons could be learned from their 'success', and the advice of the Hong Kong police was also sought.

John Alderson, then chief constable of Devon and Cornwall, who represented the liberal pole of police opinion, expressed grave doubts about this trend: 'There has to be a better way than blind repression. . . . We must not advance the police response too far ahead of the situation. It is even worth a few million pounds of destruction rather than get pushed too far down that road' (*Sunday Telegraph* 12 July 1981).

In the end this more balanced approach prevailed over Lord Scarman's inquiry, set up by the government in the wake of the Brixton riots (Scarman 1981). Neither the tougher methods available after 1981 nor the wider Scarman-inspired reforms were able to avert even more serious urban riots in 1985, in the West Midlands, Liverpool, and Brixton. The most serious conflict occurred on the Broadwater Farm estate in Tottenham North London. Firearms were used against the police, and plastic bullets deployed (but not used) by them. Most tragically there was the savage hacking to death of PC Keith Blakelock, the first Met police officer to be murdered in a riot since PC Culley in the 1833 Coldbath Fields case. After the riots, the Met commissioner, Sir Kenneth Newman, warned that he would use plastic bullets should such violence occur again. His successor, Sir Peter Imbert, argued in a Howard League lecture in 1987 that the 'winning by appearing to lose' strategy had to be abandoned in the face of regular disorder of such magnitude, or it would amount simply to losing all the time.

Serious public disorder occurred again in an industrial context at Wapping in 1986–7, during picketing, by print workers protesting at their displacement by new technology and non-union staff, outside the News International plant. Many complaints of undue violence were made against the police, and the Police Complaints Authority upheld some of them after an investigation. Other apparently unjustified uses of tough public-order tactics occurred during the policing of hippie convoys converging on Stonehenge.

During 1990 anti-poll-tax demonstrations were the source of severe public order clashes, especially following a rally in Trafalgar Square on 31 March. Damage, looting, and violence fanned out from Trafalgar Square to neighbouring areas in central London, with tourists, theatre-goers, and shoppers caught up in the mêlée. Despite the levels of violence and disorder, criticisms of police abuse and overreaction surfaced quickly, and a Trafalgar Square Defendants' Committee was formed. In October 1990 a breakaway group from a south London anti-poll-tax rally marched on Brixton prison to support those sentenced for the Trafalgar Square troubles. This led to serious disorder, with forty-five police officers injured and 105 arrests.

During the 1990s the greatest public order concerns were not industrial or political conflicts. A 'moral panic' developed about disorder occurring in a variety of leisure contexts. In 1988 ACPO had raised fears about growing disorder in rural areas caused by 'lager louts' with 'too much beer in their bellies and money in their pockets'. Subsequent Home Office research questioned the idea of disorder growing in rural areas (as distinct from towns in county force areas), and the alleged connection with affluence (Tuck 1989). In 1989–90 there was great police concern about the spread of 'acid-house' parties, and the violence they stimulated, as several officers were seriously injured in raids. The most serious violence and disorder in a leisure context occurred in September 1991, in riots on the Blackbird Leys estate, Oxford, and Meadow Well estate, Tyneside, after police attempts to curb joy-riding (B. Campbell 1993). In the mid-1990s there arose a variety of new forms of political protest, against specific issues such as live animal exports and the building of new roads in rural areas. These united groups with long experience of the hard end of public order policing with middle-aged, middle-class people, including many women, who would tradition-ally have been stalwart police supporters. The combination created especially acute policing problems. Since the late 1990s there has been a resurgence of left-wing protest about financial globalization and its consequences of deepening inequality, including major clashes in the City of London in 1999, 2000, and 2009 (with counterparts in the USA in Seattle and Washington).

During the 1970s and 1980s the British police response to riots undoubtedly became tougher, with more resort to technology, equipment, and weaponry. Darth Vader displaced Dixon in riot control tactics.

Apart from the growing use of riot control hardware, there has been a rapid proliferation of firearms use by the police in Britain (McKenzie 1996; Squires 2000; Waddington and Wright 2008; Squires and Kennison 2010). Although still unarmed (apart from the traditional truncheon) on routine patrol, the frequency with which firearms are issued to the police has escalated inexorably, as has the firepower of the guns used. Many forces now deploy armed response vehicles (ARVs) which can be used on orders from headquarters. The number of occasions when guns are fired by the police remains small by international standards, and the rules and accountability mechanisms have been tightened on numerous occasions, following a series of egregious wrongful shootings. These stretch from the Stephen Waldorf debacle[7] in 1983 to the killing of Jean Charles de Menezes, an innocent Brazilian electrician, in July 2005 in the wake of the London terrorist bombings. Most police officers wish to remain unarmed for routine work, but there is some growth of support for arming. Whatever the justification in terms of the growing violence faced by police in public order and routine patrol work, the traditional unarmed image of the British bobby has been undermined. Debate has raged about whether militaristic tactics aggravate or alleviate the violence they are supposed to deal with (e.g. the exchanges between Jefferson 1987, 1990, 1993 and P. Waddington 1987, 1993).

Accountability?

Until relatively recently the independence of the British police from control by elected governmental institutions was often seen as a virtue, although there has also been a long-standing radical critique arguing that it was anomalous in a democracy. In the USA several generations of police reformers regarded the British model of insulation from political control as a solution to problems of corruption and partisanship.

As policing became more controversial in Britain in the 1970s and 1980s, so perception of the mechanisms of accountability changed. The old mystical substitute of police identification with the public came under strain as the police were seen as unrepresentative in terms of race, gender, and culture. Throughout the 1980s radical critics sought to reform police governance so as to make police policy-making fully accountable to the electoral process. Until the mid-1990s, all governments have wanted to maintain the constitutional status quo regarding police governance. They have, however, become increasingly concerned to render the police more accountable for their use of powers and, even more crucially, the effective use of resources.

At the same time it was becoming increasingly evident that local accountability to police authorities has atrophied. It was being replaced by a degree of central control amounting to a de facto national force. (These issues will be fully explored in Chapter 7.) The perceived lack of adequate accountability was a major factor undermining legitimacy in the 1970s and 1980s.

Non-partisanship?

The spectacle of James Anderton, Manchester's chief constable, or representatives of the Police Federation, preaching at the drop of a helmet about the sinking state of our national moral fibre became familiar in the 1970s. It was hard to appreciate quite how novel a departure from tradition this was (Reiner 1978, 1980; McLaughlin and Murji 1998; Loader and Mulcahy 2003: chap. 7).

When, in 1965, the Police Federation, then a humble professional association rather than the media opinion leader it became, launched at a press conference a pamphlet, *The*

Problem, which argued for police pay rises to help the fight against crime, the authorities were aghast. The official side of the Police Council hammered the Federation for its 'unprecedented breach of faith', while one member was quoted by the Federation's *Newsletter* (April 1996: 40) as saying, 'I never thought I would see the day when the representatives of law and order would be advocating anarchy.'

By 1980 the police, at all levels from chief constable down to the rank and file, seemed to set the terms of debate on law and order and social policy (Thompson 1980). This change was heralded by the Marksist revolution at Scotland Yard, when Sir Robert Mark delivered his controversial Dimbleby lecture on BBC television in 1972.

In 1975, the Police Federation launched an unprecedented campaign for 'law and order'. It aimed 'to harness the public's growing concern about the state of crime and public order in Britain into a programme for positive action'. The Federation modelled itself on the liberal pressure groups of the 1960s that had successfully campaigned for reform of the law on capital punishment, homosexuality, and abortion. The intention was to mobilize 'the silent majority', to influence politicians to support the 'rule of law,' and to reverse the liberalizing trend in penal and social policy. The campaign was condemned by many as a dangerous departure from the tradition of police non-involvement in politics. The Federation justified itself by asking, 'What is "political" about crime?' It claimed the right to comment on legislation and policies which 'affected the working lives of police officers, who might have strong views on it'. In 1978, the Federation relaunched the campaign specifically to influence the 1979 general election. A stream of strikingly similar and much-publicized pronouncements appeared from police spokesmen and Tory politicians as part of what the media dubbed the 'great debate' on law and order. Two high points, which marked the increasingly explicit political involvement of the police, occurred near the election. A fortnight before polling day, Robert Mark hit the headlines with a broadside comparing the relationship between the Labour Party and the trade unions to 'the way the National Socialist German Workers' Party achieved unrestricted control of the German state'. The way that the media structured the debate in the terms set by what the *Daily Mail* called 'The gospel according to Sir Robert Mark' was neatly illustrated by the headline chosen by the *Evening News* to report Prime Minister James Callaghan's response, 'JIM PUTS IN THE JACKBOOT', precisely echoing Mark's imagery. The day after Mark's intervention, the Police Federation placed a long advertisement in most national newspapers under the heading, 'LAW AND ORDER'. It blamed government policies for rising crime and urged support for a set of proposals, ranging from higher police pay to stiffer penalties. The police–Tory symbiosis was underlined when, four days later, the shadow Home Secretary, William Whitelaw, gave a six-point pledge on law and order, which matched all the Federation's points. Despite this, Jim Jardine, the Federation's chairman, disingenuously claimed that the £21,000 series of advertisements had not been intended to sway voters. If not, it was a cavalier waste of his members' money.

In the event the advertisements proved to be an investment which reaped handsome dividends. On the first working day after the Conservative election victory, Federation leaders were summoned with urgency to Downing Street to be told that the new government would immediately implement in full the pay increase recommended by the Edmund-Davies committee (which in 1978 had recommended a generous inflation-proof formula that Labour was introducing in two stages). Symbolizing the more open accord between the police and the new Conservative government, the Federation broke with the tradition that their parliamentary adviser was drawn from the opposition party, and reappointed Eldon Griffiths, a Conservative MP noted for abrasive speeches on law and order. Some members were distressed that the Federation had 'nailed its flag for all to see to the Conservative Party mast', but the Federation justified the move by 'his commitment to the policies which the Police Federation had been putting forward on law and order'. In March 1982 when the Met released its annual crime statistics, it analysed them by the race of robbers as identified by victims, highlighting the stereotype of the black mugger. This was an unprecedented use of official statistics in a manner that had clear political implications. It was widely interpreted at the time as an attempt to 'mug' Scarman (Sim 1982).

In the same week there was a hysterical speech by James Anderton, condemning 'an enemy more dangerous, insidious and ruthless than any faced since World War Two', and exposing an alleged 'long-term political strategy to destroy the proven structures of the police'. The Police Federation fuelled the growing panic by an advertisement in most national newspapers arguing for the restoration of capital punishment. Police pressure on law and order was echoed by growing criticism from the Tory right of Whitelaw's supposedly 'soft' approach to crime. (The dying tradition of cross-party accord received a last hurrah at a conference on community policing held at Exeter University in March 1982. Unable to address the audience in person, Merlyn Rees, the former Labour Home Secretary, sent along instead a speech by William Whitelaw, his Conservative opposite number, to be read out, as it exactly expressed his views!) The March 1982 events were the high watermark of overt police lobbying for law and order. McNee's successor as Metropolitan commissioner, Sir Kenneth Newman, avoided the high-profile politicking of his predecessors, as have subsequent chief officers (Savage *et al.* 2000: 50). During the late 1980s the love affair between the Tories and the police cooled as public expenditure cuts began to bite on the police, and they feared a hidden agenda of incipient privatization (Rawlings 1991). For its part Labour tried hard and ultimately successfully to repair broken bridges. The party's leader, Neil Kinnock in an interview in *Police Review* in 1986, said he had a childhood ambition of becoming a policeman. Labour spokespersons assiduously attended Police Federation conferences, and criticized the Tories for cutting police expenditure. In March 1990, during the critical Mid-Staffordshire by-election, Federation leaders appeared on a Labour platform. It would be exaggerating to claim that the police switched partisan loyalties. Rather there was a gradual return to cross-party consensus on law and order. However this occurred largely because the 'New Labour' that emerged in the 1990s accepted many of the policy changes of the Thatcherite years in law and order as in other areas. Its electorally successful soundbite

'Tough on crime, tough on the causes of crime' increasingly emphasized the former. This was especially marked during the contest in toughness on law and order between the Home Secretary, Michael Howard and the Shadow Home Secretary Jack Straw before the 1997 general election (Downes and Morgan 2007; Reiner 2007a).

The prototype of the outspoken chief constable, Sir James Anderton, retired in 1991. He had become even more controversial in the late 1980s for his supposedly divinely inspired utterances on aids and other topics, as well as his suspension, on the basis of rather dubious corruption allegations, of his deputy, John Stalker, who was investigating some shootings by the RUC in Northern Ireland (Stalker 1988). Despite this he retained the loyalty of his force throughout. A *Police Review* cartoon on his resignation well expresses their ambivalence: as Anderton is seen departing the station, one PC says to another: 'I'm sorry to see him go in a way. He was the only Chief Constable I've ever known who thought someone else was God!' By then most chief constables had come to believe overt police interventions in political and social debates were unwise. Nonetheless, the years of partisanship had tarnished, possibly irretrievably, the sacred aura hitherto enjoyed by the British police of being, like the Queen, above party politics.

The service role?

The service role continued to be paid lip-service by chief constables. Indeed, a current of police thinking, especially after the 1981 Scarman report, stressed that, contrary to the growing image of the police as primarily crime-fighters, much if not most uniformed police work (measured by time or number of incidents dealt with) consisted of service calls for help. This approach, pioneered in the 1970s by John Alderson, then chief constable of Devon and Cornwall, and his philosophy of community policing (Alderson 1979, 1984, 1998), subsequently became an influential movement among progressive police chiefs in the USA and elsewhere (Skolnick and Bayley 1986, 1988; Fielding 2002, 2009; Brogden and Nijhar 2005; Savage 2007: 55–9, 128–41).

The devaluing of the service role by rank-and-file culture (summed up thus by one PC, 'this idea of performing a public service is a load of cobswobble as far as I'm concerned' (Reiner 1978: 213–17), was problematic for police legitimacy. After the Scarman Report endorsed a kind of community policing philosophy this became the orthodox analysis of the police role for all chief constables (Reiner 1991: chap. 6). The decline in public support in the late 1980s led to a redoubling of the effort to define policing in service and consumerist terms, in the Met's Plus Programme and the ACPO Statement of Common Purpose and Values (Waters 1996; Squires 1998; Savage 2007: 136–41).[8] However, these efforts were largely overturned by the Conservative government's reform package launched in 1993, which explicitly sought to prioritize 'catching criminals' (in the words of the 1993 White Paper on Police Reform) as the primary if not sole job of policing. New Labour's Crime Reduction Programme continued this emphasis, albeit in a somewhat modulated form (Savage 2007: 185–6; Reiner 2007a: 136–9).

Preventive policing?

Peel's original conception of policing emphasized patrol by uniformed constables as fundamental. This notion of the bobby on the beat as the essential bedrock of the force, to which all other specialisms are ancillary, remains a philosophy to which most chief constables pay constant homage. However, it is potent as symbol rather than practice (N. Walker 1996). Despite the rhetoric, specialist departments proliferated, and foot patrol was treated as a reserve from which high-flying potential specialists could be drawn, and a Siberia to which failed specialists could be banished. Beat work was an apprenticeship through which all police officers must pass, but seldom wished to stay in or return to. The Unit Beat reorganization represented a move towards specialization within the patrol function itself. It unintentionally glorified the thrills of car chases, combat, and capture (Holdaway 1977, 1983). Relationships between panda car drivers and the public were more likely to be restricted to conflict situations than with old-style foot patrol. As a uniformed inspector put it to me: 'Before UBP you heard there was a fight round the corner, and by the time you got there, they were probably tucked up in bed together. Today the policeman is there in seconds, while it's still going on, and he has to sort it out.' Since the 1960s the meaning of crime prevention has shifted (Gilling 1997, 2007; Crawford 1997, 1998, 2008; Hughes 1998, 2006; Hughes and Edwards 2002; Byrne and Pease 2008). Originally it referred to the 'scarecrow' function of regular uniform patrol. In the 1960s this was transmuted into a notion of prevention as pre-emption (as patrol became a 'fire brigade' emergency service). Pre-emption meant two things. First it meant the strategy, built into the Unit Beat system as its bedrock, of collecting and coordinating the low-level information provided by patrolling and area constables, who were to be evaluated by the quality and quantity of information they accumulated. A central role in the system was given to the collator, the station-based officer whose task was to assemble and monitor the information provided from the streets. This largely consisted of hunches based on the political and personal proclivities of individuals who aroused the idiosyncratic suspicions of local police. With the proliferation of computers in police forces (and the growth in capacity of the Police National Computer) this information has become more centralized and readily available, as well as acquiring an insidious status as 'hard data'. The development of 'intelligence-led', risk-oriented, inter-agency, and 'partnership' policing methods has accentuated the breadth and depth of pre-emptive surveillance and analysis in all police forces (Marx 1988, 1992; Fijnaut and Marx 1996; Maguire and John 1996a, 1996b; Dunnighan and Norris 1999; P. Gill 2000; Maguire 2000, 2008; Tilley 2008; Cope 2008).

The second meaning of pre-emption is the development of specialist crime prevention departments, providing advice to citizens on methods of minimizing the risk of victimization, and alerting them to the dangers of some kinds of offences. At first crime prevention departments were Cinderellas of the service, low status, low budget, and low key. However, as crime prevention became increasingly central to the government's law-and-order policy in the 1980s so they blossomed into belles of the ball (Bottoms 1990; Reiner and Cross 1991: chap. 1). The impact of such vaunted crime prevention efforts as Neighbourhood Watch was mixed however (Bennett 1990; Forrester *et al.* 1988; McConville and Shepherd 1992).

In the view of some critics the community policing philosophy, emphasizing both service and crime prevention work, was itself only a more covert (and there fore insidious) means of penetrating communities to acquire information (Gordon 1984). Its equally proactive cousin 'Problem-Oriented Policing' (H. Goldstein 1979, 1990; Tilley 2008) has been subject to the same accusation, although it purports to be more finely targeted, aimed at specific problems. What seems clear is that the pursuit of greater crime prevention effectiveness has meant a proliferation of proactive tactics, and specialist and plainclothes units, reversing the original strategy of Peel, Rowan, and Mayne. These policies are themselves a response to the undermining of the eighth ingredient of legitimation.

Police effectiveness?

Police effectiveness is a notoriously slippery concept to define or measure. But the official statistics routinely produced by police forces and published by the Home Office seemed to record an inexorable rise in serious offences and decline in the clear-up rate from the mid-1950s to the early 1990s. Whereas in the mid-1950s there were less than half a million indictable offences recorded as known to the police in most years, this rose above half a million for the first time in 1957. By 1977 it was over 2 million, by 1982 more than 2.5 million, and by 1992 5.4 million. Recorded crime fell in the 1990s for five consecutive years after 1993, although it began to rise again thereafter, falling again more recently (Reiner 2007a: chap. 3). Before the Second World War the percentage of crimes recorded as cleared up was always over 50 per cent. By the late 1950s it had dropped to about 45 per cent, and by the end of the twentieth century was around 25 per cent.

The inadequacy of all these figures has long been well known (Maguire 2007; Reiner 2007a: chap. 3). Many crimes are not reported to the police, so increases in the rate may mean a greater propensity to report rather than suffer victimization. The clear-up rate is affected by many determinants apart from detective effectiveness, including massaging the figures (M. Young 1991; H. Taylor 1998a, 1998b, 1999; Davies 1999b). Nonetheless it is hard to argue that the recent recorded trends (in particular the spectacular rise since the 1950s) do not correspond to basic changes in the same direction. They are certainly associated with what is widely described as a growing public fear of crime and a popular sense that police effectiveness is declining (Hope and Sparks 2000; Stenson and Sullivan 2000; Ditton and Farrall 2000; Farrall and Lee 2008; Farrall *et al.* 2009), giving rise to a 'reassurance policing' agenda (Innes 2006; Crawford 2007). Police legitimacy was further undermined by their apparent inability to deal with crime in the suites as well as in the streets. As the salience of fraud problems grew in the 1980s, so there was increasing concern about police incompetence or partiality in this area, accentuated even more recently by the 'credit crunch' and recession (Levi 1987, 2008; Karstedt and Farrall 2006; Nelken 2007).

In the 1980s the Home Office Research Unit produced a growing volume of evidence (paralleling earlier American findings) indicating that current methods of patrol and detection were of dubious effectiveness (R. Clarke and Hough 1984). Taking a lead from this (as well as the Scarman Report) several chief constables attempted to redirect methods of policing towards a restoration of public confidence and cooperation—a new social contract, as Sir Kenneth Newman called it (Reiner 1991: chap. 7; Savage 2007: 127–41). During the 1990s there was, however, a rebirth of police and political belief in the possibilities of crime control by the police, in particular using innovative methods, with some support from criminological researchers (Chapter 5). Whatever the outcome of these debates is, there can be no doubt that public concerns about apparently declining police effectiveness, and the new tactics and law and order campaigns they stimulated, were a major factor in declining police legitimacy during the 1960s and 1970s.

THE SOCIAL CONTEXT OF DECLINING POLICE LEGITIMACY

Police activity has always borne most heavily on the economically marginal elements in society, the unemployed (especially if vagrant), and young men, whose lives are lived largely in the street and other public places. Such powerless groups have aptly been named 'police property' (Cray 1972; Lee 1981). They are excluded from full 'citizenship' and bear the brunt of policing. Whereas the incorporation of the working class modified their systematic resentment at policing, police conflict with the residuum at the base of the social hierarchy remained. The police themselves recognize this and their argot contains a variety of derogatory epithets for their regular clientele drawn from this stratum. In California they are 'assholes' (Van Maanen 1978), in Canada 'pukes' (Ericson 1982), in London 'slag' or 'scum' (Policy Studies Institute 1983, iv: 164–5), and on Tyneside 'prigs' (M. Young 1991). Drawn mostly from the respectable working class, the police are responsive to their moral values and scorn those whose lifestyles deviate from or challenge them. But, however conflict ridden, relations between the police and 'slag' are not usually politicized. Membership of the marginal strata is temporary (youths mature, the unemployed find jobs) and their internal social relations are atomized, so a sense of group identity is hard to develop. Moreover, police action against them has majority support, even (perhaps especially) from the respectable and stable adult working class (B. Johnson 1976).

One crucial factor which politicized policing after the 1960s was the development of social strata with a consciousness of antagonism towards (and from) the police. This was primarily the product of the development of more self-conscious youth cultures, the return of long-term unemployment, and the increasing militancy of industrial conflict in the 1970s and early 1980s.

A more crucial change, however, was the catastrophic deterioration of relations with the black community. There is a long history of police prejudice against black people and complaints of racial harassment. By the mid-1970s clear evidence had mounted of black men (especially black youths) being disproportionately involved in arrests for certain offences, partly (though not only) because of police discrimination. A vicious cycle of interaction developed between police stereotyping and black vulnerability to the situations that attract police attention (Chapter 5). Unlike the traditional marginal strata, however, black people have a clear identity and consciousness of being discriminated against. Furthermore, the common experience of discrimination in other areas of social life meant many 'respectable' black adults share an identification and common cause with black youths in their struggles with the police (McLaughlin 2007: chap. 6). The consequential disastrous ebbing away of black confidence in the police was crystallized by the Stephen Lawrence case, which dramatically illustrated the failure of the police to protect black people, who are in fact disproportionately victimized by crime. Research on police–public relations suggests clearly that while these remain harmonious with the majority of the population (including most of the working class) they tend to be tense and conflict ridden with the young, the unemployed, the economically marginal, and black people (Policy Studies Institute 1983, i: 314–15, iv: 162–8; Skogan 1994; Bucke 1997; Fitzgerald *et al.* 2002. It should be noted that there are recent signs that the ethnic differences in trust in police are diminishing: Myhill and Beak 2008; Walker *et al.* 2009: Table 5.19). A crucial factor politicizing policing after the 1970s was a growth in the size of these vulnerable groups, primarily because of increasing social exclusion resulting from free-market policies (E. Currie 1998a, 1998b; I. Taylor 1999; J. Young 1999; Reiner 2007a, 2007b), and a heightening of their self-consciousness as targets of policing.

This reflected profound changes in the political economy of Western capitalism. Long-term structural unemployment (increasingly never-employment) re-emerged, leading to the *de-incorporation* of increasing sections of the young working class, especially among discriminated-against minorities, 'who are being defined out of the edifice of citizenship' (Dahrendorf 1985: 98). A new underclass formed not simply as a result of unemployment, but because of unemployment's apparent structural inevitability. There is much debate about the popular concept of an underclass, and its conservative, culturalist version has unacceptable connotations of 'blaming the victim'. But the structurally generated formation of a completely marginalized segment of society is a major source of the huge growth recently of crime, disorder, and tensions around policing. Unemployment is certainly not linked to crime or disorder in any straightforward, automatic way, as the Conservatives are ever ready to tell us. But there is much evidence, since the 1970s, at any rate, that unemployment is a key part of the explanation of crime and disorder (Reiner 2007a: chap. 4; Hale 2009).

Conflicts between the socially marginal and the police are perennial, although the socially excluded are now more numerous than during the post-war boom. However, the key shift feeding into political debate was a long-term cultural change in the opinion-forming middle class. The police lost the confidence of certain small but crucial sections of the influential 'talking classes', what may be described roughly as the *Guardian-* or *Independent*-reading circles. This process of a developing gulf between the police and some educated middle-class opinion had a variety of roots, stretching back to the invention of the car (Weinberger 1995: chap. 4). But the most crucial developments were the growth of middle-class political protest from the early 1960s (CND, the anti-Vietnam War demonstrations, the 1960s student movement and counterculture, the 1990s live animal export and environmental protests), and the politicization of forms of marginal deviance which involve some middle-class people, notably drug-taking and homosexuality. This conflict with highly articulate and educated sections of the population was of enormous significance in converting policing into an overt political issue.

POLICING AS NECESSARY EVIL? PRAGMATIC POST-LEGITIMATION 1992–

The earlier sections of this chapter charted the process of police legitimation in the century after 1856, and its reversal from the 1960s to the early 1990s. This third section will argue that the politics of policing after 1992 moved 'beyond legitimation'. Without recovering the status they had acquired by the middle of the twentieth century, the police have become less racked by principled political conflict and popular suspicion than in the late 1970s and 1980s. Controversy and complaint are pragmatically focused on the failure of police to achieve their widely agreed mission of crime control rather than any critique of their overall purpose or place or fairness. This reflects the deeply embedded consensus on the politics of law and order that developed after New Labour's espousal of the rhetoric of toughness (Downes and Morgan 2007; Reiner 2007a: chap. 5).

The Stephen Lawrence case, the main *cause célèbre* of the 1990s, illustrates this. Although it raised once again the vexed issues of police racism and discrimination, these were manifest above all in the police failure to clear up the murder of a young black man, not in abuse of powers. The concern was a failure to deliver public protection from crime in an equitable and efficient way, rather than the allegations of heavy-handed policing that had dominated earlier controversies.

The politics of policing has become highly febrile, full of sound and fury—but signifying nothing clearly. Peter Manning has stressed the extent to which policing is better interpreted dramaturgically than in terms of rational accomplishment of instrumental objectives (Manning 1997, 2003). The legitimatory performance played out in the first century and a half of the new police saw them as providing security and order by fair, legalistic, minimum force tactics. Although this covered up a backstage reality of widespread corruption and malpractice, the front-of-house mythology was of the best police in the world, paragons of virtue in terms of integrity and effectiveness.

The politicization of policing that developed from the 1960s to the early 1990s was largely about principled disputes between fundamentally conflicting concep-tions. These could be characterized somewhat simplistically in terms of the contrast between crime control and due process models of criminal justice as formulated by the American law Professor Herbert Packer (Packer 1968), which remains an important influence on contemporary debates (Sanders and Young 2007a, 2007b, 2008). On the one hand, a 'law and order' lobby including many police chiefs, the Police Federation, and the Tory party under Margaret Thatcher, regarded crime and disorder as running out of control and saw toughening of police powers and penal policy as the solution, characterizing due process legal safeguards as 'handcuffs' on effective policing. An opposing civil liberties lobby encompassed many lawyers and much of the ('Old') Labour and Liberal Parties. It saw adequate legal safeguards for suspects as not only an important aspect of the rule of law on principle, but necessary to ensure the correct people were convicted. It was also associated with a social democratic analysis of crime and disorder that stressed the deep social roots of these problems and regarded policing and punishment as important but partial and short-term symptom relief rather than fundamental solutions (Reiner 2006). Whatever the virtues of this position, it proved an electoral albatross around Labour's neck in the 1980s as huge increases in crime and disorder fed public concerns for immediate crime suppression. During the late 1980s and early 1990s Labour began to shed its electoral 'hostages to fortune', embracing the police and the 'law and order' (Downes and Morgan 2007). A sharp break occurred when Tony Blair became Shadow Home Secretary in 1992, and made a pitch to capture the law and order issue for Labour with the famous slogan 'tough on crime, tough on the causes of crime', the now legendary soundbite that may have been 'borrowed' from its original author Gordon Brown (Newburn and Reiner 2007). It captured the mood of national soul-searching about crime and moral decline in the wake of by the tragic 1993 murder of Liverpool toddler James Bulger. The cunning of the catch-phrase text was its ambiguity, allowing everyone to see what they wanted in it. 'Tough on crime' could mean evidence-led effective crime prevention . . . or tough punishment of criminals. 'Tough on the causes of crime' seemed to be a nod to the traditional social democratic idea that crime had deep-root causes in society, economy, and culture, but was always interpreted narrowly in practice. The political payoff lurked in the subtext: a double-whammy of toughness locked into one short, sharp sentence, cutting away at a stroke the accusation that Labour was 'soft and flabby on crime' (in the words of the 1992 Conservative election manifesto). Despite the Conservative fightback with Home Secretary Michael Howard's slogan 'prison works' and a redoubling of penal toughness, Blair succeeded in turning the tables on the Tories for some six years during which MORI polls showed Labour as the party in which the public had most confidence on law and order. But 'Labour's hold on being the best party to deal with crime was short-lived, and by 2000 the more familiar pattern of a Conservative lead returned' (Duffy et al. 2008: 18), despite falling crime rates at least as measured by the British Crime Survey (BCS). Police recorded crime rates rose from 1997 until 2004–5, largely because of changes in the Home Office counting rules, but these too have been declining in recent years (Reiner 2007a: 67–75). The contrast between overall declining crime and the public's perception of increasing risk has given rise to the government's 'reassurance agenda' seeking to plug the gap (Hough 2003, 2007a, 2007b; Millie and Herrington 2005; Innes 2006; Crawford 2007b). The new cross-party consensus on the principles of law and order has been accompanied by sharp partisan conflict about delivery, with mutual attacks on the record and policies of the other, and much opportunistic borrowings and political cross-dressing.

Recent quantitative survey data on public confidence on policing indicates not only the reassurance paradox, but increasing volatility and ambivalence, with concern about crime victimization outweighing issues of fair treatment. BCS ratings of the police as doing a good job declined from 64 per cent in 1996 to 48 per cent in 2004–5, but have since risen to 53 per cent. Throughout the period this positive evaluation is far greater (roughly double) that of all other criminal justice agencies (Allen *et al.* 2006: 9; A. Walker *et al.* 2009: chap. 5). Surveys continue to show that those with contact with the police have less favourable views than those without such contact. Victims' assessments are lower than those who had police-initiated contact. Black and ethnic minority respondents have more positive overall ratings of the police than whites, based largely on higher perceptions of effectiveness (57 per cent compared to 53 per cent rate the police as doing an excellent or very good job), although slightly fewer (81 per cent compared to 84 per cent) say the police treat people with respect (A. Walker *et al.* 2009: 104). These ratings do not vary significantly by household income or most other socio-economic indicators (ibid.: 2009: 125). However a recent IPSOS/MORI national survey for the HMI Report on the Policing of the G20 protests found a fairly sharp variation in assessments of the police by social class: 69 per cent of A–B respondents had favourable views of police contrasted with 56 per cent of D–E (HMIC 2009: 81). There was a similar variation by age: 69 per cent of 65+ age group had favourable opinions compared to 54 per cent of 15–24. Gender made less difference: 67 per cent of women favourable contrasted with 60 per cent of men.

The major qualitative research by Loader and Mulcahy on interpretations of policing in English culture underlines the variety of visions ranging from 'defenders of the faith' who cling to the Dixon ideal, through a complex array of less positive sensibilities including 'the disenchanted', 'agnostics', and 'the hopeful' to the most alienated, the 'atheists' who have lost trust in the police as a source of security or justice (Loader and Mulcahy 2003: chap. 3). The massive social upheavals of recent decades have disturbed all perceptions and relations with policing, but diagnoses and prognoses differ considerably, and are ambivalent and volatile. This is indicated too by changing mass-media representations of policing, in news/documentaries and entertainment. These have shifted from being almost entirely positive about police integrity and effectiveness in the two decades after the Second World War, through a phase of much more critical images, to an overall more favourable picture since the 1980s—but a much more complex and varied one, running the gamut from extremely hostile to overwhelmingly laudatory (Reiner *et al.* 2000, 2001, 2003). 'Stories are bifurcated between counter-critical ones, which seek to return as far as possible to the values of consensus, and those which represent a hopelessly disordered beyond-good-and-evil world' (Reiner *et al.* 2001: 190).

How can this new pragmatic and brittle politics of policing beyond legitimation be analysed in terms of the same dimensions that were used to explain the rise and fall of legitimacy in the previous 150 years? Recent developments in the eight police elements of legitimation will be reviewed, as well as the vast, complex changes in political economy and cultural context.

POLICING POLICY AND FRAGILE RE-LEGITIMATION

Bureaucratic organization?

An element in the successful legitimation of the British police after 1829 was their representation as embodiments of impersonal, rational authority: a tightly disciplined, rule-governed bureaucracy, with professional standards achieved through selective recruitment, training and promotion determined by merit. The deconstruction of this was precipitated by major corruption scandals, and by failure of training and education standards to keep pace with outside advances.

There has been no recurrence of corruption scandals on the scale of the 1980s and 1990s, although corruption is a permanent danger and concern (Punch 2009). There have certainly been numerous *causes célèbres* involving what Sir Paul Condon, then Metropolitan Police Commissioner, in the 1990s referred to as 'noble cause corruption'. Perhaps the most egregious recently have been the the 2005 shooting of the innocent Brazilian Jean Charles de Menezes in the wake of the July bombings in London, and the recent brutality allegations arising out of the 2009 G20 protests (HMIC 2009). Although both aroused considerable concern they have not had the de-legitimating effects of the 1970s/1980s scandals, in part because they have been outweighed by anxieties about crime and terrorism.

The pluralization of policing, in terms of the proliferation of agencies apart from the Peelian police (notably private security), and the internal diversification due to greater specialization, civilianization, and the burgeoning of the 'extended police family' represented by Police Community Support Officers and other developments (Crawford 2008), all complicate the image of police as a single omnibus bureaucracy. The impact of attempts to make the police more 'businesslike' through New Public Management models replaces the bureaucratic image with a more entrepreneurial one in which individuals and units are tested and ranked against each other.

Perhaps most fundamentally, the extent to which the police did represent an impersonal bureaucratic notion of state authority has become a liability rather than a source of legitimation in a more individualistic neo-liberal culture, and the prevailing narratives governing police reform have shifted accordingly (Bevir and Krupicka 2007). There is an unfortunate Catch-22 for the police here. If they are caught out in malpractices contradicting bureaucratic, rule-bound expectations this causes de-legitimating crises. But the notion of disciplined, bureaucratic rule-followers is also problematic in the more individualistic, free-wheeling, consumerist culture of 'liquid modernity' (Bauman 2000, 2007). The BCS and other surveys test public attitudes to policing by questions tapping whether people see the police delivering the bespoke, individually tailored services they desire. The uniform, 'one-size fits all' notions of legalistic justice that made for legitimation in the nineteenth and early twentieth centuries would now attract opprobrium as delivered by 'jobsworths'.

Rule of law?

The idea that police operations are governed by principles of due process legality has been crucial to their legitimation in Britain. Until the 1970s the predominant rhetoric expressing this was the increasingly threadbare notion of the police as 'citizens in uniform', without any significant legal powers beyond those of the ordinary citizen. The 1981 Report of the Royal Commission on Criminal Justice and the ensuing 1984 Police and Criminal Evidence Act (PACE), which clearly gave the police a battery of powers not available to ordinary citizens, replaced this with the principle of a 'fundamental balance' between investigative powers and safeguards for suspects intended to ensure they were used fairly and minimally. Whether it achieved this in reality has been the subject of prolonged controversy (Cape and Young 2008), although the prevailing view is that PACE transformed the treatment of suspects (the evidence will be examined in Chapter 7).

However, since the hegemony of the new tough politics of law and order after 1992, the old debates have shifted to another register. *Causes célèbres* about police malpractice, excessive force and abuse of powers still occur regularly. But the thrust of legal and policy development has been to enhance police powers and resources, not only without corresponding safeguards but watering down existing ones. In a context of heightened sense of crisis about crime and terrorism, this has happened with little questioning from the courts or public and political debate, although there have been two significant counter-examples: the 1998 Human Rights Act, and the 2002 establishment of the Independent Police Complaints Commission (critically assessed in G. Smith 2004a, 2005).

The extent to which, in the new climate of exceptionalism, crime/terror control values outweigh due process considerations is underlined by the fate of the last two Royal Commissions to be held (probably for ever): the Royal Commission on Criminal Procedure (RCCP) which reported in 1981 and was the inspiration for PACE, and the Royal Commission on Criminal Justice (RCCJ) reporting in 1993. Both followed major miscarriage of justice scandals. Both reports sought to implement the principle of balanced powers and safeguards, but the legislative impact (immediate in the case of the RCCJ, long term with the RCCP) has been the erosion of safeguards over police powers.

The details of the post-1992 trend towards boosting police powers coupled with reductions of safeguards are discussed in Chapter 7. But the new underlying rationale is demonstrated most explicitly in the Home Office's 2002 terms of reference for the first of two recent reviews (the second was established in 2007) of PACE: 'To ensure that the legislation remains a useful tool supporting the police and providing them with the powers they need to combat crime.' It was specifically intended to: 'simplify police procedures; reduce procedural or administrative burdens on the police; save police resources; speed up the process of justice'. Although lip-service is still paid to the importance of safeguards and the need for balance, the overwhelming rhetoric is about the need to rebalance on behalf of protecting victims and enhancing police efficiency in the face of new levels and kinds of threat. Safeguards are seen as encumbrances, rather than necessary protections. The one-sided focus on police 'needs' and 'efficiency' is continued in the aims of the 2007 Review *Modernising Police Powers*: 'The aim of this review is to establish from police and those who work with them, as well as the public whether the act and the codes of practice are still appropriate, proportionate, and relevant to the criminal justice system.' The 2002 review resulted in some dilution of PACE safeguards and expansion of powers. The Criminal Justice Act 2003, for example, extends detention powers without a magistrate's authority to 36 hours for all arrestable offences not just serious ones, and permits stop and search for criminal damage. No doubt the 2007 Review will result in further extensions of powers and reduction of safeguards.

What is evident in these and other examples explored fully in Chapter 7 is a new legitimatory rhetoric about police powers. It is the Dirty Harry discourse of the lesser evil, the need in emergencies to adopt tactics that would not normally be justified: but which then become routine. This is justified by a pervasive sense of crisis and exception that was heightened of course by the terror attacks in London in 2005, and before that 9/11 in the USA and in many other parts of the world in the last decade, but had already developed over the last twenty years in relation to both traditional and new forms of crime.

Strategy of minimal force?

We have seen that a crucial aspect of the legitimation of the British police was the minimal force, 'win by appearing to lose' strategy. The militarization of public order tactics and the increasing issue and use of firearms in the 1970s and 1980s, was a focal point of de-legitimation. During the 1990s the issue of excessive use of force seemed to recede somewhat. However, this was very much a false illusion. In the background social and policy developments were preparing the ground for the *causes célèbres* which have occurred recently, above all the tragic shooting of Jean Charles de Menezes in 2005 and the policing of demonstrations like those at the 2009 London G20 (Waddington and Wright 2008; Squires and Kennison 2010).

During the 1990s, with scarcely any public discussion or awareness, there was an increase in the deployment of ARVs that permanently carried firearms, and a massive escalation in the firepower available to police (McKenzie 1995; Waddington and Wright 2008: 473–4; Roberts and Innes 2009). There have also been a number of shooting incidents in which the police have been accused of over- or under-reaction, and in which enquiries by the Police Complaints Authority or its successor the Independent Police Complaints Commission (IPCC) have criticized inadequate command and control rather than the individual officers at the scene (Markham and Punch 2007). There has also been a growing deployment of defensive equipment and 'non-lethal' weaponry (body-armour, enhanced truncheons, incapacitant sprays, tasers) indicating at least the anticipation of higher levels of force in routine policing (Waddington and Wright 2008: 468–9).

In the public disorder context the escalation of violent conflicts and the militarization of police tactics appeared to abate after the 1990 poll tax riot in Trafalgar Square. Confidence grew among the police in Britain, the USA, and internationally that a new strategy of 'negotiated management' rather than 'escalated force', aiming at cooperation rather than confrontation with demonstrators and recognizing the human rights of protestors (Waddington 1994; della Porte and Reiter 1998) was proving successful at preventing or de-escalating violent conflict. There were certainly instances of controversy alleging excessive use of force, notably in relation to demonstrators against live animal exports in the mid-1990s, but this was widely seen as due to such protests attracting middle-aged, middle-class former police supporters experiencing the rougher side of policing for the first time. But behind the scenes tactics were being developed that contained the seeds of current controversy. During the 1980s militaristic tactics had proved ineffective as well as de-legitimating. The 1990 poll tax riots 'prompted a minor revolution in police tactics that only came to public prominence a decade later' (Waddington and Wright 2008: 472). This was the pre-emptive containment of what were regarded as potentially disorderly crowds within tight static cordons—what has come to be known as 'kettling'—in a number of anti-globalization or climate change protests in London in the 2000s. The legality of this tactic, justified by the police as stemming from their common law powers to prevent a breach of the police, was challenged as violating the right to liberty set out in the European Convention on Human Rights, Article 5. The House of Lords has ruled recently that the tactic was lawful, provided it was used in good faith, was proportionate to the situation, and used for no longer than was reasonably necessary (*Austin & another* v. *Commissioner of Police of the Metropolis* [2009] UKHL 5). However, this ruling is currently under challenge at the European Court of Human Rights ('Metropolitan police's "kettling" tactic challenged in European court' *Guardian* 20 July 2009). The use of kettling at the April 2009 G20 protests arguably exceeded the conditions of legality set out in the House of Lords' judgment, and the controversial operation that resulted in the tragic death of Ian Tomlinson, and several other highly publicized cases of apparent brutality caught on video, is under review by a variety of bodies, including the parliamentary Home Affairs Committee, the Joint Parliamentary Committee on Human Rights, HM Inspectorate of Constabulary, and the IPCC (HMIC 2009: 16).

The case that above all raised concerns about police use of force was the killing of the innocent Brazilian electrician Jean Charles de Menezes on a tube at Stockwell station on 22 July 2005. He had been mistakenly identified as a terrorist by the surveillance operation mounted after the failed bombings the previous day (and of course this was only two weeks after the carnage caused by suicide bombers on 7 July). He was shot several times in the head with hollow-point bullets at point-blank range while in the grip of a surveillance officer. This brought to light a hitherto secret tactic (developed by the US National Institute for Justice) for dealing with suspected suicide terrorists, Operation KRATOS. The IPCC investigation cogently defended the development and legality of the tactic in the highly difficult and dangerous circumstances of responding to suicide terrorists, but also showed that it had not been put into operation at Stockwell—the tragic killing was the product of a series of unjustifiable cock-ups (IPCC 2007). There was also much to be criticized in the Met's handling of the aftermath of the shooting which involved at best contradictory statements and management failures, at worst deliberate cover-ups and lies (IPCC 2007).

The escalation of controversy about police use of force is likely. In addition to the continuing risk of terrorist incidents, the economic collapse will fan the political conflicts already presaged by the anti-globalization protests of the last decade. This in turn is certain to result in more cases of unjustified or mistaken use of force, and these will gain high, instant publicity because of the proliferation of video-recording devices as has been shown by many examples from the 1991 Rodney King beating (Lawrence

2000) to the 2008 London G20 clashes. While each such case sparks a storm of controversy, it is arguable that they do not have the general de-legitimating effect of the 1970s/1980s militarization of policing. There seems to be a deep diversity of opinion, but a widespread mood of pragmatic acceptance that tougher tactics—risking mistakes and malpractice—are necessitated by the problems the police face. This is illustrated by the recent Ipsos MORI survey for the HMI inquiry into the policing of the G20 protests. Opinion was evenly divided over the overall handling of the protest: 46 per cent thought it was policed well, 45 per cent not well; 51 per cent thought most or all police had handled it appropriately, with only 7 per cent saying most or all police had behaved inappropriately. The survey showed majority support for the use of force as justified not only to restrain or respond to violence but to prevent disruption to transport and normal business (HMIC 2009: Annex E). This exemplifies the prevalence of pragmatic, necessary evil legitimation discourse.

Accountability?

Since 1992 the notion of accountability has shifted away from holding police power in check, to 'businesslike' notions of efficient, effective and economic policing. The Conservative reforms heralded by the Sheehy Report and Police White Paper of 1993, partially realized in the 1994 Police and Magistrates' Courts Act, began in earnest the application of New Public Management to the police. Considerably extended by New Labour after 1997, there has been a transformation of the meaning and extent of police accountability (discussed in detail in Chapter 7). Accountability has become accountancy. While the doctrine of constabulary independence remains intact as legal principle, the practice of policing has become much more regulated by central government. But this accountability has been modelled on private sector ideas and implemented by quasi-market mechanisms, seeking to achieve economical and efficient delivery of crime control above all else. 'Calculative and contractual' accountability (Reiner and Spencer 1993) has penetrated police policy and practice in a way that no earlier model did. Similar developments have occurred in the USA and elsewhere, most famously in the NYPD Compstat model of constant answerability of police commanders for current crime trends (Weisburd *et al.* 2003; M. Moore 2003; Jones and Newburn 2006b), which has become influential throughout the world. This is the quintessence of pragmatic legitimation: the police are constantly on trial in terms of performance not principle, and trust is always conditional.

Non-partisanship?

Policing is inherently political because it involves the exercise of power. But it is not necessarily *politicized* in the sense of being the subject of party political controversy, or of the partisan mobilization of the police themselves. The initial legitimation of the police presented them as separate from government and politics, as expressed in the doctrine of constabulary independence. During the 1970s the police were politicized as law and order became a political issue, and the police became a Tory-leaning partisan political lobby. This alignment weakened in the late 1990s, as ACPO reined in partisan speech, presenting a corporate professional front through 'a presumption of compliance' with collectively agreed policies (Savage *et al.* 2000: chaps. 6, 7). Paradoxically this culminated during 1993–4 in the most vigorous lobbying in ACPO history, supporting the other staff associations' campaign against the Sheehy Committee and *Police Reform* White Paper 'businesslike' restructuring (Savage 2007: 144–56). However, while pitched against a Conservative government's proposals the police campaign attracted considerable cross-party support and was not explicitly partisan. Especially after Michael Howard replaced Kenneth Clarke as Conservative Home Secretary in 1993 the government was more open to the police case and the 1994 Police and Magistrates' Courts Act made many concessions to it. On the other side, New Labour was also favourable to much of the NPM agenda, and in office after 1997 have implemented the 'businesslike' reform agenda with at least as much rigour as the Tories had (Savage 2007: chaps. 3, 5). Their commitment to this was signalled early on by the 1999 Local Government Act and its 'Best Value' scheme which 'raised the culture of performance management to another level altogether' (ibid.: 110). The collection and analysis of performance indicators and the 'league tables' they generated became ever more rigorous and sophisticated (Long 2003; Golding and Savage 2008).

Since the early 1990s the politics of policing has reflected the new politics of law and order. Partisan consensus on crime control principles, disguised by fierce conflict over delivery. In recent years, in particular since the 2005 general election, when the former Home Secretary and his Shadow of 1992–3—Michael Howard and Tony Blair—faced each other as party leaders, there have been ever more examples of political cross-dressing.

Strident accusations of politicization of the police have been hurled by Labour and the Conservatives at each other. In 2005 the Conservatives accused the Labour government of inducing the Metropolitan Commissioner and other police chiefs to lobby Parliament in support of the proposals to extend detention limits for terror suspects to 90 days ('Ministers Dragged Police into Politics, say Tories' *The Times* 11 November 2005). Accusations of politicizing the police came from the Tories again after the November 2008 arrest and detention of Damian Green, the Shadow Immigration Minister, during an investigation into leaked government documents ('Timeline: The Damian Green Affair' *Guardian* 20 January 2009). The resignation of Sir Ian Blair as Met Commissioner on 2 October 2008 prompted an orgy of accusations that the new Conservative London Mayor Boris Johnson was politicizing the police. Johnson's predecessor as Mayor, Labour's Ken Livingstone, claimed: 'This makes the role of the Metropolitan Police Commissioner much more political' (*Daily Telegraph* 3 October 2008). The defeat of the Labour government's proposals in 2008 to introduce direct elections to police authorities aroused a storm of mutual accusations of politicizing the police. Home Secretary Jacqui Smith 'accused the Conservatives of fuelling worries over politicisation in the wake of the Damian Green arrest and resignation of Sir Ian Blair. . . . Shadow Home Secretary Dominic Grieve said: "The danger of politicisation of the police comes from the micro-management that has been the hallmark of the Labour government over the last ten years"' (*Daily Telegraph* 18 December 2008. This 'micro-management' is the continuation by Labour of the 'businesslike' NPM approach pioneered by the Conservatives).

Controversy about the politicization of the Met by the Tory Mayor Boris Johnson flared again in September 2009. 'Kit Malthouse, the deputy mayor for policing, has declared that he and Johnson "have our hands on the tiller" of the Metropolitan police and have an electoral mandate to influence what it does. He asserted that the Johnson regime had "elbowed the Home Office out of the picture" and would no longer act as a rubber stamp to whatever the force proposed, insisting: "We do not want to be a passenger on the Met cruise"' ('Tories Claim: We Have Seized Control of Scotland Yard' *Guardian* 3 September 2009). The new Commissioner, Sir Paul Stephenson, backed by several other police chiefs responded with a stout reassertion of constabulary independence. But the governance of policing is evidently increasingly politicized.

These episodes indicate an orgy of political cross-dressing compared to the previous positions of the parties on these issues. Throughout the 1970s and 1980s Labour accused the Conservatives of politicizing the police for their own partisan advantage. Local democratic accountability was then seen as a left–Labour issue, opposed by the Conservatives. In 2005 election of local police chiefs was advocated by the Tories, but Labour hit back with its own proposals to strengthen local accountability only to be accused in turn of politicizing policing. The ninety-day detention debate saw the Tories donning the civil libertarian mantle that had been one of Labour's electoral 'hostages to fortune' in the 1980s. The Conservatives have also flirted with another of old Labour's 'hostages to fortune', the social democratic root cause theory of crime, most prominently in David Cameron's short-lived 'hug-a-hoodie' phase. More recently the Conservatives blamed government economic policies when the statistics indicated that crime was beginning to rise again in response to the credit crunch (as forecast by Home Office analyses). The Labour Home Secretary Jacqui Smith responded with an assertion of solely individual responsibility for crime that echoed Margaret Thatcher's rhetoric of the 1980s. 'I don't think there's any justification just because it's a difficult economic time for someone to commit a burglary. I'm not the sort of person who thinks these things are inevitable' ('Britain Unprepared for Recession Crime Wave, Opposition Claims' *The Independent* 23 January 2009). The febrile partisan assertion of superiority in fighting crime, the dizzying policy and rhetorical cross-dressing, disguise the fundamental consensus on law and order principles since 1992. The police remain deeply embroiled in political controversy, but in pragmatic terms of who promotes their effectiveness best, not any principled differences.

Service role?

The legitimation of the police was accomplished in part by encouraging them to perform services in addition to crime prevention, representing them as helpers as well as enforcers. This was part of the ideal image of the British bobby, encapsulated by the Dixon of Dock Green mythology at the height of their legitimacy. Research has repeatedly shown that the majority of calls for police help are not explicitly crime related, and that the police are really 'the secret social service' (Punch 1979). As police legitimacy began to wane an increasingly influential response from police chiefs and policy-makers around the world has been the movement to reform forces on a 'community policing' model. This protean term clearly encompasses a variety of meanings, but paramount is the mood music of restoring friendly relations with the public, a 'cherry pie' promise (Brogden 1999) that renders it beyond principled critique (Klockars 1988). Since 1992 the hegemony of the politics of law and order has transmuted the meaning of the service role. Instead being a velvet glove of uncontentious friendly services legitimating the iron fist of coercive policing, now, as the title of an episode of *The Bill* once put it, 'force is part of the service'. Public service is presented in the language of protection against crime, disorder and anti-social behaviour. This interleaving of service with the themes of reassurance and protection is illustrated by the website for Police Community Support Officers (PCSOs), the members of the 'extended police family' introduced by the 2002 Police Reform Act (Crawford 2008: 155–6). This declares: 'Police Community Support Officers are members of support staff employed, directed and managed by their Police Force.... Their primary purpose is to improve the community and offer greater public reassurance. In support of regular police officers they will work within a targeted patrol area to provide a visible and accessible uniformed presence; work with partners and community organizations to address anti-social behaviour, the fear of crime, environmental issues and other factors which affect the quality of people's lives. For example; reporting vandalism or damaged street furniture, reporting suspicious activity; providing crime prevention advice, deterring juvenile nuisance and visiting victims of crime.' The specific examples of service delivery cited all relate to crime and disorder issues.

A further example is the new public service agreement for police being proposed by the government. This seeks to move beyond simple measures of crime control performance by developing a broader test of public confidence. But this is seen entirely in crime and disorder terms. 'There will be only one top down numerical target for the police service—confidence—which will measure the extent to which the police and their partners (CDRPs) are tackling the crime and ASB issues that matter to people locally.... We know what will drive progress on this single national target—confidence—good, local policing that finds out what people are worried about, tackles it and tells them what has been done. Justice Seen, Justice Done. . . . We will collectively work to support them and others as they seek to improve the quality of life in stronger local communities' ('A Summary of the New Performance Landscape for Policing' Home Office Website 7 July 2009). In short, in the pragmatic post-legitimation framework the service role has been assimilated into reassurance about crime and disorder reduction rather than as a balance against police force.

Preventive policing?

Crime prevention was the priority for the new police according to Peel's celebrated 1829 instructions. The idea had resonances of the broad conception of 'police', as the whole gamut of social, economic and cultural processes making for domestic peace and security, derived from eighteenth-/nineteenth-century political economy and science of police (Neocleous 2000a, 2000b). But in practice the preventive role of police was narrowed to the scarecrow effect of uniform patrol and the supposed deterrent consequences of detection. As discussed above, in the last thirty years prevention in a new pre-emptive sense staged a comeback, through such fashions as Neighbourhood Watch, problem-oriented, and community policing.

The salience of crime prevention as pre-emption was reinforced and transformed as the politics of law and order became ever more prominent since the early 1990s. This was stimulated by the 1980s crime explosion despite the Thatcher government's boosting of police powers and resources, which prompted the search for alternative strategies. At the same time, research on traditional policing tactics suggested that they had limited impact on crime (as discussed further in Chapter 5), and prevention as pre-emption promised to be cheaper—a not insignificant attraction for a government averse to public expenditure.

Three levels of crime prevention have been distinguished in the literature: *primary*—addressing social and other factors conducive to crime; *secondary*—targeting at risk people and places; *tertiary*—changing known offenders, victims, hotspots to reduce reoffending. The 1991 Report of the Home Office's Morgan Committee proposed a much more wide-ranging approach, reconceptualizing crime prevention as community safety and advocating partnership between all relevant agencies under the leadership of the local authority to tackle all three levels of prevention. In short, tough on crime *and* its causes. However the Conservative government's new enthusiasm for prevention took a narrow form. It focused on 'responsibilizing' citizens (Garland 2001) through Neighbourhood Watch and the Special Constabulary. It also encouraged the spread of situational and physical security measures, notably CCTV, in which the UK became a world leader (Norris and Armstrong 1999; Goold 2004, 2009; Norris and McCahill 2006; Crawford 2007: 892).

New Labour in opposition embraced the Morgan Report, and its flagship legislation in the area, the 1998 Crime and Disorder Act went some way to implementing its community safety approach (Hughes and Edwards 2002; Crawford 2007: 893–9; G. Hughes 2006; Gilling 2007; Byrne and Pease 2008). It placed a statutory duty jointly on local authorities and the police to work with other relevant agencies in Crime and Disorder Reduction Partnerships (CDRPs), required to develop strategies for tackling crime. The Act was followed by a well-funded Crime Reduction Programme to support local partnerships and evaluation of their crime prevention efforts, aimed at reflexively developing and disseminating evidence-based strategies. In the event these laudable aims were frustrated by by government pressures to show quick success, and 'less was learned about what works than about the reasons for implementation failure' (Crawford 2007: 894–5). Many of those involved in monitoring the programme contributed to a 2004 Special Issue of *Criminal Justice* documenting the sacrifice of the programme on the altar of short-term results (Hough 2004; Maguire 2004; Hope 2004). The Crime Reduction Programme has been replaced by a series of initiatives aimed at community safety and reassurance but constantly vitiated by political short-termism, as well as a perceived government need to emphasize tough talk and spectacular initiatives in the face of tabloid pressure (Newburn and Reiner 2007).

Effectiveness?

The effectiveness of policing in controlling crime is hard to assess and remains much debated, as Chapter 7 will elaborate. But the conjunction of the spread of the New Police in the second half of the nineteenth century and a long-term decline in crime statistics created a widespread perception of police as protectors against crime. This was a crucial element in their legitimation. Conversely, the remorseless rise of recorded crime from the mid-1950s until the early 1990s was an important element in declining public confidence (although the statistics exaggerate the real increase in victimization except for the 1980s and early 1990s—Reiner 2007a: chap. 3).

The period since the early 1990s, in which the politics of tough law and order became embodied as a new cross-party conventional wisdom, is remarkable for the dissociation between different measures of crime and public perceptions. Recorded crime peaked in 1992 at just over 5.5 million; it had fallen back to 4.5 million by 1997 when Labour took office. Major counting rule changes introduced in 1998 and 2002 make comparison of the subsequent figures especially fraught, but on the new rules (which undoubtedly exaggerate the increase) a new peak of just under 6 million offences were recorded by the police for 2003–4. This has now fallen back again, to 4.7 million in 2008–9 (Walker *et al.* 2009: 1).

Comparing the police recorded trend with that shown by the British Crime Survey (BCS) suggests a much more complex picture (Reiner 2007a: chap. 3). Whereas in the first decade after the BCS began in 1981 the trend it portrayed confirmed the huge explosion of crime indicated by the police recorded statistics, after the early 1990s the series began to diverge. The BCS continued to chart a rise until 1995, but the police data fell from 1992 to 1997. As crime peaked in the early 1990s, insurance companies made claiming more onerous, discouraging reporting by victims, and more 'business-like' managerial accountability for policing implicitly introduced incentives against recording, so the police figures fell while victimization was still rising. Home Secretary Michael Howard was certainly tough on the causes of recording crime, even if not on crime itself. After New Labour came to power in 1997 the two measures continued to diverge—but in the opposite direction. BCS recorded crime has fallen rapidly and in 2008–9 was below the level of the first BCS in 1981 (Walker *et al.* 2009: 1–2). Because of major counting rule changes, the police recorded statistics rose from 1998 up to 2004, since when they have declined again. The divergence between the series sparked a politicization of the crime statistics especially during and since the 2005 general election, as the police figures make the Conservative record look good and Labour bad, while the BCS has the opposite implication. So the Labour government focuses on the BCS as the more reliable index of trends, while the Conservatives and sympathetic think-tanks (Dennis and Erdos 2005; Green *et al.* 2005) emphasize its limitations (Reiner 2007a: 73–5).

It seems clear that overall crime has fallen substantially in the last fifteen years, although more unevenly and less spectacularly on the police recorded data. But public perceptions about crime and confidence in police effectiveness do not reflect this—the basis for the 'reassurance agenda'. The proportion of people interviewed by the BCS who think crime has risen nationally has not fallen below 58 per cent since 1996, and in

2008–9 is at 75 per cent—the highest in thirteen years (Walker *et al.* 2009: Figure 5.1). On the other hand, the proportion thinking crime has risen in their local area is always substantially lower, and has fallen for the last six years to 36 per cent in 2008–9 (ibid.). The mismatch between these images is probably because perceptions of national trends are mainly shaped by media focus on spectacular crimes whereas people are more aware of crime reductions in their own area.

There is a rational kernel to the public's failure to be reassured. The dramatic overall fall in the BCS under New Labour also masks increases in some of the most alarming offences. Murder and other serious crimes of violence have increased in the last thirty years, and are now a higher proportion of all crimes. During the 1960s and early 1970s annual recorded homicides remained between 300 and 400, but this has roughly doubled. In 1976 just 5 per cent of recorded offences were classified as violent, but by 2007–8 this had increased to 19 per cent. Recorded robberies have risen sharply since the early 1990s, although they have been falling (erratically) in the last few years from a peak in 2001–2. So the trends are certainly not as rosy as the BCS total suggests. It is also the case that in so far as the decline in volume crime is the result of more effective security routines and paraphernalia they are subject to a paradox: the very measures that contain victimization serve as constant reminders of risk (Zedner 2003: 165).

The Labour government has been reluctant to claim credit for its crime control success, partly because of fear that the tabloids which routinely stoke fears about rising crime would once more castigate Labour as out of touch and soft on security. Anxiety about again being saddled by its old 'hostages to fortune' makes the government misrepresent the sources of its success. A recent review by the Prime Minister's Strategy Unit concluded that 80 per cent of the crime reduction was due to economic factors, although this estimate is somehow omitted from the version of the report currently on the Cabinet website, which concentrates almost entirely on criminal justice solutions (Solomon *et al.* 2007). Thus Labour has been successful in reducing crime, even with its very cautious approach to containing inequality and exclusion. But it is so locked into the politics of law and order that this is a success that dare not speak its name. In any event the economic collapse since credit crunched in late 2007 make it likely on the government's own econometric modelling that crime will once more begin to rise, as recent quarterly figures on some volume crime seem to confirm ('Credit Crunch Could Lead to Crime Wave, Home Office Warns Downing Street' *Daily Telegraph* 31 August 2008; 'Burglars Back in Credit Crunch Crime Wave' *The Independent* 24 April 2009).

The last twenty years have been extremely volatile in terms of the appearance of police effectiveness in crime control. With the demise of social democratic criminology as Labour espoused the politics of tough law and order (Reiner 2006), pressure mounted on the police to actually deliver the crime control and security they had always claimed as their mission. Although the general trends in crime could be interpreted as evidence that they have largely succeeded (although other factors really did the heavy lifting), the febrile context of intense partisan competition about delivery places them on a tightrope where they are constantly exposed to the appearance of failure.

SOCIAL CONTEXT OF FRAGILE RE-LEGITIMATION

The vital precondition for police legitimation was the broader story of the gradual incorporation of the working class, the main structurally rooted source of opposition to the new police, into citizenship, not only legal but also political and socioeconomic (Marshall 1950; Bulmer and Rees 1996). Conversely, the de-legitimation of the police between the late 1960s and the early 1990s was only partly a consequence of shifts in policing. These were shaped primarily by deeper transformations in political economy and culture, as indicated earlier. The displacement of the post-Second World War Keynesian and welfare state consensus by neo-liberalism during the 1970s had profound reverberations for crime, criminal justice, and policing. The return of massive inequality and social exclusion drove crime up and politicized law and order (Dahrendorf 1985; Downes and Morgan 2007).

The embedding of neo-liberalism after the advent of New Labour in the early 1990s accentuated and consolidated the new tough law-and-order strategies (Reiner 2007a). There was a remorseless rise in imprisonment and a broader hardening of penal policy (Newburn 2007c; Lacey 2008), as well as the expansion of police powers and resources. The politics of policing has become increasingly febrile and volatile. Principled debate about the purposes and democratic governance of policing was attenuated. Their role as the front line of crime control and order maintenance within a pluralized policing landscape became unquestioned. But partisan debate about tactics and who delivered policing most effectively became ever more heated. The first decade of New Labour was a period of rising prosperity, relatively full employment (although with an ever more sharply divided dual labour market), some diminution of poverty although not inequality overall. As seen in the previous section, this resulted in a considerable reduction of overall crime. But in the highly volatile party political competition about law and order the focus was on the aspects of crime that were not reducing, and on new threats, above all terrorism. This will be exacerbated considerably with the economic collapse since 2007. Sadly unemployment and long-term exclusion, poverty, inequality are all likely to escalate, and drive up crime and disorder just as they did in the 1980s. The police will be expected to turn back a tide that they have little chance of controlling, despite considerable advances in policing and community safety tactics.

CONCLUSION

This chapter has analysed the construction of police legitimacy during the late nineteenth and early twentieth centuries in the face of widespread opposition to the establishment and spread of the New Police. It has also traced their subsequent de-legitimation up to the early 1990s. The embedding of a politics of tough law and order as the hegemonic discourse about crime control has resulted in a decline of principled debate about policing, but a ferocious partisan competition about what works and who delivers best. Throughout police history their effectiveness and legitimacy has been dependent fundamentally on wider trends in political economy and culture. The dominance of neo-liberalism in the last thirty years has brought greater insecurity and anxiety despite the apparent benefits in terms of economic growth and individual autonomy. The economic collapse precipitated by the credit crunch after 2007 has brought the dark side of the neo-liberal model to the fore, and will pose policing and criminal justice with massive new problems. The fragile and pragmatic legitimation of policing since 1992 will be under enormous strain and is likely to teach policy-makers and public alike the old lesson that the police cannot be the basis of order and security. It remains as true as in ancient times that the road to peace lies through social justice not policing (Bauman 2005: 1).

NOTES

1. Some other police forces have a commanding place in their country's popular culture, for example the FBI (R. Powers 1983; Potter 1998). Canadians often point out that their most characteristic national emblem is the Mountie (Walden 1982). But in each case it is an elite force that is accorded prestige; the 'Yard' plays the same role in British popular mythology, but the mundane bobby is also a cornerstone of national pride, unmatched by the treatment of any other country's routine patrol force.

2. Too much weight should not be placed on Gorer's survey based on a self-selected sample of readers of the *People*. But it is worth noting (as Gorer does) that the *People* had a wide readership, and a disproportionately working-class one.

3. This is the standard Weberian distinction. Weber (1964: 327) emphasizes that the nature of legitimacy 'subjectively . . . may vary, especially as between "suBMission" and "sympathetic agreement"'. In other words, seeing an authority (like the police) as legitimate does not necessarily imply agreement with the concrete content of rules or their specific enforcement. It only means acceptance on some minimal basis of the authority's right to make or enforce rules. (For critical analyses and discussion of Weber's concept of legitimacy, see: Beetham 1991; Lassman 2000.)

4. The stance of compromise and co-option between classes, rather than outright conflict, was a wider historical pattern in English political development. 'Governing in the context of rapidly growing industrial capitalism, the landed upper classes . . . avoided serious defeat by well-timed concessions. This policy was necessary in the absence of any strong apparatus of repression' (B. Moore 1967: 39).

5. I am using the Weberian concept of bureaucracy as the pursuit of administrative rationalization in an organization. This is to be contrasted with the pejorative image of red tape, bungling, and faceless oppressors, although these may well be dysfunctional consequences of the Weberian model.

6. The West Yorkshire police issued 'personal protective equipment', i.e., cricket boxes and jockstraps. Class discrimination within the police was complained of when it was discovered that those for sergeants and inspectors were bigger than those for constables!

7. Waldorf, an innocent man, was mistaken for an escaped prisoner and shot many times at close range; fortunately, he survived.

8. The Plus Programme was launched in the late 1980s by the Met's commissioner, Sir Peter Imbert, as an attempt to convert the whole force to a community-policing and service ethic. The ACPO statement was an attempt to define the police mission in service terms. It began: 'The purpose of the police is to uphold the law fairly and firmly; to prevent crime; to pursue and bring to justice those who break the law; to keep the Queen's Peace; to protect, help and reassure the community; and to do all this with integrity, common sense and sound judgement' (Savage 2007: 140).

PART III

SOCIOLOGY OF POLICING

4

COP CULTURES

From the start of empirical research on policing researchers have sought to understand how police officers see the social world and their role in it. This was of particular interest because of the considerable discretion exercised by police officers, suggesting that there was extensive scope for their actions to deviate from the law or organizational policy. The idea of 'cop culture' developed as a means of understanding police practices, although there is not a one-to-one correspondence between attitudes and behaviour, as a challenging critique of the concept of police culture has recently stressed (P. Waddington 1999a: chap. 4, 1999b). Waddington notes that social psychology has long recognized the gap that frequently exists between attitudes and behaviour. Many observational studies of police work have shown that officers regularly fail to enact in practice the attitudes they articulate in the canteen or in interviews, for example with regard to race (see, for example, Policy Studies Institute 1983, iv: chap. 4). An important distinction has been made between 'cop culture'—the orientations implied and expressed by officers in the course of their work—and 'canteen culture'—the values and beliefs exhibited in off-duty socializing (Hoyle 1998). As Waddington points out, the latter clearly has an important function of tension release, which is why it so often characterized by mordant gallows humour (M. Young 1995).

There are many reasons why expressed attitudes may not be translated into action. They may not be genuine statements of belief but stated to please interviewers or to fit in with colleagues or to let off steam. Even if they are genuine and deeply held, there may be constraints against them being acted out. A racially prejudiced officer, for example, may not act in a discriminatory way because of fear of sanctions. Perspectives are complex and ambivalent, and vary in texture in different situations. An officer who expresses racist views in the canteen context may be genuinely sympathetic to the plight of an ethnic minority victim and offer support. Conversely, officers who are not prejudiced may still act in discriminatory ways, as the now common concept of institutionalized racism implies (analysed further in Chapter 5). But while the link between ideas and action is far from straightforward, this does not mean that people's perspectives—complex, ambivalent, and fluid as they may be—bear *no* relation to their practices. After all, 'language is itself a form of practice' (Loftus 2007: 195). Interpreting actors' frames of reference and worldviews—their culture—is a useful element in understanding what they do, although it certainly cannot be the whole story. This is confirmed by research showing that officers holding perspectives closer to the 'ideal-type' of 'traditional' police culture are more likely to engage in violence, holding constant other relevant factors including situational ones such as the violence offered against the officer, and the policies and style of departmental management (Terrill *et al.* 2003).

The *Oxford English Dictionary* defines the 'anthropological' meaning of culture as 'the whole way of life of a society: its beliefs and ideas, its institutions and its systems, its laws and its customs'. Cultures are complex ensembles of values, attitudes, symbols, rules, recipes, and practices, emerging as people react to the exigencies and situations they confront, interpreted through the cognitive frames and orientations they carry with them from prior experiences. Cultures are shaped, but not determined, by the structural pressures of actors' environments (what Chan (1997) following Bourdieu's usage calls the 'field, which shapes the "habitus"—the lived strategies or dispositions "triggered" by the encounter with a particular field'—Wacquant 1992: 19). Cultures develop as people respond in various meaningful ways to their predicament as constituted by the network of relations they find themselves in, which are in turn formed by different more macroscopic levels of structured action and institutions. Police officers, for example, interpret and act and interact in networks of relations structured by various increasingly distant processes and institutions—their shifts, neighbourhoods, Basic Command Units, the police organizations that emerged through the complex historical developments sketched in the last two chapters. Each actor's responses shape the situations that others act within. In short, to paraphrase Marx: people create their own cultures, but not under conditions of their own choosing.

Police culture—like any other culture—is not monolithic, and is embodied in individuals who enjoy autonomy and creativity. There are particular variants— 'subcultures'—that can be discerned within broader police culture, generated by distinct experiences associated with specific structural positions (ranks, specialisms, areas, etc.), or by special orientations officers bring with them from their past biographies and histories. In addition, cultures vary between forces, shaped by the differing patterns and problems of their environments, and the legacies of their histories. Nonetheless, it will be argued that police forces in modern liberal democracies do face similar basic pressures that shape a distinctive and characteristic culture, discernible in many parts of the contemporary world, albeit with differing emphases across time and space, and with internal variations. This is because they face certain common problems arising from the bedrock elements of their role and the constraints of legality—although the precise intensity and form of these vary greatly.

It is a commonplace of the now voluminous sociological literature on police operations and discretion that the rank-and-file officer is the primary determinant of policing where it really counts: on the street. As James Q. Wilson put it, 'the police department has the special property . . . that within it discretion increases as one moves down the hierarchy' (J. Wilson 1968: 7). It has often been claimed that legal rules and departmental regulations are marginal to an account of how police work operates, and a tenet of the highly practical culture of policing is 'You can't play it by the book.' The core laws enforced by the police often seem to be the 'Ways and Means Act' and 'contempt of cop'. The original impulse for much of the early research on police discretion in the 1960s and 1970s was a civil libertarian concern about the extent and sources of police deviation from due process of law through their espousal of a 'crime control' model (Packer 1968. For a sample of these classic studies, see Reiner 1996a).

In the late 1970s this approach came under fire from a structuralist critique, pioneered most notably and effectively by Doreen McBarnet (1978, 1979) which had a considerable influence over many empirical studies in the 1980s.[1] She argued that civil libertarians failed to distinguish between abstract rhetoric about the general values underpinning the rule of law, and concrete legal rules: there is 'a distinct gap between the substance and the ideology of law' (McBarnet 1981: 5). The rights of suspects presumed by ideological rhetoric are not clearly encapsulated in statutory or common law rules giving them practical effect. The laws governing police practice are sufficiently permissive to give officers a wide range of discretion. The courts have often seemed ready to accommodate extensions of the rules to legitimate police practice. Police routinely violate the law, but a purely cultural analysis makes the low-level operatives 'the "fall-guys" of the legal system taking the blame for any injustices' (ibid.: 156). Responsibility ought to be placed on 'the judicial and political elites' who make rules of sufficient elasticity to assimilate departures from idealized values of due process legality, which the law effectively condones or even demands. McBarnet's detailed examination of the content and operation of the rules of criminal procedure is of immense value. But it does not displace the need for analysis of police culture and the situational pressures on officers' discretion. To say that the laws governing police behaviour are 'permissive' is only to suggest that they do not even purport to determine practical policing (contrary to legal ideology). That leaves considerable leeway for police culture and the social and situational pressures on officers to shape police practice (Mastrofski 2004).

Legal rules are neither irrelevant to nor completely determining of police practice. The Policy Studies Institute (PSI) study (1983) usefully distinguished between three types of rules in terms of how they impact on practice. 'Working rules' are those that police officers actually internalize so that they become the effective principles guiding their actions. 'Inhibiting rules' have a deterrent effect—officers must take them into account in their conduct, because they are specific, likely to be enforced, and refer to visible behaviour. 'Presentation rules' are used to impart an acceptable gloss to actions undertaken for other reasons. The relationship between any of these sets of rules and the law is problematic. Legal rules may well be used presentationally, rather than being operational working rules or inhibitors. They then act as an ideological façade whereby the public at large can turn a blind eye to the messy realities of policing.

This all means that the standard legalistic response to revelations of police malpractice—slap on a new rule—may be irrelevant or even counter-productive. On the other hand, formal 'black-letter' law is far from irrelevant to police practice. Legal rules may be 'inhibiting' or become the 'blue-letter' law of police 'working' rules—or dead letters—depending on a variety of factors. These have been illuminated above all by research on the complex impact of the 1984 Police and Criminal Evidence Act, examined in Chapter 6. The culture of the police—the values, norms, perspectives, myths, and craft rules that inform their conduct—is neither monolithic, universal, nor unchanging. There are differences of outlook within police forces, according to such individual variables as personality, gender, ethnicity, sexuality, generation, or career trajectory, and structured variations according to rank, assignment, and specialization. The organizational styles and cultures of police forces vary between different places and periods. Informal rules are not clear-cut and articulated, but are embedded in specific practices and nuances, modulated by particular concrete situations and the interactional processes of each encounter.

Nonetheless, certain commonalities of the police outlook can be discerned in the reports of many studies in different social contexts. The very fact that these are observed at many times and places suggests that they are *not* a common culture that has been diffused and transmitted. Rather its themes and tropes are constantly reinvented and reproduced because they are rooted in constant problems that officers face in carrying out the role they are mandated to perform, at any rate in industrial capitalist societies with a liberal–democratic political ethos (at the very least authority, danger, and political pressure, in Skolnick's seminal 1966 formulation that is elaborated below). Cop culture offers a patterned set of understandings that helps officers cope with the pressures and tensions confronting the police. Successive generations are socialized into it, but not as cultural dopes, passive or manipulated learners of didactic rules. The process of transmission is mediated by stories, legends, jokes, exploring models of good and bad conduct, which through metaphor enable conceptions of competent practice to be explored prefiguratively (Shearing and Ericson 1991). Elements of the culture survive because of their 'elective affinity', their psychological fit, with the demands of the rank-and-file cop condition, while other aspects change as the contexts and characteristics of officers develop.

COP CULTURE: THE CORE CHARACTERISTICS

The *locus classicus* for discussing the core police culture remains Skolnick's (1966) account of the policeman's 'working personality'.[2] What needs to be added to his discussion is the analysis of variations around his model, within and between police forces (Paoline 2003). Skolnick's portrait also failed to draw out the political dimensions of police culture, which reflects and perpetuates the power differences within the social structure. The police officer is a microcosmic mediator of the relations of power in a society—a 'street corner politician' (Muir 1977). The values of the police culture act as 'subterranean processes in the maintenance of power' (Shearing 1981a). There is also the need to consider changes that have impacted on policing in the forty years since this original analysis (Skolnick 2008 offers his own reflections on this).

Skolnick synthesized earlier sociological research with his own findings to construct a pioneering sketch of the police 'working personality' (Skolnick 1966: chap. 3). This referred not to an individual psychological phenomenon (as the term 'personality' misleadingly implies) but to a socially generated culture. It was a response to a unique combination of facets of the police role: 'two principal variables, danger and authority,

which should be interpreted in the light of a "constant" pressure to appear efficient'
(Skolnick 1966: 44).

The 'danger' in the police milieu is not adequately represented by quantitative estimates of the risk of physical injury, although these are not small. People in
other occupations—say, steeplejacks, miners, deep-sea divers, anyone working with
asbestos—may be exposed to higher risks of job related disease or death. But the police
role is unique in that its core tasks require officers to face situations where the risk lies
in the unpredictable outcome of encounters with other people (Crank 2004: chap. 8).
The police confront the threat of sudden attack from another person, not the more
calculable risks of physical or environmental hazards. The extent of seriousness obviously varies. But the police officer faces, round every corner she turns or behind every
door whose bell she rings, some danger, if not of firearms at least of fists. Hence coping with violence is a recurring feature of police culture (Westmarland 2001a, 2001b;
Waddington and Wright 2008).

Danger is linked to authority, which is inherently part of the police milieu. It is because
they represent authority that police officers face danger from those recalcitrant to its
exercise. Traditional British police tactics were directed towards minimizing the use of
force. But in individual encounters this is liable to be challenged when authority has
to be exercised over someone. And the decline of deference has made police authority
increasingly questioned. Danger and authority are thus interdependent elements in the
police world, and cop culture develops adaptive rules, recipes, rhetoric, and rites to cope
with those tensions.

Skolnick postulates a third environmental element producing cop culture: 'the
pressure put upon individual policemen to "produce"—to be efficient rather than
legal when the two norms are in conflict' (Skolnick 1966: 42, 231). Undoubtedly police
officers experience external political pressure for 'results', more or less so at different
times according to particular moral panics or trends in crime statistics. Under the pressure to get 'results' in the form of clear-ups, police may well feel impelled to stretch their
powers and violate suspects' rights.

Skolnick overemphasized the degree of external compulsion in this. Public expectations of the police are themselves inflated by police propaganda about their capacities as
professional crime-fighters, which they have elevated as their core mandate (Manning
1997). Police officers are for the most part intrinsically dedicated to the goals of 'maintaining order' and 'fighting crime'.

MISSION—ACTION—CYNICISM—PESSIMISM

A theme observed in studies of cop culture is a sense of mission. This is the feeling that
policing is not just a job but a way of life with a worthwhile purpose, at least in principle.
'It's a sect—it's like a religion, the police force' (constable, cited in Reiner 1978: 247). The
purpose is conceived of as the preservation of a valued way of life and the protection of
the weak against the predatory. The core justification of policing in many officers' eyes
is victim-centred. 'Speaking from a policeman's point of view it doesn't give a damn if

we oppress law-breakers, because they're oppressors in their own right' (constable, cited in ibid.: 79).

The mission of policing is not regarded as irksome, but as fun, challenging, exciting, a game of wits and skill. Many commentators have stressed the hedonistic, action-centred aspects of cop culture (Holdaway 1977, 1983; Policy Studies Institute 1983, iv: 51–6; Westmarland 2001a, 2001b). The main substance to which the police are addicted is adrenalin (Graef 1989). But the thrills of the chase, the fight, the capture, the 'machismo syndrome' (Reiner 1978: 161), although rare highlights of the work, are not merely a sport. They can be so uninhibitedly and delightedly engaged in because they are also seen as worthwhile. In a policeman's own eyes he is one of the 'good guys' and it is this which gives him the licence for action. He is not just a racing-driver or boxer in a blue uniform.

This moralizing of the police mandate is in many respects misleading. It overlooks the mundane reality of everyday policing, which is often boring, messy, petty, trivial, and venal. It permits the elision of the universally approved elements of the police task (apprehending a murderer, say) and the political role of policing in upholding a specific state and social order. The 'sacred canopy' (Manning 1997: 21) often drawn over policing can be a tool of the organization, protecting and advancing its interest in gaining more resources, power, and autonomy from independent scrutiny. Nevertheless, it is important in understanding police work that it is seen as a mission, a moral imperative, not just another job. This makes its established practices more resistant to reform than if they were merely self-serving.

The elements of mission in the police perspective are reflected in their sense of themselves as 'the thin blue line', performing an essential role in safeguarding social order. The myth of police indispensability, of their essential social function 'to protect and serve', is central to the police worldview. Much police wrongdoing can be attributed to misguided pursuit of a 'noble cause', the Dirty Harry dilemma of achieving essential ends by tarnished means (Klockars 1980).

Nevertheless, police officers tend to acquire a set of views which have been rightly described as 'cynical', or 'police pessimism' (Niederhoffer 1967; Vick 1981). Officers often develop a hard skin of bitterness, seeing all social trends in apocalyptic terms, with the police as a beleaguered minority about to be overrun by the forces of barbarism (Reiner 1978: chap. 11). This pessimistic outlook is only cynical in a sense—in the despair felt that the morality which the police officer adheres to is being eroded on all sides. It is not a Wildean cynicism which knows the price of everything and the value of nothing. Rather it resembles a Marxian account of commodity fetishism: price has sadly masked value. The very strength of the hardboiled outlook of policemen derives from the resilience of their sense of mission. Cynicism is the Janus face of commitment.

The salience of a sense of mission obviously varies between police officers. It was much more evident in the type I labelled the 'new centurions' (after the title of Joseph Wambaugh's seminal 1971 police novel) than those the argot calls 'uniform-carriers', who shirk the work as much as possible (Reiner 1978: chap. 12). But many (if not most) 'uniform-carriers', with their quintessentially cynical views ('It's the survival of the fittest . . . You've got to look after No. l . . . The policeman should exploit his job to the full advantage'), became that way precisely because of the effects of career disappoint-ment destroying a prior sense of mission.

Undoubtedly many policemen see their combat with 'villains' as a ritualized game, a fun challenge, with 'winning' by an arrest giving personal satisfaction rather than any sense of public service. But this cynical view may well function as a self-protecting shield to reduce the anxiety that the thief-taker's many failures would otherwise induce.[3] One constable advised me:

All police work's a game. You get the people who do wrong and the people that try and catch them. Sometimes the wrong-doers get caught, sometimes they don't. If they get caught and copped, if they get nicked and weighed-off, fair enough. If they don't there's no point getting emotionally involved.

Cynicism about thief-taking as a game is thus functionally analogous to the role of humour as tension-release, expressed in the motto 'If you can't take a joke you shouldn't have joined this job' (Reiner 1978: 216–17; M. Young 1995).

The characteristic police outlook is this subtle and complex intermingling of the themes of mission, hedonistic love of action, and pessimistic cynicism. Each feeds off and reinforces the others, even though they may appear superficially contradictory. They lead to a pressure for 'results' which may strain against legalistic principles of due process. *Pace* Skolnick's account, this pressure for 'efficiency' is not primarily derived externally but is a basic motivating force within police culture. It does, however, relate to other facets of cop culture—suspicion, isolation/solidarity, conservatism—in the way Skolnick suggests.

SUSPICION

Most police officers are aware that their job has bred in them an attitude of constant suspicion that cannot be readily switched off.[4] Suspicion is a product of the need to keep a lookout for signs of trouble, potential danger and clues to offences. It is a re-sponse to the danger, authority, and efficiency elements in the environment, as well as an outcome of the sense of mission. Police need to develop fine-grained cognitive maps of the social world, so that they can readily predict and handle the behaviour of a wide range of others, in frequently fraught encounters, without losing authority (Rubinstein 1973: chaps. 4–6; Holdaway 1983: chaps. 6–7; Kemp *et al.* 1992). Police stereotyping has been the subject of many critiques. They suggest that stereotypes of likely offenders become self-fulfilling prophecies as people with those characteristics are dispropor-tionately questioned or arrested, leading to a vicious cycle of deviance amplification (J. Young 1971). However, stereotyping is an inevitable tool of the suspiciousness endemic to police work. The crucial issue is not its existence but the degree to which it is reality based and helpful, as opposed to prejudiced and discriminatory—and thus not merely unjust but also counter-productive.

While police suspiciousness and stereotyping are inescapable, the particular categories informing them reflect the structure of power in society. This serves to reproduce that structure through a pattern of implicit—sometimes explicit—class, race, and gender discrimination.

ISOLATION/SOLIDARITY

Many commentators have emphasized the marked internal solidarity, coupled with social isolation, of police officers (Clark 1965; Westley 1970: chap. 3; Reiner 1978: 208–13; Crank 2004: section III). They have been referred to as 'a race apart' (Banton 1964), 'a man apart' (Judge 1972), 'a beleaguered minority' (Alex 1976).

Certainly, many police officers report difficulties in mixing with civilians in ordinary social life. These stem from shift work, erratic hours, difficulty switching off from the tension engendered by the job, aspects of the discipline code, and the hostility or fear that citizens may exhibit to the police. Social isolation is the price paid for Peel's policy of elevating the British police as symbols of impersonal authority, and recruitment policies aimed at severing officers from their local communities (W. Miller 1999: 26–8). Internal solidarity is a product not only of isolation, but also of the need to be able to rely on colleagues in a tight spot, and a protective armour shielding the force as a whole from public knowledge of infractions. Many studies have stressed the powerful code that enjoins officers to back each other up in the face of external investigation (Westley 1970: chap. 4; Shearing 1981b; Punch 1985, 2009; Skolnick and Fyfe 1993). The offences that colleagues shield are not necessarily major infractions to be protected from external eyes. Rank-and-file solidarity is often aimed at concealing minor violations, what Cain (1973: 37) called 'easing behaviour', from the attention of supervisory officers.

Despite the tendency towards solidarity and isolation there are many conflicts *inside* the police organization. Some are structured by the rank hierarchy and the force division of labour, say between uniform and detective branches. Internal conflicts may often be overridden by the need to present a united front in the face of external attacks, but not always. The fundamental division between 'street cops' and 'management cops' can be reinforced in the face of external investigation (Ianni and Ianni 1983). 'Management cops' are derided by the 'street-wise' operational officers. The depth of the gulf is due to the different, often contradictory, functions of the two levels. 'Management' has to project an acceptable, legalistic, rational face of policing to the public. This may mean complicity with misconduct, hearing, seeing, and saying nothing. But when reform pressures become intense, 'management' may be forced into confrontation with the 'street'. To an extent, however, the apparent gulf and conflict between 'street' and 'management' orientations is functional for the organization itself. It allows presentational strategies to be adopted by management levels in real ignorance of what these might cover up, while at the same time the sacrifice of some individuals as 'bent' ratifies the effectiveness of the disciplinary process as a whole.

The 'them' and 'us' outlook which is a characteristic of police culture makes clear distinctions between types of 'them' (as well as of 'us'). The police perspective on social divisions in the population clearly reflects the structure of power, filtered through the specific problems of police work (Reiner 1978: chap. 11; Shearing 1981a; J. Lee 1981; Holdaway 1983: chap. 6; M. Young 1991; Loftus 2007, 2008, 2009).

The social structure as perceived by the police is one in which the hard class distinctions of the past have been eroded. Many policemen subscribe to an ideal of egalitarianism (epitomized by remarks such as 'nothing would give me greater pleasure than being able to nick the Lord Mayor'). At the same time they are acutely aware of the status distinctions which do exist (and need to be finely tuned to them in giving and expecting the appropriate level of deference): 'You deal with everybody here. From the basic form of human life in the jungle conditions of the bad areas, to the elite of the town. The posh dinner parties that go on. You have to handle them all' (uniformed constable). Society does not bestow fair and equal chances. As one constable remarked to me: 'It's hard for a kid if his mother's tomming it, and his dad's always in the boozer.'

The crucial divisions for the police do not readily fit a sociologist's categories of class or status, although they do display a continuing contempt towards the poor (Loftus 2007). They are police-relevant categories, generated by their power to cause problems, and their congruency to the police value system (Norris 1989; M. Young 1991). The fundamental division is between rough and respectable elements, those who challenge and those who accept the middle-class values of decency that most police revere. But finer distinctions within these categories can be made as generated by the police problematic. Seven key groups can be distinguished, each of which is discussed in the following sections.

'Good-class villains'

'Good-class villains' are professional (or at least experienced) criminals (Policy Studies Institute 1983, iv: 61–4). Pursuing them is seen as worthwhile, challenging, rewarding, indeed the *raison d'être* of the policeman's life, however infrequently the ordinary officer may encounter such cases. Moreover, the villains are likely to play the game with the same understandings as the police (Hobbs 1988, 1995). While obviously wishing to evade arrest, they do not normally challenge the basic legitimacy of the police. Relations with them may well be amicable—indeed, this may be cultivated by both sides for favours—the thin end of the corruption wedge.

'Police property'

'A category becomes police property when the dominant powers of society (in the economy, polity, etc.) leave the problems of social control of that category to the police' (J. Lee 1981: 53–4). They are low-status, powerless groups whom the dominant majority see as problematic or distasteful. The majority are prepared to let the police deal with their 'property' and turn a blind eye to the manner in which this is done. Examples might be vagrants, skid-row alcoholics, drug addicts, the unemployed or casually employed residuum, youth adopting a deviant cultural style, ethnic minorities, gays, prostitutes, and radical political organizations. The prime function of the police has been to control and segregate such groups, and they are armed with a battery of permissive and discretionary laws for this purpose, added to recently by the Crime and Disorder Act 1998's creation of the Anti-Social Behaviour Order—ASBO and other elements of New Labour's anti-social behaviour, street-crime, and respect agendas such as Penalty Notices for Disorder (Ramsay 2004, 2008; Squires and Stephen 2005; R. Young 2008; Squires 2008; Burney 2009). The concern with 'police property' is not so much to enforce the law as to maintain order using the law as one resource among others. Stop and search has been a traditional and controversial tactic in this, that has expanded in scope and been added to in recent years by a battery of street powers.

A major pitfall for the police is to mistake a member of a higher-status group for police property. The danger is reinforced in policing ethnic minority groups where the police officer is not as attuned to the signals of respectability. It is also a problem that has become accentuated for the police with the growth of respectable middle-class involvement in 'deviant' activities. The demonstrator or pot-smoker may turn out to be a university professor or lawyer.

'Rubbish'

'Rubbish' are people who make calls on the police which are seen as messy, intractable, unworthy of attention, or the complainant's own fault. Domestic disputes are a common sort of call traditionally regarded as 'rubbish' by many police officers: 'With domestic disputes, the husband and wife going hammer and tongs, you've got to separate them, calm them down before you go. And you're not doing a policeman's job, you're doing a socialist's [sic]' (Reiner 1978: 214–15, 244–5). The tendency not to treat domestic violence seriously has generated reform attempts such as mandatory arrest policies in many countries, with disputed evidence of patchy improvement (Sherman 1992a; Sheptycki 1993; Hoyle 1998; Skogan and Frydl 2004: 231–2; Heidensohn 2008: 661). 'Rubbish' are essentially people from the 'police property' groups presenting themselves as victims or clients for service, as they often do. Indeed, a major finding of crime surveys is the social isomorphism of victims and offenders (Hoyle and Zedner 2007: 465–6).

'Challengers'

'Challengers' are defined by Holdaway (1983: 71–7) as those whose job routinely allows them to penetrate the secrecy of police culture, and gives them power and information with which they might challenge police control of their 'property'. Doctors, lawyers, journalists, and social workers are in this position (as are police researchers!). Efforts will be made to minimize their intrusion, and presentational skills used to colour what they see. The Scarman-inspired development of schemes for lay visitors to police stations was an attempt to ensure regular penetration of the backstage areas of the police milieu by organized 'challengers'. PACE attempted to facilitate access by relevant 'challengers' such as duty solicitors or 'appropriate adults'. The extent to which this has succeeded in piercing the low visibility which shrouds police decisions on the street and in the station remains debatable (see Chapter 7).

'Disarmers'

'"Disarmers" are members of groups who can weaken or neutralise police work' (Holdaway 1983: 77–81). They are groups who are hard to deal with as suspects, victims, witnesses, or in service work, because they are perceived as socially vulnerable and so allegations by them against the police may receive special sympathy, such as children or the elderly.

Anyone may turn out to be an unexpected 'disarmer' because of the limitless naivety of the public, so the officer has to be wary of every encounter. One constable told me of an incident where he let off with a warning a man doing 65 mph in the city, who explained that his wife was in labour. 'A fortnight bloody later he writes to the chief constable. He explains all the circumstances and wants to thank me. I got dragged in there and given the thickest bollocking ever for condoning him going at 65 m.p.h. He dropped me right in it' (Reiner 1978: 246).

'Do-gooders'

'Do-gooders' are principled anti-police activists who criticize the police and organize to limit their autonomy (ibid.: 221–3). The prime example is the 'National Council for the Prevention of Policemen Doing Their Duty' (the National Council for Civil Liberties, now renamed Liberty). 'We're going through a spate of do-gooders who do no good! . . . They shout and shout to create problems or they'd be out of a job' (uniformed constables, ibid.). From the police perspective, the development in the 1980s of police-monitoring groups represented a proliferation of such 'do-gooders' (Jefferson et al. 1988; McLaughlin 1994).

Politicians

Politicians are regarded suspiciously (Reiner 1978: 76–81). They are remote and unrealistic ivory-tower idealists, corrupt self-seekers, secret subversives, or simply too weak to resist villainy. Unfortunately, however, they have the power to make law. The lawyers and judges involved in its administration tend to be made from the same cloth and are regarded as no better. 'The trouble is the Government think they're legislating for educated men . . . But the people here are animals, they're thick . . . MPs are out of context altogether . . . They live in a different world. I mean, every meal these politicians have is a six-course one!' (uniformed constable, ibid.)

Beset by all these threatening elements, the police become a solidary group: 'We're a tight-knit community. We've got to stand by each other because we're getting it from all angles. We get it from outside, the general public, we get it from solicitors, from QCs, we get it from our own bosses' (ibid.: 246).

Running through the police perception of the social structure is a distinction between the powerless groups at the bottom of the social hierarchy who provide the 'rubbish' and the 'police property', and the respectable strata, each with distinct segments which in different ways threaten police interests. Police culture both reflects the wider power structure and reproduces it through its operations.

POLICE CONSERVATISM

The evidence we have of the political orientations of police officers suggests that they tend to be conservative, politically and morally. Partly this is due to the nature of the job. The routine 'clients' of the police are drawn from the bottom layers of the social order. But control of the lumpen elements is not necessarily something which even politically conscious members of the working class would be averse to. However, in their public order role, and even more so in the work of their specifically political 'high policing' sections, the police have been routinely pitted against organized labour and the Left (Lipset 1969; Skolnick 1969; Bunyan 1977; Brodeur 1983, 1999; J. Morgan 1987; Marx 1988; Weinberger 1991, 1995: chap. 9; Vogler 1991; P. Gill 1994; Brewer *et al.* 1996; Mazower 1997; Huggins 1998; Hinton 2006). Furthermore, the force has from the start been constructed as a hierarchical, tightly disciplined organization. Thus the police officer with a conservative outlook is more likely to fit in. Processes of selection and self-selection lead police officers to be conservative.

However, there are contradictory pressures at work. Fiscal and political prudence from the start dictated pay and recruitment policies which meant that the bulk of officers were drawn from the working class, and these processes still operate today. Even chief officers come predominantly from working-class origins (Reiner 1991: chap. 4; Wall 1998). The police are an employee group whose grievances over pay and conditions of work have generated militancy and trade union organization analogous to that of other workers, although more commonly police unions have been a force for reaction (Reiner 1978; Judge 1994; Finnane 2002; Marks and Fleming 2006a, 2006b; Sklansky 2007). The 'deradicalization' of the policeman was not automatic, but had to be constructed (and continuously reconstructed), as Robinson (1978) cogently argued.

In the USA there has been copious historical evidence of police political support for the right and the far right. Skolnick (1966: 61) summed up his interviews and observations thus: 'A Goldwater-type of conservatism was the dominant political and emotional persuasion of police' (see also Bayley and Mendelsohn 1968: 14–30; Lipset 1969). These attitudes have been openly translated into political campaigning. Police associations have on numerous occasions actively lobbied for reactionary political candidates, and in support of specific right-wing policies (Skolnick 1969: chap. 7; Alex 1976; Reiner 1980; Bernstein *et al.* 1982). On the other hand, black and other police associations representing minorities have been a force for progressive reform in the UK and USA (Holdaway 2009).

There is little evidence of British police officers' political views. When I attempted to interview police in the 1970s about their political attitudes this was prohibited by the Home Office, as it was claimed that it would impugn the traditional notion of the police as outside any form of politics (Reiner 1978: 11, 283; 1979b). I have seen an unpublished 1977 dissertation by a police officer who interviewed a sample of colleagues in a northern city force, using the questions I had been prohibited from asking. He found that 80 per cent described themselves as Conservative—18 per cent of whom were to the right of the party. The remainder were evenly divided between Labour, Liberal, and 'don't know'. Of his sample, 80 per cent had voted in all recent elections. A slight rightward shift was indicated by the fact that 9 per cent had moved from Labour or Liberal to Conservative between 1974 and 1977, with no movement in the opposite direction. Despite this, 64 per cent affirmed that the police should remain politically neutral at all times, 21 per cent wished for the right to join a political party without taking an active role, while 12 per cent wished to be able to take an active part in politics.

More recently, a survey was conducted of 286 serving Metropolitan Police officers which included questions on voting patterns and intentions (Scripture 1997). This found that of those who had voted in the 1979, 1983, 1987, and 1992 general elections the overwhelming majority had supported the Conservatives (respectively 79 per cent, 86 per cent, 74 per cent, and 74 per cent: ibid.: 172). However, only 44 per cent intended to vote Conservative at the 1997 general election. This was probably a result of police disenchantment with the Conservative government's reform package aimed at subjecting the service to market disciplines, embodied in the 1993 Sheehy Report and the Police and Magistrates' Courts Act 1994.

The trend in the 1970s towards more open involvement in political debate of chief constables and the Police Federation has already been described. It clearly expressed views which were symbiotically related to Conservative Party policies, and echoed (at a less explicit level) the American 'blue power' political campaigning of the 1960s and 1970s. This changed in the 1990s with New Labour's embrace of law and order, and in the 2000s there have even been Tory accusations of some police chiefs being too close to Labour and complaints in the conservative press of PCs becoming too PC.

Apart from specific party politics, the police have tended to hold views on moral and social issues which are conservative. 'Cops are conventional people . . . All a cop can swing in a milieu of marijuana smokers, inter-racial dates, and homosexuals is the night stick' (cited in Skolnick 1966: 61). A 1960s survey of New York police attitudes found that the two most disliked categories of people after 'cop-fighter' were the homosexual and the drug addict (Niederhoffer 1967). I found similar support for a narrowly conventional morality in my interviews with British police (Reiner: 1978: chap. 11. See also J. Lee 1981 for Canadian evidence). Undoubtedly the very fact that some gay and lesbian police officers can now 'come out', and indeed form their own representative association, indicates a measure of progress in the last quarter of a century. However, they still experience discrimination, and homophobia remains in police culture even if it is expressed more covertly (M. Burke 1993; Paddick 2008). The social philosophy of chief officers also tends to the conservative, albeit less stridently expressed for the most part and with recent signs of change.

Although there is an obvious elective affinity for police officers between their role as upholders of authority and conservative politics and morality, this is by no means a constant. During the early and mid-1990s, as the Conservative government increasingly applied to the police its market-oriented approach to public services, so police sympathy at all levels appeared to swing towards more radical views, and this continued at least in the heyday of New Labour. This not only involved sharing concern about incipient privatization and more rigorous controls on public expenditure with other services, but extended to an increasing sympathy for analyses of crime and other social problems in terms of social justice rather than individual responsibility (D. Rose 1996: chap. 6).

MACHISMO

The traditional police world is one of old-fashioned machismo (Graef 1989: chap. 6; M. Young 1991: chap. 4; Fielding 1994; Westmarland 2001a, 2001b). Sexism in police culture is reinforced by routinized 'sexual boasting and horseplay', often at the expense of women colleagues (Policy Studies Institute 1983, iv: 91–7). Policemen are not notorious for their aversion to illicit heterosexual activities. As one constable told me, 'Policemen have one of the highest divorce rates in the country. There's always a bit of spare round the corner, because of the glamour of the job' (Reiner 1978: 212).[5]

Nor are policemen notably abstemious from alcohol, despite widespread contempt for users of other drugs. One hazard of police research is taking mental notes while sinking under a bar as the consumption of pints mounts. Police alcoholism has been a perennial problem since the early days of the force. The alcoholic and sexual indulgences of police are products of the masculine ethos of the force and the tension built up by the work, charted by the novels of Joseph Wambaugh, with their central theme of policing as a morally (even more than physically) dangerous occupation. The decidedly non-puritanical ethos about heterosexual behaviour, drinking, and gambling can expose police officers to strains, tensions, and charges of hypocrisy when enforcing laws in these areas. This helps explain the greater propensity for police corruption in the enforcement of vice laws.

It has always been tough for women police officers to gain acceptance. The establishment of employment for policewomen in the first place came only after a protracted campaign (Carrier 1988). Despite formal integration, they continue to experience discrimination (S. Jones 1987; Heidensohn 1992, 1994, 2008: 646–56; Dunhill 1989; J. Brown 1997, 2003; J. Brown and Heidensohn 2000; Silvestri 2003, 2007). The difficulties they face in achieving higher rank were illustrated by the highly publicized action claiming sex discrimination brought by Alison Halford, former assistant chief constable in Merseyside (Halford 1993). However, since then a number of women chief officers have been appointed, and there are now three women chief constables and twelve assistant chiefs. The number of women police has tripled since the early 1990s from under 11,000 to over 33,000—but this is still only 23 per cent (Heidensohn 2008: 655).

RACIAL PREJUDICE

An important aspect of police conservatism has been racial prejudice. A large number of American studies have demonstrated police suspiciousness, hostility, and prejudice towards blacks, and vice versa (Crank 2003: chap. 18). Such prejudice has been considerably diluted by the increasing recruitment of black and other ethnic minority officers in recent decades (Skogan and Frydl 2004: 312–14), although this has not significantly affected the practices of policing, which does not result primarily from prejudice (ibid.: 147–52). The issue of racial bias and discrimination remains a hot issue in US policing, most recently in the ongoing controversies over racial profiling and police stops for the 'moving violation that many blacks know as D.W.B.: Driving While Black' (Gates 1995; Walker 2004: 140–3). Ironically the Harvard Professor Henry Louis Gates who coined the phrase 'Driving While Black' in a 1995 magazine article became the subject of news headlines fourteen years later, when he was arrested on suspicion of breaking into his own house, and President Obama criticized the police for racism ('Henry Louis Gates Jr: Every Black Man's Nightmare' *The Independent* 4 August 2009).

It is usually argued that police racial prejudice is a reflection of the racism of American culture generally, and especially the social groups from which most police are drawn (lower middle or working class with no more than high-school education). Bayley and Mendelsohn (1968) summed up their own and many other studies: 'Are policemen prejudiced? The answer is yes, but only slightly more so than the community as a whole. Policemen reflect the dominant attitudes of the majority people towards minorities' (p. 144). (See also Westley 1970: 99–104; Skolnick 1966: 81–3; Skolnick and Fyfe 1993.) American police have also been prominent in political opposition to the civil rights movement and in support for far-right political organizations with a racist character.

There is similar evidence from many studies of British police racial prejudice. It is noteworthy that the documentation of this prejudice pre-dates by many years official police allegations or statistical data claiming a problem of black over-involvement in crime. Up to the early 1970s police arrest statistics indicated *under*-involvement of black people in crime compared to their proportion in the population (Lambert 1970). Nonetheless, Cain's and Lambert's studies of city forces in the early and late 1960s show a clear pattern of rank-and-file police prejudice, perceiving blacks as especially prone to violence or crime, and generally incomprehensible, suspicious, and hard to handle (Lambert 1970; Cain 1973: 117–19). My own interviews in Bristol in 1973–4 found that hostile and suspicious views of blacks were frequently offered quite spontaneously in the context of interviews concerning police work in general (Reiner 1978: 225–6). Of my sample, 25 per cent volunteered adverse comments (35 per cent in the central division which included St Paul's, an inner-city area with high tension between black people and the police; it was the scene of the of the first ghetto riot in 1980). One uniformed constable summed up the pattern: 'The police are trying to appear unbiased in regard to race relations. But if you asked them you'd find 90 per cent of the force are against coloured immigrants. They'd never want you to do that research and come up with that sort of finding.' Later work, conducted in a period during which black crime and especially mugging became heated political issues, confirms the evidence of prejudice (Holdaway 1983: 66–71, 1996; Policy Studies Institute 1983, iv: chap. 4; Reiner 1993; Lea 1986; Jefferson 1993; Whitfield 2004, 2007; Rowe 2004; Phillips and Bowling 2007: 434–41). However, the extent to which racists views are expressed openly and virulently has generally lessened (Foster *et al.* 2005), although deeper prejudiced feelings remain in the culture of white officers, who resent some of the reform efforts (Loftus 2008; Foster 2008). The reduction of openly expressed prejudice is partly a result of changes in the demographic character of forces, such as more recruitment of ethnic minority officers (albeit still a disproportionately small number especially at more senior levels: Henry 2007: 92–9; Bowling *et al.* 2008: 624–8), the influence of black and other minority police associations (Holdaway 2009), more officers with higher education (Lee and Punch 2006; Punch 2007), and a greater emphasis on multiculturalism in training and the official force ethos since the 1981 Scarman Report and the 1999 Macpherson Report (Macpherson 1999; Rowe and Garland 2003, 2007; Loftus 2009: chap. 2).

The extent of the change was vividly and dramatically called into question, however, by the 2003 BBC documentary *The Secret Policeman* which broadcast undercover film of a number of Greater Manchester Police recruits at the training centre displaying virulent racial prejudice (McLaughlin 2007: chap. 6; Holland 2007). This created a storm of controversy about the apparent failure of the post-Macpherson reforms. Two subsequent official enquiries, the 2004 Morris Report for the Metropolitan Police Authority and the 2005 Calvert-Smith Report for the Commission of Racial Equality, documented the failure of the Macpherson reforms to achieve much more than cosmetic change—indeed they may have stiffened the resentment of a more sophisticated group of 'stealth racists' who avoided sanctioning by eschewing overt racist sentiments. In Calvert-Smith's sharp conclusion, the police force was 'like a perma frost—thawing on the top, but still frozen solid at the core' (cited in McLaughlin 2007: 167–8).

It cannot be assumed, however, that police prejudice translates into behaviour expressing it. As the seminally important PSI study put it:

Our first impression after being attached to groups of police officers was that racialist language and racial prejudice were prominent and pervasive . . . on accompanying these officers as they went about their work we found that their relations with black and brown people were often relaxed or friendly. (Policy Studies Institute 1983, iv: 109; Henry 2007: 84–92)

American research suggests a similar pattern of disjunction between prejudice and discriminatory behaviour (Black 1970, 1972; P. Waddington 1999a, 1999b; Skogan and Frydl 2004: 122–6).

Police racial prejudice is in part a reflection of general societal prejudice. The consensus of social research (in Britain and in the USA) suggests that, contrary to popular belief, police recruits do not have especially authoritarian or prejudiced personalities (Skolnick 1969: 252; Reiner 1978: 157; Scripture 1997; P. Waddington 1999a: 102–4; Skogan and Frydl 2004: 128–30), although such revelations as the *Secret Policeman* documentary might suggest otherwise. Rather, they share the values of the social groups from which they are drawn—the lower middle and respectable working classes, which constitute the bulk of society. This is, of course, a double-edged finding, for while police recruits may not be more authoritarian than the general population, the 'normal' degree of authoritarianism is disturbing in an occupation which wields considerable power over minorities. As Stuart Hall commented trenchantly, chief constables would not state so cavalierly the equally true proposition that the police force must contain its fair share of criminals (S. Hall 1979: 13). It must be noted furthermore that prejudiced views are not unknown among chief constables themselves (Reiner 1991, especially 204–10).

One influential article challenged this orthodoxy, with considerable impact on the Scarman Report (Colman and Gorman 1982). The authors administered psychological tests intended to assess dogmatism, conservatism, and authoritarianism, as well as specific views on race relations, to samples of police recruits, probationer constables, and a civilian control group socioeconomically matched to the police groups. They found that 'the police force attracts conservative and authoritarian personalities, that basic training has a temporarily liberalizing effect, and that continued police service results in increasingly illiberal/intolerant attitudes towards coloured immigration'. Their results have been severely criticized on methodological and substantive grounds (P. Waddington 1982b). The control groups had a higher average level of education, which could be at least part of the explanation for the more 'authoritarian' police recruit attitudes. Other studies of recruits do not suggest the police attract individuals with radically distinct value systems compared with matched civilian control groups (Cochrane and Butler 1980; Brown and Willis 1985). What the research does reveal is that (although not necessarily sharply distinctive from the population norm) the police recruits did manifest hostile attitudes to ethnic minorities. Such attitudes seem to be accentuated with work experience, after a temporary liberalizing effect during training (Fielding 1988). The changes in selection and training following Scarman may have had some impact, but effects did not seem to survive practical policing experience to a significant extent. Unfortunately the same fate seems to be meeting the post-Macpherson diversity training reforms, with changes being primarily at a cosmetic level (Rowe and Garland 2003; Henry 2007: 96–7). Unless the pressures generating traditional cultural attitudes alter as a result of more profound transformations in the social structural context of police work, reforms in the selection and training of individual officers' cannot achieve much of substance (American and Australian experience confirms this; see Chan 1997, 2003; Skogan and Frydl 2004: 141–7).

Overall, it is necessary and sufficient to explain the police outlook on ethnic minorities (and other issues) by the police function, and the circumstances of police work, rather than by peculiarities of individual personality. Even if at some times and places distinctive personality types are attracted to policing, it is the nature of police work that determines the attraction. The crucial source of police prejudice is societal racism, which places ethnic minorities disproportionately in those least privileged and powerful social strata, with exposed public on-the-street lifestyles, that are most prone to the limited kinds of crimes the police concentrate on. So they disproportionately become police 'property'. This structural feature of police–ethnic-minority relations bolsters any prior prejudice police officers have (Jefferson 1993; Reiner 1993; Fitzgerald 2009).

PRAGMATISM

The final element of police culture to note is the very pragmatic, concrete, down-to-earth, anti-theoretical perspective which is typical of the rank and file, and indeed chief constables (with a growing number of exceptions). This is a kind of conceptual conservatism.

Police officers are concerned to get from here to tomorrow (or the next hour) safely and with the least fuss and paperwork, which has made them reluctant to contemplate innovation, experimentation, or research. This has changed in recent years with the impressive growth of a significant body of practice-oriented research, through such bodies as the Home Office's Police Research Group and Research and Statistics Directorate, the Police Foundation, and police forces themselves (Reiner 1992a; J. Brown and Waters 1993; J. Brown 1996; Cope *et al.* 2001; Cope 2008). The limits of much in-house police research were, however, underlined by a study of its early incarnations, which questioned the tendency to find favourable 'foregone conclusions' (Weatheritt 1986). This is less true of current work, due in part to a significant influx of graduates and indeed some experienced civilian researchers into police research departments (J. Brown 1996; Reiner and Newburn 2007), but resistance to analytic approaches remains (Cope 2004). A research-based approach became mandatory with the requirements of the 1998 Crime and Disorder Act and the Crime Reduction Programme to analyse locally and evaluate crime patterns and the effectiveness of crime reduction strategies, although as seen in the last chapter the evidence-led programme quickly became overwhelmed by political pressures to show quick results (Hough 2004; Maguire 2004; Hope 2004).

One review of the psychological literature on 'police personality' indicated that, while the evidence on such overtly political issues as distinctive authoritarianism or racial prejudice among policemen was mixed, it did seem that police officers have a markedly 'empirical' cognitive structure (Adlam 1981: 156). Training innovations, especially for senior ranks, have moved towards less didactic techniques to try and counter this and encourage reflective and analytic skills (Adlam 1987; Savage *et al.* 2000: 107–12; Villiers and Adlam 2003; Savage 2007: 111–12; Mawby and Wright 2008: 233–6), but it is likely that pressures to show measurable short-term crime control results in the climate of law-and-order politics will undercut the training reforms and reinforce the traditional cultural pragmatic short-termism.

VARIATIONS IN COP CULTURE

Police culture is not monolithic, and there is both structured and individual diversity. The organizational division of labour is related to a variation in distinct types of perspective around the core elements of the culture. This has been noted by a variety of studies that have developed typologies of different police orientations and styles (Foster 2003; Skogan and Frydl 2004: 130–3; Manning 2007; Cockcoft 2007).

Muir's (1977) study, for example, used sensitive observations of twenty-eight police officers in an American city. It was unique in sociological studies of the police in centring on the question 'What makes a police officer good?' rather than on the more common analysis of deviation. Muir approached this by considering the way police officers dealt with the problem of handling coercive power. The good cop has to develop two virtues. 'Intellectually, he has to grasp the nature of human suffering.

Morally, he has to resolve the contradiction of achieving just ends with coercive means'
(Muir 1977: 3–4). Intellectual vision can be 'cynical', that is, based on a dualistic division of people into 'us' and 'them', fault-finding, and individualistic; or 'tragic', seeing
mankind as of one unitary substance and moral value, seeing action as complexly
produced by chance, will, and circumstance, and recognizing the important but fragile
nature of social interdependence. Moral understanding may be 'integrated', that is,
accommodating the exercise of coercion within an overall moral code; or 'conflict-
ual' where it creates guilt because it is not related to basic moral principles. The two
dimensions yield a fourfold typology of police officer. The 'avoider' (with cynical perspective and conflicted morality) shirks duties; the 'reciprocator' (tragic perspective
and conflicted morality) hesitates to use coercive power even when appropriate; the
'enforcer' (cynical perspective and integrated morality) acts in the heat of conflicts and
without understanding the need for restraint; the 'professional' (tragic perspective and
integrated morality) is the 'good' cop. He or she is able to use violence where necessary
in a principled way, but is adept at verbal and other skills that enable solutions to be
resolved without coercive force wherever the opportunity exists.

Muir's four types were similar to those found in my own research: the 'bobby', the
ordinary copper applying the law with discretionary common sense to keep the peace;
the 'uniform-carrier', the completely cynical, disillusioned time-server who'll 'never
answer the phone if he can help it—it might be a job at the other end!'; the 'new centurion' (see Wambaugh 1971), dedicated to a crusade against crime and disorder, seeing
crime control as the central function, and emphasizing the street cop as the repository
of all truth, wisdom, and virtue; the 'professional' policeman, ambitious and career-
conscious, with an appropriately balanced appreciation of the value of all aspects of
policing from crime-fighting to sweeping the station floors, equipping him for the
largely public relations functions of senior rank (Reiner 1978: chap. 12).

Other studies have identified very similar perspectives, albeit with different labels
(Broderick 1973; Walsh 1977; Shearing 1981a; M. Brown 1981). The types seem to be as
follows (translating the other authors' labels into my terminology):

(i)   The 'bobby' (= Broderick's 'optimist' = Walsh's 'street-cop' = Muir's 'profes-
       sional' = Shearing's 'wise officer' = Brown's 'professional').

(ii)   The 'new centurion' (= Broderick's 'enforcer' = Walsh's 'action-seeker' = Muir's
       'enforcer' = Shearing's 'real officer' = Brown's 'crime-fighters').

(iii) The 'uniform-carrier' (= Broderick's 'realist' = Walsh's cynical 'street-cop' =
       Muir's 'avoider' = Shearing's 'cautious officer' = Brown's 'service type 1').

(iv)   The 'professional' (= Broderick's 'idealist' = Walsh's 'middle-class mobile' =
       Muir's 'reciprocator' = Shearing's 'good officer').

The differences in nomenclature reflect differing purposes of particular studies, as
well as conflicting conceptions of the 'good' police officer—is it possible to play it by
the rules (Broderick), must we resign ourselves to the tragic inevitability of coercive
power (Muir), or is the apparent conflict of roles ideologically functional for class control (Shearing)? This leads to explicitly opposed notions of the 'professional': the ideal

embodiment of legalistic policing (Broderick), the wise, empathetic but untutored intuitions of Dixon-style beat work (Muir), a legitimating ideology for individual and collective social mobility (Reiner).

But the same underlying types are postulated in all these studies: an alienated cynic, a managerial professional, a peacekeeper and a law-enforcer. These correspond with the basic organizational division of labour between management and rank and file, and between CID and uniform patrol. But they also stem from differing individual personalities, initial orientations to the job, and varying career ambitions and tra-jectories. The differing perspectives are already discernible in samples of uniformed patrol officers, prefiguring future career developments (Reiner 1978).

The culture of chief constables itself varies, with different perspectives typically related to the pattern of previous careers, the character of the force, and the experience of particular generations (Reiner 1991: chap. 12). Overall, British chief officers do not have fundamentally different cultural styles from the rank and file, having come from similar backgrounds and worked their way up the force hierarchy (M. Young 1993). However, they are more likely to espouse different policing philosophies, shaped by the need to accommodate to pressures from governmental and social elites. In the 1980s the conventional wisdom of chief officers was moulded by the Scarman Report (Reiner 1991). During the 1990s, however, it increasingly adopted a managerialist, 'businesslike' flavour, as the 'bureaucrat' became the 'business manager' (Savage et al. 2000: 86).

The differing orientations do not seem related to demographic characteristics such as ethnic group and gender, although the huge changes in the demographic make-up of police forces around the world have led some to hope for benign cultural changes (Sklansky 2006). No research on these issues exists in Britain as yet. But American work suggests there is no clear tendency for black officers to be different in work style from whites (Alex 1969), or to be less punitive towards other blacks (P. Waddington 1999a: 111–12; Skogan and Frydl 2004: 148–50). It may be, though, that increasing the propor-tion of black officers changes the whole ethos of a department in ways which cannot be discerned in individual comparisons, in particular when organized into representative associations (Holdaway 2009).

Nor is there much evidence of differences in policing style between male and female officers, in particular because the pressures on women to adapt to the traditional ethos of masculinity seems to outweigh the counter-pressures coming from reform attempts to remodel policing (Heidensohn 1992, 1994, 2008; Skogan and Frydl 2004: 151–2). Again, though, it is plausible that raising the proportion of women in the department might dilute the masculine ethos. Even more significantly the recent increase in women at command levels may alter leadership styles and the organizational ethos, although the evidence so far is mixed (Brown 2003; Silvestri 2003, 2007). On the other hand, the whole burden of the argument of this chapter is that the culture of the police depends not on individual attributes but on elements in the police function itself. Research on differing department styles and reform attempts implies that there is some scope for change, although this is constrained by the social and political context in which the department is embedded (Chan 2007; Foster 2003; Klinger 2004).

VARIATIONS IN ORGANIZATIONAL CULTURE

The *locus classicus* for considering differences in the styles of whole police organizations is J. Q. Wilson's (1968) study, *Varieties of Police Behaviour*. Wilson suggested that three departmental styles could be distinguished. The 'watchman' style emphasized order maintenance and the patrolman perspective. Bureaucratization, standardization, and professionalization were barely developed, and political influence was rife. Patrol officers had much discretion in handling their beats. The 'legalistic' style operated with a law enforcement approach, attempting to impose universalistic standards impartially on all communities in the city. The organization was bureaucratic and professionalized. The 'service' style prioritized the consensual, helpful functions of the police. If it has to deal with law-breaking, it attempts to do so by cautioning, not prosecution. There is much stress on public relations and community involvement. Although partly a product of departmental policy choices, the styles reflected social and political balances. 'Legalistic' departments replaced 'watchman' ones either after a corruption scandal bringing in a reform administration, or as a result of a slower process of change in the balance of power between class elements, elevating groups with an interest in rational universalistic authority as a framework for long-run planning. It could run into paradoxical difficulties if introduced in an adverse social context. For example, while less racially discriminatory, the 'legalistic' style enjoined higher levels of law enforcement, and might thus adopt aggressive methods of patrol which blacks experienced as harassment. The 'service' style only developed in middle-class suburban communities with a value consensus. Subsequent American research on the effect on police practices of changes in organization and style suggests that these can have significant impact on patterns of arrest, use of force and other significant practices. However, the political economy, social structures and political cultures of different areas seem to be the driving forces behind variations in police practices, rather than freely chosen organizational policies, as Wilson's typology itself implies (Klinger 2004; Skogan and Frydl 2004: chap. 5).

There is not much British evidence about differences in culture between police forces. Cain's (1973) study of a rural and a city force in the early 1960s indicated that country police were more closely integrated into the communities they policed. The city officers were much more closely interdependent with their police colleagues, and alienated from the populations they policed with more abrasive encounters. This was probably a consequence of the different conditions of policing in rural and urban areas rather than a function of organizational styles readily open to policy change. Urban/rural differences in style are a frequently recurring motif (Shapland and Vagg 1988; Shapland and Hobbs 1989; Loftus 2009).

S. Jones and M. Levi (1983) collected data on police and public attitudes in two forces whose chief constables stood at opposite poles in the spectrum of police debate. Devon and Cornwall's chief constable, John Alderson, was the foremost exponent of the 'community policing' philosophy, emphasizing the importance of a close and positive relationship between police and public as the essential precondition of effective policing, and seeing the police role as a broad one with a strong social service component. Manchester's James Anderton had the highest public profile of all chief constables, standing for a tough law-and-order approach.

Jones and Levi found that on a variety of indicators the public in Devon and Cornwall had more favourable opinions of their police than people in Manchester. Moreover, the police in Devon and Cornwall had a more accurate perception of their public standing than the Manchester police, suggesting a closer relationship. One common criticism levelled against the community policing policies of John Alderson was that, while they might be appropriate for tranquil rural counties, they would be impracticable in a city. Jones and Levi found, however, that the force contrast held true when Plymouth (the second largest city in the south-west) was compared to Wigan (a relatively small northern country town), although Plymouth did have the lowest levels of expressed public satisfaction in Devon and Cornwall. This suggests that, while it is indeed harder to cultivate positive police–public relations in cities, organizational culture and style are also important variables.

Some of the clearest evidence of the possibility of successful change in police culture comes from an important ethnographic study (Foster 1989) comparing two inner-city London police stations. In one, substantial reforms in policing style and practices were introduced, altering the culture in the direction intended by the Scarman Report's espousal of a community policing philosophy. The key ingredient of this achievement was the overall commitment and solid backing of the whole management hierarchy. In the other station, where this was lacking, traditional police culture remained resilient. A similar message of the possibilities of reform even in tough city areas is provided in a study of six innovative police chiefs in the USA, who set out to reorient their departments in a community policing direction (Skolnick and Bayley 1986). However, it is left somewhat unclear how far this translated successfully into sustained change in practices on the ground. Chan's (1977, 2003) influential accounts of attempts to change police culture by reforms in organization, recruitment, and training underlines the limited possibilities in the absence of fundamental transformation of the police role.

Altogether it seems that there are significant differences in the culture of policing between different areas. What is less clear is the extent to which the differences are the products of policy choices which can effectively be made in areas with different social and political structures and cultural traditions. Do societies get the policing they deserve, or can they do significantly better or worse? It is impossible to foreordain the degree of freedom facing reform strategies, although it is undoubtedly never very great. But the variations found in departmental style imply that the emphasis on the autonomy of rank-and-file culture in the interactionist research tradition needs qualification, as the work of McBarnet suggested some thirty years ago (McBarnet (1978, 1979). Nonetheless the resilience of cop culture even in extreme situations is shown by Brewer and Magee's 1990 study of routine policing in Northern Ireland. Recent observational work replicating the pioneering research of the 1960s–1980s has shown the survival of many of the facets of the culture described then, despite the massive reform efforts stemming from Scarman, Macpherson, and so many other reform initiatives, with changes superficial or partial at best. Westmarland (2001a, 2001b) and Silvestri (2003, 2007) show the stubborn survival of the masculine ethos. Loftus's important recent ethnographic study of a British force finds many of the themes found in the classic research conducted decades ago still alive and kicking, despite the determined efforts of governments and police elites (Loftus 2007, 2008, 2009, 2010). It confirms the embeddedness of police culture in the deep structure of policing an unequal society, with policy reforms producing at best cosmetic alterations.

CONCLUSION

There seem to be certain commonalities in cop culture as discovered by many studies in several different places and periods. These arise from basic elements in the police role in liberal democracies: the fundamental remit to control crime and disorder in unequal, divided societies while adhering to principles of the rule of law. The salience of these pressures varies across time and space: it is greater in contemporary neo-liberalism than it was in the post-war heyday of social democracy. There are also structured variations within forces according to the internal division of labour, as well as individual differences of interpretation and style.

Police culture and its variations are reflections of the power structures of the societies policed. The social map of the police is differentiated according to the power of particular groups to cause problems for the police, and their differential propensity to visibly commit the limited types of crime that the police, and the criminal justice system to which they are the main gateway, in practice deal with: street crimes involving an element of trespass on persons or property (Reiner 2007a: chap. 2). The least powerful elements in society become police 'property'. The power structure of a community and the views of its elites are important sources of variation in policing styles (with 'divided' societies constituting an extreme case: Brewer 1991). The different orientations within the police reflect the two ways police organizations have to face in a class-divided hierarchical social order: downwards by the rank and file, to the groups controlled with varying degrees of gusto or finesse; and upwards by the professional police chiefs, to the majority public and elite who want an acceptable gloss to be placed on what is done in their name.

Police culture is neither monolithic nor unchanging. But the predicament of the police in maintaining order and enforcing the law in liberal democracies generates a typical cultural pattern, albeit with variations around it. This may be finessed but is remarkably resilient, because it facilitates the accomplishment of policing in such societies. Officers vary in their responses, however, according to structural factors like their role in the organizational division of labour, their own demographic background, and their individual personalities and interpretations. Nonetheless the nature of police work does seem to generate a recognizably similar basic culture in all forces that have been studied. Fundamental change in this requires not just reforms aimed at individual officers (for example in selection and training), nor grand policy declarations, but a reshaping of the basic character of the police role through wider social transformation of the structures of economic inequality and power.

NOTES

1. McBarnet's critique was in many respects similar to Gouldner's (1968) debate with Becker (1963, 1967) and the 'labelling' perspective, which Skolnick and the other interactionist studies of rank-and-file policing were part of. Her arguments for a structuralist analysis of the operation of police discretion, rather than a culturalist one, were developed by Shearing (1981a, 1981b), Ericson (1982, 1993), M. Brogden and Brogden (1983), and the rigorous attempt to develop a Marxist analysis of policing in Grimshaw and Jefferson (1987). For attempts at synthesis between interactionism and structuralism, see McConville et al. 1991; Reiner and Leigh 1992; D. Dixon 1997.

2. The police world remains aggressively a man's world, notwithstanding equal opportunities legislation in the USA and Britain (Westmarland 2001a, 2001b; Silvestri 2003, 2007; Skogan and Frydl 2004: 147–52; Heidensohn 2008). Although forces have sent women on routine patrol for many years now, they still face formidable barriers of an informal kind in 'breaking and entering' into this male preserve (Ehrlich 1980). To talk of policemen was thus not sexist shorthand but a literal description when the early studies were conducted.

3. It also serves to resolve the Dirty Harry problem, whereby 'policing constantly places its practitioners in situations in which good ends can be achieved by dirty means'. This is 'a genuine moral dilemma . . . from which one cannot emerge innocent no matter what one

does' (Klockars 1980: 33). Cynicism is a clearly possible psychological result.

4. Suspicion does not only develop out of the intrinsic conditions of police work; it has been deliberately encouraged by training. Skolnick cited an American manual giving detailed guidance for field interrogations which begins, 'Be suspicious. This is a healthy police attitude.' Among the Catch-22 tips for signs of the 'unusual' subject who should be stopped are: '7. Exaggerated unconcern over contact with the officer. 8. Visibly "rattled" when near the policemen' (Skolnick 1966: 45–6). A similar guide to the 'abnormal', embracing most of the population, was an English manual by David Powis, a former Metropolitan assistant commissioner. Suspicious types included political radicals or intellectuals who 'spout extremist babble', or people in possession of a 'your rights' card (Powis 1977: 92).

5. I well remember the experience in 1971 (soon after I began research on the police) of attending a conference where, after the learned seminars a local officer took me, two other sociologists, and two out-of-town policemen to a local drinking club. There were about fifty men there, and just three women—two strippers and the barmaid. To the amazement of the observing but not participating sociologists, at the end of the evening the three policemen managed to walk off with the three women, whom they had been assiduously chatting up while fending off discussion of police culture.

5

DEMYSTIFYING THE POLICE: SOCIAL RESEARCH AND POLICE PRACTICE

Various conflicting political mythologies about policing have obscured understanding. The 'repressive state apparatus' myth flourished in the radical criminology of the 1970s and 1980s. It depicted the police as an essentially oppressive political force creating crime and criminals through labelling. In this view, community safety requires the curbing of police power (see, for instance, Scraton 1985, 1987; Farrell 1992). It echoed the long tradition of opposition to the modern police analysed in Chapters 2 and 3, but has largely disappeared from mainstream political discourse (although the post-2007 economic collapse may result in a resurgence of deep social and political conflict and revive such perspectives on policing). In recent years, however, its antithesis has dominated debate. This is the 'law and order' myth which portrays the police as an effective force for the prevention and detection of crime, and advocates police power as the panacea for law enforcement and public order problems. This has always been the primary representation of policing in the mass media (Chapter 6), and in both police and popular culture. It was the position espoused by the Conservatives and the police in the late 1970s, at first controversially (Downes and Morgan 2007). Since the early 1990s, it has become the hegemonic, almost unquestioned perspective, after neo-liberalism became the embedded political consensus. The erstwhile parties of the democratic left were born again as 'New', pushing out of mainstream debate the possibility of welfarist and Keynesian policies to tackle the root causes of crime and disorder in political economy and culture (Reiner 2006, 2007a: chap. 5). Rhetorically at least a variety of 'third way' mythologies about policing also burgeoned in the 1990s, reflecting the broader quest for social policies 'beyond left and right' espoused by Blair's New Labour, Clintonian New Democrats, and other self-styled middle-way governments seeking to distance themselves from the truncheon-rattling rhetoric of 1980s Thatcherites and Reaganites. 'Community policing' remains a fashionable label internationally in police policy discussions, largely because of its apparently benign and uncontentious 'cherry pie' connotations (M. Brogden 1999). The fundamental premise is that effective police work is possible only on the basis of public consent and cooperation. In some political and police rhetoric this innocuous proposition became a broader mythology of policing as social service, delivering good works to a harmonious community of satisfied customers. In so far as this idyll is not realized in today's harsh and conflict-ridden world, policy must be aimed at restoring it. This has flourished in uneasy tension with other new policing strategies of a tougher kind, and indeed community policing is increasingly interpreted as a crime control strategy. Its apparent antithesis, 'zero tolerance' policing, which itself became a worldwide slogan in the mid-1990s, has itself been represented as a variety of community policing by some exponents.

A more forensic version of 'third way' policing is the 'magic bullet' myth, epitomized by the flourishing *CSI*-led genre of scientific detection programmes. Through the appliance of science, by research and analysis on policing problems, it is possible to develop tactics delivering precisely the right degree of force necessary for effective yet legitimate crime control and order maintenance. This smart crime reduction narrative is a sophisticated version of the 'law and order' myth. It believes that intelligently targeted policing can, using laser-like precision, excise crime and disorder with minimal negative side effects for civil liberties or social justice. At one level it is impossible to question the project. Who but Al Capone and his disciples would prefer stupidity-led to intelligence-led policing? As with community policing, the question marks are not over the desirability of the approach but its feasibility as a strategy for achieving public safety and security.

What all the mythologies oversimplify or ignore is the extent to which policing reflects the conflicts and contradictions of the wider social structure, culture, and political economy. Policing alone cannot achieve an orderly society, whether this is seen as desirable or repressive. On the other hand it can never operate in the fully harmonious way implied by some prophets of community policing.

Research evidence, as opposed to presumption, about what the police do (and analysing the determinants, effectiveness, and fairness of their actions), has proliferated in the USA, Britain, and elsewhere in the last four decades. However, reforms and alternatives to current practice remain inconclusive and highly contested. Police work is more complex, contradictory, indeed confused, than any of the mythologies allows.

The research evidence about police practice will be considered in this chapter in relation to three specific questions. What is the police role? How effectively is it performed? How fairly is it performed? There has been a clear dialectic in the development of police research since its origins in the early 1960s about all these issues. Early research emphasized a debunking of the pre-research conventional wisdom about policing, offering an antithesis to the tacit thesis implied by popular assumptions. More recently the critical deconstruction offered by early research has itself been called into question, although not to the extent of rehabilitating the original conventional wisdom. Rather, a degree of synthesis between the rational kernel of pre-research common sense and its debunking by early research has developed, albeit increasingly bedevilled by the hegemonic politics of law and order.

WHAT IS THE POLICE ROLE?

An old chestnut of debate about the police role has been whether the police are best considered as a force, with the primary function of enforcing the criminal law, or as a service, calming a sea of social troubles. The starting point for debate was the empirical 'discovery' that the police (contrary to popular mythology) operate not mainly as crime-fighters or law-enforcers, but rather as providers of a range of services to members of the public, the variety of which beggars description.

Banton (1964), on the basis of an analysis of field diaries kept by a sample of Scottish policemen, observation, and interviews (both in Britain and in the USA) concluded (p. 127):

The policeman on patrol is primarily a 'peace officer' rather than a 'law officer'. Relatively little of his time is spent enforcing the law in the sense of arresting offenders; far more is spent 'keeping the peace' by supervising the beat and responding to requests for assistance.

Cumming *et al.* 1965 found in an analysis of phone calls by the public to an American force that over half involved demands for help or support in relation to personal and interpersonal problems, in which the police performed as 'philosopher, guide, and friend'. This was replicated by Punch and Naylor (1973) in an analysis of the calls by the public to the police in three Essex towns. In a 'new town', 49 per cent were service calls, in an 'old town' 61 per cent, and in a 'country town' 73 per cent. Of the service calls, the largest categories were 'domestic occurrences' (such as family disputes or noisy parties) and 'highway accidents'. J. Martin and G. Wilson (1969) found that only 28 per cent of duty time in provincial forces (and 31 per cent in the Met) was spent on crime-related work. Similar results have been confirmed in subsequent studies (McCabe and Sutcliffe 1978; Antunes and Scott 1981; P. Morris and Heal 1981: chap. 3; Ekblom and Heal 1982; Hough 1989; Bennett and Lupton 1992; P. Waddington 1993a, 1999a: chap. 1; Bayley 1994, 1996; Police Foundation/Policy Studies Institute 1996; R. Morgan and Newburn 1997; Johnston 2000: chap. 3; Wright 2002: 90–5; Skogan and Frydl 2004: 57–63). There has been no data from government or academic researchers assessing the nature of calls to police in recent years (since Waddington 1993). The focus of policy, research and public political debate have been on crime and its control. Nonetheless the British Crime Survey continues to analyse the nature of contacts between public and police. It shows that even now only about half the contacts initiated by the public concern crimes (J. Allen *et al.* 2006: Table 2.02). The rest are largely unequivocal service contacts ('asking for advice or information' or 'social chats'—about 10 per cent of public-initiated contacts), or ambiguous mixes of service, order maintenance and potential crime ('reporting suspicious person/circumstances, disturbance, alarms', 'reporting accidents/emergencies, missing persons/property, giving information') accounting for well over half the citizen-initiated contacts (as the percentages are of people contacting the police, and some did so more than once, the percentages of reasons add up to more than 100).

The empirical findings about the nature of police activity bolstered a liberal argument which became the orthodoxy among progressive police administrators, chiefs, and commentators. This was that 'is' meant 'ought'. The police were de facto social workers, although not recognized as such. They were a 'secret social service' (Punch 1979b). But because this was covert and seldom articulated, there was a need for the police to be better trained and organized to cope with the work that anyway accounted for most of their activity. If the law-and-order panacea for police problems was bigger guns, the liberal's was a sociology degree.

Some argued that the mandate of crime prevention should mean more than the traditional techniques of patrol and detection. They should collaborate with other social service agencies and government to tackle the underlying social causes of crime, as well as the symptoms (Stephens and Becker 1994). In British police circles this view was championed above all by John Alderson, chief constable of Devon and Cornwall, in his community policing philosophy (Alderson 1979, 1984). By the late 1980s this had become the new post-Scarmanist orthodoxy of nearly all chief officers (Reiner 1991: chap. 6). The *Operational Policing Review* mounted in 1989 by all three staff associations seemed to indicate public preference for a more community-oriented style of policing. This inspired the 1991 'Statement of Common Purposes and Values' in which the police staff associations committed themselves to a mission based on the idea of service. Following the Plus Programme in the Met, HM Inspectorate and ACPO aimed to reconstruct police culture and practice around an ethic of 'quality of service' service to the consumer (*Policing* Special Issue on 'The Way Ahead', autumn 1991; I. Waters 1996; Savage 2007: 127–41).

While this consensus was emerging at the top, there was a developing underswell of protest in the police rank and file. Research had shown that street-level police culture rested on an action and crime-fighting orientation. This was pithily summed up by one American patrolman: 'Every time you begin to do some real police work you get stuck with this stuff. I guess 90 per cent of all police work is bullshit' (Reiss 1971: 42). The 1990 *Operational Policing Review* survey of national samples of senior and rank-and-file police confirmed that this gulf still existed. While senior ranks favoured community policing initiatives, the operational ranks remained wedded to a 'strong' crime-fighting approach. However, the 1993–4 reform package—the White Paper, the Sheehy Report, the Police and Magistrates' Courts Act 1994—explicitly sought to restructure the police on a 'businesslike' model aimed at the sole priority of 'catching criminals' (Savage 2007: chap. 3; McLaughlin 2007: 96–7, 182–7). Although the New Labour government reemphasized the importance of police partnership with local government and other agencies, it continued to prioritize crime reduction as the primary purpose of policing. Its National Policing Plans prioritized crime above all other issues. The 2005–8 Plan has as its 'five key priorities' to:

- reduce overall crime—including violent and drug-related crime—in line with the Government's Public Service Agreements (PSAs);
- provide a citizen-focused police service which responds to the needs of communities and individuals, especially victims and witnesses, and inspires public confidence in the police, particularly among minority ethnic communities;

- take action with partners to increase sanction detection rates and target prolific and other priority offenders;
- reduce people's concerns about crime, and anti-social behaviour and disorder; and
- combat serious and organised crime, within and across force boundaries. (*National Policing Plan 2005–8* Home Office 2004: 1).

The National Community Safety Plans which have sought to incorporate policing into a broader partnership/community safety programme continue the crime focus (*National Community Safety Plan 2008–11* Home Office 2009). The addition of 'increasing community confidence' as a target focuses on measuring public assessments of crime control performance.

The force–service debate that has long bedevilled discussions of the police role rests on a false dichotomy: there is an excluded middle, of first-aid order maintenance. To clarify this, let me define the basic concepts. There are two dimensions underlying the distinction between aspects of police work: (a) is there consensus or conflict between the civilians and the police in an interaction? And (b) does the police action invoke the legal powers of arrest, prosecution, and so on? Putting the two dimensions together yields a typology of four possible types of police intervention (Table 5.1).

The first cell (law enforcement in a consensus situation) is a controversial area. If there is genuinely no conflict about desired outcomes between civilian and police participants in an interaction, there is no need for the invocation of legal powers, which are inherently coercive. However, the police regularly stop and question and/or search people, or detain them at police stations 'assisting with enquiries', without formally exercising their legal powers, claiming that the compliance of citizens has been voluntary. There must be doubt about how often such 'voluntary' compliance is whole-hearted and genuine, and how often it is based on ignorance about rights, and bluff by the police (D. Dixon *et al.* 1990; McKenzie *et al.* 1990; D. Dixon 1997).

The categories are all 'ideal types' and concrete incidents can be classified into them only after a contingent process of interaction in which different outcomes are possible. Take an incident I observed where police were called out because of incessant barking of a neighbour's dog. The police officer discovered that the owners were not in and climbed over the back garden fence to investigate, because the dog sounded in distress.

Table 5.1 Dimensions of police work

	Police use legal powers ('law officer')	Police do not use legal powers ('peace officer')
Consensus	'voluntary compliance'	'service'
Conflict	'law enforcement'	'order maintenance'

In the course of this the owners returned. The neighbours and the constable explained what had happened, and everyone was satisfied. The outcome was a good example of 'service' work. But it is possible that the neighbours might have got into an argument about the propriety of involving the police, and an 'order maintenance' situation developed. Depending on many factors, but primarily the officer's orientation to his job, his assessment of the moral characters of the disputants, and his skills at defusing conflict, it is quite possible that the eventual outcome would have been an arrest for assault. Then the outcome would have been classifiable as 'law enforcement' work. The nature of a police intervention is not foreordained by the initial 'call for service' made by a member of the public.

In terms of these more precisely defined types, most police work is neither social service nor law enforcement, but order maintenance—the settlement of conflicts by means other than formal law enforcement. Moreover, this is accomplished in the main by the distinctive police capacity, which is not legal powers of arrest nor social work skills, but 'the capacity for decisive action', as Bittner has put it. 'The policeman, and the policeman alone, is equipped, entitled and required to deal with every exigency in which force may have to be used' (Bittner 1974: 35; Brodeur 2007). The police mandate is the very diffuse notion of order maintenance, what Bittner (ibid.) has graphically called 'a solution to an unknown problem arrived at by unknown means'. But beneath the diversity of problems and means is the core capacity to use force if necessary (Klockars 1985; Waddington and Wright 2008). This does not mean that the police typically (or even often) use coercion or force to accomplish the resolution of the troubles they deal with. The craft of effective policing is to use the background possibility of legitimate coercion so skilfully that it never needs to be foregrounded (although of course excessive use of force has been problematic in many jurisdictions, cf. Belur 2010). Several observational studies have given impressive accounts of how 'good' patrol officers can maintain peace in threatening situations, with their legal powers (including force) as a latent resource (Bittner 1967; Muir 1977; Kemp *et al.* 1992). The successful police officer draws on the authority of her office, as well as her personal and craft skills in handling people, rather than coercive power—although sometimes this will not be possible. These skills are not adequately recognized, rewarded or understood, largely because popular and police preconceptions about the nature of the police task have precluded analysis of the craftsmanship involved in effective peacekeeping (Bittner 1983; Bayley and Bittner 1984; Norris and Norris 1993; Reiner 1998; Wright 2002: chap. 3).

However, order maintenance is just as problematic in terms of social and political justice as the higher-profile issue of crime control (P. Hall 1998). The observational studies that vividly depict many examples of good peacekeeping work fail to grapple with these problems adequately. For example, Chatterton (1983: 211–15) gives a detailed account of the calming down of a domestic dispute without the arrest of the husband, who had assaulted his wife. In Chatterton's analysis this was ultimately due to the officer exercising his sense of the justice of the man's position. As he described the case, an arrest accomplishing 'legal' justice would have been both unjust and troublesome to all concerned.

This clearly raises the problem of whether we can rely on the personal sense of justice of patrol officers, and how its exercise can be made accountable. The typical handling of domestic 'disputes' as non-criminal, order-maintenance matters, rather than assaults, has been criticized effectively for many years by feminists, and has produced change in forces around the world. One common reaction has been the encouragement of mandatory arrest policies, shifting this large category of calls unequivocally into 'law enforcement'. There has been much debate about the effectiveness and desirability of such innovations (Sherman and Berk 1984; S. Edwards 1989; Hanmer *et al.* 1989; Sheptycki 1993; Sherman 1992b; Hoyle 1998; Chesney-Lind 2002; Maxwell *et al.* 2002; Skogan and Frydel 2004: 231–2; Heidensohn 2008: 661). The issues of achieving and reconciling fairness, effectiveness, and accountability are just as acute for order-maintenance work as for the areas of law enforcement where they have been most widely discussed. That order maintenance is the core of the police mandate is attested to in a variety of ways. It is reflected in the pattern of specific demands placed upon the police by calls for service. Most involve some element of conflict, not harmonious service requests like fetching cats out of trees, but do not relate unequivocally to a criminal offence. Second, it was a core mandate historically. The main *raison d'être* for the 'new police' was crime prevention by regular patrol (that is, intervention in situations before crimes occurred) as well as order maintenance in the sense of crowd control. The unique character of British policing lies partly in merging the tasks of law enforcement and order maintenance (including crowd and riot control) into the same organization.

However, to say that the primary police role is order maintenance is not to give the police responsibility for all elements of social order. Their task is the emergency maintenance of order, not the creation of its preconditions, as the broadest philosophies of community policing seek (Alderson 1979, 1984). As P. Waddington has put it: 'The police are the social equivalent of the AA or RAC patrolmen, who intervene when things go unpredictably wrong and secure a provisional solution' (P. Waddington 1983a: 34). In this analogy, they are neither service-station mechanics nor car-makers. But, like the AA, they have a role in advising on policy relevant to their duties and cooperating with other agencies.

The influential 'new left–realist' school of criminologists in Britain argued for a 'minimalist' policing approach (Kinsey *et al.* 1986). They argued that police intervention should be confined to cases where there was clear evidence of law-breaking, and then should take the form of the invocation of legal powers and criminal process (Johnston 2000: 48–50). Only in this way, it was claimed, could police work be fully accountable to the law. This ignores, however, the large bulk of calls for service which are not unequivocally reports of crime. On a 'minimalist' strategy this would mean either not responding to such requests, or forcing the police response into a Procrustean bed of legalism untempered by discretion.

Recent empirical work suggests that a growing proportion of calls for police service, at least in urban areas, are indeed reports of crime or 'potential crime' (T. Jones *et al.* 1986; Shapland and Vagg 1988: 36–9; Shapland and Hobbs 1989. This is also true in a number of other countries; see Bayley 1985: 120–7). This may partly be a result of reconceptualization of some types of incident (such as domestic disputes) into the criminal category, by citizens, police, and researchers. The classification of domestic dispute calls into the 'service' category by early researchers, following the lead of traditional police culture, was of course quite wrong. Such calls, and those to other conflicts, are actual or potential crimes. It is also clear, however, that criminal victimization has been rising since the early police studies, at any rate until the mid-1990s, as well as more being reported by victims (Reiner 2007a: chap. 3). Certainly recorded crime rates have risen dramatically and constitute a greater pressure on the police. Forces have responded by increasing the number of specialists with law-enforcement functions (Dorn *et al.* 1991a, 1991b; Audit Commission 1993; Loveday 1997, 2006; Murji 1998; Maguire 2000). Nonetheless uniformed patrol still constitutes the bulk of personnel deployment (Tarling 1988: 5; Bayley 1994; Morgan and Newburn 1997; Skogan and Frydl 2004: 57–63; Mawby and Wright 2008: 231–3, 238–41), augmented in recent years by the advent of the police 'extended family' notably the Police Community Support Officers created by the Police Reform Act 2002 (Johnston 2007), of which there were over 16,500 in March 2009 (*Police Service Strength 13/09 England and Wales* Home Office 2009: 1). As discussed earlier, under both the Conservatives and Labour, during the 1990s government sought to define the police mandate in crime-control terms. However, uniformed patrol remains the bedrock of policing, and this will continue to be preoccupied with order maintenance, rather than criminal investigation. This is recognized in the emphasis given in recent years to the 'neighbourhood policing' programme and the 'reassurance agenda', although these are discussed almost entirely in terms of security against threats of crime and antisocial behaviour. 'Neighbourhood policing today is about fighting crime more intelligently and building a new relationship between the police and the public—one based on active co-operation rather than simple consent' (*Neighbourhood Policing your police; your community; our commitment* Home Office 2005: 5).

It has recently been argued in an influential study that in contemporary 'risk society' the police task has shifted away from being primarily order maintenance or crime control (Ericson and Haggerty 1997), and this has become an increasingly influential perspective (Johnston 2000; Wright 2002: chap. 5; Rowe 2008: chap. 9). The police have become knowledge workers, whose main function is to broker information about risks to public and private organizations concerned with the regulation and governance of people and territories. Ericson and Haggerty provide a rich account of police work involving the accumulation, analysis, and transmission of knowledge about risk to other institutions, and the impact of IT on this. Their analysis is based on extensive observation and interviews, and certainly establishes the significance of risk-related information processing in contemporary policing. However, the extent to which this has supplanted order maintenance or crime control remains debatable. Their data was derived from theoretical sampling of police with 'knowledge–work roles' (Ericson and Haggerty 1997: 128). This concentration on what they regard as the prototypical aspects of policing is theoretically justifiable to allow analysis of police knowledge–work. It does mean, however, that the material cannot itself establish empirically the extent to which this now characterizes police work in general. In any event, the police function of knowledge-brokering derives from their traditional patrolling and surveillance activities, and their power as the specialist carriers of the state's monopoly of legitimate force. It is this that gives them uniquely privileged access to risk knowledge. Order maintenance remains the core function of the police, and one which they are still primarily deployed towards.

Both the Bittner conception of policing as emergency order maintenance deploying the capacity for legitimate force, and Ericson and Haggerty's analysis of policing as risk information-brokering, agree that popular and political notions of the police as crime-fighters do not accord with what the police actually do, or what they are called upon to do in practice. The justifying *raison d'être* of the new police was indeed the prevention of crime, and this remains the dominant representation of policing in the media, which is the main source of information about the police for most people (Fitzgerald *et al.* 2002; J. Allen *et al.* 2006: Table 2.21). But in practice, once the resource of patrolling officers was established, the effective demand for them expressed by calls and other public-initiated contacts, as distinct from the abstract demand for them reported in surveys of what the public expect of the police, is not mainly crime related. The paradox is that what the police have in practice been called on to do the most—responding to people in trouble of diverse kinds of emergency, is castigated as 'fire-brigade' policing—and police reforms have been dedicated primarily to boosting their performance in reducing and clearing-up crime. To regard the primary task of the police as crime control comes at the expense of their more diffuse peacekeeping role. It poses dangers, not least for the police themselves, for there are inherent limitations to the possibilities of substantial crime reduction through policing. Seeing crime as the be all and end all of the police mission is to dispatch them to pursue a quixotic impossible dream.

HOW EFFECTIVE ARE THE POLICE?

The police were part of a process that made cities less violent, crime ridden, and disorderly during the nineteenth century. The precise contribution of the police to this, compared with general processes of social pacification, is hard to pinpoint, but it was probably significant. The impact–effect of creating a regularly patrolling force increased the risks facing offenders at least for a time. The nineteenth-century police established a baseline of order and crime control that their presentday counterparts continue to maintain more or less successfully.

Since the Second World War in most industrial countries there has been a dramatic rise in recorded crime rates (alleviated in the last fifteen years, but likely to be resumed in the wake of the 'credit crunch'), public fear of crime, and anxiety about law and order as a public issue (I. Taylor 1997; Hollway and Jefferson 1997; Reiner 2007a; Stenson and Sullivan 2001; Garland 2001; Jackson 2004; Downes and Morgan 2007; Hale and Fitzgerald 2009; Farrall *et al.* 2009). Discussions about criminal justice policy have usually reflected the law-and-order myth that given adequate resources and powers the police could tackle the problem of rising crime. The only opposition to the law-and-order lobby was on the civil libertarian principle that police effectiveness must not be bought at too high a price by the undermining of civil rights. However, in the 1970s and 1980s research in the USA and Britain began to question the assumption that increased police power and resources can control crime (R. Clarke and Hough 1980, 1984; P. Morris and Heal 1981; Heal *et al.* 1985; Bayley 1994; Morgan and Newburn 1997). This caution-ary attitude to the effectiveness of increased police spending struck a harmonious note with the fiscal parsimony of the conservative regimes dominant in Britain and North America, if not with their traditional soft spot for the guardians of law and order (Reiner and Cross 1991: chap. 1). It also chimed in with the more general mood of 'nothing works' in criminal justice (S. Cohen 1997a; Garland 2001: 61–3).

STUDIES OF TRADITIONAL POLICING

Patrol studies

Since 1954 many studies have been carried out in the USA and Britain aimed at evaluating the effectiveness of foot and car patrol in crime-control work.[1] The initial American research suggested that crime rates did decline if patrol strength was signifi-cantly increased. However, this early work was flawed methodologically and through data-rigging by the police (P. Morris and Heal 1981: 21–2). Some small-scale research conducted by the Home Office in the 1960s suggested that when an officer was intro-duced to patrol a hitherto uncovered beat recorded crime decreased, but that there was no significant further reduction from increasing the number of officers on the beat (P. Morris and Heal 1981). The most sophisticated study of motorized patrol was the celebrated Kansas City preventive patrol experiment (Kelling *et al.* 1974). This eval-uated the effects of systematically varying patrol strengths between five sets of three beats, matched demographically, in crime rates, and in patterns of demand for police services. In each set one beat was chosen at random for 'normal' levels of patrol and acted as 'control' beat. Another set was designated for 'proactive' patrol, and patrolled two or three times as frequently as the 'controls'. In the third set 'reactive' patrol was carried out, with cars entering only in response to specific calls for service. The study found no significant differences between the areas in reported crime, rates of victi-mization, levels of citizen fear, or satisfaction with the police. It was as if the level of preventive patrol made no difference to any policy goals at all. The experiment was subject to methodological criticism by Larson (1976) and others (Skogan and Frydl 2004: 226), who claimed that the design of the study was not adhered to in practice, and visible police presence in the experimental and control areas was much the same. But the study (after some very hostile early responses from American police chiefs) came to be generally accepted as establishing that increasing car patrol by itself (at least within feasible limits) is not significantly related to crime levels.

Nor is this surprising:

Crimes are rare events and are committed stealthily—as often as not in places out of reach of patrols. The chances of patrols catching offenders red-handed are therefore small ... a patrolling policeman in London could expect to pass within 100 yards of a burglary in progress roughly once every eight years—but not necessarily to catch the burglar or even realize that the crime was taking place. (Clarke and Hough 1984: 6–7)

If the preventive patrol car does not have much of a 'scarecrow' function and is unlikely to come across crimes in progress, might not faster response to emergency calls increase the chances of apprehending criminals? After all, many of the technological developments in policing in the last twenty years—cars, radios, command and control computers—have been geared to this end. But again, research suggests that few if any offenders are caught as a result of faster response by police. The main reason is that most offences (70–85 per cent) are discovered some time after the event, and most victims do not call the police immediately (R. Clarke and Hough 1984: 8–9). There is some evidence, however, that if fast response can be directed accurately to the minority of cases reported while they are in progress it can make an impact (Jordan 1998: 69; Skogan and Frydl 2004: 226–7).

In recent years it has commonly been argued that car patrol may even be counter-productive with regard to crime control. It cuts the police off from non-adversarial contacts with the public, thus reducing cooperation and information flow. Cars may also accentuate the hedonistic action elements in police culture, producing a fruitless overreaction to incidents (Holdaway 1977, 1983).

The limited utility (and evident expense) of car patrol stimulated a renewed enthusiasm for foot patrol in Britain and the USA. Early studies of foot patrol suggested it was no more effective than motorized patrol (Clarke and Hough 1984: 6). But the 1981 Police Foundation study of foot patrol (based on surveys in twenty-eight cities and an experiment in Newark, New Jersey) had modestly encouraging results. The Newark experiment was based on sets of matched beats of which some were randomly to discontinue foot patrol, some to continue it, and some to introduce it for the first time. Crime levels (measured by victimization surveys and recorded crime rates) were not affected by the varied patrol methods. But in other respects the foot patrols had beneficial effects. Fear of crime declined, confidence in neighbourhood safety increased, and citizens evaluated police services more positively. Foot-patrol officers were more satisfied with their work, had a more benign view of citizens, a more community-oriented conception of policing, and lower absenteeism rates. However, the study was not able to indicate whether these attitudes led to or resulted from the officers' assignment to foot patrol. Altogether, while confirming that polic-ing had little impact on crime rates per se, the foot-patrol experiment did imply that it had a beneficial impact on the communal sense of security and order.

The research inspired the highly influential 'broken windows' hypothesis, that policing *could* impact on crime by preventing spirals of neighbourhood decline through timely intervention to prevent minor nuisances tipping over into broader, more embedded, and serious problems (J. Wilson and Kelling 1982; Skogan 1990; Kelling and Coles 1998). This idea was the theoretical inspiration for what came to be known in the 1990s as 'zero tolerance' policing (Bowling 1999b; Dennis 1998; R. Burke 1998, 2004; Weatheritt 1998; Innes 1999a; Stenson 2001; Dixon and Maher 2005; Jones and

Newburn 2006b: chap. 6; Punch 2007). It has also informed New Labour's emphasis on its antisocial behaviour and respect agendas, from the 1998 Crime and Disorder Act onwards (Ramsay 2004, 2008; Hough *et al.* 2005; Crawford 2007: 886–7; Squires 2008; Millie 2008; Burney 2009). For all its influence on policy-makers and its popularity with the media searching for quick fixes, the empirical and theoretical basis for the 'broken windows' thesis has been effectively challenged (Sampson and Raudenbush 1999; Harcourt 2001; Taylor 2001; Crawford 2007a: 886–7; von Hirsch and Simester 2006; Bottoms 2007: 553–7; Sampson 2009).

The hypothesis that there is a causal link between minor disorder or incivilities and higher levels of more serious crime at the very least needs considerable qualification. The ecological association between areas suffering from 'broken windows' and crime is the product of structural and consequent cultural features of deprived and excluded neighbourhoods, such as poverty and lack of 'collective efficacy', trust and cohesion, resulting in both high crime *and* disorder (Sampson and Raudenbusch 1999). The interpretation of physical occurrences such as the legendary 'broken windows' as signs of broader danger and trouble is also a much more complex and contingent process, varying not only because of subtle social psychological processes, but with demographic factors (ethnicity, gender, age, class), historical cultural residues about the characteristics of places, personal and collective experiences and perceptions of wider insecurities such as unemployment or cultural change (Girling *et al.* 2000; Sampson 2009). The development of the 'signal crimes' perspective by Nigel Fielding and Martin Innes, which analyses the capacity of specific types of minor nuisance, disorder or crime to act as symbols of much deeper threats, has informed the government's recognition of this in the reassurance agenda, and the subsequent neighbourhood policing and community safety programmes (Innes and Fielding 2002; Innes 2003b, 2006; Crawford 2007). Whether these will succeed in diminishing crime and disorder and producing a greater public sense of security has yet to be seen. For all the merits of the initiatives themselves they are going to be confronting more adverse circumstances as the post-2007 economic collapse exacerbates the structural sources of crime and disorder.

The possibilities of limiting crime by routine police patrol strategies remain limited, for reasons spelled out years ago by the Audit Commission (Audit Commission 1996; Morgan and Newburn 1997: 126). They calculated that on then current police strength, a patrolling officer typically covers an area containing: 18,000 inhabitants, 7,500 houses, 23 pubs, 9 schools, 140 miles of pavement, 85 acres of parks or open space, and 77 miles of road. The clear lesson is that the number of potential targets of crime, especially in urban areas, is simply too large to be effectively covered by police patrols of any feasible visibility and frequency. Limited police resources can be proactively focused on the most probable targets for criminal victimization or offending through intelligence or crime-pattern analysis improving the impact of policing (Maguire 2000, 2008; Tilley 2008; Ratcliffe 2008), but even the most effective policing within feasible levels of resourcing cannot achieve miracles unless wider economic, social, and cultural currents are flowing in their favour, as happened during the late nineteenth and early-twentieth centuries.

The persistent popular faith in police patrol as a guarantor of safety is no doubt encouraged by the consequences of two extreme levels of policing presence. Police strikes have often been associated with greater crime and disorder (Skogan and Frydl 2004: 224), suggesting that in the complete absence of police danger rules. It is worth noting, however, that this experience is not universal. There have been some police strikes, even in large cities—notably London in 1918—that did not result in any discernible increase in crime (Reiner 1978: 5–6). The relationship between withdrawal of police and crime is not inevitable, but shaped by other social and cultural factors.

On the other hand, the popular gut feeling that if only there was a police officer at every doorstep crime would disappear (however undesirable and indeed impossible such omnipresent policing might be) is supported by recent econometric studies showing reductions of routine crime during saturation policing in the wake of terrorist attacks or alarms (Di Tella and Schargrodsky 2004; Klick and Tabarrok 2005; Draca *et al.* 2008). Fascinating as the recent terrorism policing results are, it is problematic to extrapolate from the very sharp short-run visible increases in police that they analyse to the consequences of the more modest variations in cover that are economically and politically feasible as long-run levels. The notion that there is a calculable elasticity of crime rates in relation to changes in police numbers that is constant at all levels from zero police to saturation, including the rather thin cover that is the normal experience, is dubious.

Although feasible variations in the quantity of patrol may not affect crime levels, it has long been argued that qualitatively different, innovative policing styles or strategies might do (Wilson 1975: chap. 5; Sherman 1992a, 1993; Sherman *et al.* 1997, 2002; Weisburd and Eck 2004). I shall examine the evidence about this after considering research on the effectiveness of traditional detective work.

STUDIES OF DETECTION

The lack of success of criminal investigation work is in one sense apparent from the low (and declining) proportion of crimes reported to the police that are cleared up. Before the Second World War the clear-up rate for recorded offences was usually over 50 per cent, but it is now down to 28 per cent (A. Walker *et al.* 2009: 133–4). The clear-up rate varies widely for different crimes. It remains high for homicide (92 per cent), but is lower than in the past for violence against the person (47 per cent), and for sexual offences (31 per cent), mainly because of changes in Home Office counting rules that include less serious instances in these categories and that only look at sanction detections in place of the looser 'cleared-up' classification. Detection rates are far lower for property offences, which constitute the vast majority of all recorded crimes. Sanction detection rates are around 21 per cent for robbery, 13 per cent for burglary, 11 per cent for thefts of or from cars, and 14 per cent for criminal damage (A. Walker *et al.* 2009: 136).

The clear-up rate is a notoriously problematic measure of detective effectiveness, although considerable steps have been taken to improve matters—at the cost of making the figures look worse (Audit Commission 1990b; Gill 1997; Maguire 2007). For one thing the denominator—crimes known to the police—can vary independently of offending behaviour if a higher or lower proportion of victimizations is reported by the public and/or recorded by the police. The British Crime Surveys show that fluctuations in victim reporting and police recording practices have indeed been major factors underlying the rise of recorded crime rates in recent decades, as well as the fall in the mid-1990s (Hough and Mayhew 1983; Reiner 2007a: chap. 3; A. Walker *et al.* 2009: 24–42). The falling clear-up rate is in large part a reflection of rising recorded crime levels rather than declining detective efficiency. Since the 1970s police manpower has increased, from around 107,000 to 141,859 on 31 March 2009 (Reiner 2007: 134–5; Bullock 2008), but the absolute number of crimes cleared up increased even more, so that crimes cleared-up per officer has grown. This may indicate an increase in detective efficiency, despite the fall in the proportion of recorded crimes cleared up. One British study has attempted to quantify the relationship between possible increases in manpower and likely improvements in clearup rates. From a comparison of the clearup rates of different forces in England and Wales, this concluded that a 10 per cent increase in overall manpower, directed entirely to the CID, would raise the clear-up rate by less than 1 per cent (Burrows and Tarling 1982; Tarling and Burrows 1985).

It is, however, fundamentally problematic to see the clear-up rate in itself as an index of police efficiency or effectiveness. Studies of the work of detectives show that many, probably most, of the crimes recorded as cleared up are not solved as a result of investigative effort. Only a relatively small number of major incident enquiries fit the model of 'classical' detection, starting from the crime itself and systematically investigating those with motive and opportunity to commit it (Maguire and Norris 1992; Ericson 1993; Innes 2003a, 2007; Maguire 2008).

Critical analysis of police investigative activity has indicated that it much of it traditionally follows one of two patterns, both of which have the discriminatory and invidious social consequences of stigmatization and criminalization of vulnerable groups through a process of 'deviance amplification' (Matza 1969; J. Young 1971). The first method is what Matza called the 'bureaucratic' mode, which echoes the famous lines uttered at the end of *Casablanca* by police chief Claude Rains: 'Round up the usual suspects.' In this mode successful detection depends upon knowledge of persistent offenders or of the 'underworld' (Hobbs 1988, 1995). Crimes are solved by culling the group of people 'known' to commit offences of a certain type, or by cultivation of informants. The second method is that of stereotyping and suspicion. People are apprehended because they fit the investigator's preconceived notion of particular kinds of offender. Vice work is especially likely to rely on both the bureaucratic and suspicion methods, because the discovery and clear-up of vice offences relies entirely upon proactive policing as there are no cooperating 'victims'. Similarly, the more minor and vague 'public order' offences, which form a high proportion of patrol arrests, are heavily dependent on 'suspicion'. But the majority of offences are not cleared up by either of these modes of detection.

A major finding of studies of the process by which detectives clear up crimes is that information is their lifeblood (Gill 2000; John and Maguire 2003, 2007; Maguire

2008). The quality and quantity of information immediately provided by members of the public (usually the victim) to patrol officers or detectives when they arrive at the scene of a crime is a prime determinant of success. If adequate information is provided to pinpoint the culprit fairly accurately, the crime will be resolved; if not, it is almost certain not to be (Chatterton 1976; Sanders 1977; Greenwood *et al.* 1977; Bottomley and Coleman 1981; Burrows and Tarling 1982; Maguire and Norris 1992; Innes 2003a, 2007; Foster 2008). The crucial importance of initial information highlights not only the central role of the public in clearing up offences, but also the important part played by the uniformed branch. Nearly two-thirds of crimes are cleared up almost immediately, as a result of the offender still being at the scene when the police arrived, or being named or fully and accurately described by victim or witnesses (Steer 1980). In such cases, however, the task of detectives may be far from straightforward, as they will be responsible for working up the case for court (Maguire 2008: 440–1).

With serious crimes, especially homicide, even if a suspect is indicated from the outset, a major enquiry team will be set to process it, under the leadership of a senior investigating officer (Smith and Flanagan 2000). In the case of 'self-solvers' this will be small scale and probably shortlived. But in those serious cases that detectives call 'who-dunits', where the culprit is not known, the major enquiry team will be larger scale and depending on the nature of the case—how much publicity it attracts, if it appears to be part of a series so there is continuing danger to the public, how intractable it proves—the team may continue for months or even years in rare instances (Innes 2003a, 2007).

The routine work of detectives is handled in local CID offices who will receive reports of crimes recorded every day. Most will not offer any serious leads and will be tacitly dropped. The need to grade cases more formally according to their prospects of solvability became apparent during the 1980s as crime levels grew and so did the pressure on the police to enhance their appearance of efficiency, effectiveness, and economy. But first attempts to screen out cases according to explicit criteria of formality attracted condemnation when they were revealed to the public. However, as New Public Management (NPM), target specification, and monitoring intensified in the 1990s, more formalized systems came to be adopted, culminating in the 2000s when a formal operating system, the Volume Crime Management model (VCMM) became standard. This is based on 'a crime management unit which oversees key functions carried out by a number of specialist units . . . call handling, initial scene attendance, crime screening, forensics, suspect handling and evidence review' (Maguire 2008: 452–3). Some types of crime come to be deemed so important that they become the subject of specialist squads. Such specialist squads to deal with vice, drugs, and other specific offence types have been common in local forces for decades (Lee and South 2008: 501–4). Since 1964 when nine regional crime squads were established to target organized crime that was thought to be becoming more mobile across force boundaries, there has been an a movement to greater inter-force coordinated specialist squads. This culminated in the 1970s in the establishment of national units such as the Central Drugs and Immigration Unit at Scotland Yard. In the 1990s these were superseded by the National Criminal Intelligence Unit (1992) and the National Crime Squad (1998). Both were incorporated into the Serious and Organised Crime Agency in 2005, which is 'a new hybrid policing and intelligence agency' (Lee and South 2008: 503), representing 'a paradigm shift in policing' (Harfield 2006) aimed at harm reduction rather than law enforcement (Levi 2007: 772). It has both national responsibilities to tackle high-level crime and a global scope as the UK office for Interpol and Europol, forming the main UK node in the proliferating network of international policing cooperation (Sheptycki 2002, 2007; Goldsmith and Sheptycki 2007; Walker 2008; Bowling 2009).

Research in the past has emphasized the significant proportion of crimes deemed to be cleared up by 'secondary' means, that is the questioning of suspects and offenders in order to elicit admissions that they have committed other crimes for which they will not be charged separately. Before the Police and Criminal Evidence Act 1984 (PACE) some studies suggested that as many as 40 per cent of property offences were cleared up by being 'taken into consideration' (TIC) when offenders were sentenced for other offences (Lambert 1970). Steer (1980) and Bottomley and Coleman (1981) found a lower proportion of TICs (20 and 25 per cent, respectively), and nationally, around 26 per cent of clear-ups were by TIC (Burrows and Tarling 1982). PACE made it harder to use legally dubious 'tactics' of interviewing suspects which had led them to admit large numbers of offences to be TIC (Irving and McKenzie 1989). This has resulted in the development of new techniques of investigative interviewing seeking to respect legal and ethical criteria (Williamson 2006; Gudjonsson 2007). Only about 8 per cent of clear-ups are now by TIC according to the BCS (A. Walker *et al.* 2009: 134).

Scandals about manipulation of the clear-ups attributed to TIC and 'prison write-offs' (where detectives question convicted prisoners in order to get them to admit other offences) have occurred regularly. A prominent example occurred in Kent in the late 1980s (*Observer* 8 October 1989). Such dubious ways of clearing the books by massaging the statistics had been rife for many years in other forces (P. Gill 1987; M. Young 1991; H. Taylor 1998a, 1998b, 1999). Revelations in several forces in the late 1990s suggested that the government's increasing emphasis on meeting performance targets may have led to the revival of statistical book-cooking (Davies 1999b). Indeed a police force that is assiduous in its crime recording may appear inefficient in comparison with less scrupulous neighbours (Farrington and Dowds 1985). The Home Office recently switched to publishing clear-up rates mainly in terms of 'sanction detections', i.e. ones where there is a formal sanction of some sort attached, but this includes TICs (A. Walker *et al.* 2009: 132).

Thus only a small proportion of crimes are cleared up by investigative techniques bearing any resemblance to either the 'classical' or the 'bureaucratic' modes beloved by fiction. Most solved cases are essentially self-clearing. This does not mean that detectives are useless or inefficient. 'The detective has a variety of skills. These include gathering information from the public; locating suspects; interviewing and, on the basis of information derived from both the public and suspects, of preparing cases for the prosecution' (P. Morris and Heal 1981: 33). There is also of course the relatively small but significant category of cases where the perpetrator is not initially known ('whodunits' in detectives' jargon) but are nonetheless successfully cleared up by methods including the 'classical' and 'bureaucratic' modes and the construction and exploration of possible narratives explaining the crime (Innes 2003a, 2007). However, the pressure on detectives to achieve more 'primary' clear-ups (not based on post-arrest or sentence interviewing) has led to increasing use of innovative methods which may themselves be ethically, legally, and practically problematic. These include proactive tactics such as undercover work, technological surveillance, and informers who are themselves offenders (Marx 1988, 1992; Audit Commission 1993; Greer 1995; Maguire and John 1996a, 1996b; Fijnaut and Marx 1996; Sheptycki 2000; Norris and Armstrong 1999; Dunnighan and Norris 1999; Norris and Dunnighan 2000; Heaton 2000; Maguire 2000; Billingsley *et al.* 2000; Clark 2007). There is scope for more effective management and coordination of the detective function (Maguire 2008), especially through 'case-screening' to distinguish crimes according to 'solvability' (and whether they should be allocated to CID or uniformed branches for investigation), more professional leadership of major enquiries (Smith and Flanagan 2000), and more effective proactive 'targeting' of some serious offences and offenders (Cope 2008). However, given the proliferation of recorded crimes and other demands for service relative to police resources (Audit Commission 1993; R. Morgan and Newburn 1997: 57), and the constraints on legitimate tactics in a liberal democracy (Weisburd *et al.* 1993), the prospects of successful investigation will always be limited.

INNOVATORY POLICING STRATEGIES

The evaluative research showing that old police tactics have little effect in reducing crime stimulated advocacy of a variety of innovative policing strategies. Three broad strands can be distinguished in these innovative approaches: 'hard cop', 'good cop', and 'smart cop'. Each of these is pitched at remedying a key perceived defect of traditional patrol and detective work. In practice, they frequently are combined or merge into each other.

Hard cop

Hard-cop tactics are premised on the assumption that over sensitivity to civil liberties, human rights, 'political correctness' have undermined police effectiveness by restraining their use of forceful and vigorous tactics (Hitchens 2003). An early version proposed in the 1970s was 'aggressive' patrol, championed by James Q. Wilson in the USA. A cross-sectional study of twenty-three police departments purported to show that patrol aggressiveness produced a greater likelihood of arrests for robbery, and thus lower robbery rates through a deterrent effect (J. Wilson and Boland 1978). The findings were criticized by a later study which showed that robbery rates increased (rather than declined) with greater police expenditure over time (Jacob and Rich 1980). Wilson and Boland's (1981) reply argued that their thesis concerned the effects on crime of aggressive patrol as a structural characteristic of departmental style, and was not refuted by longitudinal data about relatively small, short-term fluctuations in police expenditure. However as Jacob and Rich replied (1981), this limits the significance of the original claim. 'Aggressive' patrol becomes not a readily adoptable tactic, but a structural element of departmental style which can be altered (if at all) only in line with more fundamental reforms of municipal government and wider socio-political change. Subsequent reviews of experiments targeting 'hot spots' for aggressive crackdowns suggested some success, but primarily if tougher policing was combined with problem-solving approaches of a broader kind (Sherman 1992a; Jordan 1998; Skogan and Frydl 2004: 236–40).

A substantial absolute number of mainly petty offences can be uncovered by stop-and-search methods (P. Waddington 1999a: 50). However, as the 'hit' rate of successful searches is usually small (less than one in ten) the price in alienation of some sections of the public (primarily young males, especially blacks) is very high. After the disastrous 'Operation Swamp', a saturation police operation aimed at reducing robbery, which was launched shortly before the 1981 Brixton riots and widely regarded as a pre-cipitating factor, the British police broadly accepted Lord Scarman's message, which was reinforced by the 1999 Macpherson Report on the Stephen Lawrence case. Any marginal gains in law enforcement due to aggressive tactics are not worth the cost in endangering public tranquillity. However, the pressure induced by the heating up of the politics of law and order in the 1990s undercut this, and has been accentuated by concerns about terrorism in the 2000s, so stop-and-search powers and tactics have expanded.

'Hard cop' tactics were epitomized in the 1990s and early 2000s by the espousal around the world by some politicians, police chiefs, and much of the media of the sup-posed effectiveness of zero-tolerance policing (Jones and Newburn 2006: chap. 6). Many claimed that the celebrated crime drop in NYC was due to zero tolerance (Dennis 1998). However, close analysis did not confirm this, as the timing of the New York City fall did not fit the zero-tolerance explanation (Bowling 1999b; Karmen 2000). Crime also fell in other US cities where zero tolerance had not been adopted (and indeed fell around the world in the 1990s), albeit usually not as sharply as in New York, suggesting the drop had wider and multiple sources (R. Burke 1998, 2004; Weatheritt 1998; Karmen 2000; Levitt 2004; Dixon and Maher 2005; Eck and Maguire 2006; Zimring 2007; Punch 2007). 'Zero tolerance', i.e. strict enforcement of minor 'quality of life' offences, was itself part of broader changes in New York policing, including hiring more police, and above all rigorous performance management through Compstat which owed more to the other innovative models (Weisburd *et al.* 2003; Moore 2003). Zero tolerance is not really a transportable model except as rhetoric promoting more vigorous use of police powers: full enforcement of all laws all the time is a logical and economic impossibility. Zero tolerance, like all aggressive tactics has a downside of exacerbating brutality, discrimina-tion, and alienation of those targeted so it might in the longer term increase crime.

Good cop

'Good cop' strategies were epitomized by community policing, which as argued earlier has no clear central definition, but plays pleasant mood music of peace and goodwill that's hard to resist. It is predicated on an analysis of the ills of contemporary policing as due to declining public consent and cooperation. It thus aims to restore legitimacy and public support, partly to enhance crime control through encouraging cooperation, partly as good in itself. Community-oriented strategies became the central post-Scarman orthodoxy in

Britain, and increasingly throughout the world. As one review put it trenchantly: 'police departments in the western world can only remain legitimate if they genuflect before the altar of "community policing"' (Herbert 2000: 114).

The team-policing schemes that flourished in the USA in the early 1970s were progenitors of this approach, but had ambiguous messages (Skogan and Frydl 2004: 182–3). The problem was that they were never really tried. Initial indications about crime rates and community cooperation were encouraging; but organizational problems, in particular lower-rank hostility, frustrated full sustained implementation. Unfortunately this has been echoed by many subsequent evaluations of similar community-oriented approaches.

Community-policing schemes have proliferated since the 1980s in several American cities under a number of progressive police chiefs (Skolnick and Bayley 1986, 1988). While there have been some notable success stories, the outcome of community policing in the USA remains uncertain and variable (Bayley 1994, 1998; Skogan and Hartnett 1997; Herbert 1997, 2000; Skogan 2003, 2006; Skogan and Frydl 2004: 232–5).

The record of British initiatives in the community-policing direction is similarly patchy (Tilley 2008: 375–9). Many schemes have received positive in-house evaluations, but these are usually by partisans, and suffer from the 'foregone conclusions' syndrome of predictably happy endings (Weatheritt 1986: 18–19). Independent evaluations of community-policing innovations seem to have the opposite tendency (Pawson and Tilley 1994; Bennett 1994). 'Nothing works' has been the bottom line of studies of a variety of such tactics. These included focused patrol (Chatterton and Rogers 1989), sector policing (B. Dixon and Stanko 1995), and neighbourhood watch (Bennett 1990; McConville and Shepherd 1992).

In many if not most of these cases the problem lies in 'programme failure', difficulties in implementing the schemes as intended, and it is far from established that community-style strategies in general, or specific tactics like neighbourhood watch in particular, cannot work. It is difficult to measure the effect of innovations on broad outcomes like recorded crime or victimization rates, which are affected by numerous factors besides the policing initiative, and truly experimental research designs which could overcome this problem in principle are hard to arrange. This difficulty blights even the one celebrated case of a rigorously evaluated scheme with a positive result: the Kirkholt Burglary Prevention project which used 'cocoon neighbourhood watch', intensive mutual watching of houses immediately adjacent to houses already victimized at least once (Forrester *et al.* 1988). The key to the Kirkholt success was its 'smart' element.

Smart cop

The Kirkholt experiment is a pointer to the key concept on which 'smart' policing initiatives pin their claims. Traditional tactics fail in large part because they spread scarce police resources much too thinly across all victims, targets, and perpetrators of crime, whether in the form of preventive or detective activities. Improvements in crime reduction and detection can occur through proactive, problem-oriented, and intelligence-led approaches (A. Leigh *et al.* 1996; Maguire 2000, 2008; Williamson 2008; Tilley 2008; Cope 2008; Ratcliffe 2008). 'Smart' policing hopes that by analysing crime and disorder patterns it is possible to target prevention and detection efforts at the most likely victims and offenders. This would allow adequate levels of protection to be offered to the most likely victims, and the apprehension of offenders together with sufficient evidence to achieve convictions. While such approaches are likely to be more effective than traditional ones, there remains doubt about their efficacy in achieving substantial degrees of crime reduction (Jordan 1998). There is also considerable potential for unethical practices and encroachments on civil liberties, for example through intrusive forms of surveillance, and the abuse of informers and other undercover tactics (Marx 1988, 1992; Greer 1995; Fijnaut and Marx 1996; Norris and Armstrong 1999; Norris and Dunnighan 2000; Sheptycki 2000b, 2000c; Billingsley *et al.* 2000; Goold 2004, 2009). Nonetheless, government's search for 'magic bullets' has encouraged the proliferation of such approaches.

A crucial difficulty in evaluating policing innovations is the absence of reliable and valid measures of police performance (Reiner 1998). One of the most methodologically self-conscious projects to evaluate policing initiatives concluded that measures of good practice could be developed meaningfully only in relation to specific areas of police work, not globally, and were inescapably political (Horton 1989). Nonetheless, since the 1980s successive governments' hunt for value for money in public services has led to the search for more adequate performance indicators in policing (Audit Commission 1990a, 1990b). HM Inspectorate of Constabulary in particular have developed an ever more elaborate matrix of indicators for their annual assessments of forces (Bradley *et al.* 1986; Hough 1987; Weatheritt 1993; Butler 1992; R. Morgan and Newburn 1997; Savage *et al.* 2000: chap. 1; Savage 2007: chaps. 3, 5). It is unlikely that these have overcome the possibly intractable problems of measuring police effectiveness.

Altogether research on crime control implies that the police more or less successfully maintain a bedrock of effectiveness. Neither more of the same nor any innovative tactics are likely to improve their capacity for detection or prevention to any substantial degree. Crime levels are the product of a variety of factors and processes: labelling i.e. shifting definitions of criminality; social, economic, cultural, psychological pressures, and seductions shaping motivations towards crime; the ebb and flow of opportunities and means to offend; the varying constraints of informal as well as formal controls (Reiner 2007: chap. 4). Policing is only one aspect of the last of these. Although obviously it is impossible to calculate this, we can conceive of societies at particular times having long-run equilibrium levels of 'normal' crime, shaped by all these processes. Poor policing may result in higher, pathological levels of 'surplus' crime, and police reform in such a context can appear to produce spectacular results by returning the level to its base of normality (perhaps this accounts for some of the New York 'miracle' in the 1990s). And especially smart or tough policing may suppress the rate below the long-run norm. But this would be vulnerable to failures of police to maintain their supercharged form, or to exacerbated crime pressures, for example because of economic downturns. This is not to argue that police do not have many indispensable functions: responding to a variety of troubles, including crimes, and symbolizing social concern for justice and for the plight of victims. But it is chimerical to see them as *the* primary means of controlling crime levels.

HOW FAIR ARE THE POLICE?

Perceptions of injustice or discrimination in policing have perennially been the most potent threat to their legitimacy. Since the 'discovery' by early research on the police that they routinely exercise considerable discretion in enforcing the law, there has been a plethora of work on the pattern and determinants of this. A central concern has been the question whether discretion really meant discrimination. Do police discriminate against ethnic and other minorities, women, and the socially less powerful, when dealing with them as suspects, victims, or fellow employees?

RACE AND POLICING

What is discrimination?

This issue is more complex and harder to resolve than most polemics imply. Contrary to the implications of much radical criticism of the police, the evidence of a pattern of social differentiation in the use of police powers from which the young, the lower working class, and blacks suffer most—although undeniable—does not in itself establish discrimination (D. J. Smith 1997; P. Waddington 1999a: 49–50; Webster 2007). The radical critique implies that the differential exercise of police powers against the socially disadvantaged and relatively powerless is the product of bias, stereotyping, and the amplification of the apparent deviance of these groups (D. Chapman 1968; Cashmore and McLaughlin 1991). On the other hand, more conservative writers claim that this unjustly vilifies the police. The differential exercise of powers reflects not police discrimination but the varying deviance of different social groups (Wilbanks 1987). If studies of police culture reveal hostile attitudes to minority groups, this may be the product, not the determinant of police work (P. Waddington 1999a: 118–19). Both positions embody an element of truth, but it has been clouded by abrasive either/or polemics. There is a complex interaction between police discrimination and the differential criminogenic pressures experienced by different social groups (Jefferson 1993; Reiner 1989a, 1993; Fitzgerald 2001, 2009).

Some terminological issues must be resolved before the evidence can be reviewed, because the debates are hugely vexed by competing, contradictory, and confused usage of key concepts. I shall adopt the following definitions:

(a) 'Prejudice': the belief that all or most members of a particular group have certain negative attributes, a preconception which is carried into encounters with individuals in the category who may or may not actually have these traits. Examples are 'The people here are animals' (constable, quoted in Reiner 1978: 80), and 'All coppers are bastards'.

(b) 'Bias': the view that some types of people should have preferential treatment because of inherently superior entitlement, regardless of merit or specific conduct.

(c) 'Differentiation': a pattern of exercise of police powers against particular social categories, which varies from their representation in the population (such as a disproportionate arrest rate of young black males).

(d) 'Discrimination': a pattern of exercise of police powers which results in some social categories being overrepresented as targets of police action even when legally relevant variables (especially the pattern of offending) are held constant.

The attitudinal characteristics of prejudice and bias may, but need not, result in differentiation or discrimination. They may not be translated into action if legal, ethical, organizational, or situational constraints preclude this. Nor does differentiation necessarily indicate discrimination. It may result from legally relevant differences between groups, for example, varying patterns of offending.

Types of discrimination

Even when the police do discriminate, in the sense of treating people differently without any legal justification, this may not be the product of prejudice, bias, or unilateral police decision-making. It can be the product of situational, interactional, or institutional processes that result in discriminatory treatment by the police of different groups, even though there is no intention or wish to do so. Anti-discrimination law operates with a binary distinction: direct vs. indirect. According to the Department of Business, Innovation and Skills, 'Direct discrimination means treating one person less favourably than another on the grounds of sex, race, disability, sexual orientation, religion/belief, or age. . . . Direct discrimination may be overt or covert'. Indirect discrimination is defined as: 'applying a provision, criterion or practice which disadvantages people of a particular group (defined by sex, race, disability, sexual orientation, religious belief or age). Indirect discrimination is illegal if it cannot be justified as a proportionate means of achieving a legitimate aim'. This is close to the sociological definition of institutional discrimination discussed below.

The legal categories are essentially normative. Discrimination occurs if someone belonging to certain groups is treated less favourably than those from other groups, irrespective of motive or whether the differentiation was 'direct' or 'indirect'. The only justification would be a normative one based on the legitimate requirements of the relevant selection process. So it is no defence to say that a black person was arrested because an officer genuinely believed he was more likely to commit crimes, but it would be if she had either actually committed a crime or if there was an objectively reasonable basis for suspicion. Ignoring the motives or processes leading to discrimination may be desirable legally and morally. But in order to understand why discrimination occurs, and thus what policies might reduce or eliminate it, analysing the social and psychological sources of discrimination is important.

Discriminatory processes

It is possible analytically to distinguish at least six types: categorical, statistical, transmitted, interactional, and institutional discrimination (the first two were originally distinguished by Banton 1983).

'*Categorical discrimination*' refers to invidious treatment of members of a group purely on account of their belonging to a certain social category, regardless of the relevance of this to any particular performance criteria. It is the most straightforward, explicit, and direct form of discrimination.

'*Statistical discrimination*' refers to differential treatment of members of a group because of a stereotyped belief that they are disproportionately likely to have certain characteristics, but without reference to the specific behaviour of individual members. An example is police stopping, say, long-haired youths or young black men disproportionately because of the belief that they are more likely to get a 'result'. This does not constitute a legally valid basis for 'reasonable suspicion', and is explicitly ruled out by the Code of Practice on stop-and-search powers under PACE (D. Brown 1997: 20). Nonetheless, it is undoubtedly a tacit, unexpressed factor in stop-and-search practices (ibid.: 22). It is an example of statistical rather than categorical discrimination against black people per se.

'*Transmitted discrimination*' occurs when the police act as a passive conveyor belt for wider social prejudices. For example, white citizens' racial prejudice may make victims label attackers disproportionately as black, leading the police to search for black suspects. The significance of this is indicated by the fact that victim identification of the ethnic group of their assailant (for those offences where there is some contact between them) roughly matches the pattern of stops and arrests (Fitzgerald 1999, 2001; Waddington *et al.* 2004; Henry 2007: 85–7).

'*Interactional discrimination*' results from a process of interaction when non-criminal aspects of the behaviour of a member of the public (say, the rude demeanour of a suspect) produces a differential outcome such as arrest which is dubiously justifiable legally. Observational studies have often noted that a key factor triggering the use of police powers is 'contempt of cop' (P. Waddington 1999a: 153–5). There is substantial evidence that young black men have more negative attitudes than other groups towards the police (Bucke 1996; Clancy *et al.* 2001; Sharp and Atherton 2007), mirroring the long-standing police prejudice directed towards them. It is likely that many police encounters with young black men generate a vicious spiral of hostility culminating in an arrest (D. Brown 1997: 56; Henry 2007: 87–9).

'*Situational discrimination*' occurs when the socio-economic position or lifestyle of members of a group disproportionately expose them as targets of police suspicion. A classic early paper on the sociology of policing noted that legal powers are structured by the institution of privacy, which is itself related to class inequality (Stinchcombe 1963). So someone getting drunk or high on drugs in their living room is unlikely to come to the attention of the police, but the same intoxication in the streets could end up in police custody. A controversial recent example is the concept of 'availability' for stop and search. Much of the disproportionate use of stop and search powers against young, black, and ethnic minority, less affluent men is statistically explained because they spend more of their time in public places than other groups (Fitzgerald 1999, 2001; MVA and Millar 2000; Miller *et al.* 2000; Waddington *et al.* 2004; Delsol and Shiner 2006; Stenson and Waddington 2007; Henry 2007: 84–7; Bowling and Phillips 2007).

'*Institutionalized discrimination*' has been said by sociologists to occur when the consequences of universalistically framed organizational policies or procedures work out in practice as discriminatory, because of the structural bias of an unequal society, or because of inherent but irrelevant differences between different groups. A height requirement for recruitment, for example, means that fewer women or candidates from some ethnic groups will be selected, and is discriminatory if not justifiable by the needs of the work. A policy whereby heavy policing of specific areas was automatically triggered by street crime rates above a standard threshold could be institutionally discriminatory if social and economic discrimination pushed more ethnic minority people into living in deprived high crime areas.

The concept of institutional discrimination has long been a politically controversial one. Lord Scarman considered two possible interpretations in his 1981 Report on the Brixton Disorders. One was official discrimination that occurs 'knowingly, as a matter of policy'; the second was indirect and unintended: 'practices may be adopted by public bodies as well as private individuals which are unwittingly discriminatory' (Scarman 1981: para. 2.22). Scarman adopted the former definition and came to the conclusion that it did not occur in the Metropolitan Police. However, he did clearly show that the police were discriminatory in the second, institutionally mediated, sense. The latter interpretation is the standard one used by most sociological analyses, and I have used it above. The Macpherson report on the Stephen Lawrence case adopted a much wider but more amorphous definition, and concluded that the Met *were* institutionally racist in its sense. Macpherson's definition of 'institutional racism' was: 'The collective failure of an organisation to provide an appropriate and professional service to people because of their colour, culture, or ethnic origin. It can be seen or detected in processes, attitudes and behaviour which amount to discrimination through unwitting prejudice, ignorance, thoughtlessness and racist stereotyping which disadvantages minority ethnic people' (Macpherson 1999: para. 34). It is noteworthy that the emphasis is on failure to provide a service, and this reflects the inquiry's focal concern with the discriminatory treatment of black victims. The discriminatory use of powers against them as suspects, which had been the focus of most controversy until the Lawrence case, is swept into the broader range of discriminatory behaviour in the second sentence. Stress is clearly on the *unconscious* processes that bring about the objectively identifiable outcome of discrimination. But the notion of 'collective failure of an organisation' runs together a variety of different ideas. Does it mean overtly discriminatory organizational policy (the narrow definition suggested by Scarman which he rejected)? Or the concept as

I defined it—the unintended consequences of impartially framed policies? Or that the behaviour of a sufficient number of members is discriminatory, consciously or not, to justify labelling the organization as a whole racist? Or that the organization has failed to train or discipline some members who are racist?

The ambiguity accounts for the polarized response to the verdict. While after varying degrees of soul-searching most police leaders accepted it and the consequent need for radical change, many officers resented the implication of collective guilt. Much hostility to the findings lingers, overtly or in the form of studied misunderstandings (Marlow and Loveday 2000; Foster *et al.* 2005; McLaughlin 2007: chap. 6; Rowe 2007; Loftus 2007, 2008, 2009; Foster 2008). This is in part structured by vested interests, but it is also facilitated by the amorphousness and ambiguity of Macpherson's formulation, which lends itself to criticism even by some who are sympathetic to its intentions (Singh 2000; Lea 2003; Souhami 2007; Stenson and Waddington 2007; Henry 2007: 80; Webster 2007).

Against this it must be stressed that the finding of institutional racism was welcomed by most black and ethnic minority people as an unequivocal vindication of the depth and range of their mistreatment by much policing over decades, as victims, as suspects, and as police officers. The stigmatization clearly acted as a spur to vigorous organisational reform attempts in all police forces, but above all the Met. The Home Affairs Committee's assessment 'Ten Years On' testified to the appreciation of Macpherson that many BME witnesses expressed to it. 'The use of the term "institutional racism" …was absolutely critical in shaking police forces up and down the country out of their complacency. The consequence of that has been that police forces have paid a lot of attention; they have put a lot of resources in' (House of Commons Home Affairs Committee: *Macpherson Report—Ten Years On* 17 August 2009: para. 3). While it has become commonplace to contrast Macpherson favourably with Scarman, largely because of the symbolism of espousing the concept of 'institutional discrimination', this fails to take account of the different political contexts in which they operated and the strengths of Scarman's report itself, which points to issues that Macpherson neglects. Scarman was trying to make comprehensible to a then unreconstructed police force, harbouring racial prejudice at all levels, and to Margaret Thatcher's government in the salad days of its revolutionary fervour, how their policies had resulted in rioting without precedent for a century. His reforms did succeed in changing the culture of at least the senior police ranks to an extent that made them more receptive to Macpherson's blunter verdict. Macpherson by contrast was reporting to the New Labour government in its idealistic early days. Furthermore he was concerned not with widespread violence by police and rioters, but the failure to bring to justice the murderers of an entirely innocent teenager, attacked solely for being black, a model victim—a cause that aroused near-universal public sympathy. Nonetheless, Scarman, who had to soft-peddle the terms in which he couched his criticism of the police (though not the substance), included crucial themes in his analysis that are largely absent from Macpherson. While Macpherson is certainly tough on the police, he is soft on the causes of racist policing. His focus is primarily on the police organization and the individuals within it. Scarman, however, located the

sources of both the rioting and police racism in the wider structures of racism and disadvantage that generated them. Having discussed the concept of discrimination, what
is the empirical evidence about racial discrimination in policing?

Race discrimination in policing: the evidence

All these forms of discrimination may operate at either the policy level of senior echelons
or rank-and-file discretionary decisions on the street. The two are interdependent.
Rank-and-file discrimination, for example, may produce a higher recorded crime rate
in areas with a high black population, which might trigger differential deployment
policies, leading in turn to even higher recorded crime rates.

The weight of the research evidence supports the following propositions:

(1) There is a clear pattern of differentiation in police practice. Young males,
     especially if they are black and/or unemployed or economically marginal, are
     disproportionately subject to the exercise of police powers.

(2) Part of the disproportionate police exercise of powers against young, black,
     economically excluded men can be explained by their disproportionate involve-
     ment in some offences (mainly minor and marginal ones), as a result of their life
     circumstances (Waddington 1999a; Fitzgerald 2009). Even given this, however,
     there is evidence of police discrimination not explicable by differential offending.

(3) Part of this police discrimination is 'transmitted', 'interactional', or
     'institutionalized'; that is, although not based on criteria sanctioned by law, it
     does not result from individual bias. For example, if a person approached by the
     police for a minor offence, over which the officer would normally not proceed,
     fails 'the attitude test' (is not sufficiently deferential) he might be sanctioned
     nominally for the offence, but really for 'contempt of cop'.

(4) However, there is also evidence of 'statistical' and 'categorical' discrimination.
     Statistical discrimination violates legal specifications of adequate grounds for
     'reasonable suspicion', but it arises out of a concern to police effectively. In Shear-
     ing's terminology it is 'organisational police deviance', in that it is 'designed to
     further organisational objectives rather than promote personal gains' (Shearing
     1981b: 2). Statistical discrimination is a good example of what Sir Paul Condon
     referred to as 'noble cause corruption'. 'Categorical' discrimination, the transla-
     tion into practice of bias, is illicit from any point of view. While it is probably a
     significant factor, albeit perhaps not as much as in the past, it is hard to isolate by
     either statistical or observational analysis (Reiner 1993).

(5) The evidence reviewed in Chapter 3 documented police bias and prejudice.
     However, as argued there, these attitudes are not the product of prior peculiari-
     ties of the individual personalities of police officers, but are a reflection of wider
     societal prejudice, accentuated by the characteristics of police work. There is
     also evidence casting doubt on the extent of translation of police prejudice into
     discriminatory practice (Waddington 1999b).

I shall now examine some of the research that establishes the above propositions.

Differentiation/disproportionality

The police stop and search, arrest, charge, and use physical force against young, black, lower-status males disproportionately to their representation in the population. At the same time, they have disproportionate contact with them as victims or complainants for violent offences (Policy Studies Institute 1983, i: 62–4, 124–6; Fitzgerald and Hale 1996; Bowling 1999a; Fitzgerald 1999, 2009; Clancy *et al.* 2001; Bowling and Phillips 2002, 2007; Rowe 2004; Phillips and Bowling 2007; Bowling *et al.* 2008).

The North American evidence supports these points, as does research in many other countries (J. Lee 1981; Chan 1997). A 1973 study of stops in Dallas found that young and/or black males were stopped more than proportionately to their representation in the population or in arrest statistics (Bogolmony 1976). Young, black, and/or lower-class suspects are more likely to be arrested (Black 1970, 1972; D. A. Smith and Visher 1981; Skogan and Frydl 2004: 122–6). Blacks are more likely than whites to be killed by police (Meyer 1980; J. Fyfe 1981, 2002; Binder and Scharf 1982; Skolnick and Fyfe 1993; Geller and Toch 1996; Skogan and Frydl 2004: 258–62). British evidence points in the same direction (Choongh 1997: 52–9). Being young, male, black, unemployed, and economically disadvantaged is associated with a higher probability of being stopped, searched, arrested, detained in custody, charged, making complaints against the police (especially of assault), and failing to have these complaints substantiated.[2]

Differential arrest rates of the young, male, black, and economically marginal are found by all research after the mid-1970s (until then the evidence is clear that black people were disproportionately less likely to be arrested than white people; see Lambert 1970; Lea and Young 1984). The first study, and one of the most systematic, was the Home Office analysis of the 1975 Metropolitan Police statistics (Stevens and Willis 1979). This showed higher black than white arrest rates in all offence categories, but especially for assault, robbery, 'other violent theft', and 'other indictable offences'. Asians were underrepresented in all offence categories except assault, although this has altered since then, and the outbreak of rioting involving young Pakistanis in several Northern cities in 2001, and the 2005 London bombings, did much to 'question the benign stereotype of the law-abiding "Asian"' (Fitzgerald 2009: 414; see also Pantazis and Pemberton 2009).[3] This pattern of disproportionate arrests of black people compared with white has continued, and indeed worsened in the last decade (Fitzgerald 2009: 416). A major change in recent years has been the increasing use of police powers against Asians, with stop and search proportions now exceeding their representation in the population, and arrest rates coming close to it (Fitzgerald 2009: 416).

Unemployed or unskilled working class young men, especially if they are black, are also much more likely to be detained in police custody after arrest and before being charged (R. Morgan *et al.* 1990; Reiner and Leigh 1992; Choongh 1997: 52–9; Phillips and Brown 1998: chap. 1; Phillips and Bowling 2007: 440). Once in custody, black prisoners were twice as likely to be strip searched (Newburn *et al.* 2004). Juveniles who are working class (C. Fisher and Mawby 1982) or black (S. Landau 1981; S. Landau and

Nathan 1983; Fitzgerald 1993; D. Brown 1997: 66; Phillips and Brown 1998: chap. 6) are less likely to be cautioned than to be charged and prosecuted.

Black people were more likely to make serious complaints under the systems preceding the IPCC, especially of assault (Stevens and Willis 1981; Maguire and Corbett 1991). On the other hand, ethnic minorities and the unemployed or economically marginal were less likely to have their complaints substantiated (Box and Russell 1975; Stevens and Willis 1981; Box 1983: 82–91). Black people were more likely to claim knowledge of police use of excessive force on the basis of personal experience (Policy Studies Institute 1983, i: 26–57). Unsurprisingly, ethnic minorities viewed the complaints system even less favourably than whites did (D. Brown 1997: 230). The data continues to show that black people are more likely to make complaints to the IPCC, and in particular complaints about excessive force. Thus people classified as 'white' are 91.3 per cent of the population according to the 2001 Census, but make only 63 per cent of complaints against the police (Gleeson and Grace 2008: 23). Black people are 2.2 per cent of the population but 7 per cent of complainants (ibid.). Asians 4.4 per cent of the population and 6 per cent of complainants (ibid.). Black people are more likely than the other groups to complain of assault by police: 19 per cent of black complainants compared with 16 per cent of whites and 13 per cent of Asians (ibid.: 18). White people express more confidence in the IPCC than ethnic minorities, but the gap is narrowing and the majority of ethnic minority people interviewed expressed confidence (Inglis 2009: 6).

Altogether the evidence shows that the groups upon whom the differential exercise of police powers falls disproportionately are those characterized as 'police property'. It remains to be seen, however, to what extent the clear pattern of police differentiation involves discrimination—that is, use of police powers unjustified by legally relevant factors—and further what kind of discrimination is involved.

Discrimination

To a large extent the pattern of differentiation described so far can be accounted for by differential rates of offending or other legally relevant variables. The degree of police discrimination is less than what would be implied by a superficial reading of the social distribution of stops, arrests and other exercises of police power.

This is least true, however, of the lower-level occasions of police intervention, especially street stops, where the police operate with higher levels of discretion than at later stages of the criminal justice process. In some early American research black youths constituted a much higher proportion of stops of 'innocent' than of 'guilty' suspects (Piliavin and Briar 1964: 212). The likelihood of police stopping black males was disproportionate not only to their representation in the population, but also in arrest statistics (Bogolmony 1976: 571). Such patterns continue in later research, and the issue of disproportionate, possibly discriminatory, stops and arrests of black young men is highly controversial in the USA today, centring on the issue of 'racial profiling' (Skogan and Frydl 2004: 191–2, 317–23).

British data suggests that a roughly equal proportion of stops and searches of whites and blacks produces a 'result' in the sense of the recording of or arrest for an offence (Willis 1983: 1; Policy Studies Institute 1983, i: 116; Phillips and Bowling 2007: 435), although it must be stressed that the 'hit' rate for all stops is low (around 10–12 per cent): most people stopped are innocent of an offence (Fitzgerald 1999). When age, class, and other socioeconomic and demographic variables are controlled for, much of the ethnic variation disappears. The disproportionality is largely the result of differences in 'availability' due to lifestyle, economic disadvantage, and demography (D. Brown 1997: 19–27; Fitzgerald 1999, 2001, 2009; MVA and Millar 2000; Waddington *et al.* 2004; Henry 2007: 84–7; Phillips and Bowling 2007: 436–41). Much of the disproportionate stopping of black men is also the direct result of victims' descriptions of their assailants (Policy Studies Institute 1983, iv: 110; Fitzgerald 1999, 2001; Waddington *et al.* 2004; Henry 2007: 86). Thus much of the disproportionate stop rate for young black men is the product of transmitted, structural, or institutional racism. However, it is also likely that some of the ethnic differences are the result of categorical discrimination. Black and Asian people are much more likely than white to be stopped and searched under powers given the police since PACE which permit stops even when there is no 'reasonable suspicion' (s 60 Criminal Justice and Public Order Act 1994; s 44 Terrorism Act 2000; cf. Phillips and Bowling 2007: 435–6). They are much more likely to be stopped on suspicion of drug offences, where the police are acting proactively and with wide discretion (Quinton *et al.* 2000: 16–17), and to be strip searched after detention (Newburn *et al.* 2004). In short, black people are disproportionately stopped and searched when the police are operating with high rather than low discretion (Fitzgerald 1999, 2001), suggesting that categorical discrimination is occurring (Delsol and Shiner 2006; Bowling and Phillips 2007). Whatever the type of discrimination generating the disproportion, once it is in play it will exacerbate mutual suspicion and negative stereotyping of each other by police and ethnic minorities, leading to further statistical and interactional discrimination.

American studies of arrest patterns generally show that much, but not all, of the disproportionate arrest rate of blacks, youths, and the lower class can be accounted for by differences in the seriousness of offences which are alleged—a legally relevant criterion (Black 1971; D. A. Smith and Visher 1981; P. Waddington 1999a: 49–50; Skogan and Frydl 2004: 191–2). With regard to physical abuse of suspects, and especially the most controversial issue of police shootings, the American evidence is mixed. While some studies find that most of the disproportionate shooting rate of blacks is accounted for by varying arrest patterns, the weight of the evidence suggests that black and lower-class suspects are victims of police force more often than would be expected on the basis of arrest or other legally relevant differences (Meyer 1980; Skolnick and Fyfe 1993; Fyfe 2002; Skogan and Frydl 2004: 258–62).

In Britain the evidence also suggests that the disproportionate arrest rate of young black males is partly the product of police discrimination. However, it is also due in part to differential rates of offending (largely attributable to the age-profile and socioeconomic deprivation, as measured by such indices as unemployment or home-ownership rates, of the black population. See Stevens and Willis 1979; Policy Studies Institute 1983, i: 121, 71–5, iii: 96–7; Fitzgerald 1993, 2001, 2009; D. Brown 1997: 55–6; Phillips and

Bowling 2007: 436–41; Henry 2007: 84–7). The precise balance of these two factors is hard to ascertain. But the role of police discrimination can be adduced from the fact that blacks were most heavily arrested for offences which allow particular scope for selective perception by police officers: 'other violent theft' and 'sus'—for which the black arrest rate was fourteen or fifteen times the white (Stevens and Willis 1979). However, several studies (Stevens and Willis 1979; Henry 2007: 86–7) point to victim identifications of the race of offenders as supporting the claim that the disproportionate black arrest rate reflects varying involvement in offences, as well as police stereotyping (although victim identifications may themselves be, at least in part, a consequence of public stereotypes). However, the extent of the black–white arrest differential is so great that it would be implausible to attribute it all to police discrimination. Stevens and Willis (1979: 28–34) calculated that, on the hypothesis that black and white crime rates were identical, and the arrest imbalance was entirely due to 'mistaken' arrests of blacks, 76 per cent of all black arrests would have to be 'mistaken'. It remains true that the disproportionality in arrests is so great that it is difficult to believe that it is entirely the product of differences in legally relevant variables (Phillips and Bowling 2007: 438–41).

Lea and Young (1984), in the book that pioneered the 'left–realist' analysis of crime, accepted the validity of the Home Office and PSI analyses. They explained the disproportionate black arrest rate as the consequence of two mutually reinforcing processes: 'increased . . . black crime and police predisposition to associate blacks with crime become part of a vicious circle' (Lea and Young 1984: 167; see also Lea 1986).

Lea and Young were subjected to a torrent of criticism for this, accusing them of capitulating to 'the weight of racist logic' and of lending 'sociological credibility to police racism' (Gilroy 1982, 1983; Scraton 1985, 1987). In this plethora of vituperation there was no serious attempt at a rebuttal of Lea and Young's argument. Any such engagement with the issue of explaining the black arrest rate as the outcome of anything but a protean and all-pervasive racism was dismissed as 'empiricist haggling over official crime statistics' (Gilroy 1983: 146). But this sort of characterization of all police and all aspects of policing as equally and undistinguishably racist precluded any serious analysis of how and why policing changes, and of separating out potentially positive developments within police strategy and thinking. The state and its coercive apparatus, the police, were blanketed together as a monolithic reflex of the racist logic of capital.

Against this position Lea and Young mounted several powerful arguments. First, for many years during which there was clear evidence of widespread prejudice in the police force, official arrest statistics (which probably exaggerate black involvement in crime) did not depict blacks as arrested disproportionately. That was the clear conclusion of Lambert's (1970) study of Birmingham crime statistics in the late 1960s, and of the police evidence to the House of Commons Select Committee on Race Relations in 1971–2. But by the time of the 1976–7 Commons Select Committee on Race Relations and Immigration the police were claiming that the position had changed, and that there was a disproportionately high rate of young black crime.

Apart from the implausibility of the changing black arrest pattern in the 1970s being the result of a sudden shift in police thinking, Lea and Young stressed that it would be strange if the life circumstances of young blacks did not produce some increase in offences. 'The notion that increasing youth unemployment . . . a high young population in the black community . . . racial discrimination and the denial of legitimate opportunity, did not result in a rising rate of real offences is hardly credible' (Lea and Young 1984: 167–8).

All this is not to deny that 'moral panics' are often created by the practices of the police, the judicial apparatus, and the media. This was shown, for example, by *Policing the Crisis*, with its detailed account of the 'mugging' scare of 1972–3, and its construction by police, judiciary, and media (S. Hall *et al.* 1978). However, there can be little doubt that during the 1970s 'mugging' (robberies involving street attacks on strangers) became more prevalent, and was a not insignificant risk for vulnerable categories of people in some areas (although not for the population overall). Black overrepresentation in arrests for this were unlikely to be the product exclusively of police policy or prejudice. Indeed *Policing the Crisis*, for all its emphasis on the moral panic associated with mugging as symbol of increasing state and societal authoritarianism, did not deny its underlying reality (ibid.: 390).

It seems clear that the disproportionate black arrest rate is the product both of black deprivation and of police stereotyping—and of the interaction between these factors amplifying both. To recognize that the police statistics have some basis in a reality of black crime, which is itself related to structures of institutionalized and direct discrimination in economic and social life, is important (Fitzgerald 2001, 2009; Rowe 2004: chap. 9; Stenson and Waddington 2007; Henry 2007: 84–92; Webster 2007). It underlines the point that more needs to change than just setting straight mistaken police stereotypes or prejudices, or even organizational reforms in selection, training, and greater recruitment of ethnic minority officers.

However, some evidence of pure police discrimination was furnished by S. Landau's two studies (1981; S. Landau and Nathan 1983) of the processing of juvenile offenders by the Metropolitan Police. The first concentrated on decisions by station officers about whether to charge offenders immediately or refer them to the juvenile bureau. Holding constant the legally relevant variables of offence type and previous criminal record, blacks were more likely to be charged immediately than to be referred to the juvenile bureau.

Landau's later study examined the decisions of the juvenile bureau itself about whether to charge or caution those referred to it. He noted that, given the assumption that the earlier police decision would have screened out the 'worst' cases, it might be expected a priori that more people would be cautioned in those categories which are treated more harshly at the earlier stage. But in fact for 'crimes of violence' and 'public order' offences blacks were more likely to be treated harshly at both stages: they were less likely to be referred to the bureau, and less likely to be cautioned by it, holding constant the nature of the offence and past record. This might partly be accounted for by a lesser likelihood that cases involving blacks satisfied the legal preconditions for the cautioning process: an admission of guilt, and the consent of the victim. But part of the difference is 'pure' discrimination not explicable by 'legal' factors.

A similar conclusion emerges from data about complaints (dating from before the establishment of the IPCC in 2002). Some, but not all, of the class and ethnic differences can be accounted for by legally relevant factors (Stevens and Willis 1981). Black complainants were disproportionately involved in trouble with the police at the time of the complaint. Police were more likely to allege suspect's provocation (that is, assault or violent struggling) as a justification in the cases of black complaints of assault by the police. Altogether, blacks (and other vulnerable groups like young unemployed men) were more likely to have the characteristics of 'discreditability' which made it improbable that their complaints will be substantiated (Box and Russell 1975).

The evidence clearly suggests that part but not all of the social differentiation apparent in the exercise of police discretion is accounted for by legally relevant factors like offence patterns, so the extent of discrimination of any kind is less than the disproportionality in the use of police powers indicates. While some pure 'categorical' bias undoubtedly exists, much discrimination is transmitted', 'interactional', 'institutionalized', and 'statistical'.

Transmitted discrimination. The role of 'transmitted' discrimination (that is, where the police act as transmitters of public discrimination) is indicated in several ways in the research. It is implied in the key role of victim and witness information and identification in the clear-up of crime. It is also indicated in the significance attached by police to victim specifications of the race of their assailants in the case of crimes like robbery (Fitzgerald 1999, 2001; Henry 2007: 86). American research has also underlined the central importance of complainants' wishes as a determinant of arrest decisions, after controlling for legal variables like offence seriousness (Smith and Visher 1981: 173).

Interactional discrimination. Many researchers have stressed the context and process of interaction itself (especially the respect accorded by a suspect, which may itself depend upon the officer's approach) as a crucial determinant of police decision-making (P. Waddington 1999a: 153–5). Such penalizing of 'contempt of cop' is not, of course, a valid legal basis for arrest. But many apparently legally proper arrests may result from the suspect's failing the 'attitude test', thus incurring sanctions for an offence which might otherwise be overlooked. This is largely a result of the cop cultural imperative that the police officer should appear to maintain control, especially in public situations—which is why the presence of bystanders often increases the probability of arrest or the use of force (Smith and Visher 1981: 172–3; Waddington 1999a: 154).

Institutionalized discrimination. A key example of institutionalized discrimination is the directing of extra police resources or more aggressive tactics to 'high-crime' areas suffering from social deprivation. The result will be a greater probability of stop and search, arrest, and so on, for those people living there who are vulnerable to police attention, such as young black and/or unemployed men (Blom-Cooper and Drabble 1982).

Another example is the use of indices of the risk of reoffending (which themselves are an example of 'statistical' discrimination) in a routine way to determine decisions such as cautioning or charging. These indices of 'problem family' backgrounds and the like, even if used universalistically by the police bureaucracy, will result in discriminatory decisions (S. Landau and Nathan 1983: 143–5; Phillips and Bowling 2007: 440–1).

Finally the long-standing complaints about police inattention to racial attacks are partly due to unthinking application of standard preconceptions and procedures which assume individual motivations for offences. The 'normal' procedures of the police institution may indirectly disadvantage ethnic minority victims (Home Office 1981; Bowling 1999a; Bowling and Phillips 2002: chap. 5; Rowe 2004: chap. 6; Phillips and Bowling 2007: 424–8). As the Stephen Lawrence case made clear so dramatically, however, the failure to deal adequately with racist crimes may often be due to more direct forms of discrimination. The Macpherson Inquiry revealed many instances of incompetence and malpractice, which it attributed in large part to institutionalized racism in the Metropolitan Police (Macpherson 1999; Marlow and Loveday 2000; Rowe 2007; McLaughlin 2007: chap. 6).

Statistical discrimination. This is pinpointed in several studies as a major cause of discrimination in stop-and-search, due to stereotypical police presuppositions that particular groups (including young black men) are more likely to be offenders (Stevens and Willis 1979: 31–3; Willis 1983: 25; Policy Studies Institute 1983, iv: 230–9; Fitzgerald 1999; Phillips and Bowling 2007: 436–7), although it has been questioned by others (Waddington *et al.* 2004; Henry 2007: 85–6). Stereotyping is certainly not a legally acceptable basis for 'reasonable suspicion', indeed it is explicitly rejected as such in the PACE Code of Practice. Stops based on statistical discrimination are a form of 'noble cause' corruption. They derive from a concern with effective policing, however misguided (as well as illegal) this might be in that frequent stops and searches of innocent people magnify hostility to the police in vulnerable groups, and in the end undermine law enforcement.

Categorical discrimination. Undoubtedly much discriminatory use of police powers is a reflection of categorical bias of the kind found in police culture. However it is hard to pinpoint it as a separate factor from the overall context of encounters. That is why observational studies of policing tend to emphasize the absence of pure discrimination which cannot be justified or at least explained in some sense by the process and context of encounters (Reiner 1993). At the same time observational studies do portray a prevalence of prejudiced opinions, which are not necessarily directly translated into police practice (Black 1971; Holdaway 1983; Policy Studies Institute 1983, iv: chap. 4; P. Waddington 1999a: chap. 4). But it is likely that prejudices do also over-determine the conflict-ridden character of many police encounters with black people, generating the perceived 'contempt of cop' that is the trigger for some discriminatory arrests. Bias and prejudice also underlie the failure to recruit, retain and promote ethnic minority officers in proportion to their numbers in the population, due in large part to their experience of discrimination at the hands of white officers, although some progress has been made as a result of decades of official initiatives directed at this issue (Holdaway 1996, 2009; Cashmore 2001; Bowling and Phillips 2002: chap. 9; Rowe 2004: chap. 2; O'Neill and Holdaway 2007; Bowling *et al.* 2008: 624–8).

GENDER AND POLICING

The issue of gender discrimination has also been a vexed one. A clear distinction between the debates about race and sex discrimination is that women generally are disproportionately *infrequently* at the receiving end of police powers, whereas one of the key questions in relation to race is the disproportionate policing of black people as suspects. The very small proportion of female suspects or offenders at every stage of the criminal justice process is one of its most striking and consistent patterns (Heidensohn and Gelsthorpe 2007). It does not follow, however, that the police do not deal with women suspects in discriminatory ways. Police officers tend to view women with a conventional imagery, bifurcating them as either 'wives' or 'whores' (M. Brogden *et al.* 1988: 119–20; Heidensohn 2008). The low rate of formal processing of women as suspects masks a complex web of discrimination. Some women may escape suspicion because 'chivalry' places them outside the frame of likely offenders in the stereotypes of investigating officers (Heidensohn and Gelsthorpe 2007: 399–400). Yet others, such as teenage girls behaving in sexually precocious or deviant ways, or prostitutes, may be dealt with by the police at a lower threshold of entry into the system because they violate the officers' codes of acceptable behaviour, or may be seen paternalistically as in need of 'protection' from themselves (M. Brogden *et al.* 1988; Dunhill 1989). There is much clearer evidence of police discrimination in their treatment of women as victims of crime. Calls to domestic disturbances have always been a significant part of the police workload, but notoriously have tended to be treated by officers without recourse to criminal proceedings, even when evidence of assault is present (S. Edwards 1989; Hanmer *et al.* 1989). 'Domestics' were seen as messy, unproductive, and not 'real' police work in traditional cop culture (Reiner 1978: 177, 214–15, 244–5; M. Young 1991: 315–16). This issue has become highly charged since the 1970s, and around the world police forces have attempted to improve their response to domestic assaults, with debatable results (Sheptycki 1993; Sherman 1992b; Hoyle 1998; Maxwell *et al.* 2002; Chesney-Lind 2002; Skogan and Frydl 2004: 231–2; Heidensohn 2008: 660–3).

There has also been much concern about insensitive or even hostile treatment of rape victims, an issue dramatically highlighted in 1982 by a celebrated episode of Roger Graef's TV documentary on the Thames Valley Police which showed a very disturbing interrogation of a rape victim (BBC 1, 18 January 1982). Despite considerable improvements since then (Blair 1985), the treatment of rape victims by police remains deeply problematic (Hanmer *et al.* 1989; Gregory and Lees 1999; Lees 2002; Temkin 2002; Walby and Allen 2004; J. Jordan 2004; Temkin and Krahe 2008).

It is also clear from a growing volume of evidence that women are discriminated against as police officers, in terms of career prospects as well as harassment in the job. Until the 1980s, discrimination within police forces was open and institutionalized in the existence of separate departments carrying out radically different functions. This itself followed from widespread resistance within (and outside) the force to the initial recruitment of policewomen in the early decades of the twentieth century (Carrier 1988). Since the Sex Discrimination Act 1975, women have been formally integrated into the same units as male officers, and the proportion in the force has risen to its current level of approximately one-quarter (Bullock 2008). Nonetheless, the continuation of discrimination has been documented by numerous studies.[4] The issue was vividly highlighted by the much-publicized action brought by the former assistant chief constable of Merseyside, Alison Halford, alleging discrimination against her in her attempts to be promoted (Halford 1993), although since her action a number of women have become chief constables (there are currently three women chief constables out of the forty-three in England and Wales, and 13 per cent of ACPO rank officers are women; cf. Bullock 2008).

Many commentators have argued that the unequal employment and promotion of policewomen is important not only as an issue of justice, but to dilute the machismo element in police culture, which has been seen as an important source of abuse. Research evidence in the USA and Britain to date does not confirm that most women officers police differently from their male colleagues, but rather that they tend to be influenced by the traditional culture of masculinity (Heidensohn 1992, 1994; Westmarland 2001a, 2001b; Silvestri 2003, 2007; Skogan and Frydl 2004: 151–2), but this could change as numbers increase further. A related issue of discrimination relates to the treatment of gays and lesbians, as victims or suspects or as police officers. Although again the position has certainly improved in the last two decades, there remains evidence of continuing bias and discrimination (M. Burke 1993; Williams and Robinson 2004; Rowe 2008: 109–11).

CONCLUSION

The pattern of discrimination and the map of the population found in police culture are isomorphic. They are interdependent, and bound up within the wider structure of racial and class disadvantage. Although it may sometimes be that discrimination is associated with prior individual police attitudes of a prejudiced kind, the fundamental processes are structural. Even if recruits were not especially prejudiced at the outset, the evidence on the impact of the experience of policing suggests they tend to become so.

The young 'street' population has always been the prime focus of police order-maintenance and law-enforcement work (Loader 1996; M. Lee 1998; McAra and McVie 2005). The processes of racial disadvantage in housing, employment, and education lead young blacks to be disproportionately involved in street culture (Fitzgerald 2001, 2009; Stenson and Waddington 2007). They may consequently become engaged in specific kinds of street crime, for reasons that have already been indicated. At the same time, the relative powerlessness of ethnic minorities and lower-working-class youth means that the police may be less constrained and inhibited in dealing with them. In times of economic crisis and competition for jobs and other resources, the majority group (especially the white working class) may indeed benefit from the effects of over-policing of blacks, because black stigmatization as criminal, the acquisition of criminal records, reduces their competitiveness (Johnson 1976: 108). For all these reasons, the economically marginal ethnic minorities, and especially their youth, are prone to become 'police property' (J. Lee 1981). These structural aspects are the hard core of police conflict with the underclass who still constitute their main clientele (Crowther 2000a, 2000b; Loftus 2007, 2009). But they are exacerbated by cultural factors such as police prejudice, which, if reflected in verbal and other abuse, can make even normally uncontroversial service work fraught with tension. Finally, once conflicts become common a vicious cycle develops whereby police officers and their 'property' approach encounters with pre-existing hostility and suspiciousness, and interact in ways which only exacerbate the tension.

Overall, this chapter has argued that contrary to popular, police cultural and media images, the primary mandate in practice of the police is emergency order maintenance, for which they are entrusted as specialists in (if not monopolists of) the use of legitimate force on behalf of the state. At certain times and places much if not most of their role will be service work, but since the 1970s the crime demands have been increasing. Their effectiveness in law enforcement is apparently declining, but this is largely because of pressures on crime rates arising from wider social and cultural processes. Attempts to measure police effectiveness remain bedevilled by the absence of adequate performance indicators even in relation to crime work, and certainly for the broader aspects of policing. The exercise of police powers has throughout history been operated primarily against the economically and social marginal, especially those from ethnic minorities, and it still is. The growth in the size of 'police property' groups that has resulted from government economic and social policy since the 1980s has been the major factor undermining police effectiveness and legitimacy, and the apparently discriminatory use (or, rather, misuse) of powers. Sadly the economic collapse since 2007 is likely to exacerbate this vicious spiral of social and criminal injustice feeding into each other (Cook 2006).

NOTES

1. In addition to the experimental studies reported in the text, there have been attempts to discover the relationship between aggregate levels of crime and policing by econometric analysis (McDonald 1976: chap. 6; Carr-Hill and Stern 1979; P. Morris and Heal 1981: 16–18). These early studies found a *positive* relation between police force size and crime rate, which they attributed to the recording phenomenon: the more police, the more crime recorded. Subsequent econometric studies generally found either little or no relation between police force strength and crime levels (Eck and Maguire 2005). One problem bedevilling the research was untangling the complex causal interrelations that are likely to exist between police and crime levels. A priori it could be that increases in police numbers reduce crime by enhancing potential offenders' fear of apprehension as well as incapacitating some by arrest. But increasing crime rates could have the political effect of boosting expenditure on police and thus produce a positive relationship between police numbers and recorded crime. An influential recent study by Levitt sought to untangle this by using electoral cycles to estimate the proportion of changes in police personnel that was attributable to this political effect. His results suggest

that marginal increases in police strength *do* result in less crime (Levitt 2004). Despite the ingenuity of this method, it is still possible that there are uncontrolled sources of variability in crime rates not tapped by the calculations. So it cannot really be taken as dispelling the implications of the experimental studies cited in the text, especially as they are in line with plausible theoretical reasons questioning the possibility of impacting on crime by changing police numbers alone, except at the extremes of no police or saturation policing (Skogan and Frydl 2004: 224–5).

2. Evidence showing disproportionate stops and searches of young males, the unemployed, and black people, is presented by many studies including: A. Brogden 1981: 44–52; Willis 1983: 14; Policy Studies Institute 1983, i: 95–102, iii: 96–7; J. D. Brown 1997: 19–27; Bucke 1997; Fitzgerald 1999, 2001; Bowling and Phillips 2002: 138–47; Rowe 2004: chap. 5; Waddington

et al. 2004; Phillips and Bowling 2007: 434–8; Henry 2007: 82–7; Bowling *et al.* 2008: 617–19.

3. On past low Asian involvement as suspects with the police, see: Jefferson *et al.* 1992; Fitzgerald 1993; Bucke 1997. The later increase is analysed in Phillips and Bowling 2007: 435–6; Fitzgerald 2009: 413–14. Other evidence for disproportionate arrests of blacks, young males, and the unemployed is found in: Policy Studies Institute 1983, i: 118–26, iii: 88–91; Jefferson *et al.* 1992; Fitzgerald 1993; D. Brown 1997: 55–6; Phillips and Brown 1998: chap. 1; Phillips and Bowling 2007: 438–41; Bowling *et al.* 2008: 621–2.

4. For evidence of discrimination against women police officers, see: S. Jones 1987; Graef 1989: chap. 6; M. Young 1991: chap. 4; Heidensohn 1992, 1994, 2008; Fielding and Fielding 1992; Fielding 1994a; C. Martin 1996; J. Brown *et al.* 1999; Brown and Heidensohn 2000; Westmarland 2001a, 2001b; Silvestri 2003, 2007.

6

MYSTIFYING THE POLICE: THE MEDIA PRESENTATION OF POLICING

Mass-media images of the police are of considerable importance in understanding the political significance and role of policing. We have seen that neither uniformed patrol nor plainclothes investigation work is very successful in crime control. However, their symbolic significance is profound (N. Walker 1996; Manning 1997, 2001, 2003; Loader 1997; C. P. Wilson 2000; Loader and Mulcahy 2003). They signify that there exists an agency charged with apprehending offenders, so that there is always some prospect (however small statistically) of penal sanctions. In Chapter 3 we saw that the architects of the British police tradition were concerned to construct an image of the bobby as the embodiment of rational legal authority. The nineteenth-century conflicts about the establishment and acceptability of the police were played out in the media of the day, the press, the novel, and the music hall (W. Miller 1999: chap. 5). Popular literature and journalism began to feature the exploits of police 'detective officers' from the mid-1840s, and Dickens 'virtually appointed himself patron and publicist to the Detective Department' (Ousby 1976: 65–6). Since then there has been a continuing concern with constructing and maintaining a favourable image of policing as a benign, honourable, and helpful service, which in today's mediated world has become an increasingly professionalized PR operation (R. C. Mawby 1999, 2002a, 2002b).

In large, complex, and class-divided societies, however, the experience of different segments of the population with the police is uneven. Police activity bears most heavily upon a relatively restricted group of people at the base of the social hierarchy, who are disproportionately the complainants, victims, or offenders processed by the police. Politically, though, the most crucial sectors for determining police prestige, power, and resources are the majority higher up the social scale, whose contacts with the police (and certainly adversarial encounters) are confined mainly to the police's traffic-control functions. For these strata the mass media are the main source of perceptions and preferences about policing. Moreover, even in the lower-status groups where police contacts are more frequent, contacts are largely restricted to a distinct segment: young males. Attitudes to the police of the women and older men in these groups is crucial, in particular for the flow of information, and the probability that routine encounters can be conducted relatively peaceably.

There is much evidence that the mass media shape most people's views of the police and frame political debate (Cavender 2004). In the *Policing for London* (PFL) survey, for example, 80 per cent said the news media were their principal source of information about the police, contrasted with only 20 per cent citing 'direct experience'. While 'word of mouth' was the second most prominent source of information (43 per cent), it is striking that 29 per cent mentioned 'media fiction' as their main source (Fitzgerald *et al.* 2002: Figure 6.1, 78). According to the BCS, 59 per cent of people get their information about the police in general from TV and radio news, 39 per cent from newspapers, and 23 per cent TV documentaries, contrasted with only around 20 per cent who cite personal experience or word of mouth. Although media fiction is less cited than in PFL, it still accounts for 10 per cent as their source of information (Allen *et al.* 2006: Table 2.21). So Sir Ian Blair, the former Commissioner of the Metropolitan Police, was spot on when he joked in his Dimbleby lecture on BBC TV in 2005 that 'Lots of people in this country are actually undertaking a permanent NVQ on policing—it's called *The Bill*'. The media representation of policing feeds back into policing practice via its effect on public perceptions, in 'media loops' (Manning 1998). A striking example was the declaration by Sir Stephen Lander, newly appointed chairman of the Serious and Organised Crime Agency, that SOCA's priorities would be set by the 'brainboxes in the Home Office' according to analysis of the prominence of different kinds of crime, measured by column inches in the press ('UK's Crime-Fighting Agency Will Use the Press to Set Agenda' *The Independent* 10 January 2005).

The media-constructed image of policing is thus vital for the attainment of 'consent'. This image does not float free of the actualities of policing, but it is not a mirror reflection of them either. It is a refraction of the reality, constructed in accordance with the organizational imperatives of the media industries, the ideological frames of creative personnel and audiences, and the changing balance of political and economic forces affecting both the reality and the image of policing.

The crucial political significance of media presentations of policing has long been recognized by police officers. There are many examples of use of the media by police to construct 'crime waves' as devices for accruing organizational prestige and resources (Fishman 1978; S. Hall *et al.* 1978; Christensen *et al.* 1982; R. Powers 1983; Potter 1998; Surette 2007: chap. 4). More recently they have begun to use the media more systematically as a means of presenting a desirable image, and even as an investigative resource (Fishman and Cavender 1998; R. C. Mawby 1999, 2002a, 2002b; Innes 1999b, 2003b). The long tradition of respectable anxiety about subversive media effects is embodied in continuous demands for censorship and control. Conceptions of the political and social implications of media presentations of crime and law enforcement can be broadly divided into two opposing perspectives (Reiner 2008: 315–16).[1] The first view holds that the media ought responsibly to inculcate respect for legal and moral norms and their appointed guardians. Commercial exigencies, however, exert constant pressure to pander to base appetites and emotions, leading all too often to sensationalist and exploitative glorification of the criminal and denigration of the police. The opposing view regards the media as propagators of a dominant ideology

sanctifying the existing institutions of the social order, the laws by which their operations are expressed, and the repressive apparatuses that maintain them. Struggles for
or against dominant values and rules are transformed by the media into metaphysical
confrontations of universal good and evil. They are thus depoliticized, as is the role of
the police as an arm of the state.

Both the 'subversive' and the 'hegemonic' view of the role of media images of law
and order are too simple. In an unequal and hierarchical society, competition in
presenting ideas is as structurally loaded as all conflicts. Very broadly, the weight of
images portrayed by the mass media will be supportive of the existing social order
in any relatively stable society. But the demands of credibility and comprehension
produce a reflection in media presentations of changing patterns of conflict. Images
across the range of media may be contradictory, or even present a consensus for reform
at particular times. The key to understanding the content of the media is knowledge
of the organizational dynamics, ideology, and professional imperatives of the productive personnel and institutions (Ericson *et al.* 1987, 1989, 1991; Schlesinger *et al.* 1994;
Colbran 2007, 2009a, 2009b).

This chapter will examine the pattern and implications of media presentations of the
police, both in purportedly 'factual' and in fictional products.[2]

'FACTUAL' IMAGES

Sir Robert Mark, Commissioner of the Metropolitan Police in the early 1970s, initiated
a policy of unprecedented openness between the Met and the news media. He justified
this by referring to the relationship between police and journalists as 'an enduring,
if not ecstatically happy, marriage'. Overall the treatment of the police by the news
media has been such as to legitimate their role and activities, but this outcome has
been neither smooth nor unruffled. Conflict has frequently arisen between police and
journalists over specific issues, and many police officers have a genuine sense of the
media as biased against them. These perceptions are not unfounded. The media, even
while reproducing perspectives fundamentally legitimating the police role, nonetheless criticize and question many particular police actions and individual officers. So
long as that is not carried too far, the existence of the media as apparently independent, impartial and ever-vigilant watchdogs over state agencies on behalf of the public
interest is conducive to the legitimation of these apparatuses (but not all individuals
working within them). The process of legitimation could never be effective if the media
were seen as mere propaganda factories.

Law and order is a staple of news reporting. The amount of attention given to crime
news is generally greater in popular than in 'quality' media (Roshier 1973; Williams and
Dickinson 1993; Reiner *et al.* 2000, 2001, 2003). The proportion of news devoted to
crime, and especially to criminal justice and policing, has tended to increase over time
(Reiner *et al.* 2000, 2001, 2003). News reports are predominantly about specific crimes,

rather than trends, causes, or remedies. The amount of attention given crime bears no relationship to trends in crime statistics (Roshier 1973).

There are structured differences between the characteristics of crime and criminals reported by the media, and the picture conveyed by official statistics, victimization, or self-report studies (Allen *et al.* 1998; Reiner *et al.* 2000, 2001, 2003). The American criminologist Surette has dubbed this 'the law of opposites': 'The media's crime and justice portraits will be the opposite of what is true' (Surette 2007: 202). With the caveat that the criminal statistics used to compare media representations with are themselves problematic measures of 'truth', systematic divergences have been consistently documented by British and American research:

(i)   The media over-report and sensationalize serious crimes, especially murder, crimes against the person, or ones with a sexual element. This may not be surprising, although two Norwegian studies show it is not a universal phenomenon, varying in different political cultures (Hauge 1965; Green 2008). But it has ideological consequences for perceptions of the police role.

(ii) The media concentrate on crimes which are solved. Offences which are reported by the media at the time of their occurrence are disproportionately the serious offences of interpersonal violence which have the highest clear-up rates. Most other offences are reported only after an arrest. Indeed, reports are frequently based on trials, especially the opening prosecution stage and the judge's summing-up and sentencing.

(iii) Offenders reported in the media are disproportionately older adults, and from a higher social class than their counterparts in reality. (The same is true of victims.)

In short, the news media present a picture of crime which is misleading in its focus on the serious and violent, and the emphasis on older, higher-status offenders and victims. Reporting also exaggerates police success in detection.

The corollary of this is a presentation of the police that is without doubt generally favourable. The police are cast in the role they want to see themselves in—as the 'thin blue line' between order and chaos, the protectors of the victimized weak from the depredations of the criminally vicious. The media (with particular inflections ranging from the more liberal 'quality' organs like the *Guardian* or *The Times*, to the more overt vigilantism of the popular tabloids) generally support the police role and even extensions of police powers. As one study concluded, 'the news media are as much an agency of *policing* as the law enforcement agencies whose activities and classifications they reported on' (Ericson *et al.* 1991: 74).

Chibnall's study (1979) of Fleet Street crime reporters found that they explicitly saw it as their responsibility to present the police in a favourable light. A typical quote was: 'If I've got to come down on one side or the other, either the goodies or the baddies, then obviously I'd come down on the side of the goodies, in the interests of law and order' (Chibnall 1977: 145).

Since the 1980s this picture has altered considerably. Specialist crime reporters used to be found only on tabloid newspapers, and they tended to see themselves as extensions of the working team of detectives whose crime-busting exploits they glamorized and celebrated. More recently, reflecting the politicization of 'law and order', broadsheet newspapers, as well as the BBC and ITV, have employed specialist correspondents in the criminal justice area, although often under labels such as 'home affairs' or 'legal' correspondents rather than crime specifically (Schlesinger and Tumber 1994). This has gone hand in hand with an increase in the proportion of crime-related stories in the broadsheets, and a shift towards stories concerned with criminal justice issues (Reiner *et al.* 2000, 2001, 2003).

In the last couple of years another profound change in crime-news production has become apparent: the virtual disappearance of court reporters (Davies 1999a, 1999b, 2008: 77–9). This is due in part to the increasing news emphasis on celebrities, to a point where even the sensational murder story is squeezed out (unless there is also a celebrity element, as in the murder of Jill Dando). It is also a result of the more commercial orientation of the multimedia conglomerates that own an increasing number of news outlets, which has restricted editorial budgets severely. The result is that many crime and criminal-justice stories, cases, and issues fail to get aired at all, even in the sensational manner that used to be a core news staple.

Nonetheless, belief in their watchdog role has led reporters to pursue assiduously stories of police wrongdoing. The most notable example was *The Times's* (1969) revelation of widespread corruption in the Metropolitan Police, which sparked off the major scandals of the 1970s. But police corruption stories were traditionally located within a 'one bad apple' framework, implying that the discovery and punishment of the rare evil individual was proof that the police institution remained wonderful. As the number of corruption scandals proliferated, it became increasingly difficult to maintain the 'one bad apple' mode of legitimation. The metaphor increasingly became the 'rotten barrel', and in the late 1990s the 'poisoned trees', from which the 'bad apples' came (Punch 2003).

However, media reporting has continued generally to place corruption stories in a framework that legitimates the police institution at the same time as reporting widespread deviance. The main legitimatory device now is the 'scandal and reform' narrative. Simultaneously with reports of malpractice, there are accounts of the reforms the police and government are undertaking to ensure that future wrongdoing will be prevented (Schlesinger and Tumber 1994). A good example is a front-page story which reported serious corruption in the National Crime Squad and other elite investigative units, which also reported on the fundamental reforms of the complaints process introduced to deal with the problem (*Observer* 14 May 2000: 1–2).

The sources of this basically favourable framework of news about the police are threefold. First, a variety of concrete organizational pressures underlying news production have unintended pro-police ideological consequences. The tendency to report cases at the stage of the trial derives partly from the economy of concentrating reporters at institutional settings like courts, where newsworthy events can be expected to occur regularly, but it results in exaggerating police success. The police control much of the information on which crime reporters rely, and this gives them a degree of power as essential accredited sources. The institutionalization of crime reporters itself became a self-generating cause of regular crime news, and over time they developed a symbiotic relationship with their reliable contacts, notably the police (Chibnall 1977: chaps. 3, 6; Schlesinger and Tumber 1994). The need to write reports to meet the deadlines of news production contributes to their event orientation, the concentration on specific crimes at the expense of analysis of causal processes or policies (Rock 1973: 76–9). Considerations of personal safety and convenience lead cameramen covering riots typically to film from behind police lines, which structures the image of the police as vulnerable 'us' confronting menacing 'them' (Murdock 1982: 10–89). These and other production pressures lead to a pro-police stance quite independently of any conscious bias (Ericson *et al.* 1987, 1989, 1991; Schlesinger and Tumber 1992, 1993, 1994).

Second, the professional ideology of reporters, their intuitive sense of news-worthiness, what makes a 'good story', can be analysed as a system of values which both emphasizes crime incidents, and underlies their particular representation (Chibnall 1977: 22–45; Hall *et al.* 1978; Greer 2003, 2009a: 186–8, 2009b: Part 3; Jewkes 2004). Such emotional elements of perceived newsworthiness as immediacy, drama, personalization, titillation, and novelty are conducive to an emphasis on violent and sensational offences (S. Brown 2003).

These processes are most apparent in the handling of explicitly political issues with law-and-order dimensions, such as coverage of political demonstrations or terrorism (A. Clarke and Taylor 1980; Mythen and Walklate 2006a, 2006b). This was shown in a detailed behind-the-scenes study of the production process of news reports about the 27 October 1968 anti-Vietnam War demonstration outside the US Embassy in Grosvenor Square, London (Halloran *et al.* 1970). The media constructed their reporting around the issue of violence, crystallized in the famous 'kick photo', showing a policeman being held and kicked by two demonstrators, which appeared prominently on most front pages the day after the event (S. Hall 1973). This achieved the subordination of the wider political questions involved in the demonstration to one dramatic incident of anti-police brutality. Similarly, news coverage of the May Day 2000 'anti-capitalist' rally in London concentrated above all on the daubing of the Cenotaph and Winston Churchill's statue, occluding discussion of the issues the protestors sought to highlight. The professional values of newsworthiness are a crucial determinant of the character of crime and police reporting, quite independently of any overtly political considerations.

The recent proliferation of video cameras means that footage fitting the values of news-worthiness but filmed by citizens and showing police violence is increasingly available, so that framing from the police side is challenged. From the beating of Rodney King in 1991 to the 2009 G20 protests in London amateur film has documented police brutality (Lawrence 2000; HMIC 2009). The Norwegian criminologist Thomas Mathiesen has dubbed this 'synopticon' as it mitigates the panopticism of the authorities (Mathiesen 1997), and Canadian engineering professor Steve Mann has called this phenomenon of citizen recording challenging official surveillance 'sousveillance' (Mann *et al.* 2003).

Third, the nature of law-and-order coverage is also profoundly affected by the explicit political ideology of the press, which is predominantly conservative. The broadcasting media are dominated by a viewpoint representing the 'moderate middle', taking for granted certain broad beliefs and values—what Stuart Hall succinctly called 'a world at one with itself'. The master concepts of news ideology include such notions as the 'national interest', the 'British way of life', and the 'democratic process'. These are seen as threatened by mindless militants or terrorists manipulated by a minority of extremists representing violence and subversion, with only the 'thin blue line' to save the day. Both straightforward crime and political conflict are predominantly presented as the same pathology, with the police celebrated as guardians of the normal.

The police, however, often see themselves as denigrated and under attack in the news media. Criticisms of the press are frequently made by police spokesmen, as epitomized in Robert Mark's complaint in a speech to the London Press Club in 1974 that 'Without doubt the most abused, the most unfairly criticized and the most silent minority in this country' were the police.

Part of the explanation of this discrepancy between police views and content analyses of media presentations lies in police officers' anxiety about the headline revelations of police malpractice, which is not assuaged by 'one bad apple' or 'scandal and reform' editorializing. Criticisms are perceived bitterly, while favourable comments seem less salient. Because of anxieties about their coverage, and realization of its importance, the police have tried to handle their relations with the media carefully (Chibnall 1979; Crandon and Dunne 1997; R. C. Mawby 1999, 2002a, 2002b; Innes 1999b, 2003b). Scotland Yard opened a press office in 1919, largely because of fears about unauthorized leaks produced by reporters bribing officers. Since then relations between the press and the police have fluctuated. The advent of Sir Harold Scott as commissioner in 1945 marked a high spot in police—press cordiality, the dawn of the 'golden age' of crime-reporting (coinciding with the 'golden age' of public confidence in the police), when a few detectives, notably Robert Fabian, achieved superstar status.

The late 1950s *causes célèbres* which heralded the Royal Commission on the Police marked a new strain on police—press cordiality, as the police became concerned about media highlighting of their peccadilloes. However, the mid-1960s were glowing ones for press treatment of the police. The reorganization of the police was welcomed as a modernizing breakthrough, and their gang-busting successes against the Krays and Richardsons duly celebrated. The high point in press eulogizing of British police virtue was the laudatory way their handling of the counter-cultural manifestations of the spirit of 1968 (notably Grosvenor Square) were contrasted with repressive foreign heavy-handedness.

The police—press accord was threatened by the 1969 and later corruption scandals, but Mark dealt with these not by shutting out the media, but manipulating them skilfully through a policy of openness, enunciated in a memorandum of 24 May 1973. This was part of a coherent strategy of reform intended to fend off threats to police independence (Chibnall 1979).

Following Mark's replacement by Sir David McNee as commissioner in 1977, relations with the media became more abrasive. A number of incidents led to harsh police
criticism of the media, especially the BBC. The most prominent *cause célèbre* was the
virulent police reaction to the *Law and Order* series of TV plays written by G. F. Newman,
broadcast in April 1978. The Prison Officers' Association and the Metropolitan Police
for a time withdrew facilities from the BBC in protest.

The abrasiveness in police—press relations in this period was not so much a
consequence of personalities, of McNee being a less adroit media manipulator than
Mark, as a symptom of the politicized state of policing. The 1979 general election saw
an intensification of partisan police interventions in politics (I. Taylor 1980; Reiner
1980; Downes and Morgan 2007). The media were used by the law-and-order lobby
to construct a climate conducive to their demands, but at the same time there was an
undercurrent of questioning of police practices, perceived most clearly by the police
themselves (McLaughlin and Murji 1998; Loader and Mulcahy 2003: Part III).

These contradictory currents became especially acute and apparent in media
coverage of the 1981 urban riots in Brixton and Toxteth and their aftermath (Sumner
1982; Tumber 1982). Wren-Lewis's detailed analysis (1981–2) distinguished three
different discourses in media coverage. The 'law-and-order discourse' portrayed the
clashes as an inexplicable eruption of sheer hooliganism requiring firm repression by
an adequately equipped police force. The 'contra-discourse' was a radical one standing
the first on its head. The riots were seen specifically as anti-police demonstrations provoked by heavy-handed police harassment. The 'social causality discourse' (favoured
by the Labour Party's leaders) emphasized the importance of the failure of government
economic policy as the root cause of discontent, but accepted the need for effective
policing to suppress the unacceptable symptoms, the street disorders. Wren-Lewis emphasized the novelty of presentation of the contra-discourse during media analyses of
Brixton. In 1981 the contra-discourse was given some prominence in the 'interpretive'
stage after the riots died down. The initial 'revelation' stage of reporting Brixton was
heavily loaded by the law-and-order discourse, carried above all by the vivid pictures of
violent clashes in the early newscasts. However, after the establishment of the Scarman
Inquiry into the April disorders, the media discussions moved into a stage of closure,
attempting to play down the contra-discourse and re-emphasized the law-and-order
discourse. When the July 1981 disorders erupted in Brixton, Toxteth, Moss Side, and
elsewhere, far less attention was allowed to the contra-discourse, and reportage was
heavily weighted to the law-and-order frame. Wren-Lewis thus pointed to the novel
appearance in media discussions of Brixton in April 1981 of some critical views on
policing. But he found a strong move to displacement of this by a pure law-and-order
discourse following the appointment of Scarman, and the July riots.

In the event, the Scarman Report incorporated elements of the contra-discourse,
seeing policing mistakes as a core factor sparking the disorders. The report united the
contra- and social causation discourses, largely rejecting the law-and-order one. It
was lapped up by the media, which gave much attention to Scarman's criticisms of
police tactics. Media coverage of the long-term impact of the riots and the Scarman

Inquiry allowed considerable scope to critical discourses, and on the whole rejected the law-and-order framework (Murdock 1982: 110–15). This was undoubtedly a major factor allowing the riots and the Scarman Report to presage a move to a climate of reform within the police during the late 1980s (Savage 2007: chap. 4).

The general coverage of police matters since the mid-1980s has become increasingly critical. Much news footage revealed apparent abuses, for example during key public order clashes (notably in the miners' strike). Even the 1990 Trafalgar Square anti-poll-tax demonstration, during which the media initially portrayed the police favourably, was subsequently subject to media analyses probing allegations of mishandling and malpractice. Above all the media were prominent in the process by which the major *causes célèbres* of police abuses leading to miscarriages of justice have been revealed, notably the Guildford Four, the Birmingham Six, and the Tottenham Three. In each case individual investigative journalists and documentaries were pivotal factors in discrediting the police evidence (Mullin 1989; Wolffinden 1989; D. Rose 1992, 1996). During the 1980s an increasing proportion of entertainment and news stories presented police integrity and effectiveness negatively, although positive images remained dominant (Reiner *et al.* 2000, 2001, 2003).

While the media played their part in the development of a crisis of confidence in policing in the early 1990s, they reflected rather than created this conjuncture. There were deeper sources of loss of faith in the police by government and opinion formers, as well as the general public, not least the convenience of the police as a scapegoat for more fundamental failures of the criminal justice system and law-and-order policy. However, the police contributed to their own problems by the way their own 'law and order' campaigns of the late 1970s and early 1980s used the media to create unrealistic expectations of what more police powers and resources could achieve.

Since 1993 there have been contradictory trends in news coverage of policing. The police themselves have tended to withdraw from overt campaigning to influence public debate in the manner of such crusading chief constables as Sir James Anderton. Instead they have adopted a more corporate approach to cultivating a favourable public image, through the Association of Chief Police Officers (Reiner 1991; Wall 1998; Savage *et al.* 2000; Loader and Mulcahy 2003: chap. 7). The overall presentation remains highly-favourable to the police mission, increasingly defined exclusively as crime control, and the capacity of innovations such as 'zero-tolerance' policing to deliver results. However, the favourable media presentation of policing is volatile and increasingly challenged, constantly liable to be sabotaged by scandals or spectacular failures. The Stephen Lawrence case, which united the issues of police ineffectiveness, racism, and corruption, epitomized the brittle character of the representation and public standing of the police in the 1990s. The brief lull of optimism that the 1999 Macpherson Report's reforms had quelled the poison of police racism was shattered by the 2003 BBC documentary *The Secret Policeman* which showed vivid undercover footage of virulent police racism (McLaughlin 2007: chap. 6). What is clear is that media presentation of police issues is now much more unstable, complex and contradictory than either the 'hegemonic' or the 'subversive' perspectives imply.

FICTIONAL IMAGES

Crime and law enforcement have always been staples of the mass entertainment media. Historians of detective fiction are fond of tracing roots back to the Bible and Greek mythology, seeing Cain and Abel or the Oedipus myth as crypto-crime stories (Sayers 1928). In the eighteenth century there was a flourishing trade in broadsheets, ballads, 'memoirs', and novels about the exploits of highwaymen like Dick Turpin or Jack Sheppard, and thief-takers like Jonathan Wild. But the real take-off in crime and detective fiction occurred with the formation of modern police forces in Europe in the early nineteenth century. There was a mushrooming output of fictionalized memoirs of ex-detectives from the Sûrete or the Bow Street Runners. The prototype was the publication in 1828–9 of the *Mémoires* of Vidocq, a thief turned thief-taker who ran the Paris police detective bureau after 1817. Modern detective fiction is usually traced back to Edgar Allan Poe's trilogy of short stories about C. Auguste Dupin, the archetypal ratiocinative sleuth, starting with *The Murders in the Rue Morgue* (1841). The birth of detective fiction coincided with the development of modern police forces. Both can be traced to anxieties of similar kinds among the respectable literate strata, fears about the threat to social order represented by the 'dangerous classes' (Ousby 1976; J. Palmer 1978; Priestman 2003; Knight 2003). They embody similar models of the solution to these concerns about conspiracy and subversion: the unfailingly resourceful individual symbolizing a superior ideal of self-disciplined rationality, who is symbiotically related to a well-ordered bureaucratic organization Brown 2003: chap. 3; Valier 2004: chap. 1; Valverde 2006: chap. 5).

Since the mid-nineteenth century crime and detective fiction has been a prominent part of the output of all the dominant mass media. Popular heroes, including Sherlock Holmes, Charlie Chan, the Saint, Dick Tracy, Sam Spade, whatever medium they originated in, remain perennial favourites in all entertainment forms: novels, pulp magazines, comics, theatre, cinema, radio, television. About a quarter of all fictional works sold in Britain and America are crime stories. During the last fifty years in Britain about 25 per cent of the most popular television programmes, and around 20 per cent of all cinema films have been crime stories (Allen *et al.* 1998: 60–1).

Crimes and police officers are even more ubiquitous than that, appearing in almost all fiction, from Punch and Judy through Dostoyevsky to *Singin' in the Rain* (with Gene Kelly dancing round a bewildered cop). None of these is without some significance for images of the police, but I shall concentrate on the crime genre specifically as the richest source of such conceptions.[3] In this genre (fictions with crime and law enforcement as the central thematic elements) a broad division can be drawn between criminal tales (in which the central character is a person or persons—professional or amateur—engaged in criminal activity) and law-enforcement stories (in which the central character is a crime-fighter, whether amateur or professional).

Some work has analysed quantitatively the content of prime-time crime shows in American TV (Pandiani 1978; Lichter *et al.* 1994). A striking finding was the remarkably similar pattern of representation of crime, criminals, and law-enforcers between news coverage and fiction (and consequently a similar pattern of divergence from official statistics). Four important structural characteristics were found in TV crime shows:

(i) Most crimes depicted were serious, involving considerable violence, large-scale theft, or extensive damage to property. Murder, assault, and armed robbery constituted about 60 per cent of all TV fiction offences.

(ii) Criminals were rational and purposive, not impulsive, confused, drifting, or driven. They were high-status, middle-aged, white men. Their main motive was greed, although they usually had to engage in violence to achieve their ends.

(iii) Law-enforcers were more likely to be amateur than professional, although this is no longer the case. If professional police, they were usually detectives. They were predominantly unattached, economically comfortable, white males in middle adulthood.

(iv) The law-enforcers almost invariably solved or foiled the crime(s), usually through the exercise of remarkable skill, daring, and increasingly scientific expertise.

All these elements are the precise opposite of the pattern of real offending and policing. On the other hand, the characters, themes, and milieux have similar features to most other prime-time TV entertainments, which portray predominantly comfortable-to-affluent middle-class, middle-aged lifestyles.

These are the basic features of the crime genre which constitute the core myth of law and order around which numerous variants can be constructed. Crime is portrayed as a serious threat, certainly to the property and person of individual victims, but often extending to the social order per se. However, the forces of law and order can and do regularly contain it. They are thus portrayed as essential and valuable, even pivotal, institutions in our society. Furthermore, although crime seldom prevails, criminals are formidable and worthy foes of the law-enforcers. They are not defeated because they are unintelligent, resourceless or puny, but because of the superlative prowess and dedication of the law-enforcers.

Around this core myth, however, there are varied permutations, with radically conflicting perspectives on the virtue, justice, likeability, and sympathy accorded to law-enforcers, the criminal justice system, and offenders. There are also changes over time in the basic pattern of representation of crime. Since the Second World War there has been a broad tendency towards media narratives which are more critical of the police, increasingly questioning their integrity, and their effectiveness in dealing with crime (Lichter *et al.* 1994; Powers *et al.* 1996; Sumser 1996; Allen *et al.* 1998; Reiner *et al.* 2000, 2001, 2003). Rule-bending by law-enforcement protagonists is no longer presented as a regrettably necessary evil as in the Dirty Harry films of the 1970s–1980s. It is routinely and unquestioningly engaged in because of the magnitude and emergency of the threats (24), or by officers who are themselves criminal law-breakers putting down not only even worse criminal threats but the few honest cops they encounter (*The Shield*), and even in *Dexter* by a police forensic scientist who happens to be a serial killer eliminating less likeable serial killers.

There have been numerous scholarly analyses of crime films.[4] The fictional treatment of the police has been the subject of a handful of studies (for example, C. P. Wilson 2000), with specialist studies examining police novels (Dove 1982; Dove and Bargainnier 1986, Panek 2003), police films (Reiner 1981b; Park 1978; Inciardi and Dee 1987; Parish and Pitts 1990b; N. King 1999) and TV cop shows (Hurd 1979; Kerr 1981; A. Clarke 1992; Sparks 1992, 1993; Reiner 1994; Eaton 1995; Brunsdon 2000; Leishman and Mason 2003; O'Sullivan 2005). The paucity of studies of police fictions reflects the fairly recent elevation of the cop to hero status, coinciding with the advent of TV as the primary mass entertainment medium in the early 1950s. Novels and films with police heroes (the 'police procedurals') did not really emerge as a distinctive sub-genre until the late 1940s, so that television, since its early days in the 1950s, is the only medium where the professional police officer has always featured as an heroic figure (Reiner 2008: 320).

To facilitate discussion of the varying kinds of law enforcement story (whether in literary, film or television form), their fluctuating dominance and social meanings, I have classified them into twelve ideal-type models, shown in Table 6.1. These are distinguished by their treatment of seven elements: the hero, crime, villain, victim, social setting, the police organization, and narrative sequence.

Law enforcement narratives are connected to some other closely related genres, such as the espionage, investigative reporter or lawyer/district attorney/courtroom stories. They also have been subject to many comic or parodic treatments. The criminal protagonist side of the crime genre could similarly be analysed into different recurring patterns, although none of these leads will be pursued here.

I shall now give a brief account of the image of the police in each type.

THE 'CLASSIC SLEUTH'

The majority of detective stories between the heyday of Sherlock Holmes at the turn of the twentieth century and the 1930s were classic sleuth mysteries. The story revolves around a puzzling crime by an unknown offender—often one that was seemingly impossible to commit. There are a variety of possible culprits, but by the use of what Agatha Christie's Hercule Poirot called his 'little grey cells', the eccentric hero with supercharged neurons eliminates all the red herrings and points the finger at an unlikely culprit. The police are portrayed as bumbling buffoons or, at best, unimaginative bureaucrats, capable of handling routine offences but quite out of their depth with a case of any complexity. Their lack of perceptiveness (as well as that of the hero's companion and chronicler, the Dr Watson figure) operates as a device to show up the hero's genius. The sleuth was usually an amateur or a consulting detective. Sometimes, however, even in the 1920s–1930s 'golden age' of classic sleuth fiction he (seldom she) was a professional policeman, such as Freeman Wills Crofts's Inspector French, Ngaio Marsh's Roderick

Table 6.1 Law enforcement stories

Type	Hero	Crime	Villain	Victim	Setting	Police organization	Plot structure
Classic sleuth	Grey-celled wizard (usually amateur).	Murder by person(s)/ method unknown.	Personal motive —outwardly respectable.	Exceptionally murderable.	Respectable upper-class, often rural.	Honest, well-meaning, rule-bound plods.	Order—crime— red herrings— deduction—order restored.
Private eye	Self-employed. Motive: honour. Skill: dedication, moral intuition.	Greed and/or passion murder. Mystery not crucial.	Apparently respectable and/ or professionals. Several cross-plotting.	Not always clear. Client (i.e. apparent victim) often morally dubious.	Respectable upper-class façade masking corruption, and underworld.	Brutal, corrupt, but may be tough and efficient.	Moral disorder— private eye hired— blows, brawls, bullets, broads, and booze—use of moral sense— 'solution'—moral disorder continues normally.
Police procedural	Routine cops, using footwear, fingerprints, and forensic science.	Murder; usually for gain. Whodunit less important than how apprehended.	Usually professional, and not sympathetic.	Ordinary, respectable folk. Weak, guileless innocents.	Cross-section of urban life, including cops' homes. Procedures— order restored.	Team of dedicated professionals. Hierarchical but organic division of labour.	Order—crime(s)— one damn thing after another — use of police
Vigilante	Lone-wolf cop or amateur. Skill: ruthless fanaticism.	Bestial behaviour by habitual, not necessarily economic, criminal.	Psychopathic. Unsympathetic even if 'analysed'.	Tortured innocents, though gullible.	Urban jungle, ruled by naïve, incompetent elite.	Rule-bound bureaucrats *vs.* street-wise cops.	Rampage in urban jungle—ruthless chase—elites try to restrain vigilante— defiance—'normal' jungle life restored.

(continued)

Table 6.1 Continued

Type	Hero	Crime	Villain	Victim	Setting	Police organization	Plot structure
Civil rights	Professional, dedicated, legalistic cop.	Mystery to allow hero to exhibit professionalism.	Usually personal motive, with modicum of sympathy to justify concern for rights.	Respectable/influential: strong pressure for 'results'.	Unequal society. Money and status 'talk'.	Servants of power.	Unfair order—crime—innocent accused—professionalism—solution—fairer order.
Undercover cop	Skill is courage + symbiosis with underworld: ability to 'pass'.	Organized racket.	Professional organized structure. Leader unknown (or proof required).	Ordinary citizens.	Underworld.	Team of professionals to give hero back-up.	Order—crime—infiltration—hero's rise in racket—solution—combat—order.
Police deviance	Honest 'loner' cop.	Police brutality or corruption.	Other law-breaking cops.	Suspects or ordinary citizens.	Police station + underworld.	Rotten basket, or bad apples.	Police deviance—investigation—control of deviance or of investigator.
Deviant police	Rogue cop or Freudian fuzz.	Police protagonist's brutality or corruption.	Professional crooks who 'invite' his brutality or corruption.	Suspects, processed by protagonist, or general public.	Police station + underworld.	Generally honest but bad apple(s).	Temptation—fall of protagonist—chance of redemption—redemption/death.
Let 'em have it	Elite gangbusters.	Organized racket.	Known gang (maybe unknown leader).	Ordinary folk.	Underworld vs. overworld.	Tough combat unit.	Order—rackets—battle—victory—order.

Fort Apache	Team of routine cops.	'Raids', skirmishes with ethnic minority enemy.	Ghetto toughs, and renegade or foolish whites.	Ordinary folk.	Police outpost in hostile enemy territory.	Beleaguered minority. Camaraderie broken by discipline and deviants.	Cold war—incident—threat of all-out war—troublemakers neutralized—cold war.
Police community	Routine patrol cops: very human.	Many petty misdemeanours. Tempt cops to cynicism.	No specific person. Real villain is despairing cynicism.	Ordinary citizens. Many are unsavoury 'assholes'.	Police station/car, contrasted with city jungle and domestic tensions.	Brotherhood, 'family' of disparate types.	Picaresque. Will cop save or lose his soul?
Community police	Routine patrol bobby: very human.	Petty, if any.	Prodigal son, if any.	Ordinary folk. Salt-of-the-earth types.	Organic, integrated community.	Microcosm of larger community. Non-divisive hierarchy and specialization.	Order—everyday human problem—police use moral wisdom + social bonds—order restored.

Alleyn, Michael Innes's Inspector Appleby, and Earl Der Biggers's Charlie Chan (most of whom have featured in several types of media). But these were mostly unusual police officers, of independent means and elite education, spouting poetry, esoteric allusions, and classical quotes with the snootiest amateur sleuth. They clearly never joined police departments for anything so vulgar as a modest but secure pay cheque. Rather, the job provided them with a more predictable and plausible supply of mysterious corpses than their amateur counterparts' reliance on invitations to spend weekends at creepy country mansions. Unlike later models of fictional police, these supersleuths were in the great detective tradition, relying on brainpower not police power or firepower.

Contrary to the theory expressed by Rex Stout (creator of Nero Wolfe, and a master of the classic tradition) 'that people who don't like mystery stories are anarchists', the classical sleuth story is not really a law-and-order fable. The generally dim picture of the regular police militates against this. So does the image of a society with so ordered, predictable, and regular a daily round that the minutest deviation from routine constitutes a clue to the eagle-eyed sleuth. But above all it is a structural probability built into the plot requirements that the victim had it coming and merits no sympathy. He or she must be an 'exceptionally murderable' person, so odious a bundle of unpleasant qualities that all the other characters have ample motive for murder, supplying an abundance of red herrings (Grella 1970: 42). Furthermore, the sleuth does not want to be burdened with anything so mundane as legal requirements of proof. A good way out of this is for the murderer to be so sympathetically motivated that the sleuth, having demonstrated prowess by discovering the culprit's identity, does not turn him or her over to the police. The detective in effect acts as a vigilante, invoking a private sense of justice, not due process of law (Ruehlman 1974).

Classic sleuth stories remain popular in print, in the form of the lavish screen versions of Agatha Christie novels which were big commercial successes for the British cinema in the 1970s and 1980s, and on television. Most commonly nowadays the protagonist of the classic sleuth stories is a professional police officer. Popular series have featured P. D. James's *Dalgleish*, Ruth Rendell's *Wexford*, Colin Dexter's *Morse* (and his recent successor *Lewis*), R. D. Wingfield's *Frost*, Caroline Graham's Inspector Barnaby in *Midsomer Murders*, Ian Rankin's *Rebus*, Reginald Hill's *Dalziel and Pascoe*, and others in this mould. These classic sleuth mysteries are still enormously popular although largely ignored by critics and sociologists (an exception is Sparks 1993).

PRIVATE EYE

The novels and stories of Dashiell Hammett in the late 1920s and early 1930s, heralded a new kind of detective mystery: the tough, hard-boiled private-eye story. In the hands of his successors, notably Raymond Chandler, Ross MacDonald, and Mickey Spillane, the private eye became the dominant model of the law-enforcer during the 1940s, on screen as well as in literature. The model lives on in such characters as Robert Parker's Spenser and James Lee Burke's Dave Robicheaux (Geherin 1980), and more recently various feminist incarnations such as Sarah Paretsky's V. I. Warshawski. In Chandler's

(1944) famous puff for the superiority of the private eye over the classic mystery, its virtue is said to lie in its greater realism. This doesn't really hold water. The milieux and characters of the private eye may be more sordid and seedy, but the hero was a far more romantic figure than the sleuth, and especially in Chandler's hands became a modern knight errant, the lone man of the mean streets. Furthermore, there was a strong vein of social criticism and political commitment, usually of a radical or at least populist kind. (Spillane was an exception only in the sense that his politics were of the radical right.) The private eye was plunged into a quixotic quest through the murky corruption of a modern metropolis, by a client who more often than not was as treacherous as the initial suspects. A particular mystery might eventually be solved (although the puzzle element was never of real importance), but society itself could never be set to rights by such individual action as the hero was capable of. The police were often part of the network of corruption, on the take and/or brutal. But they were not stupid or weak. Some could even be effective law-enforcers in a bureaucratic way. The private eye's superiority was not special skill, but moral integrity and dedication compared with the corrupt run-of-the-mill cops, and an ability to violate bureaucratic procedure and cut corners.

THE POLICE PROCEDURAL

The police procedural story emerged in the late 1940s as an apparently more realistic successor to the private detective. It appeared more or less simultaneously in all media: novels, in the hands of such pioneers as Hilary Waugh in the USA, and John Creasey in England (especially his *Gideon of the Yard* series, written under the pseudonym J. J. Marric); the cinema, spearheaded by *Naked City* in 1947 (later a long-running TV series); radio and TV, with Jack Webb's *Dragnet*—the quintessential police procedural. Webb's famous catchphrase, 'Just give us the facts, ma'am', sums up the procedural's distinctiveness. The heroes were ordinary, unglamorous, routine cops, with more or less happy domestic lives, doing a job with professional skill and dedication, but no exceptional talent. They solved cases successfully because they had the back-up of an efficient organization, technological aids, and legal powers. Often they were harassed and worked on several cases simultaneously, an early device to lend an aura of verisimilitude that rapidly became a cliché. The organization was an integrated one, with differences of rank or function not leading to conflict. Authority was accepted without undue deference or resentment. Professional pride and camaraderie did not lead to alienation from the public. The cop had a private life which was meaningful and humanizing. At the level of physical detail and iconography the procedural was clearly more 'realistic' than the earlier kinds of mystery. But they really gave scarcely more accurate an account of police work in general. This remains the case in the currently fashionable variant, the forensic science stories. These feature brilliant feats of detective work using state-of-the-art wizardry and scientific expertise to foil intractable crimes. Popular examples include *CSI, Cracker, Bones, Silent Witness, Waking the Dead, Numbers, Criminal Minds*. The appliance of science resolves possible tensions about policing, as it unequivocally establishes guilt through objective techniques without anything but minimal reactive force.

THE VIGILANTE

The vigilante is either a lone-wolf cop or an aggrieved private citizen. The prototype of the former is Clint Eastwood's Dirty Harry, and of the latter the character played by Charles Bronson in *Death Wish* (1974), based on a Brian Garfield novel.

The vigilante story is an implicit denial of the procedural's values. Police procedure is impotent in the face of crime. Only the street-wise cop, understanding the vicious nature of criminals, can deal effectively with them, defying any restraints posed by legal or departmental rules and regulations. The vigilante tale is a quite explicit law-and-order fable, proposing police power as the only solution to the major menace of crime. The obvious plot device for achieving this end is the representation of ordinary city life as an urban jungle, and the specific crime/criminals focused on as especially bestial. The department is not the integrated organization depicted in the procedural. Above all it is divided by the absolute gulf and conflict between street cops and the management cops who restrain them for 'political' reasons. The citizenry, although nominally the justification for the vigilante's battle, do not adequately appreciate or support his actions, preferring to know as little as possible about the men who remove their moral garbage.

The vigilante story was a clear reflection of the law-and-order politics which Richard Nixon used to secure his 1968 presidential victory. From early 1968 until the mid-1970s—the heyday of the vigilante story—law and order was regularly named as the main domestic problem by opinion polls in America. The cop became the rallying symbol for white 'backlash' and middle-aged 'kidlash', with 'Support your local police' as the effective code words. The vigilante films were peppered with specific references to the contemporary law-and-order debate, as in Dirty Harry's attack on the controversial Supreme Court decisions of the early 1960s (such as *Miranda* and *Escobedo*) which strengthened suspects' rights. The vigilante cop model was translated for British audiences by the exceptionally popular TV series *The Sweeney*, and its derivatives like *Target*.

So successfully did the vigilante story articulate widely shared sentiments, not only about law and order but also about the counter-cultural and radical (as well as conservative) disenchantment with bureaucracy, that it came to seem *the* archetype of cop fiction (N. King 1999). Vigilante stories remained popular throughout the 1980s and 1990s, for example the *Lethal Weapon*, *Die Hard*, and *Beverly Hills Cop* film series, which were huge box-office successes (Allen *et al.* 1998: 62–3). These more recent incarnations display fashionably postmodern humour, knowing cool, and reflexivity. The prevalence of the vigilante model is why police stories are widely regarded as law-and-order mythology, although there have been radically different fictional models of policing which have been popular at different times. The vigilante tragically balancing moral values has been supplanted in the era of hegemonic tough law and order by protagonists who unhesitatingly torture and kill, and are often themselves corrupt and callous (*24*, *The Shield*, *Dexter*).

THE CIVIL RIGHTS STORY

The civil rights cop story was the opposite of the vigilante narrative. The police organization (and its political masters) were depicted as so concerned with 'results' that they trampled over due process and legal procedures. The hero was a cop in the procedural mould (who would have been happy in Jack Webb's team) but who confronted an unprofessional organization. The plot allowed the hero to prove that cops can have their cake and eat it. Only by following due process could they avoid fitting up the wrong suspect, and thereby allowing the guilty (and dangerous) villains to go free.

The quintessential example of this narrative was John Ball's 1965 novel *In the Heat of the Night*, which was made into an enormously successful, Oscar-winning 1967 film. Virgil Tibbs (Sidney Poitier) a black, big-city detective was arrested as a murder suspect merely because he was a black stranger passing through the small Georgia town of Sparta. Tibbs used his professional skills coolly and calmly to find the real culprit, teaching the sloppy and bigoted local police chief (played by Rod Steiger) that the college degree is a more effective tool of detection than the third degree.

The civil rights phase in cop stories only lasted a few years—from about 1965 to 1968. Although in general it would be misleading to see fiction as directly reflecting political events, in this case the connection was quite plain. Throughout the 1960s until 1968 the major domestic problems (as indicated by opinion polls) were seen as 'racial problems' or 'civil rights'. The emergence in 1968 of law and order as the prime domestic political issue coincided with the displacement of the civil rights by the vigilante cop story.

THE UNDERCOVER COP

Although the undercover cop tactic may be used by any style of policing, there is a special symbiosis between it and vigilantism. This is partly because it involves the hero in morally dubious practices of deception and conniving at crime (if not being an *agent provocateur*). It is also because, for it to be plausible that the hoods accept the hero as one of them, he has to have the image of a deviant. When clean-cut procedural cops like Mark Stevens in the 1948 film *Street with No Name*, or Edmond O'Brien in the 1949 *White Heat* infiltrated gangs, it was hard to credit the crooks' gullibility. It was much more plausible when James Cagney or Edward G. Robinson, with their established gangster personae, did undercover work in the 1935 *G-Men* or 1936 *Bullets or Ballots*. Indeed, what needed explaining was their employment as cops!

POLICE DEVIANCE (GOOD APPLE IN ROTTEN BARREL)

The police deviance story has affinities with the civil rights stories. It portrays the struggle of a single honest cop against a corrupt organization. The difference is that the civil rights narrative concerned the violation of rights to achieve convictions, rather than exploitation of the job for personal financial reward.

The police deviance story was very much a development of the 1970s, following the Knapp Committee investigations revealing pervasive corruption in the New York Police Department. The quintessential example was the book and film based on the experiences of Frank Serpico, the honest cop whose revelations stimulated the Knapp Commission. Many other individuals involved in those events have produced memoirs or fictionalized accounts (such as *Prince of the City* 1982). Police deviance stories continue to be a vigorous sub-genre (*Year of the Dragon* 1985; *The Untouchables* 1987; *Q. and A.* 1990; *Internal Affairs* 1990; *Cop Land* 1997; *LA Confidential* 1997; *Night Falls on Manhattan* 1997; *Training Day* 2002; *The Departed* 2006).

In Britain, too, the Scotland Yard scandals stimulated several novels and plays focusing on the issue of police corruption. Bernard Toms's *The Strange Affair*—(1968 also filmed, starring Michael York) focused, like *Serpico*, on the (unsuccessful) struggles of a lone honest policeman. G. F. Newman's *Bastard* series of novels, the *Law and Order* novels and play trilogy, and the play *Operation Bad-Apple* all explored the world of policing in a critical light reflecting the impact of the 1970s corruption scandals. More recent British television series have continued to focus on police deviance, as in *Between the Lines, Cops, The Vice, Prime Suspect,* and increasingly since the 1990s, *The Bill* (Brunsdon 2000; Leishman and Mason 2003).

DEVIANT POLICE (BAD APPLE IN CLEAN BARREL)

There are two subvariants of this category. In the 'Freudian fuzz' stories the central character is a cop who is driven into vigilante-style brutalities, which (unlike in the vigilante narrative) are not approved of. His rule-breaking is the product of the combined pressure of the general cynicism induced by police work and some special psychological weakness of the hero, which although 'analysed' by the narrative does not morally justify his actions. The quintessential example was Sidney Kingsley's play *Detective Story* and the 1951 movie version of it. (For other examples, see Reiner 1981b: 205–7.) The 'Freudian fuzz' was not a bad man, so he was allowed some chance to redeem himself, even though it usually cost him his life.

The other variant was the 'rogue cop' story, in which the protagonist was led into deviance at least partly for personal gain, although the 'invitational edge' of temptation was stressed so that his actions were seen as comprehensible if not condonable. Good examples were the 1950 Joseph Losey film *The Prowler,* and the 1954 *Rogue Cop.* Because the protagonist was not thoroughly evil, he was also usually allowed redemption through self-sacrificing death.

Where the police deviance/deviant police narratives are combined (bad apple in rotten barrel), as in G. F. Newman's work, the bleakest image of the police in popular fiction is achieved. American police deviance stories have also tended to increasing pessimism, with corruption seen as endemic rather than episodic (for example, *Internal Affairs, LA Confidential, Cop Land, Training Day, The Shield*).

'LET 'EM HAVE IT!'

Unlike the other categories there are no examples of this type with any pretensions to seriousness. It was the province of the 'B' movie, the pulp magazine or novel, the Saturday-morning cinema serial, and the comic strip. None of the moral, political, or even practical problems or dilemmas of policing was touched upon, as they are in some way by all the other categories. Rather, this type formed the bedrock imagery of 'cops versus robbers' stories from which the others constructed more complicated permutations. The stories were simple sequences of planning and executing skirmishes, raids, and battles in the 'war against crime' between police and hoodlum organizations. Examples are such G-men films of the 1930s as *Let 'Em Have It, Muss' Em Up, Don't Turn 'Em Loose,* and *Show' Em No Mercy* (vigilante stories without this being seen as a controversial stance), or the perennially popular Dick Tracy character (originating in a 1930s comic strip, but graduating to 'B' feature and serial films and radio, and revived in Warren Beatty's 1990 blockbuster film). With the growing sophistication of post-1950s cinema, this type disappeared from the large screen. But it continued in such popular TV series as *The Untouchables* or *Starsky and Hutch*, although with inflections reflecting the fashions of the day (the procedural in the former, the vigilante in the latter). Since the early 1990s there has been something of a big screen comeback, in *Dick Tracy, Lethal Weapon,* and lesser spin-offs, part of a Hollywood return to nostalgic escapist adventures which began with *Star Wars* and *Superman* in the late 1970s and continued with *Batman* in the law enforcement genre.

'FORT APACHE'

The 'Fort Apache' story was distinguishable more by its setting than its narrative structure. The quintessential example was Heywood Gould's novel *Fort Apache, the Bronx,* and the 1981 Paul Newman film it inspired. This was partly a picaresque account of the police community, partly (unsolved by the cops) murder mystery, partly a 'civil rights' story. The distinctive feature was embodied in the title. The police were portrayed as the old US cavalry, a beleaguered garrison in hostile territory. The military metaphor invited comparison with the 'Let 'em have it' sagas, but the depiction of the 'enemy' was crucially different. In the G-Men or Dick Tracy stories the hoods were unequivocally evil. In the Fort Apache type the police were opposed by people of a different race. Not only did distinctions have to be made between the 'good' and 'bad' members of it (the hero of *Assault on Precinct 13* was a black cop), but even the hostiles who attacked the police were reacting to oppression (in the liberal variants like *Fort Apache, the Bronx,* or Tony Richardson's 1982 *The Border*), or at least represented a distinct if alien culture. (Even the savage gangs who callously murdered a little girl in *Assault on Precinct 13* were shown as having a code and rituals, and had taken to the warpath because of police harassment.) Implicitly the tense relations between the police and the ghetto residents whose borders they patrolled were the products of the racism and uneven economic development of white America, although the prime focus of sympathy was the cop who had to carry the can for the sins of the majority. In all these films the evil action of renegades on both sides threatened (or produced) all-out war, although the hero struggled to contain it. Ultimately, however, the police could at best lower the temperature of the cold war between ghetto and suburb, not remove the sources of conflict. The Fort Apache stories reflect the civil rights *vs.* law-and-order debates some years on, with a pessimistic, albeit usually liberal, slant. There was little faith in the efficacy of either civil rights or repressive policies to do more than contain a 'dreadful enclosure', a sensitivity that continues with *The Wire.*

POLICE COMMUNITY

Police community stories are everyday tales of ordinary cop folk. They are best illustrated by the novels of ex-Los Angeles police sergeant Joseph Wambaugh, and their film derivatives, especially *The New Centurions, The Blue Knight, The Choirboys,* and the TV series *The Blue Knight* and *Police Story. Hill Street Blues* continued some of the same themes, with much less reverence for the police force.

Although crimes featured in these stories, they were not central to the narrative, and were mainly petty misdemeanours rather than serious offences. The true theme of the stories was the moral development of the police officer, and the internal relations of the police community. The narratives were a picaresque portrayal of the bewildering array of incidents the patrolling cop encounters. The linking question giving these episodes coherence was whether the cop could safeguard his soul, or would surrender to the besetting sin of cynicism, and take refuge in alcohol, suicide, or brutalization. While the police formed an internal community of sorts, they were divided from ordinary citizens, who if not themselves corrupt were unappreciative 'assholes' who did not back up the police. Whereas the domestic life of the procedural policeman was happy (with the occasional trivial tiff over missed Christmas dinners and the like just adding a touch of verisimilitude), and the vigilante's home life non-existent apart from casual sexual encounters, the 'blue knight' reluctantly and sadly watched his marriage and family fall apart as a necessary consequence of his higher calling. The police community stories embodied the cop culture portrayed by American sociological studies, emphasizing the social isolation and internal solidarity of the police fraternity.

COMMUNITY POLICE

Community police stories are the British equivalent of the American police community narrative, the differences reflecting the divergent images and predicaments of the bobby and the cop. The quintessential exemplar was the *Dixon of Dock Green* television series (although *The Blue Lamp,* the 1950 film that introduced PC George Dixon—and killed him off within the first hour—was much more of a straightforward crime-fighting procedural than the television series that resurrected Dixon). Although displaced by the harsher *Z Cars* and the later vigilante style of *The Sweeney,* the community police narrative staged a remarkable comeback in the 1980s in the successful *Juliet Bravo, Heartbeat,* and *The Bill* series (and other spin-offs like *Rockcliffe's Babies* or *Specials*), reflecting the new fashion for 'community policing' in the political debates about law and order (Reiner 1994).[5]

The keynotes of the community police story are an emphasis on the harmonious relations within the police force, and between it and the wider society. This perspective is shared with the procedural, which originated in the same period. But unlike in the procedural, the emphasis is on the non-crime-related tasks of the police, and even, when crime-fighting, the human rather than organizational or technological resources of the police are stressed. Like the procedural policeman (but unlike the vigilantes or police deviants), the community police not only stick to the rules but are more effective as a result.

A later variant in some British TV series was the bureaucratic police story, which focused on senior management levels of the police (for example *Waterfront Beat* and *The Chief*). These portrayed the whole gamut of police work, not just crime, and were primarily concerned with the internal politics of the police bureaucracy rather than any mystery plot. This variant clearly reflected the politicization of policing. None of these examples has been particularly successful, however, and the more immediately crime-oriented work of street-level police, especially detectives, is likely to retain its fictional centrality.

THE CHANGING IMAGE OF THE POLICE

The crucial break in the police's fictional image came in the late 1940s when for the first time routine police officers (rather than G-men and the like) begin to appear as hero figures, in the American and British procedurals, and the British community police stories. Before then the ordinary copper was a background not a leading character; a servant figure, and like other servants, public or private, socially invisible. This was illustrated well by Thomas Burke's classic 1912 short story 'The Hands of Mr Ottermole', later filmed as an episode of Hitchcock's 1950 television series. In this the mysterious mass murderer whom nobody observes was in fact a patrolling bobby, seen by everyone but noticed by none.[6]

The precondition for the emergence of the police officer as a credible figure was the professionalization of the police, and their espousal of the important social mandate of crime control (Manning 1977). Jack Webb in the 1950s received unprecedented facilities for making *Dragnet* from William Parker, chief of the Los Angeles Police Department and a leader of the professionalization movement. (James Ellroy's novel *LA Confidential* and the 1997 movie derived from it—in which the imaginary TV series *Badge of Honour* is modelled on *Dragnet*—offers a more jaundiced picture of Parker's LAPD.) Webb (1959) responded by writing a eulogistic account of the LAPD 'from the inside'. *The Blue Lamp* also began with introductory shots and voice-over emphasizing the importance of both the uniformed bobby and technological professionalism in the battle against 'the crime wave'.

If the precondition for police heroes was professionalization, the demand for them (and for professionalization) came from the notion that other informal and amateur means of peacekeeping were no longer adequate. The procedural and the community police story implied a society where order maintenance required a professional organization, but this could operate democratically, with community consent and according to the rule of law.

The deviant police and civil rights stories, which emerged in the later phases of the procedural cycle but before the vigilante boom, implied that legalistic policing was breaking down, at least for some cops in some forces. But it was still maintained as an ideal. The 1970s vigilante stories rejected the model of liberal policing altogether as naive wishful thinking. They suggested a society so deeply threatened by extremes of evil that only the most drastic and unrestrained forceful measures could save it. The police community and police deviance stories of that period pointed to the dangers of the law-and-order mentality for officers themselves.

The overall trend throughout these developments was clearly towards an increasingly critical view of policing, and the culmination of this for the US cop fictions was the Fort Apache story. Although portrayed as a gallant band patrolling the borders between civilization and the chaos that the racism and ruthless economic advance of that 'civilization' had engendered in its ghetto areas, there was little faith in the prospect of any solution, either liberal reforms or total repression. In British police fiction a similar bleak conclusion was proposed by G. F. Newman's combination of the police deviance/deviant police models in a portrait of endemic corruption and rule-breaking. The only alternatives in his world were to let the villains carry on without any regulation, or to attempt control with the inevitable consequence of the corruption of the controllers, even as they did the job as well as possible while themselves on the take. Crime control conforming to a legalistic conception was unattainable. The deepening darkness of the mood of police fictions matched the politicization of law-and-order issues in the late 1960s and 1970s, as well as a growing undercurrent of apprehension by conservatives and liberals alike (fed by criminological and penological research) that 'nothing works'.

In Britain the 1981 Scarman Report stimulated a flurry of 'community policing' initiatives. This cautious attempt at re-legitimating the police was reflected in the renewed fictional enthusiasm for community police stories like *The Bill* and *Heartbeat*, as well as such great sleuth-style police detectives as *Morse*. In the USA too, there was some softening of the police image on television in the early 1980s indicated by shows like *Hill Street Blues*, *Cagney and Lacey*, and *T. J. Hooker*. However, there was no return to *Dixon*-style harmony in the TV police image. The police community was shown with its own internal conflicts based on gender, race, age, rank, and specialism, and as dealing with a much more fragmented outside world.

During the 1980s there was a bifurcation of images of the police. Critical and vigilante narratives coexisted with nostalgic throwbacks like *Heartbeat*. As a frequently appearing police soap opera with a large team of regular characters *The Bill* represented a dialectical synthesis of 1940s–1950s consensus and 1960s–1970s critical representations (Reiner 1994). In this milieu the police are not represented automatically as either 'goodies' or 'baddies'. Their moral status is contestable, and has to be established anew in each narrative (Allen *et al.* 1998). In the 1990s and 2000s *The Bill* itself featured more stories focusing on police deviance, and there was an increasing focus on issues of corruption, sexism, racism, and homophobia in other series like *Between the Lines, Cops, Prime Suspect,* painting ever darker shades of blue (Brunsdon 2000; Leishman and Mason 2003). The style of these series was modelled on the documentary, while on the other hand many documentaries featured crime reconstructions using techniques derived from fiction to heighten dramatic effects, blurring the factual–fictional distinction in what Leishman and Mason (2003) called 'factions'.

CONCLUSION

Both the 'factual' and the fictional (and the 'factional') presentations of the police broadly legitimate the police role in presenting them as necessary and for the most part effective. But this legitimizing function coexists with increasing media criticism not only of specific police actions and individuals, but even of the whole direction of police policy, at times building up to a consensus for reform. Moreover, the media image of the reality or ideal of policing is not monolithic, either in any one period or between different times. Nevertheless, a broad threefold pattern of change can be discerned corresponding to the trends in police politicization. The culmination of the long process of police legitimation led to the 'golden age' of crime-reporting as well as consensual police fictions of the 1940s and 1950s (procedurals and community police stories). The unintended outcome of professionalism became in the late 1960s a renewed politicization. Law and order became a major political issue, reflected in (and stimulated by) news and fictional media presentations. In the early 1980s, however, there was a struggle to restore legitimacy manifested both in police policy and debate, and in media accounts, both 'factual' and 'fictional'.[7] There is no new legitimating myth, however. A more sophisticated public awareness of conflict, inside and outside the police organization, precludes anything but a pragmatic, conditional legitimation in specific narratives, challenged by others. For every *Heartbeat*-style attempt at affirmative nostalgia there are critical revisionist excavations of the police, like *LA Confidential,* as well as beyond good and evil criminal cop protagonists as in *The Shield* and *Dexter.* In a media time loop, some very popular recent television series have played with the issue of whether present or past policing was preferable (*Life on Mars, Ashes to Ashes, New Tricks*). The contrast is between the supposedly politically correct, PACE rule-bound, scientifically equipped, procedural police of today, and the corner-cutting, sexist, loud-mouthed but more human *Sweeney* model, with the latter ultimately prevailing. Excluded from the picture are the continuing prevalence of police racism, sexism, violence, and rule-breaking today, and the Dixonesque cosy community constable icons of the pre-*Sweeney* past. Having lost the automatic trust they once enjoyed, the police cannot retrieve it wholesale: public faith in policing is tentative, volatile, contradictory, and brittle, and has to be renegotiated case by case.

NOTES

1. This overlooks a fundamentally different perspective, the predominant one among media professionals themselves. With regard to news production it is the 'cock-up' theory. In relation to crime fictions it is the view of them as mere innocent 'entertainments'. The common theme to these practitioners' perspectives is the denial of social or political implication, on the grounds either that the media 'tell it like it is', or that they are 'only' stories. But media presentations are never innocent of social and political implications, though not conscious or intentional for the most part.

2. This distinction is tenuous. Crime fictions have often been at the frontiers of realism in style, while 'real-life' police are undoubtedly affected by media images. When I went on patrol in 1980 in the precinct of Los Angeles where Joseph Wambaugh's novel *The Choirboys* (and its film spin-off) was set, many officers wore belt-buckles sporting the legend 'I am a Choir Boy'. The difference between 'factual' and 'fictional' presentations has been further eroded by the rise of 'fly-on-the-wall' documentaries like those pioneered by Roger Graef in his seminal 1981 Thames Valley Police series, called simply *Police*, and the genre of 'reality' programmes (Kidd-Hewitt and Osborne 1995; Fishman and Cavender 1998; Hill 2000; Brown 2003: chap. 2; Leishman and Mason 2003: Part 3). Fictional series such as *Between the Lines* and *Cops* also blur the line by using documentary styles of filming.

3. An important kind of fiction this leaves out is children's literature (Morrison 1984). A frequent theme is that the police (however laughable or lovable) are essential for social order. In Enid Blyton's *Mr Plod and Little Noddy*, for instance, when Mr Plod is injured the Toytown populace bemoan their plight. 'Who is going to protect us against robbers?' asks Miss Fluffy Cat, and Mr Wobbly Man echoes her concern. The inconceivability to most modern people of social order without police —what I have called police fetishism—owes a lot to repetition of such stories.

4. These studies include, for analyses of crime films: McCarthur 1972; Shadoian 1977; Rosow 1978; Clarens 1997; Rafter 2006; of detective fiction, Haycraft 1941, 1946; Watson 1971; Symons 1972; Cawelti 1976; J. Palmer 1978; D. Most and Stowe 1983; Mandel 1984; Ashley 2002; Knight 2003; Priestman 2003; Horsley 2005; of detective films, Everson 1972; Tuska 1978; Parish and Pitts 1990a; of detective TV shows, Meyers 1981, 1989.

5. *Juliet Bravo* symbolized a new 1980s fashion for female cop heroes, also found in *Police Woman, Charlie's Angels, The Gentle Touch, Cagney and Lacey,* and *Prime Suspect,* for example. Other programmes and films tried to transcend the previous domination of the genre by WASP males by having a variety of ethnic minority protagonists.

6. The device of the socially invisible uniformed lackey was exploited by G. K. Chesterton in a Father Brown story in which the murderer is a similarly unnoticed postman; it is also used in the clichéd denouement: 'The butler done it.'

7. The crime genre has always presented itself as topical and bringing the public stories 'hot from the headlines'. Although with differing devices for conveying verisimilitude (all of which have a very short shelf life, rendering yesterday's forms palpably artificial), police stories have always striven for what counted as 'realism'. So it is no puzzle that the genre should so quickly register changing styles and debates in the police.

PART IV

LAW AND POLITICS

7

POLICE POWERS
AND ACCOUNTABILITY

The last three decades have seen profound changes in the legal and constitutional status of the police. Their powers and accountability have been transformed by overt developments in law, and by covert shifts in policy and practice. The landmark Police and Criminal Evidence Act 1984 (PACE) attempted a codification of police powers to investigate crime, and the safeguards over their exercise. The Prosecution of Offences Act 1985 created the Crown Prosecution Service, removing this major law-enforcement responsibility from the police, and purporting to introduce an extra element of accountability in the processing of cases (Jackson 2008). The Criminal Justice and Public Order Act 1994 (CJPOA) made further changes in this significant area, including in s 34 putting pressure on suspects not to exercise their right of silence by permitting courts to draw adverse inferences from refusal to answer questions. These statutes derived from the only two Royal Commissions to have reported in the last three decades (although the erosion of the right to silence in the CJPOA went against the specific recommendations of both Royal Commissions). Since the election of New Labour in 1997 there has been an accelerating tidal wave of criminal justice legislation, most of it expanding the powers of the police and further watering down safeguards for suspects. On the other hand, in its salad days New Labour brought in the 1998 Human Rights Act, and in the 2002 Police Reform Act (PRA) established the Independent Police Complaints Commission (IPCC) responsible for investigating serious allegations against the police.

Legal change and political practice have also transformed the doctrine of constabulary independence and police governance. The Conservative's Police and Magistrates' Courts Act 1994 (PMCA) and Labour's 2002 PRA were key legislative steps in this process. Chief constables have become less accountable to local government, while their accountability to central government has grown apace. Arguably we now have a de facto national police force, although in recent years reinvigorating local police accountability has become a mantra for all political parties.

The year 1981 was a major climacteric for the politicization of policing, most obviously because of the urban riots, unprecedented since the nineteenth century, and the ensuing Scarman Report, but also because of the Report of the Royal Commission on Criminal Procedure (RCCP) which culminated in PACE. The early 1990s were another major turning point as the New Public Management (NPM) hit the police and policing became more centralized and 'businesslike'. Police accountability was the subject of heated debate throughout the last three decades, but from the early 1990s the focus shifted from democratic and civil liberties concerns to a managerialist-cum-populist stress on efficient, effective, and economic criminal catching.

The RCCP had been announced to Parliament by Prime Minister James Callaghan in 1977. It was a response to opposing political pressures concerning police powers and accountability which had been growing for years. On the one hand, there was mounting evidence and complaint about police abuse of powers (revealed by the 1977 Fisher report on the Confait case, discussed in Chapter 3). On the other, the law-and-order lobby lamented that suspects' rights made the police operate with 'one hand tied behind their back' (as the Police Federation chairman Jim Jardine put it). The RCCP mounted an extensive programme of research, and was also inundated by evidence from the opposing lobbies. Police organizations presented a 'shopping-list' of demands for new or enhanced powers, while civil liberties groups argued for tighter control over existing police powers.

When the RCCP Report was published in January 1981 it was greeted with almost universal condemnation by the left and civil liberties groups (for examples, see the article by Harriet Harman, representing the National Council for Civil Liberties, in the *New Statesman* 2 January 1981: 6–7; Hewitt 1982: chap. 1). The police had regarded the establishment of the RCCP with, in the words of the Superintendents' Association' 'almost universal pessimism', fearing that against 'law and order . . . will be ranged the big guns of every minority group and sociological agency'. But when the Report was published the police reception was very favourable (*Police* February 1981: 3, 14–22).

In October 1982 Home Secretary William Whitelaw published the first version of the Police and Criminal Evidence Bill ('Mark I'). Supposedly based on the RCCP Report, it drew on it in a one-sided way. The RCCP proposals for greater police powers were incorporated or extended, but many of the safeguards were omitted or weakened. The RCCP had placed great weight on the concept of 'a fundamental balance' between suspects' rights and the powers of the police, making its proposals an integrated whole. Mark I aroused a storm of controversy which united the left and the civil liberties groups with a broad spectrum of middle-of-the-road and even conservative opinion. Altogether Mark I had a very rough parliamentary ride before it fell with the 1983 general election.

A revised Bill (Mark II) was introduced in the Commons in October 1983, responding to some of the criticisms Mark I. Mark II regained the support with reservations that had been accorded the RCCP by the mainstream professional law bodies, and had a much better press. The left, civil liberties groups, and many academics continued to oppose it (Christian 1983; Freeman 1984). The police reception to Mark II was distinctly cooler than to its predecessor.

The issues of police powers and accountability are of course interdependent and intimately related. The fundamental problem raised by both debates is how to regulate police actions. The police inevitably have discretion in the enforcement of laws, for at least two reasons. One is that they could never have adequate resources for full enforcement of every law. There is thus an inescapable necessity for choice about priorities. Second, even the most precisely worded rule of law requires interpretation in concrete situations. The logically open texture of rules in application makes inevitable an element of at least implicit discretion. These considerations make discretion unavoidable, but it is also desirable. Full enforcement would violate generally accepted criteria of justice, as recognized in cases where it is uncontentious that prosecutions should not occur, such as those involving exceptionally old or young offenders. In addition, criteria of what constitutes an offence are situationally and culturally variable, especially with the more amorphously defined 'public order' offences. What is accepted in Soho might scandalize in Suffolk. The Anti-Social Behaviour Orders (ASBOs) instituted by the Crime and Disorder Act 1998, for example, constitute indirect criminalization of loosely defined behaviour perceived by complainants and the police as nuisances (Ashworth 2004; Ramsay 2004).

The problem of how the discretion enjoyed by the police can be regulated exists at two levels: policy-making for the force as a whole—the assessment of priorities in resource allocation and broad overall strategy and style; and the street-level actions of rank-and-file officers. In addition, there is the task of providing channels for complaints about abuse and dissatisfaction. Before examining the recent changes in these areas, some fundamental issues about the legitimation of police powers must be considered.

FIRST PRINCIPLES: THE SIGNIFICANCE OF FORMAL POLICE POWERS

The legitimation of the British police in the nineteenth century was partly based on the minimization of their legal powers (Chapter 3). This developed into the myth of the constable as 'citizen in uniform', without any special powers beyond the ordinary citizen. The quintessential formulation was by the 1929 Royal Commission on Police Powers and Procedure (RCPP), cited with approval by the 1962 Royal Commission on the Police (RCP): 'The police of this country have never been recognized, either by law or by tradition, as a force distinct from the general body of citizens . . . the principle remains that the policemen, in the view of the common law, is only a person paid to perform, as a matter of duty, acts which if he were so minded he might have done voluntarily . . . Indeed a policeman possesses few powers not enjoyed by the ordinary citizen' (RCPP 1929: 6; RCP 1962: 11). Half a century after these sentiments were authoritatively quoted as a core principle of British policing they seem as antique as the black and white images of the Dixon-style copper. For a century and a half the misleading yet stirring ideal of the 'citizen in uniform' had legitimated the British police. Since then there have been two revolutions in the development and legitimation of police powers. PACE in 1984 replaced the 'citizen in uniform' myth with the much debated principle of 'fundamental balance' between police powers and suspects' safeguards. A little more than a decade later, this itself has been superseded by a proliferation of police powers not merely without balancing safeguards, but with a whittling away of the PACE safeguards. This has been legitimated by 'Dirty Harry' rhetoric, a supposed need to *re*balance the system in the interests of victims, because of a persisting state of emergency posed by crime, antisocial behaviour, and latterly, terrorism, accompanied by a castigation of traditional principles (barely 25 years old!) as standing in the way of modernization.

The shift in legitimatory myths reveals dramatic transformations in the politics of policing and security, and involves deep issues of principle about the relationship between state and citizens in a democratic society (Loader and Walker 2007). But in terms of policing practice, debates about police powers involve two fallacious assumptions common in public policy debate about policing. They are shared by the otherwise opposed law-and-order and civil liberties lobbies. Both emphasize law enforcement as the central police function, and adopt the rational deterrence model of classical criminology, albeit at different stages of the argument. In this sense both fail to take on board the implications of social research on the police, discussed in Chapter 5. Neither has adequately considered or explained the fundamental question 'What are police powers for?' but that issue must be addressed before it can be decided what powers are necessary and how they can be regulated.

If pushed on the issue both camps would say the police are primarily concerned with preventing and detecting crime. The historical and sociological evidence indicate that crime-fighting has never been, and cannot be the prime activity of the police, despite the mythology of media images, cop culture, and, in recent years, government policy. The core mandate of policing, historically and in terms of concrete demands placed upon the police, is the more diffuse one of order maintenance. Only if this is recognized can the problems of police powers and accountability really be confronted in all their complexity. The vaguely defined 'public order' offences like breach of the peace or the 1998 Crime and Disorder Act's ASBOs (which appear to be a scandalous embarrassment from either a crime control or due process approach) speak to the very heart of the police role. Given this, the implicit goal of many civil libertarian critiques—a precisely and unambiguously defined set of criminal offences and police powers to deal with them—becomes an unattainable chimera.

It is not just civil libertarians, of course, who discuss police powers as if the only function of policing should be crime detection. PACE was argued for by the Conservative government in 1984 as its 'main current policy initiative in the field of police powers to combat crime' (Home Office Working Paper *Criminal Justice* 1984). The 1993 White Paper *Police Reform*, New Labour's Crime Reduction Programme, and many subsequent policy statements explicitly prioritize crime control as the police mission. In Chapter 6 it was shown that the clear-up of crimes is only marginally dependent on police initiative, and largely results from information provided by the public. Changes in police powers do not significantly increase police effectiveness in crime control. There is no evidence that the rules of criminal procedure allow a significant proportion of suspects to avoid conviction, *pace* the 1979 claim of the Police Federation chairman that, if these rules had been suggested as a new board game:

'Waddingtons would have turned it down because one player, the criminal, was bound to win every time'. The RCCP's own research concluded that 'There are no obvious powers which police might be given that would greatly enhance their effectiveness in the detection of crime' (Steer 1980: 125).

If the law-and-order lobby errs in postulating the rational deterrent model with regard to policing crime (more police power + greater deterrence = less crime), the civil liberties lobby adopt the same model for policing the police. For years it has been the refrain of radical and liberal criminologists when arguing against the 'hang 'em, flog 'em' brigade that policing and penal policy have a limited and primarily symbolic role in restraining deviance. This analysis should extend to police wrongdoing. The main way that the sanctions and enforcement machinery proposed by a rational deterrence model can be effective is by the impact they have on the cultural controls in a community, including the police. It is these cultural understandings which are the immediate determinants of law-abidingness or deviation, and they are interdependent with a society's political economy, social patterns, and history (Reiner 2007a: chap. 4). What needs more precise analysis is the relationship between formal rules of law and the working rules of police conduct. How does 'blue-letter' law in action (Reiner and Leigh 1992) relate to black-letter law 'in the books', shaped by police culture and the situational exigencies and organizational sanctions of policing?

There are two competing views on this in the research literature. The interactionist largely assumed that formal rules were primarily presentational (Manning 1979; Holdaway 1979, 1983, 1989; Chatterton 1979, 1995; Punch 1979a; Fielding 1989). They are the terms in which conduct has to be justified, but do not really affect practice. It is the police subculture that is the key to understanding police actions. This culturalist perspective sometimes amounted to an extreme rule scepticism. 'Sociologists of the police have tended to treat the notion of legality as unproblematic, not because they assume the police operate according to these principles, but rather because they assume the opposite, that they are largely irrelevant in practice' (McBarnet 1979: 25).

But interactionist studies themselves point to some impact of formal rules, for example in the emphasis on rank-and-file solidarity aimed at shielding deviant practices from the senior ranks, and the need always to have a good story to 'cover your ass'. Rank-and-file subcultural autonomy is limited to a degree by formal controls, but how much, when, and in what way? Police subculture is by no means radically distinct or deviant in its values from either legal or popular morality. The police are broadly representative of the population, as is their culture (P. Waddington 1999a, 1999b; Foster 2003: 198–9).

While there is some tolerance for rule-bending as 'noble cause corruption' in police culture, that does not mean there is carte blanche for gross abuse. As implied by Klockars' exploration of the 'Dirty Harry' dilemma, the moral norms of police culture, while tolerating malpractices like 'verballing' or even physical force in some circumstances, proportion these to moral judgements of desert and necessity, even if these fall short of ideal versions of ethical policing (Klockars 1980; Kleinig 1996; Neyroud 2008). The danger of police subcultural notions of justice becomes acute, however, when there is moral conflict, confusion, or change in a society, and police ethics are at odds with those of their 'clients'. When the police deal with those regarded as 'alien', disreputable, and 'police property', the constraints of traditional communal morality are not an adequate protective guide or check. The problem in contemporary liberal democracies is less how to protect the majority, the 'public', from police oppression, than how to protect vulnerable minorities. A crucial issue for police accountability is the 'tyranny of the majority' problem. The rules of criminal procedure are dangerously stretched in relation to suspects drawn from relatively vulnerable and powerless social groups, but these constitute the vast majority of cases. 'Democratic controls' through the electoral process are not much help here. What has to be achieved is the incorporation within the operative police subculture of working procedures and norms which embody universal respect for the rights even of weak or unpopular minorities, which the rhetoric of legality purports to represent (Goldsmith 1990). The task of reform is neither just laying down the law, nor achieving majority control. It is probing what policy changes can achieve their desired objectives, bearing in mind the refracting effects of the rank-and-file subculture, and the situational exigencies structuring police work and culture (Chan 1997; D. Dixon 1997; Foster 2003).

The second strand in research literature on the police is a structuralist one. It argues that the source of police deviance is not primarily rank-and-file subcultural autonomy. The problem is the tacit encouragement, by senior officers, judges, and the state elite, of deviations from the ideal of legality. This is accomplished through a permissive structure of vaguely stated legal rules, and the accommodation of case law to police practices (McBarnet 1979, 1981; M. Brogden 1982; Jefferson and Grimshaw 1984; Grimshaw and Jefferson 1987; McConville *et al.* 1991; Ericson 1993; G. Smith 2004b). This structuralist case needs qualification in terms of specifying which rules, in which circumstances, are bent, and in what ways. The fact that police work is dispersed and of low visibility, and that judges may accommodate police practices in many judgements, so that sanctions are often effectively weak, does not mean that the formal rules have no impact or that anything goes, and regulating police work more effectively is a viable project (Reiner and Leigh 1992; D. Brown 1997; D. Dixon 1997; Chan 1997; B. Dixon and Smith 1998; Cape and Young 2008).

A prime problem in controlling police deviation from legality is the pervasiveness of conflicts of evidence about whether malpractice has occurred, due to the 'low visibility' of most practical police work (J. Goldstein 1960). In such arguments the suspect is usually at a structural disadvantage, which is why complaints are so seldom upheld (Box and Russell 1975; Goldsmith and Lewis 2000; G. Smith 2001, 2004a, 2005, 2009). A key aspect of the PACE project and subsequent developments has been a variety of tactics, from tape recording to CCTV, aimed at opening up the low visibility of routine policing (Newburn and Hayman 2001). Much of the criticism of PACE and other extensions of formal police powers rests upon what I have called 'a law of inevitable increment: whatever powers the police have they will exceed by a given margin' (Reiner 1981a: 38). As Ole Hansen of the Legal Action Group put it: 'If they exceed their present powers why should they not exceed wider powers?' (letter to *New Society* 22 January 1981: 161). But police abuse is not the product of some overweening constabulary malevolence constantly bursting the seams of whatever rules for regulating conduct are laid down. It is based on pressure to achieve specific results, using traditional techniques that may often be inadequate. The pressure is derived partly from public expectations, as mediated by the police organization and subculture. If the police can achieve their proper objects within the law, one strain making for deviation disappears. This does not mean that unacceptable practices should be legitimated. But it does suggest that the police must have adequate powers to perform the core tasks that are expected of them. It is a criminological commonplace that it is counter-productive to pass unenforceable laws because this breeds general contempt for the law. The same is true of rules of criminal procedure drawn so narrowly that the police are regularly inclined to violate them in pursuit of objectives which would probably have wide popular approval.

The art of achieving accountability. . . . is to enlist the support of the police in disciplinary activities. . . . For processes of external regulation. . . . to be more than a highly publicised morality play, the police must become convinced that they will be trusted to bear. . . . the active responsibility for ensuring correct performance. (Bayley 1983: 158)

Accountability institutions will only work if they win over and operate with internal disciplinary and self-controlling processes. Nonetheless there is a need for competent and vigorous external accountability, both to symbolize police subordination to law and democracy, and to ensure that internal disciplinary and management processes operate effectively.

Police lawlessness has always been rife. A fascinating illustration is former Met Commissioner Sir Robert Mark's autobiographical account of his youthful 'indiscretions' as a pre-war Manchester constable, such as breaking a drunken navvy's leg with an illegal truncheon (Mark 1978: 28–9). He also documented the prevalence in the late 1940s of interrogation by physical force (such as holding suspects' heads down lavatories) and the meting out of brutal summary justice to those who assaulted the police. There is much similar evidence in oral histories of policing in the first half of the twentieth century (M. Brogden 1991; Weinberger 1995). I am not suggesting that the police are now more law-abiding, rather that we don't really know what the trend is. The extent of police deviance at any time is an unknown 'dark figure'. Increasing concern is as likely to be due to changing public sensitivity and values as to a growth of real police misconduct. Public perceptions of what constitutes intolerable police behaviour are likely to have changed as deference declined in the post-war period, making complaints against the police more widely credible. Since the early 1990s pressures towards more police malpractice have intensified greatly with the new political consensus about tough law and order. At the same time concerns about police abuse have been relegated in priority compared to the new imperative of crime control. As will be seen below, this has resulted in a vast expansion of formal police powers, and a dilution of safeguards over their abuse.

The relationship between legal rules and police practice is complex. Rules do not determine practice but they are not irrelevant to it. The relationship is highly variable between times, places, and different aspects of law and practice. We cannot assume that shifts in powers correspond to changes in practice, but they are indicative of the political and social context in which the police operate, and the symbolization of the priority of crime control over due process values is of concern from a standpoint of principled legality. This will be explored by an analysis of the impact of recent legal change, above all the legacy of PACE.

POLICE POWERS: PACE AND AFTER

PACE is the single most significant landmark in the modern development of police powers. Much of its content had already been prefigured by piecemeal changes in statute and case law (and *sub rosa* police practice) in the years leading up to it. Nonetheless, as a statutory codification and rationalization of police powers and the safeguards over their exercise, it had enormous symbolic and practical importance. The Act's many critics saw it as signifying a lurch towards 'policing by coercion' (Christian 1983) or 'a draconian increase in police powers' (Lea and Young 1984: 254). The official claim was that it balanced powers and safeguards, with the 'objective of encouraging effective policing with the consent and cooperation of society at large' (Home Office *Working Paper on Criminal Justice* 1984: 15).

PACE purported to implement the RCCP's principle that 'a fundamental balance' had to be struck between 'the rights of the individual in relation to the security of the community'. This notion was built into the RCCP's terms of reference: to have regard 'both to the interests of the community in bringing offenders to justice and to the rights and liberties of persons suspected or accused of crime'. A sharp dichotomy between 'individual' and 'communal' interests is untenable. The 'communal' interest is ill served by abrogation of 'individual' suspects' rights which leads to wrongful convictions and the continued freedom of the truly guilty. An adequate framework of civil liberties is as much in the interest of any civilized community as is security from crime.

But the contrast between 'communal' and 'individual' interest as presented by the RCCP bears a kernel of truth. In any specific investigation, the tighter the protections afforded individual suspects the greater the difficulties of securing a conviction. For both the legislature and the police officer this gives rise to what has aptly been called 'the Dirty Harry dilemma' (Klockars 1980). Rules constructed too loosely undermine the pretensions of criminal procedure to sift out offenders accurately and fairly from innocent people. If they are pitched too restrictively, not only do obviously guilty offenders escape justice but police respect for the rule of law is undermined, with the counter-productive consequence that violations of due process may increase. Wherever the balance is drawn, the individual officer in some cases will confront the Dirty Harry dilemma of either violating the rules or allowing offenders of whose guilt he is convinced to go free.[1] The problem is to place the balance so that there is neither an abandonment by the legal system of its role of protecting just procedures, nor demoralization of the police through too frequent exposure to Dirty Harry dilemmas.

THE CONTENT OF PACE

How adequately PACE achieved the aspiration of a 'fundamental balance' between police powers and safeguards is highly debatable. On one hand, the Act gave the police a plethora of powers that they had not possessed before, at any rate on a statutory basis. To a degree this extension of powers was nominal rather than real, for much was a rationalization and codification of hitherto haphazard statute and common law, or a legitimation of what was already police practice.

On the other hand, the exercise of statutory powers was governed by safeguards which were set out partly in the Act itself, partly in the accompanying five (now eight) Codes of Practice. These Codes provided detailed procedures regulating stop and search; search and seizure; detention and questioning of suspects; identification parades; and tape recording of interviews (plus three later ones, on video recording, on arrest powers, and on dealing with terror suspects. See: 'Police and Criminal Evidence Act 1984 (PACE) and accompanying Codes of Practice', Home Office website, 2008). These Codes were underpinned by s 67 of PACE, which made failure to comply with them a disciplinary offence, and made a breach admissible as evidence in criminal or civil proceedings, if thought relevant by the judge(s). The Act also implemented the RCCP's solution to the difficulties of reviewing police actions posed by the low visibility of routine police work. This was to establish a variety of recording requirements for each exercise of a police power, giving reasons for what is done. There was also a requirement that interviews be contemporaneously recorded. Backing up particular safeguards for specific powers, the Act also included sections purporting to enhance police accountability more generally. There was an obligation imposed on police authorities to make arrangements for consulting the views of the local community (s 106), and Part IX established the Police Complaints Authority (PCA), which enhanced the independent element in the complaints system (and in 2002 was superseded by the IPCC).

This basic scheme, combining extension and rationalization of powers with procedural safeguards resting fundamentally on reporting requirements, ran through all the major provisions of PACE. It has been succinctly characterized as a strategy of 'authorise and regulate' (D. Dixon 2008). A clear illustration was stop-and-search powers. These were boosted by s 1, which extended nationally the power to search for stolen goods, previously only granted by local legislation in some metropolitan areas. New powers were given to stop and search for articles made or adapted for use or intended to be used for burglary, theft, obtaining property by deception, or taking a motor vehicle without authority. Finally a power to stop and search for offensive weapons (defined as weapons made or adapted for use to cause injury, or intended by the person carrying it to be so used) was provided.

Altogether, stop-and-search powers were clearly extended by PACE. There were two main safeguards over them, of debatable effectiveness. First, record-keeping: constables must make detailed records of each search, and of the reasons for it, and tell the suspect s/he has the right to request a copy within twelve months. Second, Code of Practice A specified that stops and searches must be justified by 'reasonable suspicion', for which there must be an objective basis, connected to the individual searched. It cannot arise only from an individual's membership of a category stereotyped as more likely to offend, such as black or young or long-haired people.

This same schema, combining extended powers with new safeguards based on record-keeping monitored by internal discipline, ran through all the main sections of PACE. It can be seen in the provisions on powers to arrest suspects, to enter and search their premises and seize evidence, and to detain them for questioning.

The detention and questioning sections contained a particularly complex set of safeguards, resting on the custody officer (CO), a newly created police specialism with a duty to supervise the detention of suspects (s 36). The CO (normally a sergeant, according to PACE) had the duty of informing a new detainee of his rights (to see a solicitor, to have someone informed of his arrest, and to consult the Codes of Practice). The CO must maintain a custody record on which are entered all significant events in the period of detention. A complex timetable of reviews of the necessity of detention, and of processes that can extend it up to an absolute maximum of ninety-six hours in exceptional cases, was elaborated in the Act and Code C.

THE INTERPRETATION OF PACE AT COMMON LAW

PACE clearly extended the key investigative powers of the police, subject to a regime of internal disciplinary safeguards for each power. In addition some general safeguards were introduced. Perhaps the most significant was the possible exclusion of evidence obtained in violation of PACE procedures. Confessions are admissible only if the prosecution can show they were not obtained by oppression, or by methods rendering them unreliable (s 76). Judges are obliged to warn juries of the dangers of convicting a mentally handicapped person on the basis of a confession (s 77). A more general discretion was provided for judges to exclude evidence if it appears that 'the circumstances in which the evidence was obtained' mean it would have 'an adverse effect on the fairness of the proceedings' (s 78). This rather loose discretion (a watered-down version of an amendment introduced by Lord Scarman) fell far short of the tough exclusionary rule hankered after by civil libertarians.

However, one of the surprises following PACE was the much tougher attitude adopted by the judiciary towards police breaches of the Codes than their permissive toleration of violations of the old Judges' Rules. There was some unevenness in the reaction of individual judges. Nonetheless a review of the post-PACE common law on the pivotal detention and questioning provisions concluded that 'the judges now see themselves as having a disciplinary and regulatory role in maintaining the balance between the powers of the police and the protection of suspects' (Feldman 1990: 469).

In the decade following the implementation of PACE, there was a plethora of empirical evaluations of its core aspects, largely sponsored by the Home Office (reviewed in Brown 1997). This represented an impressively 'reflexive' approach to policy in this area, embodying a dialectic of scandal, reform, research, and further reform. In the last decade such research has not taken place on anything like the same scale (Cape and Young 2008: 1–4), largely because the Home Office in the new era of tough law-and-order politics no longer sees evaluating the safeguards as requiring research—they are presumptively impediments to police effectiveness, much as Dirty Harry saw them.

PACE IN PRACTICE: THE RESEARCH VERDICT

Empirical studies of police work prior to PACE suggested that the powers of the police were formulated in so loose a fashion, and interpreted so permissively by the judiciary, that police practice frequently departed from principled statements of the 'rule of law' (McBarnet 1981). This underlay much of the civil libertarian opposition to PACE. It was feared that the police would exceed their new extended powers just as they had prior to PACE. The safeguards were expected to be ignored, relying as they did on police internal discipline and judicial discretion. These fears were exacerbated by the evidently jaundiced police views expressed towards the cumbersome paperwork of the safeguards.

The controversial character of the Act generated a considerable body of evaluative empirical research on its effects, commissioned by a variety of bodies. The evidence suggests a much more complex picture than was implied by the polarized polemics that attended the birth pangs of PACE. PACE certainly seems to have had a profound effect on the nature and outcomes of police handling of suspects. Routine practice has incorporated much of the procedures of the Codes of Practice, and many indices of suspects' access to rights indicate improvement. On the other hand, assimilation of the PACE rules into police culture and working practices has been uneven and incomplete. Much is ritualistic and presentational and affects little of substance in the experience of suspects (Adams 2000). On the plus side, research evidence suggests that:

(i) Suspects are almost invariably informed of their rights on reception at the police station (McKenzie *et al.* 1990; Morgan *et al.* 1990; D. Dixon 1997: 147–52; D. Brown 1997: chap. 6; Bucke and Brown 1997: chaps. 2, 3; Phillips and Brown 1998: chaps. 3, 4; Maguire 2002; Sanders and Young 2007: 170–1).

(ii) As a result, the proportion receiving legal advice has increased between two and four times, and is now about one-third of all suspects (Morgan *et al.* 1990; D. Dixon *et al.* 1990; D. Brown 1997, chap. 6; Bucke and Brown 1997: chap. 3; Phillips and Brown 1998: chap. 4; Maguire 2002; Sanders and Young 2007: 199–204). Some 40 per cent of suspects interviewed now receive legal advice (Bucke *et al.* 2000: 21). However, the quality of legal representation is frequently inadequate (McConville *et al.* 1994; Sanders and Young 2007: 205–14; Edwards 2008).

(iii) The special extended powers (such as denial of the right to see a solicitor) available for 'serious arrestable offences' (on the authority of senior officers or in some cases a magistrates' court) were obtained relatively infrequently, in about 2 per cent of cases (D. Brown 1997).

(iv) The extent of the use of dubious 'tactics' to extract incriminating statements by interrogation declined (Irving and McKenzie 1989; D. Brown 1997: chap. 7). Police and the Home Office have worked to develop more effective and ethical interviewing techniques (Williamson 2006; Gudjonsson 2007; Sanders and Young 2007b: 263–9; D. Dixon 2008: 32–3).

(v) Tape recording of interviews reduced arguments in court about what occurred in them, and is now welcomed by police who were long opposed to it (Willis *et al.* 1988; D. Brown 1997: 146–56). It has encouraged the innovations in interviewing cited above.

(vi) The average period of detention in police stations for all cases remained roughly the same, about six hours and forty minutes, despite the formal extension of the legal length of detention (Morgan *et al.* 1990; D. Brown 1997: 63–5; Phillips and Brown 1998: chap. 7). Just over 500 suspects per annum are detained for over 24 hours, and under 100 for more than 36 hours (Sanders and Young 2007: 180).

(vii) The PCA's supervision of the police investigation of complaints could be vigorous and active (Maguire and Corbett 1991). The PCA has now been superseded by the IPCC which has full investigative powers in serious cases.

There was also much evidence from the same research, however, which painted a more negative picture:

(i) Detention is authorized almost automatically and invariably. The idea of the custody officer as an independent check on this proved chimerical (Morgan *et al.* 1990; McConville *et al.* 1991; Phillips and Brown 1998: chap. 3; Sanders and Young 2007: 184–5).

(ii) The information to suspects about their rights is often given in a ritualistic and meaningless way. This may account for the overwhelming majority of suspects who do not take them up (Morgan *et al.* 1990). It has been claimed also that 'ploys' are frequently used to dissuade suspects from taking up their rights (McConville *et al.* 1991; Sanders and Young 2007: 200–4).

(iii) Some research suggested that the right to silence benefited serious offenders disproportionately (Williamson and Moston 1990), although other studies questioned this (Bucke *et al.* 2000: 6–7; Sanders and Young 2007: 233–5). Relatively few offenders ever exercised their right of silence, in part or completely. The proportion has declined substantially (but hardly surprisingly) since the Criminal Justice and Public Order Act 1994 permitted adverse inferences to be drawn (Irving and McKenzie 1989; D. Brown 1997: chap. 8; Phillips and Brown 1998: chap. 5; Bucke *et al.* 2000: chap. 3; Sanders and Young 2007: 229–30).

(iv) Later stages in the detention process (such as reviews, or regulating access to suspects by investigating officers) are less punctiliously followed than the reception rituals (D. Brown 1997: 62–3, 163–5). Custody officers are also less scrupulous about monitoring pre-detention events (such as delay between arrest and arrival at police stations: see Morgan *et al.* 1990; D. Brown 1997: 159–63).

(v) PACE procedures can frequently be sidestepped by securing 'voluntary' compliance with police requests. Such 'voluntary' compliance was a major method by which police operated before PACE conferred on them clear statutory powers to stop and search, and detain for questioning, as the euphemism familiar to Agatha Christie readers, 'assisting with enquiries', indicates (D. Dixon *et al.* 1990; McKenzie *et al.* 1990).

(vi) After PACE bedded in, the use of 'tactics' in interrogation increased once more, compared to its virtual elimination immediately after the Act, but did not return to pre-PACE levels (Irving and Mckenzie 1989; D. Brown 1997: chap. 7).

(vii) The provision of 'appropriate adults' and defence solicitors to assist vulnerable suspects like the mentally disordered remained inadequate (Sanders and Young 2007: 172–4, 243–5). In many cases no 'appropriate adult' was called or attended, although they usually were in cases involving juveniles (Phillips and Brown 1998: 52–7).

(viii) However adequate PCA supervision of complaints investigations may have been, public confidence and complainant satisfaction remained low, while the rank-and-file police were simultaneously alienated (Maguire and Corbett 1991; D. Brown 1997: chap. 11). The success of the IPCC in gaining public confidence seems encouraging so far, but remains problematic in the light of the continuing low rate of substantiation (G. Smith 2004a, 2005; T. Jones 2008: 711–12).

(ix) Consultative committees do more to impress police views on the public than vice versa, and act as a legitimating device more than a means of accountability (R. Morgan 1989; N. Fyfe 1992; G. Hughes 1994).

(x) The socially discriminatory pattern of use of police powers remains as marked as before. The burden of police powers still falls disproportionately on the young, economically marginal, ethnic minority males, who are the overwhelming majority of those stop/searched, arrested, detained, strip-searched (Morgan *et al.* 1990; McConville *et al.* 1991; Choongh 1997; Phillips and Brown 1998: chap. 1; Fitzgerald 1999, 2001, 2009; Fitzgerald *et al.* 2002; Newburn *et al.* 2004; Henry 2007; Delsol and Shiner 2006; Bowling and Phillips 2007).

PACE: GLASS HALF-FULL OR HALF-EMPTY?

The resilience of the social pattern of policing and its basic practices in the face of PACE is due to the unchanging role of the police, primarily as regulators of public space and those who live their lives there. PACE could do little to alter the impact of this on the culture and organization of policing, and as we will see, in the last decade policy has tilted towards unbalanced extensions of police power.

Nonetheless the Act *has* impacted on police practices, albeit unevenly and patchily. This was due in part to the symbolic consequences of the legislation, which put safeguards on a statutory basis that carried more weight with police at all levels than the Judges' Rules. It was also because of a variety of changes making punishment of breaches more likely. These included the tougher line taken by the courts, and the deterrent value of internal disciplinary sanctions (however little it may have been appreciated by outsiders). Of particular importance has been a variety of devices which began to open up the 'low visibility' backstage areas of routine policing. Key examples are the recording requirements; lay station visitors; enhanced access to solicitors (D. Brown 1997: chap. 6; Phillips and Brown 1998: chap. 4; Bucke *et al.* 2000: 21–7; Sanders and Young 2007: 199–200), and 'appropriate adults' in cases involving juvenile or mentally disordered suspects (D. Brown 1997: chaps. 9, 10; Phillips and Brown 1998: chap. 3); and the introduction of CCTV in some stations (Newburn and Hayman 2001). The legislation has achieved far more than its civil libertarian critics initially expected, if far less than they would wish.

Deterrence, symbolism, organizational, and training changes are all important in understanding how PACE affected police culture and practice. If powers are precisely rather than permissively formulated, procedures to render visible occasions of use are constructed, and supervisors and courts determined to police the police, change can occur in line with the law. Thus the booking-in procedures, which are precise, relatively visible to supervisors, and clearly enjoined in training, are religiously followed. However, the danger of precisely formulated rules is also evident here. They can be satisfied by ritualistic observance with little meaning, defeating their intended objectives.

In short, PACE accomplished significant constitutional and control functions, transforming police practices in large part. However, given the low visibility and hence inevitable discretion of much routine police work, the key changes had to be in the informal culture of the police, their practical working rules. These were affected through symbolism, training, organization, and discipline, but they are not determined by formal rules. Police culture is primarily a function of the structurally determined social role of the police, which has not altered in any fundamental way. Policing in a hierarchical and divided society can never be even in its impact, and the socially discriminatory use of police powers continues. Legal regulation alone will always be inadequate to secure legitimacy and genuine consent. In the last fifteen years, however, the hegemonic politics of tough law and order has shifted policy away from concern with achieving 'fundamental balance' between powers and safeguards, towards the continuing enhancement of powers without corresponding safeguards, and indeed with some attrition of the PACE protections. This unbalancing has been justified by a rhetoric of balancing powers in favour of victims in the face of exceptional emergencies requiring tougher policing, and a modernization of procedures not fit for purpose in the twenty-first century. Tony Blair launching the Home Office Five Year Strategy for Criminal Justice on 19 July 2004, boasted that 'We asked the police what powers

they wanted and gave them to them' in order to 'rebalance the system radically in favour of the victim . . . our first duty is to the law-abiding citizen'. And if a 'law-abiding
citizen' is wrongly suspected of a crime? New Labour's capitulation to any police request contrasts remarkably with the Thatcher government's sceptical approach to the
police 'shopping list' in the deliberations over PACE. Contrary to the implications of
Blair's modernizing discourse, the state of police powers was not a hoary Victorian
relic, but scarcely thirty years old. Never trust any policing procedures over thirty
seems to be the watchword of the 1960s generation in office. This is not because of the
civil libertarian concerns that worried many New Labour ministers in the days of their
youthful opposition to PACE, but because it is now seen as hampering crime control
by the police.

DEFINING POLICE DEVIANCE DOWN: POLICE
POWERS SINCE PACE

Since the early 1990s shift in the politics of law and order (Downes and Morgan 2007;
Reiner 2007a: chap. 5) crime control values have overwhelmed due process (Sanders and
Young 2007a, 2008). A paradoxical feature of the all-pervasive law-and-order climate is
that even some changes originally seeking to render the police exercise of powers more
accountable have the unintended consequence of legitimizing and enhancing them.

An example is the creeping de facto recognition of a power to stop and question
out of the Macpherson Report's attempt to regulate the practice, which had no clear
legal basis. The celebrated 1966 case *Rice* v. *Connolly* confirmed the principle that the
police had no power to stop someone to ask questions, although of course they regularly did this and gained 'voluntary' cooperation (in the 2001 case *Ricketts* v. *Cox* the
defendant was found guilty of obstruction for, inter alia, refusing to answer questions,
but the judgment explicitly does not overturn the earlier case, basing the conviction
on 'the totality of [Ricketts'] behaviour', not just his refusal to answer questions). The
Macpherson Report was rightly concerned that the pattern of stops seemed as racially
discriminatory as the exercise of the stop-and-search power, so they recommended
that police be required to record these along the same lines. The Home Office and the
Association of Chief Police Officers (ACPO) accepted this, and after trials the recording
of stops became required nationally, and forces began to speak of a power to 'stop and
account'. It could be argued that a power to stop and question was implicit in PACE's
conferral of stop-and-search powers. But the overall wording of PACE Part 1 suggests
that the stop must be justified by reasonable suspicion to search as well, although the
constable 'need not conduct a search if it appears to him subsequently—(i) that no
search is required; or (ii) that a search is impracticable' because suspicion was dispelled
by questioning' (s 2). There is no implication that the constable is empowered to stop
and question, other than as a preliminary to a search. However, following the government's acceptance of the Macpherson recommendation, Code of Practice A on stop and

search was amended to require that 'When an officer requests a person in a public place to account for themselves, i.e. their actions, behaviour, presence in an area or possession of anything, a record of the encounter as set out in paragraph 4.17 must be completed at the time and a receipt given to the person'. In February 2008 the *Report of the Independent Review of Policing* by Sir Ronnie Flanagan, former chief constable of the RUC, recommended as part of an attack on 'unnecessary bureaucracy' that stop-and-account recording should be drastically simplified. This proposal was adopted with alacrity by Home Secretary Jacqui Smith ('Home Secretary Responds to Flanagan Review', Home Office website, 7 February 2008), and is now in the current Code of Practice A. So an attempt to regulate a *sub rosa* procedure has culminated in a de facto recognition of a power never actually granted by legislation or case law, with reporting requirements that have been minimized to cut bureaucratic impediments to crime control. It is quite plausible to argue that the police do require the power to stop and question on the same basis as stop and search, but this has never been clearly debated and the process has been governed by an implicit and unquestioned assumption of its desirability.

A stream of legislation in the last fifteen years has remorselessly extended police powers (albeit with some extensions of citizens' rights by the Human Rights Act 1998, and the creation of the IPCC by the Police Reform Act (PRA) 2002). The process of undoing the PACE balance was heralded under the Conservatives in 1994 and has accelerated under New Labour since 1997. The Criminal Justice and Public Order Act 1994 permitted adverse inferences to be drawn from the accused's silence (against the recommendations of both the RCCP and RCCJ). Section 60 of the CJPOA introduced a stop-and-search power that could be operated without the reasonable suspicion required by PACE, if an inspector or higher-rank officer reasonably believes an area is likely to experience serious violence, or persons carrying offensive weapons. She can then authorize (for up to forty-eight hours) officers to stop and search anyone for offensive weapons, even without reasonable suspicion. Sections 61–3 also expanded public order powers to control trespassers or raves.

The Police Act 1997, one of the Conservative government's final pieces of legislation, established the National Criminal Intelligence Service (NCIS) and National Crime Squad (NCS). It also empowered police interference with property and 'wireless telegraphy' to prevent or detect serious crime.

The Crime and Disorder Act 1998 was New Labour's flagship legislation, establishing the ambitious Crime Reduction Programme to implement its ambition of joined-up, evidence-led policies to fulfil the pledge to be tough on crime and its causes. In the course of this it significantly expanded police powers. It empowered chief officers to apply for ASBOs, and to make local child curfew orders. It created new offences of racially or religiously aggravated assaults, and expanded the scope of criminal damage, harassment, and public order offences. The Regulation of Investigatory Powers Act 2000 extended powers and procedures to enable and regulate interception of communications, covert and intrusive surveillance, and covert intelligence operations.

The Terrorism Act 2000 followed the path indicated by s 60 of the CJPOA in extending stop-and-search powers without the PACE reasonable suspicion requirement.

Section 44 gave an assistant chief constable or higher-rank officer the power to authorize an area for extended powers if it is 'expedient for the prevention of acts of terrorism', subject to confirmation by the Home Secretary. The area may be as large as London, and indeed London has been authorized as such on a rolling basis since then. In designated areas, a constable can stop and search any vehicle or person for articles of a kind that could be used for terrorism, whether or not the constable has any ground for suspecting the presence of articles of that kind (s 45(1)). This has frequently been used against people where there is no suspected connection with terrorism, as in the 2006 *Gillan* case, in which the House of Lords upheld the legality of the search of peaceful protestors going to demonstrate at an arms fair in the Barbican. The Act also extends powers to cordon and control areas; to arrest and detain without warrant; and to search premises.

The Criminal Justice and Police Act 2001 extended powers to control public alcohol consumption and to protect witnesses. But its most significant contribution was the introduction of on the spot penalties for certain listed offences, Penalty Notices for Disorder (PNDs). These resulted from Tony Blair's originally ridiculed suggestion that young offenders should be marched to a cashpoint (ATM) to pay an immediate fine. After police criticism of the impracticality of that, the search for on-the-street police sanctions resulted in the PND (although they usually involve being taken to a police station). Originally directed mainly at 'safety' offences such as false alarms and drink-related disorder, the scope of PNDs has been extended repeatedly and now includes theft under £200 and vandalism under £500, and an increasing proportion are used to deal with such volume crimes (Young 2008: 166–71). They provide a welcome tool for the police to be able to clear-up volume offences without evidence sufficient for a charge, thus helping them meet ever more demanding performance targets. PNDs count for an increasing proportion of clear-ups (Young 2008: 174–7). Together with the expansion of stop and search they contribute to a growing battery of powers available to the police for regulating their 'property' on the streets without needing to overcome significant evidentiary hurdles.

Alongside this expansion of high discretion, hard-to-regulate powers, there has been a continuing erosion of PACE safeguards. This was signalled clearly by a Home Office Review of PACE instituted in 2002. Unlike the introduction of PACE, and its first major revisions in 1994, there was no public enquiry at all, let alone anything like a Royal Commission to signify that matters of constitutional moment were involved. The new climate of one-sided concern with crime control was manifest in the Review's remit: 'To ensure that the legislation remains a useful tool supporting the police and providing them with the powers they need to combat crime.' And more specifically to: 'simplify police procedures; reduce procedural or administrative burdens on the police; save police resources; speed up the process of justice'. Notions of a balance with safeguards have vanished, and there is a single-minded emphasis on what the police need to combat crime, sanitized by the aseptic language of managerialism. Issues under consideration included: giving powers to search premises without warrant or with only a superintendent's (not a magistrate's) authorization, and widening their scope; a general power of arrest for any offence, and extending the special enhanced powers for serious arrestable offences (SAOs) to all arrestable offences; creating on-street bail schemes, and qualifying the requirement to take an arrestee straight to the station; extending the detention time for any offence (not just SAOs) to thirty-six hours; stopping the custody clock if prescribed delays occur (e.g. getting solicitor or surgeon); permitting authorization of detention up to thirty-six hours by an inspector (not superintendent); removing the requirement for a magistrate to authorize detention beyond thirty-six hours; allowing a custody officer (not inspector) to conduct six- and nine-hour reviews of detention; allowing reviews by telephone.

Many of these suggestions have now been implemented in legislation. The Criminal Justice Act 2003 extends detention up to thirty-six hours for all arrestable offences not just SAOs, and empowers stop and search for criminal damage. The Serious Organised Crime and Police Act 2005 (SOCA) replaces NCS and NCIS with the Serious and Organised Crime Agency (SOCA). It allows for civilian custody officers, not police sergeants as PACE required. It creates a power of arrest for *all* offences, not just arrestable offences or those satisfying the necessity criteria of PACE s 25. It enhances powers to search premises, and gives powers to take fingerprints or foot impressions on the street. Community support officers (CSOs) are given more powers, e.g. of search. A power is given for police to impose conditions on demonstrations near Parliament.

The clear trend since 1993 has been to extend police powers, without specific safeguards. This has been confirmed by House of Lords' judgments in several cases: *Clingham* (2003) on ASBOs, *Gillan* (2006) on stop and search under the Terrorism Act 2000, *Austin* (*FC*) *and another* v. *Commissioner of Police of the Metropolis* (2009) on policing public order, legitimizing the controversial 'kettling' tactic subject to proportionality and necessity criteria. This suggests a rather different judicial attitude than in the early days of PACE, sensitive to the climate of exceptionalism and emergency. This trend is set to continue, with the 2007 establishment of another Home Office review aimed at streamlining PACE, again in the interests of liberating police procedures. 'The aim of this review is to establish from police and those who work with them, as well as the public, whether the act and the codes of practice are still appropriate, proportionate, and relevant to the criminal justice system.' To this end it considered a battery of powers relative to stop, stop and search, arrest, detention, interviewing, together with the further elimination of some PACE safeguards (for a blistering critique, see Zander 2007).

In sum, the period of legitimation of police powers by the principle of fundamental balance between powers and safeguards, supposedly enshrined in PACE 1984, lasted scarcely two decades. It has been displaced by a rhetoric of modernization to rebalance in favour of victims, supposedly justified by a new era of exceptional insecurity and threat. This same spirit animates current discussions of police accountability, as will be explored below.

CONTROLLING THE CONTROLLERS: DEVELOPMENTS IN POLICE ACCOUNTABILITY

The basic objectives and rules of criminal procedure are framed by Parliament in its enactment of substantive and procedural law. The issue of accountability is the question of how to keep police practice, in particular the operation of discretion, within that broad framework and in line with democratically decided communal values. This itself resolves into three analytically distinct functions: a 'judicial' function of determining whether specific police actions have breached legal or procedural rules; a quasi-'legislative' function of setting priorities in the allocation of resources between different legitimate policing duties; and an 'executive' one of managing the performance of these duties in as efficient and effective a way as possible. Debates about accountability revolve around how satisfactorily existing mechanisms perform these functions. Underlying the debates are differing conceptions of who should have the ultimate power of decision when there is a conflict of viewpoints over the goals and means of policing, over what range of issues accountability operates, and in terms of what political conceptions of justice should policing arrangements be evaluated (Reiner and Spencer 1993; Stenning 1995; N. Walker 2000; Loader and Walker 2007; T. Jones 2008).

Conventional police rhetoric makes much of the democratic character of the British police. As Robert Mark (1977: 56) put it: 'The fact that the British police are answerable to the law, that we act on behalf of the community and not under the mantle of government, makes us the least powerful, the most accountable and therefore the most acceptable police in the world.' This illustrates the central role played in official ideology by the notion of police accountability to the law.

There are four main ways in which the courts regulate police conduct: (i) police officers may be prosecuted for crimes, for example arising out of serious complaints alleging criminal misconduct; (ii) civil actions may be brought against police officers for damages in cases of wrongful arrest, trespass, assault, or for negligent performance of their duties; (iii) judges have discretion to exclude evidence obtained in violation of due process of law, as embodied primarily in PACE and its accompanying Codes; (iv) judicial review of police policy decisions may be sought, if they are claimed to be *ultra vires*. In practice none of these has operated very effectively. Police officers are rarely prosecuted for crimes arising out of wrongful performance of their duties (B. Dixon and Smith 1998; G. Smith 2001). The DPP and Crown Prosecution Services (CPS) have demanded stricter standards of evidence before recommending the prosecution of police officers than they require for ordinary suspects, because they believe it is harder to convince juries to convict police officers (D. Rose 1996: chap. 7). During the 1990s there was an increase in the number of officers convicted of criminal offences (other than traffic offences) from 35 in 1992 to 65 in 1998 (G. Smith 2001: 377). However, the number remains small when compared with the approximately 35,000 complaints against the police recorded per annum, or the 1,367 people awarded damages for police wrongdoing after a civil action. The burden of proof in civil actions is the lesser standard of 'balance of probabilities', but the problems of cost, time, and access to lawyers mean that such actions are rarely resorted to (and rarely successful), even though they have significantly increased in recent years. Before PACE, case law had whittled away the control functions of the judiciary. The 1979 House of Lords' *Sang* decision stated: 'It is not part of the judge's function to exercise disciplinary powers over the police or prosecution as respects the way in which evidence to be used at the trial is obtained by them.' Judicial attitudes to breaches of PACE were more robust initially, but have become more permissive following legislation creating more discretionary police powers.

THE COMPLAINTS SYSTEM AND CIVIL ACTIONS

A statutory system for complaints against the police began with the Police Act 1964. From the start it was subject to severe criticism for relying entirely on internal police investigation and adjudication. After many years of pressure to introduce an independent element, resisted by most police opinion, the Police Act 1976 established the Police Complaints Board. After studying the police report and initial decision, the Board could recommend and, if necessary, direct that disciplinary charges be brought.

The Board—a political compromise—was greeted with dismay both by the police and by civil libertarians. The latter deplored the impeccably establishment character of the Board's members, the lack of independent investigative powers, and the greater facilities for police officers to sue complainants for libel, which was won by the Police Federation during the political wrangling preceding the Act.

In the early 1980s pressure mounted for a more vigorous and independent scrutiny of allegations of serious police misconduct. The Police Complaints Board's own 1980 Triennial Report set out several recommendations to improve its functioning. The Board's new chairman, Sir Cyril Philips (who was also chairman of the RCCP), committed himself to a tougher policy, declaring that 'the existing Board had kept so low a profile that it has climbed into a ditch' (*Guardian* 19 March 1981). The Scarman Report and the Commons Select Committee on Home Affairs strongly argued for the independent investigation as well as adjudication of complaints. Finally, in a surprising volte-face, the Police Federation retracted its long-standing opposition to independent investigation, as did a few chief constables.

Despite this pressure PACE did not establish a completely independent system. Rather, it replaced the Complaints Board with the PCA, which was required to supervise the investigation of complaints alleging death or serious injury, and empowered to do so in any other case where it considered this is in the public interest. The Act also established procedures for resolving minor complaints informally, if complainants agree to this.

Research on the PACE procedures suggested that the PCA lacked the confidence of both complainants and the police (Maguire and Corbett 1991; Reiner 1991: 286–300;

D. Brown 1997: chap. 11). However, the much-maligned PCA, and the new procedures for informal resolution of minor complaints worked reasonably well, given the severe resource constraints (Maguire and Corbett 1991).

By the late 1990s pressure for fundamental overhaul of the system had mounted to a crescendo, following several years of gradual reform. The PMCA 1994, s 37 repealed the double jeopardy rule whereby officers acquitted of a criminal offence could not face a disciplinary charge which was substantively the same. In 1998 the Police (Northern Ireland) Act established a fully independent ombudsman to investigate and adjudicate complaints against the police (s 51), and it became fully operational in 2001 (Mulcahy 2008: 214).

In late 1997 the Parliamentary Home Affairs Committee (HAC) began an inquiry into police discipline and complaints. Its report, *Police Disciplinary and Complaints Procedures*, was published in January 1998 and recommended radical overhaul. It supported the principle of independent investigation. It also concluded that the terms on which officers were investigated was as important as who did the investigating. Consequently, it recommended the removal of the 'right of silence' from police disciplinary proceedings, and held that the civil, balance of probabilities, standard of proof should apply, not the criminal one of 'beyond reasonable doubt'. The HAC Report supported the earlier agreement between the Home Office and the police staff associations for a procedure to handle unsatisfactory performance by police officers. It expressed concern about CPS decisions about the prosecution of police officers, urging the DPP to give written reasons when prosecution was not recommended.

The Home Secretary's response was largely favourable, broadly accepting the HAC Report's main recommendations. On 1 April 1999 new regulations for dealing with police conduct and efficiency replaced the old discipline regulations, intended to bring the police in line with standard employment practice. Finally, after decades of pressure, the 2002 Police Reform Act established the IPCC, with the responsibility of investigating serious complaints against the police.

The IPCC investigates all cases involving death, serious injury, assault, or corruption. Forces may also refer other cases to it, and the IPCC may take over the investigation of cases if there are major matters of public interest involved. IPCC investigations are not limited to complaints but cover all allegations of possible serious misconduct, such as shootings, traffic accidents involving police vehicles, deaths in custody. The IPCC independently investigates the most serious matters. Other somewhat less serious investigations are either *managed* or *supervised* by the IPCC, the former implying closer IPCC involvement and scrutiny. Those cases deemed less serious still are subject to *local* investigation, with more distant oversight by the IPCC. The IPCC is organized into four regional divisions in England and Wales. Its investigators are drawn from a variety of backgrounds involving suitable skills, including former police officers but also such previous occupations as financial services analysis, customs and excise, and social work. A total of 28,963 complaint cases were recorded by police forces across England and Wales in 2007–08 (Gleeson and Grace 2008: vi). The most common allegations involved 'Other neglect or failure in duty' (24 per cent); 'Incivility, impoliteness and intolerance' (22 per cent); 'Other assault' (14 per cent). Of the allegations, 43 per cent were dealt with by local resolution, and 32 per cent were investigated; 14 per cent were withdrawn or discontinued. Of those investigated, 11 per cent were substantiated, and 89 per cent unsubstantiated. The statistics indicate increasing numbers of complaints since the IPCC was established, which might indicate greater public confidence in part, but is also attributable to an expansion in the number of types of staff that can be complained against, the possibility of complaining directly to the IPCC, and improved recording by forces. The substantiation rate is slightly higher than before, but remains extremely low.

The results of having a completely independent system may not be as dramatic as many hoped. The low rates of clear-up of complaints against the police were not due mainly to cover-ups by police investigators, and the focus of debate on the issue of *who* investigates neglects more fundamental questions such as what are the functions of the system and how can complainants' interests be foregrounded (Smith 2004, 2006, 2009). A key problem is the 'low visibility' of the operational situations that give rise to most complaints. Frequently they turn on conflicts of testimony between complainants and police officers, with no independent evidence. Irrespective of who does the investigating and adjudicating many are unlikely to be sustained, leaving many complainants with a sense of grievance. This problem has bedevilled attempts to establish complaints systems in all jurisdictions (Goldsmith 1991; Goldsmith and Lewis 2000).

In the light of the poor prospects of substantiation of complaints against the police, it is hardly surprising that civil actions have become a major growth industry as an alternative means of redress (B. Dixon and Smith 1998; G. Smith 2001, 2003). The door was opened when s 48 of the 1964 Police Act made chief officers, and thus police forces, vicariously liable for wrongs committed by police officers (reversing the common law position established by *Fisher* v. *Oldham* in 1930). This made it financially worthwhile to sue officers for torts. The means for suing frequently came from legal aid. The lower burden of proof in civil actions compared to the criminal standard required for complaints made the prospects of success much greater. In 1998–9 the HM Chief Inspector of Constabulary's Annual Report showed that claims against all police forces had reached 5,961 of which 1,302 were settled and 65 successful in getting damages. The total paid out for damages and settlements came to nearly £4.6 million (G. Smith 2003). Small wonder that Met policy appeared to change in the mid-1990s from settling to contesting actions. In the 1997 Appeal Court case *Thompson and Hsu* v. *Commissioner of Police of the Metropolis* the Met was successful in getting the court to suggest more restrictive guidelines for damages (B. Dixon and Smith 1998: 428). On the other hand, the grounds for civil actions were extended in 1996 by the Court of Appeal. In *Swinney* v. *Chief Constable of Northumbria* the police force was held liable for negligence, despite the stringent tests for such actions established by the House of Lords in 1989 in *Hill* v. *Chief Constable of West Yorkshire* (B. Dixon and Smith 1998: 424–6). Civil actions appear to many an attractive means of redress for police wrongdoing compared to the complaints system (G. Smith 2001, 2003).

POLICE GOVERNANCE

Some of the most contentious issues of police accountability arise in relation to the quasi-legislative and executive functions of determining the priorities and efficiency of force policy. The Police Act 1964 consolidated and rationalized the governance structure for provincial policing which had developed over the previous century. The two London forces (the Met and the City of London) retained their own accountability structures (in the former to the Home Secretary alone, in the latter to the Common Council of the City of London as well as the Home Secretary). The 1964 Act defined the general duty of the police authority as being 'to secure the maintenance of an adequate and efficient police force for the area' (section 4.1). The precise relationship constitutionally and in practice between police authority, chief constable, and Home Office has long been a complex and much-debated matter (G. Marshall 1965, 1978; Loveday 1985, 1991, 2000, 2006; Lustgarten 1986; Reiner 1991; Reiner and Spencer 1993; Jones *et al.* 1994; Jones and Newburn 1998; Walker 2000; Loveday and Reid 2003; McLaughlin 2005, 2007: chap. 7; Loveday and McClory 2007; Jones 2008). Although the 1964 Act purported to clarify and rationalize the situation, it failed to do so. Its statements were self-contradictory or vague at the crucial points. The police authority were explicitly empowered to appoint the chief constable, to secure his retirement (subject to the Home Secretary's agreement) 'in the interests of efficiency', and to receive an annual report. They could also ask for further reports on 'matters connected with the policing of the area' (section 12.2). However, the chief constable could refuse to give such a report if she deemed it inappropriate, and the dispute was to be referred to the Home Secretary as arbiter. Nor was the 1964 Act clear about the possibility of the police authority being able to instruct the chief constable on general policy concerning law enforcement in the area (as distinct from the immediate, day-to-day direction and control of the force, which is clearly precluded). Again, in cases of conflict it was for the Home Secretary to arbitrate. But the Act's thrust was to limit responsibility for 'operational' matters to the chief constables (Jefferson and Grimshaw 1984a: chap. 2). Lustgarten (1986) elegantly but devastatingly exploded this hackneyed, untenable distinction between 'operational' and 'policy' matters. The categories necessarily overlap and are arbitrary and tendentious classifications, without a basis in the Act itself.

Altogether the Act, together with the organizational changes in policing already discussed (amalgamation, technological advance, professionalization, growth of the police lobby), strengthened the power of the chief constable and the Home Office at the expense of the local authority. The police authorities paid the piper (or more precisely shared policing costs with central government) but did not call any tunes. They determined the force's establishment and rank structure, and appointed the chief constable (both subject to Home Office approval). But the chief constable had sole responsibility for deployment of the force, as well as for appointments, promotion, and discipline. The authority could dismiss the chief constable for good cause, but subject to Home Office veto. In practice most police authorities did not even use the limited powers envisaged by the Act, deferring normally to the chief constable's 'professional' expertise (M. Brogden 1977; Reiner 1991:

chap. 11). This was even more the case with the joint boards that replaced the Metropolitan authorities abolished by the 1985 Local Government Act (Loveday 1991).

In the late 1970s there developed several initiatives from the Left campaigning for police authorities to exercise their dormant powers, as well as seeking an expansion of them. Jack Straw, then Labour MP for Blackburn, introduced an unsuccessful Private Member's Bill on police authorities in November 1979. It aimed to increase the influence of police authorities (to be democratically elected by the local community, removing the JP element) over general policy issues, as distinct from day-to-day operational decisions, which would remain the chief constable's prerogative.

Controversy was particularly acute over the Metropolitan Police, for whom the authority was the Home Secretary, so that Londoners lacked even the limited form of financial accountability available in the provinces. In March 1980 Jack Straw, then a vigorous campaigner for radical police reform, introduced another unsuccessful Bill, aimed at creating a Greater London police authority to control the Met. However, it was not until 1999 that the Greater London Authority Act ended the anomalous lack of a local police authority in London, with the establishment of the Metropolitan Police Authority (MPA).

After sweeping Labour victories in the May 1981 local government elections, the GLC established a Police Committee with a strong support unit to monitor police policy. In the early 1980s several London boroughs, aided by GLC funds, established local 'monitoring groups'. Many provincial councils also moved into radical Labour hands in 1981, and there followed a series of much-publicized battles between the police authorities and chief constables, especially in Greater Manchester and Merseyside (McLaughlin 1994).

The 1984–5 miners' strike stimulated even sharper conflicts, with several Labour-dominated police authorities protesting at their lack of control over the manner of policing the strike or the extent to which the national operation produced a potentially disastrous depletion of resources for local policing needs (Fine and Millar 1985; McCabe et al. 1988; Green 1991). South Yorkshire Police Authority attempted to curb its chief constable's spending on the miners' dispute, but was stopped by a high court ruling. In September 1984, the police authority instructed the South Yorkshire chief constable to disband the mounted police unit, and most of the dog section. They justified this on financial grounds, although the chief constable (and most of the press) saw it as retaliation for the controversial use of horses in controlling pickets. The next day the Home Secretary warned the authority that it might be acting in contravention of the Police Act 1964, and the authority backed down on legal advice. Overall the miners' strike indicated that police authorities could be ignored if chief constables and the Home Office were in agreement.

Developments after the miners' strike continued this trajectory of centralization, reducing the role of local police authorities to virtual insignificance. PACE introduced a statutory requirement (s 106) that consultative arrangements be established in each force area. While apparently enhancing local accountability, pressure was exerted by the Home Office for these to take the uniform shape of consultative committees, illustrating how the growing number of nominally advisory Home Office circulars had come to be regarded as binding by most forces. Consultative committees functioned to legitimate the constitutional status quo (R. Morgan 1989; N. Fyfe 1992; G. Hughes 1994). The Local Government Act 1985 abolished the six metropolitan councils, replacing their police authorities by more quiescent joint boards (Loveday 1991).

The Court of Appeal judgment in *R v. Secretary of State for the Home Department ex. p. Northumbria Police Authority* [1988] 2 WLR 590, established that local police authorities had no power to challenge policy decisions by a chief constable if he secured Home Office support, even in spending matters. Home Office Circular 40/1986 had stated that, if chief constables were not permitted by their police authorities to purchase CS gas or plastic bullets for training in riot control, they could obtain them from a central store if the HM Inspector of Constabulary felt it necessary. The Northumbria Police Authority sought a judicial review of this circular as outside the Home Secretary's powers under the 1964 Police Act, which placed primary responsibility for 'maintaining an adequate and efficient' police force on the authority (s 4). The Court of Appeal rejected the argument. It held that the Home Secretary had power under the royal prerogative to do what he felt necessary for preserving the Queen's peace, irrespective of the Act. It also interpreted the Home Secretary's powers to supply common services under s 41 of the Police Act, and to use his powers so as to promote general police efficiency (s 28), as enabling him to override the police authority's views on necessary expenditure and equipment. This seemed to underline the impotence of local police authorities vis-à-vis the other two legs of the tripartite system of police governance, making them a figleaf of local influence in a highly centralized, de facto national structure (Reiner 1991: 25–8).

In the late 1980s and early 1990s a number of other developments continued this clear centralizing trend. Talk of a 'hidden agenda' of regionalization or even a national force was common among the police elite. Central government gained effective control of policing, but by proxy rather than the overt creation of a national force. Its instruments for this were Her Majesty's Inspectorate of Constabulary (HMIC), ACPO, the Met, and the creation of specialist national policing units.

The cutting edge of the thrust to greater centralization was the government's tightening control of the police purse strings. Concern about 'value for money' from policing, as from all public services (although rather less stringently), was a major theme of the Thatcher government throughout the 1980s. Home Office Circular 114 of 1983 signalled the government's intention to make additional police resources conditional on evidence that existing resources were being used as efficiently, effectively, and economically (the dreaded three Es) as possible. The even tougher Circular 106 of 1988 cast a chill over police managers and staff associations which has continued ever since. The alarm that permeated policing circles at all levels was indicated by the unprecedented joint study of the threat to 'traditional policing', sponsored in 1989 by all three staff associations (*Operational Policing Review* 1990).

The new financial regime was not only tighter but more centralized. The Audit Commission, the independent body established by the government to monitor local authority spending, became a key player in the policing field with a series of hard-hitting

reports aimed at enhancing value for money (Weatheritt 1993: 32–6). It argued itself
that 'The balance has now tilted so far towards the centre that the role of the local police
authorities in the tripartite structure has been significantly diminished. Accountability
is blurred and financial and management incentives are out of step' (Audit Commission
1990a).

The role of HM Inspectorate of Constabulary was considerably enhanced after
the mid-1980s, as the linchpin of a more centralized coordination of standards and
procedures (R. Morgan and Newburn 1997: 146–7; Savage 2007: 95–104). This process began in the early 1980s with the financial management initiative, and developed apace (Weatheritt 1993: 29–32). In 1987, the inspectorate launched a complex
computer-based management information system, the Matrix of Police Indicators. In
1990 inspection reports on individual forces began to be published, as well as thematic
inspections looking at issues across forces. Inspections are no longer the perfunctory
affairs of police legend, but involve the collation of considerable data on a standardized
basis, shaping police activity into centrally determined channels. Until the 1980s the
inspectorate had been something like a House of Lords for the police. It was a place to
which distinguished former chief constables could aspire after completing long, worthy
operational careers, or occasionally to which less successful ones were kicked upstairs.
The change in the role of the HMIC from dignified to effective was accompanied by a
change in the character of appointments to it. Appointments became relatively young
chief constables, in the prime of their careers, and with the prospect of advancement
in terms of operational command still ahead of them. There are also specialist civilian
HMIs.

The Home Office has also encouraged ACPO to develop a much higher profile and
expand its role, as a means of enhancing the standardization and centralization of
policing (Reiner 1991; Savage *et al.* 2000; Loader and Mulcahy 2003: chaps. 7, 8; Savage
2007: 156–63). ACPO first made a significant impact on public debate about policing
when it established and operated the National Reporting Centre as a means of coordinating the massive national mutual aid policing operation during the 1984–5 miners'
strike. It was widely argued that ACPO was acting as a medium of government control
of policing.

Successive Home Secretaries have encouraged ACPO to become the pivotal body
for harmonizing policies between forces. To deliver this enhanced function the Home
Office increased funding for the ACPO secretariat, which became more professional and
streamlined. It had until the 1960s been run entirely by serving chief officers, and until
1989 remained a shoestring operation managed by retired police officers. In October
1989 ACPO appointed a firm of management 'head-hunters' to find a suitable candidate
for the Home Office-funded post of general secretary, at a salary comparable with that
of servicing chief officers, and responsible for a policy analysis unit. Although ACPO
rules required the post to be offered first to the membership, in the event a civilian was
appointed: Marcia Barton, former secretary of the official side of the Police Negotiating
Board. ACPO is the linchpin of what has become a central 'policing policy network'.
This encompasses also the Home Secretary and Home Office civil servants, HMIC,

the Audit Commission, with some input, too, from the staff associations representing lower ranks (the Police Federation and Superintendents' Association), individual chief officers, and police authorities (Savage *et al.* 2000: Savage 2007).

There has been a proliferation of specialist national policing units. The NCIS and NCS were established by Parts I and II of the Police Act 1997, growing out of a variety of specialist national and regional organizations that had proliferated in the previous decade. They became the core agencies in the development of intelligence-led and proactive policing throughout the country, and were strongly linked with international policing bodies. Both NCIS and NCS, together with the investigative branches of the Immigration, Revenue, and Customs services, have been merged into the Serious and Organised Crime Agency (SOCA) created by the 2005 Serious Organised Crime and Policing Act. SOCA is a hybrid agency working as a policing organization but specializing in covert and intelligence-gathering activities (Harfield 2006; Savage 2007: 111–14). It has officers permanently stationed overseas in intelligence agencies, and has investigators from other jurisdictions attached to it here. SOCA is a non-departmental public body, governed by a board with a majority of non-executive members, and answerable directly to the Home Secretary, not a police authority. Its staff are civilians not police officers, although they do have an array of powers.

One of the key sources of the impetus towards centralized units and the tighter national control of policing generally was the belief that it was an essential requirement of European integration after 1992 (M. Anderson *et al.* 1995; den Boer 1999, 2002). More generally there has been concern about the growth of international crime leading to a perceived need for higher-level national (and indeed international) police bodies to cope with it, prompting an increasing development of transnational policing—as well as concerns about its accountability (M. Anderson 1989; McLaughlin 1992; Sheptycki 1995, 1997, 1998a, 1998b, 2000a, 2002; R. I. Mawby 1999; Deflem 2002; Andreas and Nadelmann 2006; Johnston 2006; Goldsmith and Sheptycki 2007; N. Walker 2008).

Concern about the quality of police leadership has been another major source of centralization in recent years. A Parliamentary Home Affairs Committee (HAC) Report in 1989 recommended central control over the careers and training of senior officers, making successful completion of the senior command course at Bramshill a condition of promotion above assistant chief constable rank. This was a formal ratification of the *status quo*, in which the Home Office already exercised a considerable measure of control over who becomes a chief constable (Reiner 1991: chap. 5). The Home Office already had power to approve the shortlist of candidates interviewed by police authorities, as well as to veto the police authority's selection, according to the 1964 Police Act. Even in the period before the Second World War, the Home Office could exercise considerable influence over chief officer appointments (St Johnston 1978: 61–3; Wall 1998).

Greater centralization is not a new development but the accentuation of a process that goes back to the initial creation of policing since 1829. Since then every major piece of legislation concerning the police has imposed greater uniformity. Nor is this just a question of the formal organization of the police. The Home Office had often been closely involved in the day-to-day operations of policing industrial disputes (Morgan 1991): the 1984–5 miners' strike was far from being a new departure. Routine crime has also been a stimulus to greater centralization, seeking more efficient coordination of the 'war against crime'. This was the rationale used by the 1962 Royal Commission Report to justify its recommendations for greater Home Office control, although it balked at the overt national force advocated in Dr A. L. Goodhart's influential dissenting memorandum. However, what Dr Goodhart and others forecast in 1962 has come about. Rejecting a *de jure* national police force, we have ended up with the substance of one, but without the structure of accountability for it that the explicit proposals embodied.

The centralizing trend became more apparent still as a result of the profound restructuring of police governance in the 1990s. Originally announced by Home Secretary Kenneth Clarke in March 1993, and published by his successor, Michael Howard, in June 1993 in the White Paper *Police Reform*, the reforms culminated in the Police and Magistrates' Courts Act 1994 (which received its Royal Assent in July after a conflict-ridden passage). The most controversial changes were to the structure of police authorities. Section 4 limited the normal size of police authorities to seventeen. The uniform size, regardless of the area or population covered, signified a departure from the conception of police authorities as representative local bodies. The specified functions of police authorities were subtly altered from the 1964 Act, s 4 formulation, which was the 'maintenance of an adequate and efficient' force. The 1994 Act changed this to 'efficient and effective'. The precise scope of this responsibility remains as gnomic as in the 1964 version, but the symbolism is obvious. The prime motif of the newfangled police authorities is that they are to be 'businesslike' bodies—the local watchdogs of the managerialist, value-for-money, private-enterprise ethos underpinning the whole reform package (McLaughlin and Murji 1997, 2001; Savage 2007: 173–83).

The democratically elected councillor component of police authorities was reduced from two-thirds to just over a half (nine out of the normal total of seventeen members). Three members were magistrates (down from one-third).

The remaining five members were appointed under an astonishingly complex and arcane procedure. The rationale running through the fourteen sections and umpteen sub-sections of the mind-numbingly labyrinthine selection game seemed to be to allow the Home Secretary as many bites at the cherry as possible, without simply letting him or her choose the members directly. The original version of the Bill did indeed do precisely that, but so overtly centralizing a measure drew the wrath of a number of former Conservative Home Secretaries in the House of Lords, who staged a revolt against it. The chair of the police authority is chosen by the members themselves. This was another concession resulting from the House of Lords revolt against the clear centralizing thrust of the original Bill: it was originally intended that the Home Secretary would appoint the chair directly. Overall the final version of the Act leaves police authorities with a slight preponderance of elected members, but this is a figleaf to hide the centralization that was nakedly apparent in the Bill as originally presented to Parliament.

The intention was to make police authorities more 'businesslike', but the business they should be doing is that of central government rather than the local electorate. This is despite the fact that the new police authorities have more explicit functions and powers than their 1964 Police Act predecessors, including duties to issue an annual policing plan for their area and local policing objectives. The chief constable had the same general function of 'direction and control' of the force as in the 1964 Act, but must exercise it with regard to the local policing plan and objectives that the authority draws up in liaison with her. This is an empowerment of the police authority compared to the 1964 Act, but it acts primarily as a conduit for the Home Secretary's priorities. The Home Secretary decided the codes of practice for police authorities, set national objectives, and performance targets which local plans must take into account, determined the central government grant to police forces which covered most of their expenditure, and directed police authorities about the minimum amount of their budgetary contribution and other matters. Despite this substantial shift of power towards central government, the PMCA was officially represented as doing precisely the opposite. This claim was based on the relaxation of the detailed controls that used to exist on how chief officers spent their budgets. Chief constables became free to allocate their budgets in whatever way they felt best suited the policing plan. The White Paper *Police Reform* (Home Office 1993) anticipated explicitly that chief officers would pay attention to the advice of the Audit Commission and HM Inspectorate of Constabulary. These bodies were encouraging devolution of decision-making to basic command units in forces on the model of schemes like sector policing in the Met (B. Dixon and Stanko 1995). It was assumed that the pursuit of nationally determined performance targets would (paradoxically) drive chief officers to devolve a considerable measure of responsibility to local commanders.

That this apparent constabulary independence would prove somewhat illusory became clear when the changes in police governance were considered in the context of the other elements of the government's police reform package. The Sheehy Inquiry into Police Responsibilities and Rewards, which reported in the same week of June 1993 as the Police Reform White Paper was published, recommended that all police officers should be appointed on short-term contracts and subject to performance related pay (PRP). The criteria for successful performance, and the assessment of whether these have been satisfied, would be governed by the Home Secretary via the new police authorities (which on the White Paper's original plan would be controlled by central government appointees).

This would have constituted a formidably centralized system of control over policing. Without abandoning the constabulary independence doctrine in any formal way, the Home Secretary would colour the use of discretion by constables by setting and assessing the criteria for performance that determine pay and job security. The police would no longer be accountable in the gentlemanly 'explanatory and cooperative' style that characterized the 1964 Police Act, nor would they be subject to the 'subordinate and obedient' style of accountability to democratically elected local authorities demanded by radical critics (G. Marshall 1978). Instead they would be subject to a new market-style discipline which can be called 'calculative and contractual' (Reiner and Spencer1993). In the fashionable terminology of new public management, the government would be 'steering' but not 'rowing' (Osborne and Gaebler 1992). While not concerned directly with the details of policing, central government could in practice penetrate the parts of policing that they could not reach hitherto, the day-to-day operation of discretion. This would be accomplished by attaching offers that could not be refused to the attainment of the targets specified in policing plans.

The clear centralization apparent in the original version of the reforms was not fully incorporated into the ensuing legislation. The PMCA reached the statute book in considerably modified form because of Peer pressure exercised mainly by Conservative former Home Secretaries. The toughest aspects of Sheehy's recommendations were defeated by a storm of opposition from police representative associations (Savage *et al.* 2000: chap. 6; Savage 2007: 144–56). The potentially centralizing thrust of the PMCA was not immediately apparent in practice. National policing plans were along 'motherhood and apple pie' lines, with key objectives that were unlikely to cause controversy with local police authorities and chief constables (T. Jones and Newburn 1997). A 1998 House of Lords' judgment, however, underlined the significance of the Home Secretary's national policing plan and objectives in setting the framework for operational policing throughout the country (*Regina* v. *Chief Constable of Sussex ex. p. International Trader's Ferry Limited* (available on the House of Lords' website). It upheld the legality of a chief constable's decision (restricting the level of police protection for live animal exporters against protestors). The decision was based in part on the chief constable's statutory obligation to pursue the objectives set by government:

The Chief Constable has operational command of the force.... But he is now also required to have regard to the objectives and targets set out in an annual plan issued by the Police Authority pursuant to section 8 [of the 1996 Police Act].... In preparing the plan, the Authority will have regard to what it perceives to be the policing priorities of its area and also to any national objectives and performance targets set by the Home Secretary under sections 37 and 38. The 1995–6 police plan said that the police would concentrate their efforts on the prevention and detection of crime and answering and attending calls from the public. The Home Secretary had also determined certain 'key objectives' which had to be included in the plan, such as increasing the number of detections for violent crime and targeting crimes which were a local problem such as drug-related criminality. (per Lord Hoffmann)

At one level these objectives are the kind of 'motherhood and apple pie' ones that nobody could dispute. However, in the case in question they were held to override both the general police duty to keep the peace (which had to be reasonably balanced against other concerns, including budgetary limitations) and also EC Treaty obligations to protect the free movement of goods.

The traditional common law doctrine of constabulary independence was given lip-service in the House of Lords' judgment, and indeed in this case it was supporting the chief constable's decisions. However, there was also recognition of the way that the Police and Magistrates' Courts Act 1994 and subsequent legislation obliged the chief constable to pursue objectives specified by central government. This left the doctrine of police operational independence an empty shell. The police were free to 'row' in any way they decided, so long as it was in the direction 'steered' by the Home Secretary.

The 1994 reforms constituted a profound transformation in the formal organization of police governance. Almost as much criticism was levelled at the style in which these changes have been carried out as their their substance. Unlike previous major changes in police accountability there was no preceding Royal Commission or major public deliberations. The reforms emanated from internal Home Office inquiries with minimal outside consultation. Although the measures were predicated on a clear, contentious conceptualization of the police role as primarily 'catching criminals' (para. 2.2 of the White Paper *Police Reform*) there was no public debate about this narrowing of the traditional police mandate. In theory and practice this had hitherto been seen as encompassing a much broader spectrum of concerns, including crime prevention and management, order maintenance and peacekeeping, emergency, and other services (see Chapter 5). The narrow emphasis on crime detection, pushed to the forefront by the White Paper, had hitherto been seen by most official enquiries as a deformation of rank-and-file police culture, to be rebutted by wise management as much as possible, not actively promoted by policy and performance targets.

Attempts to relocalize control seem like pushing a stream uphill. As 'law and order' became increasingly politicized it was ever more unlikely that governments would wish to relinquish ultimate control over policing. On the other hand, the complexly mediated mechanisms that ensured central government dominance also shielded it from responsibility for mishaps. Why should any government relinquish a position which gave it power without responsibility? This was after all an ancient if rather unroyal prerogative. The myth of a tripartite structure of governance for local policing, with constabulary independence for operational decisions, was useful for legitimating a system of de facto national control.

Under New Labour after 1997, the themes of increasing central control and businesslike modernization through NPM became ever more marked (Senior *et al.* 2007). Nonetheless, concern to give local communities effective control over policing also remained a live issue. The 1998 Crime and Disorder Act placed a new duty on local authorities for crime reduction. They were obliged in conjunction with the police to establish multi-agency Crime and Disorder Reduction Partnerships, involving all relevant local bodies in developing strategies to reduce crime and disorder. They were required to conduct audits every three years of local crime, disorder and drug problems as the basis for designing and evaluating their programmes. This partnership approach empowered local authorities as partners of the police but also made them responsible for implementation of the government's ambitious Crime Reduction Programme. The centralizing and managerialist thrust came clearly to the fore in the early years of the millennium. David Blunkett became Home Secretary in 2001, and introduced a white paper, *Policing A New Century: A Blueprint for Reform*. Blunkett established a Police Standards Unit (PSU) to measure and compare the performance of Basic Command Units (BCUs) and local partnerships, intervene as necessary with support, and to promulgate best practice. The Criminal Justice and Police Act 2001 set up a

Central Police Training and Development Authority (Centrex), incorporating national police training and wider responsibilities for promoting scientific and intelligence-led approaches (Savage 2007: 111–12). A National Centre for Policing Excellence (NCPE) was introduced as part of Centrex, to advance the reform programme (ibid.: 114–15).

The subsequent Police Reform Bill proposing sweeping measures to enhance government control of policing standards, some of which were dropped after vigorous police campaigning. But the 2002 Police Reform Act was a major landmark consolidating greater central government control over policing. Police authorities continued to have a duty to draw up local policing strategies in conjunction with the chief officer, but these had to 'have regard' to the Home Secretary's National Policing Plan and its priorities. The Home Secretary was empowered to 'issue guidance' about local strategy, and the local authorities and chief officers had a duty to take account of this. The Home Secretary acquired powers to issue statutory codes of practice and to make regulations about practices and procedures throughout the country, that were binding on local forces and not merely advisory. The Home Secretary was further empowered to compel a force to take remedial measures if it had been judged as inefficient or ineffective by HM Inspectorate of Constabulary. The Act also strengthened the powers of a police authority to suspend or remove a chief police officer, and gave the Home Secretary stronger powers to compel the authority to do this. In 2004 Blunkett tried to use these powers to require Humberside Police Authority to suspend the chief constable, after criticisms in the Bichard report on the investigation of the Soham murders. The chief and the authority did not comply, but the High Court ruled in the Home Secretary's favour. Although a compromise was reached whereby the chief returned to work briefly before taking early retirement, the case underlined the potency of central government's new powers. The PRA also accentuated the pluralization of policing by strengthening the 'extended police family': it permitted chief officers to appoint 'community support officers' and other auxiliaries, and enabled the accreditation of street and neighbourhood wardens. It also enhanced the procedures for individual police accountability by establishing the IPCC, as discussed above.

The 1994 PMCA had created powers for the Home Secretary to order amalgamations of forces to enhance efficiency. In 2004 the White Paper *Building Communities: Beating Crime* trailed the issue of amalgamating some forces to achieve greater efficiency in tackling 'Level 2' criminality (between local and national), and HMIC were asked to pursue this (Savage 2007: 119–22). The 2006 HMIC Report *Closing the Gap* duly produced a 'business case' for restructuring, supporting the consolidation of the 43 existing forces into a small number of 'strategic forces'. Home Secretary Charles Clarke espoused this enthusiastically, and chief officers and police authorities were required to propose mergers. This programme was overtaken by a series of crises in the Home Office in 2006, culminating in Clarke's replacement by John Reid and the subsequent hiving off to a new Ministry of Justice of part of the Home Office's activities. In the wake of this tumult the force amalgamation programme was put in abeyance pending further review. But the issue may well be resuscitated and the centralizing thrust of policy was apparent.

The 2006 Police and Justice Act continued these processes, with some enhancement of local police authority powers and their responsibilities to follow central government policies. The make-up of local police authorities was altered by removing the magistrate members (magistrates may try to become independent members). Authorities now normally consist of nine elected councillors, and eight independent members. The Act also diluted central government's role in the selection of independent members, who are now chosen by a local panel in compliance with central guidelines. Police authorities were given a duty to hold the chief officer to account for the performance of her functions. The Home Secretary was also empowered to place new functions on police authorities by order, and in 2008 placed duties on them to monitor their forces in respect of Human Rights and planning procedures, and to promote equality and diversity. The Act also established the National Police Improvement Agency (NPIA), incorporating Centrex and the NCPE, as well as the Police Information Technology Organisation (PITO). The NPIA had a remit to 'rationalise the landscape of national organisations', developing good practice, supporting forces in implementing change, and providing operational support (Savage 2007: 118–19). The NPIA's own priorities when it became operational in 2007 emphasized its role in identifying and planning for future policing challenges, identifying and spreading good evidence-based practice, leading change programmes, and using research and analysis to improve policing. The Act clearly developed the process of nationally governed modernization, with both empowerment and responsibilization of local authorities to promote this agenda.

At the same time concerns about increasing centralization have become more vigorous, and Labour, the Conservatives, and the Liberal Democrats have pledged to enhance local policing accountability in various ways. A major aspect of Labour's strategy in recent years for enhancing effectiveness, boosting public confidence and closing the 'reassurance gap' has been the Neighbourhood Policing programme, which includes commitments to strengthen local accountability (McLaughlin 2005b, 2007: 187–96). Labour wanted to introduce some directly elected members of police authorities, as part of its 2008 Police and Crime Bill, but was forced to back down because of opposition by local authority and police organizations ('Police Elections Plan Is Dropped', BBC News website, 18 December 2008). The Conservatives, erstwhile champions of professional police independence, have explored various schemes for direct election of police chiefs, or of commissioners to replace police authorities. The need to relocalize police accountability is currently cross-party consensus, although how to achieve it remains controversial. Whether in practice any party in office would reverse the centralizing managerialist trajectory of recent years, as long as the politics of law and order remain as heated as in recent decades, must be doubtful.

NOTE

1. The reference is to the 1971 film in which Clint Eastwood as Detective Harry Callahan is faced with the choice of violating procedures or failing to apprehend a palpably dangerous psychopathic murderer.

8

CONCLUSION: BEYOND LIFE ON MARS: A HISTORY OF THE FUTURE

Policing has been under increasing pressure in the last four decades of hegemonic law-and-order politics, as the previous chapters have indicated. Neo-liberal globalization has precipitated a fundamental break with the past in many respects, with fateful consequences for crime and criminal justice (Reiner 2007a). The transformation thesis, critically considered in Chapter 1, asserts that 'Future generations will look back on our era as a time when one system of policing ended and another took its place' (Bayley and Shearing 1996: 585). This claim rests above all on changes in the policing division of labour. The dominance of the Peelian model of state police, established against severe challenges in the nineteenth century, has been usurped by a pluralization of policing provision (Johnston and Shearing 2003). The police are increasingly cooperating and competing with a variety of other policing agencies and processes, within and between states (Sheptycki 2002). Their functions are also becoming more diverse and complex. The police are increasingly acting as 'knowledge workers', brokering information to public and private organizations concerned with regulating sundry kinds of risk (Ericson and Haggerty 1997). At the same time the police face increasing managerialist accountability for effective delivery of crime control, as well as periodic crises of legitimacy triggered by scandals about abuse of powers and force, race, and gender discrimination. The police cannot themselves do much to control crime or disorder, which is shaped by much deeper currents of culture and political economy. But the hegemony of neo-liberalism melted into air the solid bases of social order. The police were suddenly asked to deliver on the impossible mandate of crime control that they had quixotically promised for a century.

The politics of policing in the early twenty-first century is a volatile whirlpool of contradictory currents. But, as argued in Chapter 1, the transformation thesis misrepresents the past character of policing, and the sources of the current predicament. The primary sources of the crisis do not lie in defects of the Peelian model, nor is the solution a mixed economy of private security networked with public provision revamped in a managerialist businesslike style. The defects of the police in terms of effectiveness and justice that sociological research uncovered were not due to state provision, but to the dominance of the state by the interests of capital, so that the tension between policing as the reproduction of universally beneficial general order ('parking tickets') and particular partisan order ('class repression') was tilted heavily to the latter (Marenin 1983). In this light, reducing the yoke of the state over policing provision is not liberation. It is to become free of Mussolini only to be captured by Hitler.

NEW MILLENNIUM, NEW ORDER?

The transformation of policing reflected and reinforced wider shifts in social order, political economy, and culture. During the last quarter of the twentieth century profound social changes occurred, suggesting a fundamental break in the trajectory of world development analogous in its scope to the rise of industrial capitalism some two centuries earlier. Whether or not this constituted a new kind of social order with its own novel dynamic has been debated extensively (Harvey 1989, 2005; Callinicos 1989, 2006; Bauman 2000, 2007; Giddens 2002; Held and McGrew 2007; Panitch *et al.* 2006; P. Hirst *et al.* 2009). The proliferation of labels for the new conjuncture indicates the problems in characterizing the society that is emerging: postmodernity, late modernity, liquid modernity, neo-liberalism, post-Fordism, turbo-capitalism, risk society, globalization, information age. All connote undeniable aspects of current developments, but with different conceptions of their drivers, directions, and desirability. What is clear, however, is that several interrelated changes—technological, cultural, social, political/economic—coalesced during the 1970s to forge what is arguably a new political and social configuration, with profound implications for crime, order, and policing (Garland 2001; Loader and Sparks 2007).

Many (mainly conservative) commentators have invoked the long historical process usually seen as the growth of 'permissiveness' to explain rising crime, disorder, and problems for policing (Reiner 2007a: chap. 4). This theme was rehearsed many times by Tony Blair, most explicitly in a speech launching the Home Office's five-year Strategic Plan for law and order in 2004, which Blair claimed 'marks the end of the 1960s liberal, social consensus on law and order'. He explicitly blamed the '1960s revolution' for encouraging 'freedom without responsibility', when 'a society of different lifestyles spawned a group of young people who were brought up without parental discipline, without proper role models and without any sense of responsibility to or for others' (*A New Consensus on Law and Order* 19 July 2004 Labour Party). Blair's speech embodied the quintessential conservative analysis of rising crime. The Enlightenment values of personal liberty, autonomy, and self-realization were dangerously democratized by 1960s 'permissiveness'. As this spread to the masses, it brought the destruction of family, responsibility, and self-control—the bulwarks of civilization. The criminogenic consequence has been an undermining of the informal social controls and internalized inhibitions that once held deviant impulses in check. While not sharing conservatives' negative evaluation of these trends, many liberal and radical analysts would agree that there has been a long-term progress towards greater individual autonomy and 'desubordination' (Miliband 1978; Dahrendorf 1985).

The legal and policy changes that are often referred to as promoting 'permissiveness', however, represented a restructuring rather simple weakening of social control (Newburn 1992). Furthermore, some areas of deviance exhibit quite opposite trends to increasing liberalization. A clear example is drugs policy, which has toughened into a 'war on drugs' despite growing consumption of illegal drugs indicating wider popular acceptance (South 2007; Shiner 2009). In any event, while liberalization offers the potential for crime to rise if pressures or temptations increase, by itself it is no more an explanation of rising crime than failing brakes are of a car's forward motion. Changes in informal control and attitudes to authority make sense of increasing crime rates only in a context where other factors generate social strains and opportunities conducive to offending.

The inexorable rise in recorded crime that began in the late-1950s was kick-started by a number of consequences of the development of a mass consumerist 'affluent society (Reiner 2007a: chap. 4). This had several implications for the growth of property crime, which constitutes the bulk of offending. Perhaps the most obvious effect was the creation and proliferation of attractive and vulnerable criminal targets in the shape of new, widely available consumer goods. The car and its equipment, the most common 'victim' of an offence, proliferated. Mass-produced consumer durables were not only tempting to steal but relatively anonymous and untraceable and hence easier to dispose of without fear of identification. The proliferation of such consumer goods also heightened a sense of relative deprivation among those who were excluded from the new more materialistic and acquisitive culture.

The increases in recorded crime levels were accelerated further after the mid-1970s by the fallout from the fundamental shift in political economy represented by the return of free-market economics, and the deregulation of increasingly globalized markets. A clear consequence has been a rapid increase in inequality, extreme socio-economic polarization and long-term exclusion from employment (Dahrendorf 1985; Levitas 2005; Wilkinson and Pickett 2009). Between 1977 and 2006–7 the top 20 per cent of the population increased its share of total income, from 36 to 42 per cent, while the share of each of the bottom quintile group fell from 10 to 7 per cent (F. Jones 2008). The Institute of Fiscal Studies has shown that income inequality (as measured by the standard Gini coefficient) rose dramatically during the Thatcher years 1979–91, at a historically unprecedented rate. It then fell slightly in the Major years but rose again during New Labour's first term. In Labour's second and third term it remained roughly constant but rose slightly in the last couple of years to reach the highest level since records began in 1961 (Brewer et al. 2008: 27–8). The proportion of children under eighteen living in households with incomes below the official poverty line increased from 10 per cent to one-third in the Thatcher years, but New Labour did succeed in reducing this to 21.3 per cent by 2004–5. However since then it has increased again to 22.3 per cent. Poverty among working-age non-parents increased under Labour, while the proportion of the whole population living in poverty slightly fell from 1997 to 2004–5 (19.4 to 17 per cent) but has since increased again to 18 per cent (ibid.: 38). At the turn of the millennium the gap between the lowest and the highest paid was greater than at any time since records began in 1886 (I. Taylor 1999: 15). This amounts to a reversal of the long process, of more than two centuries' duration, of gradually increasing incorporation of all sections of society into a common status of citizenship, albeit with considerable—but diminishing—inequalities, which was the underpinning of police legitimation as shown in Chapter 3.

The consequences for crime and social cohesion are enormous. In many parts of the world 'lawlessness and crime have so destroyed the social fabric that the State itself has withdrawn' (S. Cohen 1997b: 234). While not threatened by such extremes of social meltdown, Britain and other industrial societies are experiencing profound shifts in the modalities of crime, order and policing.

As social exclusion, economic insecurity, and inequality grow, so the motives and opportunities for crime multiply, and the restraining effects of both formal and informal social controls are eroded. The consequences for crime and order of this social earthquake are profound and intertwined (E. Currie 1998a, 1998b; Davies 1998; Young 1999; I. Taylor 1999; Reiner 2007a). Growing exclusion and immiseration—and the perceived hopelessness of its reversal by legitimate means—not only increase pressures to offend, but also undermine the informal social controls of family, education, work, and community, and encourage a neo-Social Darwinist culture of survival of the fittest. The de-legitimation of public expenditure and collective provision by the ethos of the market weakens the state's capacity to provide either the 'soft' controls of welfare provision or effective public policing. Inequalities in access to security widen, as a burgeoning private market in policing develops.

During the 1980s, the heyday of free-market triumphalism, recorded crime rates rocketed. Although recorded crime rates fell during the mid-1990s, this was largely a recording phenomenon: the British Crime Surveys show that victimization rates continued to rise (Reiner 2007a: chap. 3). The fall in reporting and recording of crime was a paradoxical consequence of the high levels of offending. On the one hand, victims were deterred from reporting because of concern about their insurance policies. On the other hand, the police were under pressure to reduce the proportion of crimes they recorded because of the new 'businesslike' policing-by-numbers regime introduced to enhance their crime-fighting efficiency. After 1997 when New Labour took office there was a reversed divergence between the BCS and police recorded crime rates. The BCS continued to fall, until by the late 2000s it was at the lowest level since the early 1980s (Reiner 2007a: chap. 3). But due to two major changes in counting rules, the police recorded figures rose until the mid-2000s. Public concern about crime has remained high despite the overall crime fall of recent years, widening the 'reassurance gap'.

The architect of the 1993–4 reform package intended to achieve 'businesslike' policing in Britain, Conservative Home Secretary Kenneth Clarke, claimed that they amounted to the most profound reorganization since Sir Robert Peel's original establishment of the Metropolitan Police in 1829. Granting some political licence for this hyperbole, there can be no doubt that the police have experienced themselves as in deep crisis in recent decades. The crime rate increases of recent decades, and the failure of public opinion to register the last decade's overall fall, together with a variety of other axes of controversy traced in earlier chapters have prompted a seemingly endless and accelerating series of reforms (Savage 2007 is an excellent summary and analysis) with more on the horizon.

POLICING IN PERMANENT CRISIS

One interpretation of the particularity of the crisis in British policing is that the police are undergoing a normalization process. Whereas in certain respects they used to be very different from other police forces, either in Europe or in the rest of the common law world (Bayley 1985; R. I. Mawby 1991, 1999, 2008; Brodeur 1995, 1998), there is now something of a convergence in organization and style, indicated by, for example, the almost universal fashionability of community- and problem-oriented policing at least at the level of lip-service. Facing similar domestic crime problems, and indeed confronting a common problem of growing international crime, police forces are adapting in similar ways, and this is facilitated by a direct diffusion of ideas and innovations through conferences, exchanges, and increasing collaboration (Sheptycki 2002; Goldsmith and Sheptycki 2007; Jones and Newburn 2006b; Savage 2007: chap. 2; N. Walker 2008).

The modern British police were established during the first half of the nineteenth century against widespread opposition across the social and political spectrum, as shown Chapters 2 and 3. To overcome this, the architects of the British police tradition (Peel and the first two Metropolitan commissioners, Rowan and Mayne), strove to construct a distinctive organizational style and image for the police. They emphasized the idea of the police as an essentially civilian body, minimally armed, relying primarily on the same legal powers to deal with crime as all citizens shared, strictly subject to the rule of law, insulated from governmental control, and drawn from a representative range of working-class backgrounds to facilitate popular identification. This conception was succinctly summarized by an official inquiry conducted by the police staff associations: 'traditional British policing is relatively low in numbers, low on power, and high on accountability; . . . it is undertaken with public consent' (*Operational Policing Review* 1990: 4).

This image of British policing did not develop because of some peculiar affinity of British culture with civic values, as conservative historians suggest. In colonial situations (including Ireland) British policing developed on an overtly militaristic model (M. Brogden 1987). The pacific image of the British bobby was a myth deliberately constructed in order to defuse the virulent opposition to the very idea of police in early nineteenth-century Britain. Police legitimation owed at least as much to the more general long-term social process of greater social integration and consensus over the century between the 1850s and the 1950s as to any actions of the police themselves.

During the 1970s process renewed politicization appeared in growing debate about police malpractice, and an apparent change of overall tactics to a more coercive, 'fire brigade' style. Anxiety about changing police practices prompted developing civil libertarian concern about limiting police powers and rendering the police more accountable. On the other hand, throughout the 1970s the police lobbied with increasing vociferousness for more powers to deal with 'the fight against crime', and to resist 'political' control.

The post-1964 trends in police tactics were not a coherent and deliberate strategy. Many changes, notably the development of 'fire brigade' policing out of the Unit Beat reorganization, were the unintended consequence of reforms aimed at achieving quite different results. Others, such as the use of more coercive tactics in crowd control and crime-fighting, were largely reactive, ad hoc, and unimaginative responses to pressing problems.

Both police and popular culture embody views of policing and its purposes that are at odds with the reality of police work. They exaggerate the extent to which policing is concerned with serious criminal offences, and overestimate the capacity of the police to deal with criminality by detection and deterrence. In practice most demands for police interventions are calls for the resolution of a diffuse range of minor conflicts, disorders and disputes—a 'peacekeeping' function. The police's legal powers (especially the capacity to use legitimate force) are the reasons for calling the police in an emergency, rather than, say, a priest, psychiatrist, or marriage guidance counsellor. There is scope for discussion about whether 'peacekeeping' interventions are adequately and fairly handled. The police's crime fighting image has distracted attention from exploration of how the craft of 'peacekeeping' can be cultivated by training and supervision. On the crime side of police work, research shows the central role of the public (as victims and witnesses) in uncovering and clearing up offences. Only in a relatively small number of atypical (although prominent) major cases does detective work have any resemblance to popular images.

During the 1970s and early 1980s, debate about police powers and accountability became polarized between a 'law and order' and a civil libertarian lobby, both of which ignored the weaknesses of the 'rational deterrent' model (more sanctions = less offending) as a means of policing either crime or the police. The relationship between formal police powers and the extent of either ordinary crime or police malpractice is tenuous and uncertain.

The politicization of policing in the 1970s and 1980s stimulated a series of reform strategies. As new scandals arose they in turn prompted further soul-searching among police leaders and new policy initiatives. A repetitive dialectic seems to play itself out cyclically, with a thesis of tough 'law and order' prompting an antithesis in a renewed stress on the need for public consent, culminating in a synthesis based on varying tactics chosen from the coercion–consent spectrum proportionate to the requirements of particular situations. Since the early 1990s, however, the cross-party consensus on tough law and order has seen an escalating array of new powers unbalanced by safeguards. Reforms have been geared primarily to enhancing crime control effectiveness.

CYCLES OF REFORM

SCARMANIA TO NEWMANIA

The 1981 Scarman Report on the Brixton disorders became the focal point for a multifaceted reorientation of police thinking, which dominated police reform debates throughout the 1980s. The message of Scarman was far from new. He explicitly drew on Sir Richard Mayne's 1829 instructions to the New Metropolitan Police in his discussion of the 'two principles of policing' (paras. 4.55–4.60). Scarman adopted Mayne's definition of the functions of the police being 'the prevention of crime . . . the protection of life and property, the preservation of public tranquillity'. The nub of Scarman's approach was the priority of maintaining public tranquillity over law enforcement. Skilful and judicious discretion—'the art of suiting action to particular circumstances'—was the better part of policing valour.

Guided by these principles, Lord Scarman made several criticisms of the police as both background to and immediate precipitants of the Brixton disorders. Overall, he judged, 'the history of relations between the police and the people of Brixton during recent years has been a tale of failure' (para. 4.43). While not condoning the disorders, Lord Scarman outlined how the deprivations, frustrations, and racial tensions of inner-city life ensured that the 'recipe for a clash with the police is therefore ready-mixed' (para. 2.37). This had been aggravated by 'unimaginative and inflexible' police tactics, such as stop-and-search sweeps which antagonized the many innocent people who fell victim to them. These operations culminated in the notorious 'Swamp '81' which was the immediate trigger for the riots, a classic illustration of law enforcement at the expense of public tranquillity.

Lord Scarman made numerous recommendations for improving policing seeking to prevent reoccurrences of the disorders. There were several suggestions aimed at improving the calibre of individual officers, and making them less prejudiced (paras. 5.6–5.32). There were also recommendations for organizational reform: tightening discipline in relation to racially prejudiced or discriminatory behaviour (paras. 5.41–5.42), increasing consultation (paras. 5.55–5.71), increasing accountability through lay station visitors (paras. 7.7–7.10), more independent investigation of serious complaints (paras. 711–7.29), and narrowing the scope of highly discretionary powers (paras. 7.2–7.6).

The Scarman Report attracted anger from the left for his denial that racism was 'institutionalised within police practice or in British society as a whole', a striking contrast with the central conclusion of the 1999 Macpherson Report on the Stephen Lawrence case. Scarman explicitly defined 'institutional racism' as discrimination which occurs 'knowingly, as a matter of policy' (para. 2.22). Critics argued that there was plentiful evidence of the discriminatory impact of official policies (of the police and other institutions), albeit often unwitting. But there was no evidence of institutional police racism in Scarman's specified sense of deliberately adopted policy. In the broader meaning of institutional racism as the unintended consequence of organizational policies (see Chapter 5), Scarman's analysis of the disastrous impact of such strategies as stop-and-search was eloquent testimony to his awareness of the problem. But Scarman was concerned that there might be a closing of ranks against change if he attacked the 'integrity and impartiality of the senior direction of the force' (para. 4.62). His proposals were intended to deal with both widespread rank-and-file racial prejudice *and* the unwitting discriminatory impact of policies like stop-and-search.

Scarman was the trigger for a reorientation of police thinking on a wide front. Indeed, by the late 1980s his ideas had become the predominant conception of policing philosophy among chief constables (Reiner 1991: chap. 6). Scarman's principles first had practical impact through their influence on Sir Kenneth Newman's strategy for policing London, which he developed after becoming Metropolitan commissioner in October 1982. This was the prototype of similar programmes around the country over the following decade (Savage 2007: chap. 4).

Newman's strategy was intended to be a fundamental reorientation of policy and organization, aimed at achieving the same success in legitimation as Rowan and Mayne's original formulation, but in the face of new problems. This momentous historical role was explicitly avowed. Newman himself described the changes as 'the most sweeping in the Met.'s more-than-150 year history'—a claim repeated a decade later by Kenneth Clarke when he launched a diametrically opposite package of police reforms!

Newman placed great emphasis on the idea of a 'notional social contract' based on greater public involvement and a 'multi-agency' approach. Key devices for public involvement were Scarman-style consultative committees (with lay station visitors reporting back to them), 'neighbourhood watch', crime prevention panels, victim support schemes, greater use of the Special Constabulary, and attempts to recruit more black people. The 'multi-agency' approach involved police collaboration with other agencies, 'social, economic, cultural and educational', to develop solutions that 'address the root causes rather than the symptoms of crime' (*Commissioner's Report* 1983: 8). Newman's 'notional contract' also aimed at changes in police organization and culture. The key targets were more professional 'management by objectives', and the co-option of all ranks and sections into the overall strategy. Consideration was also given to the problem that has bedevilled police managerial innovations: how to incorporate the rank and file. A 'code of ethics' was formulated, and attempts made to spread its ideas through the force. A 'corporate management' style involving the rank and file in the formulation of objectives and priorities was aimed at.

The strategy was undermined by increasing polarization due to the social and economic policies of the Thatcher government. The worst enemies of the police bid for re-legitimation were not their overt critics but their apparent benefactor—a 'law and order' government that was unconcerned about destroying the social preconditions of consensus policing and the virtues of the British police tradition. The Thatcher government's policies generated rapidly increasing inequality, long-term unemployment, and political polarization. The vaunted return to 'Victorian values' was above all a return to the spectre of the 'two nations' invoked by Disraeli, and of levels of crime, violence, and disorder unprecedented since the nineteenth century. The policies that achieved police legitimation in the days of Queen Victoria had succeeded only because of the wider processes incorporating the working class into the social and political order. The last two decades of the twentieth century witnessed an accelerating de-incorporation of more and more layers of society. The young 'never-employed', especially concentrated among ethnic minorities, swelled the ranks of the 'police property' groups who have always borne the brunt of coercive policing. The implications of deepening social divisions for policing problems were widely recognized by chief constables and the rank-and-file police themselves (Reiner 1991: chap. 9; Rose 1996: chap. 6).

The late 1980s and early 1990s were vintage years for police scandals, starting with the release of the Guildford Four by the Court of Appeal in 1989. This was closely followed by a succession of similar scandals—the cases of the Birmingham Six, the Maguires, Judith Ward, Winston Silcott and the other men convicted for the murder of PC Blakelock during the 1986 Broadwater Farm riots, the troubles of the West Midlands Serious Crimes Squad, and numerous other revelations and allegations of malpractice.

The scandals were reflected in a precipitous decline in the police's poll ratings after 1989. The contrast was sharpest with the post-war period, often regarded as a 'golden age' for the police. A MORI poll for *Newsnight* in 1989 found that only 43 per cent today had 'a great deal of respect' for the police, compared with 83 per cent of a national sample asked the same question in 1959 for the Royal Commission on the Police. Fourteen per cent had 'little respect', compared to only 1 per cent on 1959. Surveys had for several years provided pointers to an erosion of support for the police especially among those who tend to be at the receiving end of police powers—the young, male, and economically marginal in the inner cities (Smith *et al.* 1983). There was also was opinion-poll evidence of a growing perception of police abuses (such as corruption, excessive force, or racial discrimination) even among the 'respectable' majority of the population.

The other source of the decline in public confidence was the police's apparent failure to deliver effectively the protection that their own propaganda had promised. Recorded crime rates increased inexorably after the mid-1950s (in part because of increased reporting by victims, but from the late-1970s this became a real crime explosion as confirmed by the new British Crime Surveys (Reiner 2007a: chap. 3). Public confidence in the police was undermined by this combination of apparent police ineffectiveness and revelations of malpractice.

Newman's successors, Sir Peter Imbert and Sir Paul Condon, continued a strategy aimed at securing the re-legitimation of the police in the face of the many factors that had eroded it, as did police chiefs around the country. In essentials their strategies were similar to Newman's, and certainly incorporated the Scarman spirit.

This coincided with the advent of 'new realism' in the Labour Party under Neil Kinnock, and subsequently Tony Blair's 'tough on crime, tough on the causes of crime' slogan which aimed to recapture 'law and order' as a political issue. In the 1990s police leaders faced much less radical opposition, as the Labour position became only subtly distinct from that of the police elite, and since 1992 has largely espoused the politics of law and order. The decline in public confidence in the police also bottomed out in the 1990s. It remained stable from the nadir of 1991 until the turn of the millennium when there was again a decline, followed by some years of slowly rising confidence since 2005 (Allen *et al.* 2006; Walker *et al.* 2009: 103–5).

CONSUMERISM

Instead of the old Labour concern to rein in police power through enhanced account-ability, the central theme of New Labour strategy for policing was effective crime reduction. There were of course still differences from either Tory or police versions of crime prevention. Local authorities, in partnership with the police themselves, became responsible for coordinating crime prevention strategy following the 1998 Crime and Disorder Act. But the police received their due weight as essential partners in crime prevention initiatives, and beat policing was accorded paramount impor-tance. The new language of managerialism became prominent in Labour thinking, as in Conservative and police pronouncements. However, the clearest theme of police reform talk in the early 1990s was the rhetoric of consumerism. Both Conservative government (Citizen's Charter) and Labour opposition (the Quality Commission) offered their rival versions. The police elite themselves rapidly latched on to this new language as a way of founding a new ethic of service to revive their flagging status, circumventing more political forms of accountability.

This was evident in the first major national response by the police to the perceived crisis of public confidence. In 1990 there appeared the *Operational Policing Review* the report of a wider-anging study of policing problems launched by an unprecedented collaboration between the three staff associations, the Police Federation, the Superintendents' Association, and the Association of Chief Police Officers (ACPO). The police assessment of the implications of their own study was that the priorities of police and public were out of kilter. The public expressed a preference for a community-oriented, service style of policing rather than an enforcement-based approach. The ensuing 'Statement of Common Purpose and Values' enshrined a philosophy of policing in which the watch-word was service. It was amplified by a 'Strategic Policy Document on Quality of Serv-ice' endorsed by the three staff associations. The public were regularly spoken of as the 'customers'—even if they were prisoners!—with the paramount concern being to satisfy their requirements through 'a service culture' (Woodcock 1991: 82; Waters 1996, 2007; Squires 1998; Savage 2007:139–41).

The early 1990s service-based, consumerist rhetoric was infinitely preferable to the tough 'law and order' promises and practices of the previous two decades, which had been the initial police reaction to spiralling crime and disorder. Nevertheless, it could not restore the police to their former high in popular esteem, its avowed aim.

'BUSINESSLIKE' CRIMINAL-CATCHING

None of this self-engineered change proved sufficient to satisfy governments. As discussed in Chapter 7, in 1993 the Home Secretary, Kenneth Clarke, launched a restructuring of police organization and accountability intended to make policing more 'businesslike' according to standards set by central government and its local appointees. This approach was embodied in the 1993 Report of the Sheehy Inquiry into Police Responsibilities and Rewards, the 1993 White Paper entitled *Police Reform*, and the Home Office *Review of Police Core and Ancillary Tasks*. The entire package was premised on an official definition of the police task as 'catching criminals' (specified in the White Paper), which reversed the notion of the priority of preserving public tranquillity as advocated by British police tradition from Peel to Scarman. The reforms were clearly directed at imposing the disciplines of the marketplace on policing.

All three staff associations strongly condemned the government's plans. At the annual conference of the Police Federation in May 1993 the ritual roasting of the Home Secretary contrasted strikingly with the enthusiastic reception for Labour's Tony Blair (*Police Review* 28 May 1993: 12–13). The political alignments over policing appeared to have turned full circle from the days when law and order was seen as a clear Tory issue, and the police were the pets of the Thatcher government.

The political space for the Conservative government's confrontation with the police was created by the erosion of public support discussed above. The police were widely perceived as guilty of systematic malpractice as well as falling down on the job, despite generous treatment in terms of pay and conditions compared to other public services throughout the 1980s. This perception was largely exaggerated: malpractice had certainly been prevalent in the past as well, though more readily covered up. Although police resources had increased they were outstripped by the growing demands placed upon the police, in terms of rising crime rates, greater disorder, heavier traffic volumes, and more emergency calls of all kinds. Whether justified or not, however, there was a decline in public confidence in the police, even though it remained robust compared to that in many other public institutions.

NEW LABOUR AND POLICING

The New Labour government elected in 1997 substantially continued the policies on policing that it inherited from the Conservatives. The new governance structure embodied in the Police and Magistrates' Courts Act 1994 remained intact, as did the quest for demonstrable value-for-money, quasi-market performance measurement and sanctions, and the prioritization of crime reduction objectives. However, there were important early departures that would not have occurred under the Conservatives. These include the establishment of the Macpherson Inquiry into the mishandled investigation of Stephen Lawrence's murder, the Human Rights Act 1998, and the reform of the complaints system (Chapter 7). Above all, the 1998 Crime and Disorder Act and ensuing Crime Reduction Programme launched a new approach, which, while not downplaying the role of the police, placed it in a broader context of policing in partnership with local government and other agencies. However, this became sacrificed within a few years to the pressures of demonstrating short-term success and eye-catching initiatives aimed at appeasing the tabloids, of which the 2002 'street crimes' summit was the quintessential example (Hough 2004; Reiner 2007a: 138; Newburn and Reiner 2007: 334–5).

THE MACPHERSON REPORT AND STEPHEN LAWRENCE

The publication in late February 1999 of the Macpherson Report on the murder of Stephen Lawrence stimulated a flood of agonizing and analysis in all sections of the media. After all the stories, plays, and interviews, there can be few people who are not aware of the basic facts about the horrific, unprovoked murder on 22 April 1993 of the 18-year-old black student by a gang of young racists.

(i)   The perfunctory reaction of many police officers who attended the murder scene, initially suspicious of the dying Stephen and of his friend, Duwayne Brooks.

(ii)   The botched police investigation, and the abortive private prosecution of three of the prime suspects, which meant that whatever evidence came to light later they would be scot-free.

(iii) The boxing of the leadership of the Metropolitan Police into an unprecedented corner in which they were compelled to issue abject apologies for their numerous sins of commission and omission in the case.

(iv)   The inspiring struggle of Stephen's parents to get at the truth of their son's death, culminating in their pyrrhic victory in the report, which concluded that the multiple failings of the police investigation, and the police's insufficiently sensitive handling of relationships with the Lawrence family and Duwayne Brooks, owed much to 'institutional racism'.

The public in general seemed understandably shocked and appalled at the catalogue of brutality, violent racism, and police incompetence and callousness that the media coverage revealed.

Yet in the light of the bitter experience of discrimination and violence against black people in this country over the last half century, perhaps the most frightening thing was that the Lawrence case was far from unique as an example of either violent racism or discriminatory policing. In his definitive book on the subject, Ben Bowling (1999a) showed that since the murder in 1959 of Kelso Cochrane there had been at least ninety murders of black or Asian people which appeared to be racially motivated. Such murders are only the tiny tip of a huge mass of cases of racial violence, intimidation, and harassment directed at all ethnic minorities. Yet this is only a part of a broader picture of 'hate crimes' directed at other vulnerable minorities (Hall 2005; Chakraborti and Garland 2009). What set the Lawrence case apart was not the brutality of the event itself, which had all too many counterparts, nor the police incompetence and racism that the inquiry uncovered. Stephen Lawrence himself was the ideal–typical pure victim, a person of impeccable character suffering an entirely unprovoked attack. Even given this, however, the clinching factor was the perceptiveness and dedication of Stephen's parents in campaigning relentlessly to achieve a measure of truth, if not justice, for their son.

The Macpherson Report, which established all this, transformed the terms of political debate about black people and criminal justice, and was a comparable landmark to the Scarman Report. Until it, attention had focused on the disproportionate rate of stops, arrests, convictions, and imprisonment of black people. Whether this was interpreted as evidence of racial discrimination in criminal justice, or of disproportionate black criminality, the primary concern was about black people as suspects. What had not featured in public awareness and political debate was the disproportionate rate at which black people suffered as victims of crime. Both sides of this issue reflect the social and geographical exclusion of black people in a discriminatory society. It has become usual to compare the 1999 Macpherson Report favourably with the 1981 Scarman Report, because it grasped the nettle of institutional racism that Scarman had denied. Macpherson was undoubtedly more hard-hitting as a critique of police failure. It succeeded in gaining official acceptance of the existence of institutionalized racism. Paradoxically, however, it was Scarman who had the keener grasp of how police discrimination is intimately bound up with wider structures of racial and social inequality and disadvantage.

With the 20:20 vision of thirty years' more experience of police discrimination in relation to race, it is clear that the Scarman Report failed to end racial discrimination in policing. This was not because of its own failings, however, but because of the lack of political commitment to achieve the transformation of black people's social and economic circumstances, as well as the reforms of police organization and policy that it called for. In the continuing absence of a fundamental attack on economic and social disadvantage experienced by black and other ethnic minority people the widespread anger and sorrow produced by the Lawrence tragedy is likely to prove equally unsuccessful in achieving a real breakthrough in the vexed relationship between black people and the police and criminal justice system.

CRIME REDUCTION AND PARTNERSHIP POLICING

The main thrust of New Labour's initial criminal justice policy, embodied in the Crime and Disorder Act 1998 and the Crime Reduction Programme, was a departure from traditional Conservative or Labour policies. As many critics pointed out, the Act contained provisions (notably the Anti-Social Behaviour Orders) which are potentially oppressive for human rights and counter-productive. Its main strategy, nonetheless, was novel and cannot be dismissed as either simply punitive or liberal but premised on a conception of citizenship reflecting the cultural changes of recent decades (Ramsay 2006, 2008). It was based on an intelligence-led, problem-solving approach, with systematic analysis and reflexive monitoring built into policy development. Its intellectual basis was a thorough review of the evidence concerning the effectiveness, costs, and benefits of the main strategies for dealing with offending: preventing the development of criminality by early childhood intervention and education, situational and community crime prevention, policing, sentencing, and alternative penal techniques (Nuttall *et al.* 1998).

Section 6 of the Act required local authorities and the police in partnership to audit local crime and disorder problems, identify their sources, and develop appropriate strategies for reducing them, with regular research evaluations of effectiveness. This was part of the 'evidence-led' Crime Reduction Programme, based on 'joined-up thinking', the realization that crime must be dealt with by wider-ranging policies than criminal justice alone. In principle this aimed to be tough on the causes of crime, not just tough on those few lottery losers of the criminal justice system who are convicted. The broad approach to policing, stressing problem-solving in conjunction with other agencies, including local government, acknowledged the research demonstrating the limits of the police's capacity to tackle crime alone. This echoed the analysis of Scarman and police chiefs influenced by him such as Newman and Imbert, which had been displaced by the emphasis solely on 'catching criminals' emanating from the Clarke–Howard reform package of 1993. Labour's initial commitment to evidence-led policy even resulted in the new hostage to fortune of changes in the counting rules for police recording of crime which were bound to result in apparent dramatic rises (Reiner 2007a: 51–3).

The problem with the Crime Reduction Programme, however, lay in its place within the overall strategy of New Labour, many other aspects of which throttled its possible success. Most obviously, the initial commitment to keep within Conservative spending plans undermined the capacity of the police, probation, education, and other social services to perform as intended, while exacerbating the pressures leading young people into crime, such as school exclusions and truancy (Downes 1998: 196–7). More generally the criminogenic consequences of failure to bring inequality and social exclusion down vastly outweighed any crime-reducing effects of the Home Office programme. New Labour's commitment to old Tory economic policy was its main hostage to fortune in crime control policy. On the other hand, the intelligence-led approach to policing and crime reduction were vulnerable to populist attacks from the Conservatives, who continued to attack Labour as 'soft' on crime, enabling them to grasp back public confidence in them as the party of law and order, despite Labour's success in bringing down overall crime (Duffy *et al.* 2008). This has resulted in Labour gradually dropping the 'tough on the causes of crime' part of its celebrated slogan focusing ever more obsessively on the 'tough on crime' element (Newburn 2007c; Reiner 2007a: chap. 5; Newburn and Reiner 2007).

THE LIMITS OF POLICE REFORM

What remains missing from all the reform strategies is a fundamental sociological analysis of the role of the police, and of the sources of their present plight. Common to all the solutions considered is an unquestioned assumption that falling public confidence has been caused by a decline in police standards. Certainly there have been many scandals revealing serious police malpractice. But do these establish that the integrity of the British police force has fallen? The extent of police abuse at any time is unascertainable, and there is always a substantial dark figure of hidden police deviance so trends cannot be reliably ascertained. What we do know is that in the 'golden age' of the mid-twentieth century, when the police were symbols of national pride, there was extensive and routinized wrongdoing behind the scenes. This is clear from police memoirs (for example, the very revealing vignettes of life in the Manchester police in the 1930s and 1940s found in Mark 1978) and from oral histories of policing (such as M. Brogden 1991 and Weinberger 1995). What prevented these abuses from being revealed at the time was the much more deferential culture of the social strata at the receiving end of policing, and of the media and the educated middle class. Complaints were less likely to be made (rather than sullenly put up with as yet another unpleasant fact of life), and they were far less likely to be given credence by opinion formers. It is plausible that what appears to be a growing amount of police malpractice is largely just a greater likelihood of it coming to light, due to a much more deep-seated cultural change: the progressive erosion of deference in the post-war period. This was accentuated by a ratcheting up of the coerciveness of police tactics in the face on increasing crime and disorder in the 1970s and 1980s.

The increase in crime and disorder problems confronting the police had profound social causes. Above all there was the growing social and economic divisions and deprivation produced by neo-liberal economic policy, which swelled the numbers of those who in Victorian times would have been called the 'dangerous classes' and came to be referred to as the 'underclass' (Crowther 2000a, 2000b). They have always constituted the prime business of the police, and have been aptly labelled 'police property'. As their 'property' and problems increased, so the police moved higher up the scale of coerciveness in their menu of tactics. This was liable to generate more malpractice, which in turn reinforced tendencies to cynicism and authoritarianism in police culture. But these were symptoms of the problem, not its prime mover. Consequently, solutions aimed primarily at changing the police will miss the mark.

At the heart of the well-intentioned solutions considered above there is a systematic failure to confront the nature of policing. The consumerist approach, in particular, implied that the police can and should be whatever market surveys revealed consumer preferences to be. But what is the 'service' that the police have historically been organized to deliver? What is the 'service' that clients effectively demand when they call for the police? Largely it is to handle disorder or crime, inherently contentious situations, even though the police typically seek to resolve conflicts without recourse to coercion. The police are the specialist repository domestically of the state's monopoly of legitimate force, and the 'service' they are predominantly called upon to provide is 'the capacity for decisive action' (Bittner 1974: 35). As the title of one episode of the TV series *The Bill* put it succinctly: 'Force is Part of the Service'.

The police are thus inherently a 'dirty work' occupation, in Everett Hughes's term (E. Hughes 1961). It is only in the most exceptional circumstances, such as the consensus climate of post-war Britain, that the police can be regarded widely as anything other than a regrettable necessity. This has always been the status of the police in even the most pacific and law-abiding countries. For the most part, the fashionable languages of managerialism, community and consumerism overlook the fact that policing is not about the delivery of an uncontentious service like any other. Their business is the inevitably messy and intractable one of regulating social conflict. They cannot control, but rather are buffeted by, prevailing social currents.

The end product of reform cannot realistically be the restoration of the status of the police as beloved symbols of national pride. The pedestal on which they stood in the middle of the twentieth century was based on unique circumstances, in particular the consensus climate of Britain during and after the Second World War. PC George Dixon was not the norm for the British police, but their finest hour. In a more egoistic, anomic, divided society they cannot function as sacred totems of a collective conscience that has become dispersed and diversified. They have become a demystified, mundane institution of governmentality, competing and cooperating with other policing forms. But in the absence of economic and social changes reversing the neoliberal thrust to greater inequality, exclusion and conflict the police will not be able to contain the pressures towards more crime and disorder.

The prospects for reversing this by 'businesslike' managerialist reforms or Labour's Crime Reduction Programme or the new policing theory hopes for a nodal network of private and public security auspices all suffer from the same problems as their 'magic bullet' tough or smart policing counterparts. The premise underlying all these perspectives is that, if properly organized, policing or security can have a significant impact on crime levels, blocking crime by uniformed patrol and other preventive measures, and detecting criminals efficiently after the event if crimes do occur.

There is, however, a substantial body of research evidence and theoretical argument, reviewed in Chapter 6, suggesting that policing resources and tactics have at best a tenuous relationship to levels of crime or the clear-up rate. Innovative strategies may have some impact in particular situations but not much effect on overall levels of crime. The police function more or less adequately as managers of crime and keepers of the peace, but they are not realistically a vehicle for reducing crime substantially. Crime is the product of deeper social forces, largely beyond the ambit of any policing tactics, and the clear-up rate is a function of crime levels and other aspects of workload rather than police efficiency.

POLICING NEO-LIBERALISM

Underlying the many specific causes of controversy over policing, such as malpractice, militarization, or apparently declining effectiveness, there are the deeper and more fundamental changes in contemporary society that were pointed to earlier in this book. The rise of a specific organization specializing in policing functions coincided with the development of modern nation-states, and was an aspect of the process by which they sought to gain centralized control over a particular territory. This was particularly true of Britain, where bureaucratic police organizations came into being comparatively late by European standards and coincided with the historical trajectory towards greater social integration after the initial impact of the Industrial Revolution. In all societies the police's symbolic functions are at least as important as their direct instrumental effectiveness in dealing with crime and disorder.

The position of the police as an organization symbolizing national unity and order was threatened fundamentally by the advent of neo-liberal political economy and those social changes often labelled as 'postmodernity', above all increasing inequality, fragmentation, and pluralism. Consumerism and the culture of cool have become the driving forces of action, narcissism, and the 'pleasure principle' displacing the puritan asceticism and discipline that were the cultural foundation of modern industrialism (Pountain and Robins 2000; Hall *et al.* 2008). The social structure of postmodernity follows the same dynamic of fragmentation, disorganization, pluralism, and de-centring (Bauman 2000, 2007). Economic changes have transformed the social framework, dispersing the centralized Fordist production systems of modern times, and polarizing the class structure into what is often referred to as the 'two thirds, one-third society', although the continuing relevance of class is occluded by multifarious dimensions of diversity (Hutton 1995; Loftus 2007, 2009).

While the majority participated (until the 2008–9 crash), albeit unevenly and insecurely, in unprecedented levels of consumption, a substantial and growing 'underclass' was permanently and hopelessly excluded (Dahrendorf 1985: chap. 3; Galbraith 1992; Crowther 2000a, 2000b). Certainly with the political dominance of free-market economic policies there has been no prospect at all of their incorporation into the general social order. In other words, the 'police property' group is far larger, and more fundamentally alienated. This economic fragmentation interacts with the long and complex process of cultural diversification, declining deference, erosion of moral absolutes, and growing 'anomia' (Dahrendorf 1985: chap. 2) to create a more turbulent, disorderly social world.

In this context, the British conception of the police as a body with an omnibus mandate, symbolizing order and harmony, became increasingly anachronistic. The British police moved towards the international pattern of high policing national units for serious crime, terrorism, public order, large-scale fraud, and other national or international problems. Local policing of particular communities remains and indeed is valorized in the Neighbourhood Policing Programme and the cross-party lip-service towards the invigoration of local accountability (McLaughlin 2005, 2007: chap. 7). But there are sharp differences between policing styles in relation to different 'communities of risk' (Johnston 2000: chap. 4). High-tech 'bubbles of security' in the gated 'communities' of the affluent, 'service'-style patrols in stable suburban areas, and paramilitary zero tolerance keeping the lid on underclass symbolic locations.

For those in society who can afford it, provision of security is increasingly privatized, often in the 'mass private property' where more and more middle-class leisure and work takes place (Shearing and Stenning 1983, 1987; Newburn and T. Jones 1999; Loader 1999; Button 2002, 2007, 2008; Rikagos 2002; Wakefield 2003). Specialized human policing in any form, however, is becoming a smaller part of an array of impersonal control processes built into the environment, technological control and surveillance devices, and the guarding and self-policing activities of ordinary citizens (M. Davis 1990, 1998; McCahill 2002; Zedner 2003, 2009; Coleman 2004; Goold 2004; Jones 2007). The police are becoming part of a more varied assortment of bodies with policing functions, and a more diffuse array of policing processes, within and between nation-states (Sheptycki 2000a, 2002, 2007; Goldsmith and Sheptycki 2007; Walker 2008; Bowling 2009).

THE LIMITS OF POLICING

Police and policing cannot deliver on the great expectations now placed on them in terms of crime control, whether by tough zero tolerance 'law and order' or intelligence-led crime reduction and problem-solving. 'Nothing works' was far too bleak and demoralizing a conclusion to draw from evaluation studies of criminal justice and police practice, as was frequently done in the 1970s. There are enough well-researched examples of targeted policing and crime prevention innovations, for example, to suggest that these can have a significant, if modest, effect on crime and fear (Weisburd and Eck 2004; Skogan and Frydl 2004: chap. 6; Tilley 2008; Cope 2008; Maguire 2008). However, the burden placed on them by governments is excessive. The kind of reductions that have been experienced through these initiatives—while welcome, and cost-effective compared to either more crime or mass imprisonment—go nowhere near reversing the increases of the last half-century. The overall crime reduction that has been occurred in recent years is largely due to factors other than policing. The cruel irony is that the Labour government knows this. A 2007 review by the Prime Minister's Strategy Unit concluded that 80 per cent of the crime reduction was due to economic factors, although this estimate was somehow omitted from the version of the report on the Cabinet website, which concentrated almost entirely on criminal justice solutions (Solomon *et al.* 2007: 14). Labour has been moderately successful in reducing crime, despite its very limited achievement in containing inequality and exclusion. But it is so locked into the politics of law and order that this is a success that dare not speak its name. And this achievement is likely to be swept away by the collapse of its economic programme built on the flimsy foundations of neo-liberal market mantras.

David Garland (1996, 2001) has cogently argued that states have adjusted their policies and rhetoric in recognition of the limits to their sovereignty in terms of crime control. There has been a bifurcation between two levels of crime-control policy and discourse. On the one hand, promulgation of detailed policies to implement best practice in crime prevention—what Garland calls the 'criminologies of everyday life'—as in Labour's Crime Reduction Programme. Such discourses are largely stripped of moral condemnation, but treat crime pragmatically, as an actuarial risk to be calculated and minimized (Feeley and Simon 1994). On the other hand, there are regular moral panics about especially horrific crimes (such as the murder of Jamie Bulger or the Soham murders), which become occasions for orgies of punitiveness and anguished Jeremiads about moral decline. The explosions of punitiveness prompted by the relatively rare, spectacular, exceptionally fear-provoking crimes symbolically assuage popular anxiety and frustration, while the 'criminologies of everyday life' are geared to provide as much limited pragmatic protection as possible against more mundane offences.

A substantial and sustained return to earlier levels of crime is simply not possible without major changes in the conditions that generated the rise in the first place. The 'realist' exploration of what works is worthwhile, but at best can have modest results unless it becomes a wedge for broader reforms. If the 'social' is indeed dead (N. Rose 1996), and a return to Keynesian-style economic policies aimed at stabilization and solidarity no longer feasible, because of globalization and changes in popular values, there is a price to be paid: living with a high-crime society permanently.

THE LONG GOODBYE

A continuation of high rates of routine crime, and the variety of security and control measures adopted to contain or reduce them, offers a highly dystopian image of the future. We are accustomed to everyday routines geared to crime prevention, with varying tactics and success depending on social location. In essence there is a vicious circle of interdependence between social divisions and exclusion, crime, and crime-control strategy. Growing social divisions fuel rising crime, which in turn generates control strategies that accentuate social exclusion. In a variety of interlocking ways crime and reactions to crime exacerbate the social divisions that generated them.

The clearest example is the social bifurcation that produces and is in turn reinforced by the flourishing market in private security, aptly described as a 'new feudalism' (Shearing and Stenning 1983). The more privileged sections of society protect themselves from the burgeoning 'dangerous classes' of the socially excluded by a variety of environmental, spatial, architectural, and technological segregation devices such as the increasingly ubiquitous CCTV cameras. Together with private policing, these provide the 'moats' seeking to secure the castles of consumerism. The wealthy flit between 'security bubbles' in 'cities of quartz' guarded not so much by police (public or private) as by more or less subtle physical and social barriers (M. Davis 1990). Inequalities in exposure to crime and disorder are exacerbated as policing and security increasingly become strategies of border control between the dreadful enclosures of the excluded and the gated denizens of the wealthy, between and within different countries.

Unable or unwilling to tackle the sources of rising crime, states and citizens react punitively on the hapless minority of criminals they encounter or apprehend. Tough new sentencing policies on the 'three strikes and out' model have swelled the prison populations of the USA, Britain, and other countries which have increasingly followed this example, to unprecedented levels (Lacey 2008). This is despite little evidence that it cuts crime to any substantial extent (Reiner 2007a: 158–61; Hedderman 2008). Nonetheless current policies will result in further huge growth of the penal empire, if only as an expression of impotent rage at the losers in the criminal justice lottery. A possible rise in vigilante activity could be the citizen counterpart of the increase in official punitiveness, striking at those suspected offenders who are at hand, as an expression of impotence in the face of crime and insecurity (Johnston 1996; Abrahams 1998; Zedner 2009: 51, 161–2).

This image of a society polarized between a gilded but insecure elite and a threatening, temporarily subjugated mass haunted dystopian visions of the future at the end of the nineteenth century, as in H. G. Wells's *The Time Machine*. They returned with a vengeance in the last quarter of the twentieth century not because of some inevitable *fin de siècle* phobia, but because of the rapid reversal of the slow march of social inclusion. The proliferation of *Blade Runner*-style imaginings of the revolt of the repressed (M. Davis 1998: chaps. 6, 7) testify to a scarcely subconscious anxiety that the burgeoning array of sophisticated surveillance and control measures cannot indefinitely hold the lid down on the expanding excluded classes.

It is hard to see how order of any kind can be maintained if we head towards the '20:80' society of two-fifths excluded from legitimate work projected by some analysts of globalization (H.-P. Martin and Schumann 1997: chap. 1). There are, of course, already many parts of the world where functioning states and civil society have weakened to the extent that a 'new barbarism' prevails (Hobsbawm 1994: 53). In such places the tenuous modern distinction between crime and politics ceases to be useful as 'low intensity warfare runs into high intensity crime' (S. Cohen 1997b: 243). Up to the beginning of the twenty-first century, such 'degree zero' collapses of order have been avoided in advanced industrial societies (Reiner 1999). However, given the huge increases in crime and disorder that have already occurred as a result of our current two-thirds/one-third societies, it is hard to be optimistic about the consequences of even more precipitous inequality and exclusion following economic collapse.

Whether this will be the shape of law and order in the twenty-first century is anyone's guess. But the prospects can be summed up by a paraphrase of Rosa Luxemburg. The choice is between some form of social democracy and at best, the barbarism of high crime rates, and a fortified society. What is clear is that the police cannot protect us from increasing insecurity, not even if they are transformed into torturing clones of Jack Bauer or a smartly allocated network of 'pick 'n' mix' policing services.

In Chapter 2, I began my account of the rise of modern policing with a quote from Raymond Chandler's *The Long Goodbye* and I shall conclude with another. In that classic 1953 private eye novel, Philip Marlowe made some prescient remarks about the prospects for policing and crime control: 'Crime isn't a disease, it's a symptom. Cops are like a doctor that gives you aspirin for a brain tumour, except that the cop would rather cure it with a blackjack' (Chandler 1977: 599). Blackjacks (tough 'law and order' policing) and aspirin (community policing) can be only temporary palliatives without more fundamental social surgery.

POSTSCRIPT: FOR SOCIAL DEMOCRATIC POLICING

The dire consequences of neo-liberalism in the economic arena have become manifest with the return of depression on a scale unprecedented since the 1930s. The holes in the neo-liberal model are widely acknowledged now even by erstwhile neo-liberal economists and policy-makers (Turner 2009). The risk society and neo-liberal 'responsibilisation' (O'Malley 1992, 2004; Garland 2001) were euphemisms for a massive 'risk shift' (Hacker 2006) from government and corporations to the mass of the population who could not carry the burden. 'When the Bush–Cheney administration proposed to replace Social Security with a system of individually accumulated, individually owned, and individually invested accounts, my first thought was that its goal was to take the Social out of Social Security. It took a few minutes longer to realise that it also intended to take the Security out of Social Security' (Solow 2008, reviewing Gosselin 2008). The news does not seem to have penetrated most criminology as yet, but there is a growing sense among economic and political analysts that the state remains needed and indeed that social democracy is as necessary as the post-war generation felt it to be. The prospects for civilization depend 'on whether the social-democratic leaders of western Europe can breathe life into the dry bones of what seemed, until recently, a dead doctrine' (Bogdanor 2009). Tawney's statement of social democratic principles, at the start of the last great depression, remains valuable for democratic and ethical politics and policing: 'its fundamental criticism of capitalism is not merely that it impoverishes the mass of mankind—poverty is an ancient evil—but that it makes riches a god . . . Socialism accepts . . . the principles which are the cornerstones of democracy, that authority, to justify its title, must rest on consent; that power is tolerable only so far as it is accountable to the public; and that differences of character and capacity between human beings, however important on their own plane, are of minor significance compared with the capital fact of their common humanity' (Tawney 1931: 197). Contrary to popular mythology and indeed the new policing theorists, even the best policing (public and/or private) cannot provide the foundations of security. But if these foundations *are* once more reproduced by inclusive economic and social policies then the police can offer what they are capable of: legitimate and effective first-aid responses to crime and emergencies. To reverse the sentiment expressed in Psalm 127 (which is one of this book's epigraphs), if the Lord *is* with the city, the watch does *not* watch in vain.

APPENDIX: CHRONOLOGY OF POLICE HISTORY

THE STRUGGLE OVER POLICE ESTABLISHMENT 1750–1829

1785	Gordon Riots and Pitt's abortive Police Bill
1786	Dublin Police Act
1792	Middlesex Justices Act
1750–1820s	Fieldings, Colquhoun: 'Science of Police'
1800	Thames River Police Act
1814	Peel's Irish 'Peace Preservation' Police
1819	Peterloo Massacre
1822	Parliamentary Committee on Police
1829	Metropolitan Police Act

DIFFUSION AND LEGITIMATION OF PEEL'S POLICE 1829–1919

1833	Coldbath Fields disorder
1835	Municipal Corporations Act
1839	County Police Act
1839	City of London Police Act
1842	Detective Dept. at Scotland Yard
1856	County and Borough Police Act
1888	Local Government Act

PROFESSIONALIZATION AND CONSTABULARY INDEPENDENCE 1919–69

1918–19	Police strikes; Desborough Committee; Police Act
1929	Royal Commission on Police Powers and Procedure
1930	*Fisher* v. *Oldham*
1934	Hendon Police College
1936	Public Order Act

1948   Oaksey Committee; Police College (now Bramshill)
1959–62   Royal Commission on Police
1964   Police Act 1964
1965–   Unit Beat reorganization; Met Special Patrol Group
1968   R v. *Metropolitan Police Commissioner ex. p. Blackburn*

POLITICIZATION OF POLICING 1969–86

1969–   Scotland Yard corruption scandals
1972   Saltley Gate
1972   Sir Robert Mark's Dimbleby Lecture
1975–9   Police Federation 'law and order' campaign
1976   Police Act 1976
1977   Fisher Report on Confait
1979–81   Royal Commission on Criminal Procedure
1981   Urban disorders; Scarman Report
1984   Police and Criminal Evidence Act (PACE)
1984–5   Miners' strike
1985   Urban disorders (Handsworth, Brixton, Broadwater Farm)
1985   Local Government Act
1986   Public Order Act

CONSUMERIST CONSENSUS: 'BUSINESSLIKE' POLICING: PRIVATIZATION, PLURALIZATION 1986–93

1983   Home Office Circular 1983/114
1987   HMI Matrix of Police Performance Indicators
1988   Home Office Circular 1986/106
1988   *Northumbria Police Authority* case
1989–91   'Guildford Four', 'Maguire Seven', 'Birmingham Six' appeals
1990   Operational Policing Review/Statement of Common Purposes
            and Values
1990   Audit Commission Report *Footing the Bill*
1990   Poll tax riots
1992   National Criminal Intelligence Service
1992   Maastricht Treaty, 'Europol'
1991–3   Royal Commission on Criminal Justice
1993   Group 4 wins contract for prisoner transportation

NEO-LIBERAL LAW AND ORDER POLITICS EMBEDDED: DEEP CONSENSUS, FEBRILE CONFLICTS. PRAGMATISM/PARTNERSHIPS VS. PUNITIVE PANICS 1993–

1993	James Bulger murdered (February)
1993	Stephen Lawrence murdered (April)
1993	Blair 'tough on crime, tough on the causes of crime'
1993	Sheehy Report; *Police Reform* White Paper
1994	Police and Magistrates' Courts Act
1994	Criminal Justice and Public Order Act
1995	Posen Review Core and Ancillary Tasks
1996	Police Act
1997	Police Act
1998	*R v. Chief Constable of Sussex ex. p. International Traders Ferry Ltd*
1998	Crime and Disorder Act
1999	Report of the Macpherson Inquiry into the murder of Stephen Lawrence
1999	Patten Report: *Policing in Northern Ireland*
2000	Terrorism Act
2000	Regulation of Investigatory Powers Act
2000	Met Police Authority (chaired by Mayor)
2001	Criminal Justice and Police Act (Centrex, PNDs)
2001	Private Security Industry Act
2001	Oldham, Burnley, Bradford riots
2001	White Paper: *Policing a New Century*
2001	New York terror attacks (9/11)
2002	Police Reform Act (PCSOs, Police Standards Unit, IPCC)
2002	Home Office PACE Review
2003	Anti-Social Behaviour Act
2003	House of Lords' case *Clingham* (on ASBOs)
2004	National Policing Plan 2005–8
2005	Prevention of Terrorism Act (March)
2005	Serious and Organised Crime and Police Act (SOCA, arrest power for all offences, search powers for PCSOs)
2005	London terror bombings (July)
2005	Jean Charles de Menezes shot dead by police (22 July)
2006	House of Lords' case *Gillan* (Terrorism Act 2000 s 44 stop searches)
2006	Terrorism Act
2006	Police and Justice Act (NPIA)
2007	Home Office PACE Review

2007	Flanagan Review of Policing
2007	Home Office Strategy: *Cutting Crime: A New Partnership 2008–11*
2007	National Community Safety Plan 2008–11
2008	Policing Green Paper *From the Neighbourhood to the National: Policing Our Communities Together*
2008	Policing and Crime Bill
2008	Met Commissioner Sir Ian Blair resigns citing loss of Mayor's confidence
2009	House of Lords' case *Austin* (on 'kettling')
2009	G20 demonstrations, death of Ian Tomlinson (1 April)
2009	HMIC Report *Adapting to Protest*

REFERENCES AND BIBLIOGRAPHY

ABRAHAMS, R. (1998). *Vigilant Citizens.* Cambridge: Polity Press.

ADAMS, C. (2000). 'Suspect Data: Arresting Research', in R. King and E. Wincup (eds), *Research on Crime and Justice.* Oxford: Oxford University Press.

ADLAM, R. (1981). 'The Police Personality', in D. Pope and N. Weiner (eds), *Modern Policing.* London: Croom Helm.

ADLAM, R., and VILLIERS, P. (eds) (2003). *Police Leadership in the 21st Century.* Winchester: Waterside Press.

ADLAM, R., and VILLIERS, P. (eds) (2004). *Policing a Safe, Just and Tolerant Society.* Winchester: Waterside Press.

ALDERSON, J. (1979). *Policing Freedom.* Plymouth: Macdonald & Evans.

ALDERSON, J. (1984). *Law and Disorder.* London: Hamish Hamilton.

ALDERSON, J. (1998). *Principled Policing.* Winchester: Waterside Press.

ALEX, N. (1969). *Black in Blue.* New York: Appleton, Century, Crofts.

ALEX, N. (1976). *New York Cops Talk Back.* New York: Wiley.

ALLEN, J., LIVINGSTONE, S., and REINER, R. (1998). 'True Lies: Changing Images of Crime in British Postwar Cinema'. *European Journal of Communication,* 13/1: 53–75.

ALLEN, J., EDMONDS, S., PATTERSON, A., and SMITH, D. (2006). 'Policing and the Criminal Justice System—Public Confidence and Perceptions: Findings from the 2004/05 British Crime Survey'. London: Home Office online report 07/06.

AMATRUDO, A. (2009). *Criminology and Political Theory.* London: Sage.

ANDERSON, D. M., and KILLINGRAY, D. (eds) (1991). *Policing the Empire: Government, Authority and Control, 1830–1940.* Manchester: Manchester University Press.

ANDERSON, D. M., and KILLINGRAY, D. (eds) (1992). *Policing and Decolonisation: Politics, Nationalism and the Police, 1917–65.* Manchester: Manchester University Press.

ANDERSON, M. (1989). *Policing the World.* Oxford: Oxford University Press.

ANDERSON, M., DEN BOER, M., CULLEN, P., WILLMORE, W., RAAB, C., and WALKER, N. (1995). *Policing the European Union: Theory, Law and Practice.* Oxford: Oxford University Press.

ANDREAS, P., and NADELMANN, E. (2006) *Policing the Globe.* Oxford: Oxford University Press.

ANTUNES, G., and SCOTT, E. S. (1981). 'Calling the Cops'. *Journal of Criminal Justice,* 9/2.

ASCOLI, D. (1979). *The Queen's Peace.* London: Hamish Hamilton.

ASHLEY, M. (2002). *Modern Crime Fiction.* London: Carroll and Graf.

ASHWORTH, A. (2004). 'Social Control and "Anti-social Behaviour": The Subversion of Human Rights'. *Law Quarterly Review,* 120/2: 263–91.

ASHWORTH, A., and REDMAYNE, M. (2005). *The Criminal Process* (3rd edn). Oxford: Oxford University Press.

AUDIT COMMISSION (1990a). *Footing the Bill: Financing Provincial Police Forces.* London: HMSO.

AUDIT COMMISSION (1990b). *Effective Policing: Performance Review in Police Forces.* London: HMSO.

Audit Commission (1993). *Helping with Enquiries: Tackling Crime Effectively*. London: HMSO.

Audit Commission (1996). *Streetwise: Effective Police Patrol*. London: HMSO.

Backman, J. (2000). 'The Hyperbola of Russian Crime and Police Culture', in A. Ledeneva and M. Kurkchiyan (eds), *Economic Crime in Russia*. Deventer, Netherlands: Wolter Kluwer.

Bailey, V. (1981). 'The Metropolitan Police, the Home Office and the Threat of Outcast London', in V. Bailey, *Policing and Punishment in the 19th Century*. London: Croom Helm.

Baldwin, R., and Kinsey, R. (1982). *Police Powers and Politics*. London: Quartet Books.

Ball, J., Chester, L., and Perrott, R. (1979). *Cops and Robbers*. Harmondsworth: Penguin Books.

Banton, M. (1964). *The Policeman in the Community*. London: Tavistock.

Banton, M. (1983). 'Categorical and Statistical Discrimination'. *Ethnic and Racial Studies*, 6/3 (July).

Bauman, Z. (2000). *Liquid Modernity*. Cambridge: Polity.

Bauman, Z. (2005). 'The Demons of an Open Society'. Ralph Miliband Lecture, 20 November. London: LSE.

Bauman, Z. (2007). *Liquid Times*. Cambridge: Polity.

Baxter, J., and Koffman, L. (1983). 'The Confait Inheritance-Forgotten Lessons?'. *Cambrian Law Review*, 14.

Baxter, J., and Koffman, L. (eds) (1985). *Police: The Constitution and the Community*. Abingdon: Professional Books.

Bayley, D. (1983). 'Accountability and Control of Police: Some Lessons for Britain', in T. Bennett (ed.), *The Future of Policing*. Cambridge: Institute of Criminology. Cropwood Papers 15. (Reprinted in Reiner 1996a: ii.)

Bayley, D. (1985). *Patterns of Policing*. New Brunswick, NJ: Rutgers University Press.

Bayley, D. (1991). *Forces of Order: Police Behavior in Japan and the United States* (2nd edn). Berkeley, CA: University of California Press.

Bayley, D. (1994). *Police for the Future*. New York: Oxford University Press.

Bayley, D. (ed.) (1998). *What Works in Policing?* New York: Oxford University Press.

Bayley, D. (2006). *Changing the Guard: Developing Democratic Police Abroad*. New York: Oxford University Press.

Bayley, D. (2007). 'Police Reform: Who Done It?' *Policing and Society*, 18/1: 7–17.

Bayley, D., and Bittner, E. (1984). 'Learning the Skills of Policing'. *Law and Contemporary Problems*, 47: 35–60.

Bayley, D., and Mendelsohn, H. (1968). *Minorities and the Police*. New York: Free Press.

Bayley, D., and Shearing, C. (1996). 'The Future of Policing'. *Law and Society Review*, 30/3: 586–606.

Beattie, J. (2001). *Policing and Punishment in London 1660–1750*. Oxford: Oxford University Press.

Beattie, J. (2006). 'Early Detection: The Bow Street Runners', in C. Emsley and H. Shpayer-Makov (eds), *Police Detectives in History 1750–1950*. London: Longman.

Beattie, J. (2007). 'Sir John Fielding and Public Justice: The Bow Street Magistrates' Court, 1754–1780'. *Law and History Review*, 25/1: 61–100.

Beccaria, C. (1963). *Of Crimes and Punishments* [first published as *Dei delitti e delle pene*, 1764]. Indiana: Bobbs-Merrill.

Becker, H. (1963). *Outsiders*. New York: Free Press.

BECKER, H. (1967). 'Whose Side Are We On?' *Social Problems*, 14/3: 239–47.

BECKETT, F., and HENCKE, D. (2009). *Marching to the Fault Line: The 1984 Miners' Strike and the Death of Industrial Britain*. London: Constable and Robinson.

BEETHAM, D. (1991). *The Legitimation of Power*. London: Macmillan.

BELUR, J. (2010). *Permission to Shoot? Police Use of Deadly Force in Democracies*. Berlin: Springer.

BENNETT, T. (ed.) (1983). *The Future of Policing*. Cambridge: Institute of Criminology. Cropwood Papers 15.

BENNETT, T. (1990). *Evaluating Neighbourhood Watch*. Aldershot: Gower.

BENNETT, T. (1994). 'Recent Developments in Community Policing', in S. Becker and M. Stephens (eds), *Police Force, Police Service*. London: Macmillan.

BENNETT, T., and LUPTON, T. (1992). 'A National Activity Survey of Police Work'. *Howard Journal of Criminal Justice*, 31/3: 200–23.

BENYON, J. (ed.) (1984). *Scarman and After*. Oxford: Pergamon.

BERNSTEIN, S., BIGELOW, B., COOPER, L., CURRIE, E., FRAPPIER, J., HARRING, S., KLARE, M., POYNER, P., RAY, G., SCHAUFFLER, R., SCRUGGS, J., STEIN, N., THAYER, M., and TRUJILLO, L. (1982). *The Iron Fist and the Velvet Glove: An Analysis of the US Police* (3rd edn). Berkeley, CA: Centre for Research on Criminal Justice.

BESSEL, R. and EMSLEY, C. (eds) (2000). *Patterns of Provocation: Police and Public Disorder*. Oxford: Berghahn.

BEVIR, M. and KRUPICKA, B. (2007). 'Police Reform, Governance and Democracy', in M. O'Neill, M. Marks, and A.-M. Singh (eds), *Police Occupational Culture: New Debates and Directions*. Oxford: JAI.

BILLINGSLEY, R., NEMITZ, T., and BEAN, P. (eds) (2000). *Informers: Policing, Policy, Practice*. Cullompton: Willan.

BINDER, A., and SCHARF, P. (1982). 'Deadly Force in Law Enforcement'. *Crime and Delinquency*, 28.

BITTNER, E. (1967). 'The Police on Skid Row: A Study in Peacekeeping'. *American Sociological Review*, 32.

BITTNER, E. (1970). *The Functions of the Police in Modern Society*. Chevy Chase, MD: National Institute of Mental Health.

BITTNER, E. (1974). 'Florence Nightingale in Pursuit of Willie Sutton: A Theory of the Police', in H. Jacob (ed.), *The Potential for Reform of Criminal Justice*. Beverly Hills, CA: Sage.

BITTNER, E. (1983). 'Legality and Workmanship', in M. Punch (ed.), *Control in the Police Organization*. Cambridge, MA: MIT Press.

BLACK, D. (1970). 'Production of Crime Rates'. *American Sociological Review*, 35: 733–48.

BLACK, D. (1971). 'The Social Organization of Arrest'. *Stanford Law Review*, 23: 1087–111.

BLAIR, I. (1985). *Investigating Rape: A New Approach for Police*. London: Croom Helm.

BLOM-COOPER, L., and DRABBLE, R. (1982). 'Police Perception of Crime'. *British Journal of Criminology*, 22/1 (April): 184–7.

BOGDANOR, V. (2009). 'Loosening Labour's Golden Straitjacket'. *New Statesman*, 19 March.

BOGOLMONY, R. (1976). 'Street Patrol: The Decision to Stop a Citizen'. *Criminal Law Bulletin*, 12/5.

BOTTOMLEY, A. K., and COLEMAN, C. (1981). *Understanding Crime Rates*. Farnborough: Gower.

Bottoms, A. E. (1990). 'Crime Prevention Facing the 1990s'. *Policing and Society*, 1/1: 3–22.

Bottoms, A. E. (2007). 'Place, Space, Crime, and Disorder', in M. Maguire, R. Morgan, and R. Reiner (eds), *The Oxford Handbook of Criminology* (4th edn). Oxford: Oxford University Press.

Bottoms, A. E., and Stevenson, S. (1990). 'The Politics of the Police 1958–1970', in R. Morgan (ed.), *Policing, Organised Crime and Crime Prevention*. Bristol: Bristol University, Centre for Criminal Justice. British Criminology Conference Papers 4.

Bottoms, A. E., and Wiles, P. (1996). 'Crime and Policing in a Changing Social Context', in W. Saulsbury, J. Mott, and T. Newburn (eds), *Themes in Contemporary Policing*. London: Policy Studies Institute/Police Foundation.

Bowden, T. (1978). *Beyond the Limits of the Law*. Harmondsworth: Penguin Books.

Bowling, B. (1999a). *Violent Racism*. Oxford: Oxford University Press.

Bowling, B. (1999b). 'The Rise and Fall of New York Murder'. *British Journal of Criminology*, 39/4: 531–54.

Bowling, B. (2009). 'Transnational Policing: The Globalization Thesis, a Typology and a Research Agenda'. *Policing*, 3/2: 149–60.

Bowling, B. (2010). *Policing the Caribbean*. Oxford: Oxford University Press.

Bowling, B., and Phillips, C. (2002). *Racism, Crime and Justice* (2nd edn). London: Pearson Longman.

Bowling, B. and Phillips, C. (2007). 'Disproportionate and Discriminatory: Reviewing the Evidence on Police Stop and Search'. *Modern Law Review*, 70/6: 936–61.

Bowling, B., Parmar, A., and Phillips, C. (2008). 'Policing Ethnic Minority Communities', in T. Newburn (ed.), *Handbook of Policing*. Cullompton. Willan.

Box, S. (1983). *Power, Crime and Mystification*. London: Tavistock.

Box, S. (1987). *Recession, Crime and Unemployment*. London: Macmillan.

Box, S., and Russell, K. (1975). 'The Politics of Discreditability'. *Sociological Review*, 23/2: 315–46.

Bradley, D., Walker, N., and Wilkie, R. (1986). *Managing the Police*. Brighton: Wheatsheaf.

Braithwaite, J. (2000). 'The New Regulatory State and the Transformation of Criminology'. *British Journal of Criminology*, 40/2: 222–39.

Bratton, W. (1998). 'Crime is Down: Blame the Police', in N. Dennis (ed.), *Zero Tolerance: Policing a Free Society* (2nd edn). London: Institute of Economic Affairs.

Brewer, J., and Styles, J. (eds) (1980). *An Ungovernable People*. London: Hutchinson.

Brewer, J. D. (1991). 'Policing in Divided Societies'. *Policing and Society*, 1/3: 179–91.

Brewer, J. D., and Magee, K. (1990). *Inside the RUC*. Oxford: Oxford University Press.

Brewer, J. D., Guelke, A., Hume, I., Moxon-browne, E., and Wilford, R. (1996). *The Police, Public Order and the State* (2nd edn). London: Macmillan.

Brewer, M., Muriel, A., Phillips, D., and Sibieta, L. (2008). *Poverty and Inequality in the UK: 2008*. London: Institute for Fiscal Studies.

Broderick, J. (1973). *Policing in a Time of Change*. Morristown, NJ: General Learning.

Brodeur, J.-P. (1983). 'High Policing and Low Policing: Remarks about the Policing of Political Activities'. *Social Problems*, 30/5 (June): 507–20.

Brodeur, J.-P. (ed.) (1995). *Comparisons in Policing: An International Perspective*. Aldershot: Avebury.

Brodeur, J.-P. (ed.) (1998). *How to Recognize Good Policing.* Thousand Oaks, CA: Sage.

Brodeur, J.-P. (1999). 'Cops and Spooks: The Uneasy Partnership'. *Police Practice and Research,* 1/3: 1–25.

Brodeur, J.-P. (2007). 'An Encounter With Egon Bittner'. *Crime, Law and Social Change,* 48/1: 105–32.

Brogden, A. (1981). 'Sus is Dead, but What about Sas?' *New Community,* 9/1 (spring/ summer).

Brogden, M. (1977). 'A Police Authority— The Denial of Conflict'. *Sociological Review,* 25/2: 325–49.

Brogden, M. (1981). 'All Police is Conning Bastards', in B. Fine, A. Hunt, D. McBarnet, and B. Moorhouse (eds), *Law, State and Society.* London: Croom Helm.

Brogden, M. (1982). *The Police: Autonomy and Consent.* London and New York: Academic Press.

Brogden, M. (1987). 'The Emergence of the Police: The Colonial Dimension'. *British Journal of Criminology,* 27/1: 4–14.

Brogden, M. (1991). *On the Mersey Beat: An Oral History of Policing Liverpool between the Wars.* Oxford: Oxford University Press.

Brogden, M. (1999). 'Community Policing as Cherry Pie', in R. Mawby (ed.), *Policing across the World.* London: UCL Press.

Brogden, M., and Brogden, A. (1983). 'From Henry VIII to Liverpool 8: The Complex Unity of Police Street Powers'. *International Journal of the Sociology of Law,* 12/1: 37–58.

Brogden, M., and Nijhar, P. (2005). *Community Policing.* Cullompton: Willan.

Brogden, M., and Shearing, C. (1993). *Policing for a New South Africa.* London: Routledge.

Brogden, M., Jefferson, T., and Walklate, S. (1988). *Introducing Policework.* London: Unwin.

Brown, D. (1997). *PACE Ten Years On: A Review of the Research.* London: Home Office. Home Office Research Study 155.

Brown, D., Ellis, T., and Larcombe, K. (1992). *Changing the Code: Police Detention under the Revised PACE Codes of Practice.* London: HMSO.

Brown, J. (1996). 'Police Research: Some Critical Issues', in F. Leishman, B. Loveday, and S. Savage (eds), *Core Issues in Policing.* London: Longman.

Brown, J. (1997). 'Equal Opportunities and the Police in England and Wales: Past, Present and Future Opportunities', in P. Francis, P. Davies, and V. Jupp (eds), *Policing Futures.* London: Macmillan.

Brown, J. (2003). 'Women Leaders: A Catalyst for Change', in R. Adlam and P. Villiers (eds), *Leadership in the Twenty-first Century.* Winchester: Waterside.

Brown, J., Hazenberg, A., and Ormiston, C. (1999). 'Policewomen: An International Comparison', in R. Mawby (ed.), *Policing Across the World.* London: UCL Press.

Brown, J., and Heidensohn, F. (2000). *Gender and Policing.* Basingstoke: Macmillan.

Brown, J., and Waters, I. (1993). 'Professional Police Research'. *Policing,* 9/3: 323–34.

Brown, L. and Willis, A. (1985). 'Authoritarianism in British Police Recruits: Importation, Socialisation or Myth?'. *Journal of Occupational Psychology,* 58/1: 97–108.

Brown, M. (1981). *Working the Street.* New York: Russell Sage.

Brown, S. (2003). *Crime and Law in Media Culture.* Buckingham: Open University Press.

BRUNSDON, C. (2000). 'The Structure of Anxiety: Recent British Television Crime Fiction', in E. Buscombe (ed.), *British Television*. Oxford: Oxford University Press.

BUCKE, T. (1996). *Policing and the Police: Findings from the 1994 British Crime Survey*. London: Home Office. Research Findings 28.

BUCKE, T., and BROWN, D. (1997). *In Police Custody: Police Powers and Suspects' Rights under the Revised PACE Codes of Practice*. London: Home Office. Home Office Research Study 174.

BUCKE, T., and JAMES, Z. (1998). *Trespass and Protest: Policing under the Criminal Justice and Public Order Act 1994*. London: Home Office. Home Office Research Study 190.

BUCKE, T., STREET, R., and BROWN, D. (2000). *The Right of Silence: The Impact of the Criminal Justice and Public Order Act 1994*. London: Home Office. Home Office Research Study 199.

BULLOCK, S. (2008). *Police Service Strength England and Wales*. London: Home Office.

BULMER, M., and REES, A. M. (eds) (1996). *Citizenship Today: The Contemporary Relevance of T. H. Marshall*. London: UCL Press.

BUNYAN, T. (1977). *The Political Police in Britain*. London: Quartet Books.

BURKE, M. E. (1993). *Coming Out of the Blue*. London: Cassell.

BURKE, R. H. (ed.) (1998). *Zero Tolerance Policing*. Leicester: Perpetuity Press.

BURKE, R. H. (ed.) (2004). *Hard Cop, Soft Cop: Dilemmas and Debates in Contemporary Policing*. Cullompton: Willan.

BURNEY, E. (2009). *Making People Behave: Anti-social Behaviour, Politics and Policy* (2nd edn). Cullompton: Willan.

BURROWS, J., and TARLING, R. (1982). *Clearing up Crime*. London: Home Office Research Unit.

BUTLER, A. J. (1992). *Police Management* (2nd edn). Aldershot: Dartmouth.

BUTTON, M. (2002). *Private Policing*. Cullompton: Willan.

BUTTON, M. (2007). *Security Officers and Policing*. Aldershot: Avebury.

BUTTON, M. (2008). *Doing Security*. London: Macmillan.

BYRNE, S., and PEASE, K. (2008). 'Crime Reduction and Community Safety', in T. Newburn (ed.), *Handbook of Policing* (2nd edn). Cullompton: Willan.

CAIN, M. (1973). *Society and the Policeman's Role*. London: Routledge & Kegan Paul.

CAIN, M. (1979). 'Trends in the Sociology of Police Work'. *International Journal of Sociology of Law*, 7/2: 143–67.

CALLINICOS, A. (1989). *Against Postmodernism*. Cambridge: Polity Press.

CALLINICOS, A. (2006). *The Resources of Critique*. Cambridge: Polity Press.

CAMPBELL, B. (1993). *Goliath: Britain's Dangerous Places*. London: Methuen.

CAPE, E., and YOUNG, R. (eds) (2008). *Regulating Policing: The Police and Criminal Evidence Act 1984—Past, Present and Future*. Oxford: Hart.

CARR-HILL, R., and STERN, N. (1979). *Crime, the Police and Criminal Statistics*. London and New York: Academic Press.

CARRABINE, E. (2008). *Crime, Culture and the Media*. Cambridge: Polity Press.

CARRIER, J. (1988). *The Campaign for the Employment of Women as Police Officers*. Aldershot: Avebury.

CARTER, A. (1982). 'The Wonderful World of Cops'. *New Society*, 23 September.

CASHMORE, E. (2001). 'The Experiences of Ethnic Minority Police Officers in Britain: Under-recruitment and Racial Profiling in a Performance Culture'. *Ethnic and Racial Studies*, 24/4: 642–59.

CASHMORE, E., and MCLAUGHLIN, E. (1991). *Out of Order? Policing Black People.* London: Routledge.

CASTELLS, M. (1996–8). *The Information Age*, i–iii. Oxford: Blackwell.

CATHCART, B. (1999). *The Case of Stephen Lawrence.* London: Viking.

CAVADINO, M. and DIGNAN, J. (2006). *Penal Systems: A Comparative Approach.* London: Sage.

CAVENDER, G. (2004). 'Media and Crime Policy'. *Punishment and Society*, 6/3: 335–48.

CAWELTI, J. G. (1976). *Adventure, Mystery and Romance.* Chicago, IL: Chicago University Press.

CHAKRABORTI, N., and GARLAND, J. (2009). *Hate Crime: Impact, Causes and Responses.* London: Sage.

CHAN, J. (1996). 'Changing Police Culture'. *British Journal of Criminology*, 36/1: 109–34.

CHAN, J. (1997). *Changing Police Culture: Policing in a Multicultural Society.* Cambridge: Cambridge University Press.

CHAN, J. (2003). *Fair Cop: Learning the Art of Policing.* Toronto: University of Toronto Press.

CHAN, J. (2007). 'Police Stress and Occupational Culture', in M. O'Neill, M. Marks, and A.-M. Singh (eds), *Police Occupational Culture.* Oxford: JAI.

CHANDLER, R. (1944). 'The Simple Art of Murder'. *Atlantic Monthly*, December.

CHANDLER, R. (1977). *The Long Goodbye.* London: Heinemann. [Originally published 1953.]

CHAPMAN, B. (1970). *Police State.* London: Macmillan.

CHAPMAN, D. (1968). *Sociology and the Stereotype of the Criminal.* London: Tavistock.

CHATTERTON, M. (1976). 'Police in Social Control', in J. King (ed.), *Control Without Custody.* Cambridge: Institute of Criminology. Cropwood Papers No. 7.

CHATTERTON, M. (1979). 'The Supervision of Patrol Work under the Fixed Points System', in S. Holdaway (ed.), *The British Police.* London: Edward Arnold.

CHATTERTON, M. (1983). 'Police Work and Assault Charges', in M. Punch (ed.), *Control in the Police Organization.* Cambridge, MA: MIT Press.

CHATTERTON, M. (1995). 'The Cultural Craft of Policing—Its Past and Future Relevance'. *Policing and Society*, 5/2: 97–108.

CHATTERTON, M., and ROGERS, M. (1989). 'Focused Policing', in R. Morgan and D. Smith (eds), *Coming to Terms with Policing.* London: Routledge.

CHESNEY-LIND, M. (2002). 'Criminalising Victimisation: The Unintended Consequences of Pro-arrest Policies for Girls and Women'. *Criminology and Public Policy*, 2/1: 81–90.

CHIBNALL, S. (1977). *Law and Order News.* London: Tavistock.

CHIBNALL, S. (1979). 'The Metropolitan Police and the News Media', in S. Holdaway (ed.), *The British Police.* London: Edward Arnold.

CHOO, A. (1989). 'Improperly Obtained Evidence: A Reconsideration'. *Legal Studies*, 9/3.

CHOONGH, S. (1997). *Policing as Social Discipline.* Oxford: Oxford University Press.

CHRISTENSEN, J., SCHMIDT, J., and HENDERSON, J. (1982). 'The Selling of the Police: Media, Ideology and Crime Control'. *Contemporary Crises*, 6.

CHRISTIAN, L. (1983). *Policing by Coercion.* London: GLC Police Committee and Pluto Press.

CLANCY, A., HOUGH, M., AUST, R., and
    KERSHAW, C. (2001). *Crime, Policing
    and Justice: The Experience of Ethnic
    Minorities.* London: Home Office.

CLARENS, C. (1997). *Crime Movies.* New
    York: Da Capo.

CLARK, D. (2007). 'Covert Surveillance and
    Informant Handling', in T. Newburn,
    T. Williamson, and A. Wright (eds),
    Handbook of Criminal Investigation.
    Cullompton: Willan.

CLARK, J. P. (1965). 'Isolation of the Police:
    A Comparison of the British and American
    Situations'. *Journal of Criminal Law,
    Criminology and Police Science*, 56/3: 307–19.

CLARKE, A. (1992).' "You're Nicked!" TV
    Police Series and Fictional Representation
    of Law and Order', in D. Strinati and
    S. Wragg (eds), *Come On Down—Popular
    Media Culture in Postwar Britain.* London:
    Routledge.

CLARKE, A., and TAYLOR, I. (1980). 'Vandals,
    Pickets, and Muggers'. *Screen Education*,
    36 (autumn).

CLARKE, R., and HOUGH, M. (1980). *The
    Effectiveness of Policing.* Farnborough:
    Gower.

CLARKE, R., and HOUGH, M. (1984). *Crime
    and Police Effectiveness.* London: Home
    Office Research Unit.

CLARKE, R., and MAYHEW, P. (eds) (1980).
    Designing Out Crime. London: Home
    Office Research Unit.

COCHRANE, R., and BUTLER, A. J. (1980).
    'The Values of Police Officers, Recruits
    and Civilians in England'. *Journal of Police
    Science and Administration*, 8: 205–11.

COCKROFT, T. (2007). 'Police Culture(s):
    Some Definitional, Methodological
    and Analytical Considerations', in
    M. O'Neill, M. Marks, and A.-M. Singh
    (eds), *Police Occupational Culture.*
    Oxford: JAI.

COHEN, P. (1979). 'Policing the Working
    Class City', in B. Fine, R. Kinsey, J. Lea,
    S. Picciotto, and J. Young (eds),
    Capitalism and the Rule of Law. London:
    Hutchinson.

COHEN, S. (1972). *Folk Devils and Moral
    Panics* (2nd edn). London: Paladin/
    Oxford: Martin Robertson, 1980).

COHEN, S. (1979). 'The Punitive City'.
    Contemporary Crises, 3/4.

COHEN, S. (1985). *Visions of Social Control.*
    Cambridge: Polity Press.

COHEN, S. (1997a). 'The Revenge of the
    Null Hypothesis: Evaluating Crime
    Control Policies'. *Critical Criminologist*,
    8: 21–5.

COHEN, S. (1997b). 'Crime and Politics: Spot
    the Difference', in R. Rawlings (ed.), *Law,
    Society and Economy.* Oxford: Oxford
    University Press.

COHEN, S., and SCULL. A. (eds) (1983).
    Social Control and the State. Oxford:
    Martin Robertson.

COHEN, S., and YOUNG, J. (eds) (1973). *The
    Manufacture of News.* London: Constable
    (2nd edn, 1981).

COLBRAN, M. (2007). 'Representations of
    the Police and Crime on "The Bill": The
    Effect of Changing Working Processes
    and the Changing Role of Police Co-
    Operation on the Show' (presented
    at the British Society of Criminology
    Conference, London: LSE, September).

COLBRAN, M. (2009a). 'Representations
    of Policing on "The Bill": The Process
    of Constructing Storylines' (presented
    at the British Society of Criminology
    Conference, Cardiff University, July).

COLBRAN, M. (2009b). 'Representations
    of the Police on "The Bill": The Effect
    of the "Media Loop"' (presented at
    the American Society of Criminology
    conference, Philadelphia, November).

COLEMAN, R. (2004). *Reclaiming the Streets: Surveillance, Social Control and the City.* Cullompton: Willan.

COLMAN, A., and GORMAN, L. (1982). 'Conservatism, Dogmatism and Authoritarianism in British Police Officers'. *Sociology,* 16/1: 1–11.

COLQUHOUN, P. (1795). *A Treatise on the Police of the Metropolis.* London: J. Mowman.

COLQUHOUN, P. (1800). *Treatise on the Commerce and Police of the River Thames.* London: J. Mowman.

COLQUHOUN, P. (1806). *Treatise on Indigence.* London: J. Mowman.

COOK, D. (2006). *Criminal and Social Justice.* London: Sage.

COPE, N. (2004). 'Intelligence Led Policing or Policing Led Intelligence? Integrating Volume Crime Analysis into Policing'. *British Journal of Criminology,* 44/2: 188–203.

COPE, N. (2008). '"Interpretation for Action?": Definitions and Potential of Crime Analysis for Policing', in T. Newburn (ed.), *Handbook of Policing.* Cullompton: Willan.

COPE, N., INNES, M., and FIELDING, N. (2001). *Smart Policing? The Theory and Practice of Intelligence-Led Policing.* London: Home Office.

COX, B., SHIRLEY, J., and SHORT, M. (1977). *The Fall of Scotland Yard.* Harmondsworth: Penguin.

CRANDON, G. (1990). 'The Media View of the Police'. *Policing and Society,* 6/4: 578–81.

CRANDON, G., and DUNNE, S. (1997). 'Symbiosis or Vassalage? The Media and Law Enforcers'. *Policing and Society,* 8/1: 77–91.

CRANK, J. P. (2004). *Understanding Police Culture* (2nd edn). Cincinatti, OH: Anderson Publishing.

CRAWFORD, A. (1997). *The Local Governance of Crime.* Oxford: Oxford University Press.

CRAWFORD, A. (1998). *Crime Prevention and Community Safety.* London: Longman.

CRAWFORD, A. (2006). 'Policing and Security as "Club Goods": The New Enclosures', in J. Wood and B. Dupont (eds), *Democracy, Society and the Governance of Security.* Cambridge: Cambridge University Press.

CRAWFORD, A. (2007a). 'Crime Prevention and Community Safety', in M. Maguire, R. Morgan, and R. Reiner (eds), *The Oxford Handbook of Criminology* (4th edn). Oxford: Oxford University Press.

CRAWFORD, A. (2007b). 'Reassurance Policing: Feeling is Believing', in A. Henry and D. Smith (eds), *Transformations of Policing.* Aldershot: Avebury.

CRAWFORD, A. (2008). 'Plural Policing in the UK: Policing Beyond the Police', in T. Newburn, *Handbook of Policing* (2nd edn). Cullompton: Willan.

CRAWFORD, A., LISTER, S., BLACKBURN, S., and BURNETT, J. (2005). *Plural Policing: The mixed economy of visible patrols in England and Wales.* Bristol: Policy Press.

CRAWSHAW, R., DEVLIN, B., and WILLIAMSON, T. (1998). *Human Rights and Policing.* The Hague: Kluwer.

CRAY, E. (1972). *The Enemy in the Streets.* New York: Anchor.

CRITCHER, C., and WADDINGTON, D. (eds) (1996). *Policing Public Order: Theoretical and Practical Issues.* Aldershot: Avebury.

CRITCHLEY, T. A. (1970). *The Conquest of Violence.* London: Constable.

CRITCHLEY, T. A. (1978). *A History of Police in England and Wales* (2nd edn). London: Constable (1st edn, 1967).

CROWTHER, C. (2000a). 'Thinking about the "Underclass": Towards a Political Economy of Policing'. *Theoretical Criminology*, 4/2: 149–68.

CROWTHER, C. (2000b). *Policing Urban Poverty*. London: Macmillan.

CUMMING, E., CUMMING, I., and EDELL, L. (1965). 'The Policeman as Philosopher, Guide and Friend'. *Social Problems*, 12/3: 276–86.

CURRIE, E. (1998a). *Crime and Punishment in America*. New York: Holt.

CURRIE, E. (1998b). 'Crime and Market Society: Lessons From the United States', in P. Walton and J. Young (eds), *The New Criminology Revisited*. London: Macmillan.

DAHRENDORF, R. (1985). *Law and Order*. London: Sweet & Maxwell.

DALEY, H. (1986). *This Small Cloud*. London: Weidenfeld.

DAVEY, B. J. (1983). *Lawless and Immoral: Policing a Country Town 1838–57*. Leicester: Leicester University Press/ New York: St Martin's Press.

DAVIES, N. (1998). *Dark Heart*. London: Verso.

DAVIES, N. (1999a). 'Getting Away With Murder'. *Guardian*, 11 January, 'Media' section: 4–5.

DAVIES, N. (1999b). 'Watching the Detectives: How the Police Cheat in the Fight against Crime'. *Guardian*, 18 March: 12.

DAVIES, N. (2008). *Flat Earth News*. London: Chatto & Windus.

DAVIS, J. (1984). 'A Poor Man's System of Justice: The London Police Courts in the Second Half of the 19th Century'. *Historical Journal*, 27/2.

DAVIS, M. (1990). *City of Quartz*. London: Vintage.

DAVIS, M. (1998). *Ecology of Fear*. New York: Metropolitan Books.

DEFLEM, M. (2002). *Policing World Society*. Oxford: Oxford University Press.

DELLA PORTA, D., and REITER, H. (eds) (1998). *Policing Protest*. Minneapolis, MN: University of Minnesota Press.

DELLA PORTA, D., PETERSON, A., and REITER, H. (eds) (2006). *The Policing of Transnational Protest*. Aldershot: Ashgate.

DELSOL, R., and SHINER, M. (2006). 'Regulating Stop and Search: A Challenge for Police and Community Relations in England and Wales'. *Critical Criminology*, 14/3: 241–63.

DEN BOER, M. (1999). 'Internationalisation: A Challenge to Police Organisations in Europe', in R. Mawby (ed.), *Policing Across the World: Issues for the Twenty-first Century*. London: UCL Press.

DEN BOER, M. (2002). 'Towards an Accountability Regime for an Emerging European Police Governance'. *Policing and Society*, 12/2: 275–90.

DENNIS, N. (ed.) (1998). *Zero Tolerance: Policing A Free Society* (2nd edn). London: Institute of Economic Affairs.

DENNIS, N., and ERDOS, G. (2005). *Cultures and Crimes: Policing in Four Nations*. London: Civitas.

DI TELLA, R., and SCHARGRODSKY, E. (2004). 'Do Police Reduce Crime? Estimate Using the Allocation of Police Forces After a Terrorist Attack', *American Economic Review*, 94/1: 115–33.

DITTON, J., and FARRALL, S. (eds) (2000). *The Fear of Crime*. Aldershot: Dartmouth.

DIXON, B., and SMITH, G. (1998). 'Laying Down the Law: The Police, the Courts and Legal Accountability'. *International Journal of the Sociology of Law*, 26: 419–35.

DIXON, B., and STANKO, E. A. (1995). 'Sector Policing and Public Accountability'. *Policing and Society*, 5/2: 171–83.

Dixon, D. (1997). *Law in Policing*. Oxford: Oxford University Press.

Dixon, D. (2008). 'Authorise and Regulate: A Comparative Perspective on the Rise and Fall of a Regulatory Strategy', in E. Cape and R. Young (eds), *Regulating Policing*. Oxford: Hart.

Dixon, D. and Maher, L. (2005). 'Policing, Crime and Public Health: Lessons for Australia from the "New York Miracle"'. *Criminal Justice*, 5/1: 115–44.

Dixon, D., Coleman, C., and Bottomley, K. (1990). 'Consent and the Legal Regulation of Policing'. *Journal of Law and Society*, 17/3: 345–62.

Dixon, D., Bottomley, A. K., Coleman, C. A., Gill, M., and Wall, D. (1990). 'Safeguarding the Rights of Suspects in Police Custody'. *Policing and Society*, 1/2.

Dodsworth, F. M. (2007). 'Police and Prevention of Crime: Commerce, Temptation and the Corruption of the Body Politic, from Fielding to Colquhoun'. *British Journal of Criminology*, 47/3: 439–54.

Dominick, J. (1978). 'Crime and Law Enforcement in the Mass Media', in C. Winick (ed.), *Deviance and Mass Media*. Beverly Hills, CA: Sage.

Donajgrodski, A. P. (1977). '"Social Police"' and the Bureaucratic Elite', in A. P. Donajgrodski (ed.), *Social Control in Nineteenth Century Britain*. London: Croom Helm.

Dorling, D. (2004). 'Prime Suspect: Murder in Britain', in P. Hillyard, C. Pantazis, S. Tombs, and D. Gordon (eds), *Beyond Criminology*. London: Pluto.

Dorn, N., Murji, K., and South, N. (1991a). 'Mirroring the Market—Police Reorganisation and Effectiveness against Drug Trafficking', in R. Reiner and M. Cross (eds), *Beyond Law and Order: Criminal Justice Policy and Politics into the 1990s*. London: Macmillan.

Dorn, N., Murji, K., and South, N. (1991b). *Traffickers: Drug Markets and Law Enforcement*. London: Routledge.

Dove, G. (1982). *The Police Procedural*. Bowling Green, OH: Bowling Green University Popular Press.

Dove, G., and Bargainnier, E. F. (eds) (1986). *Cops and Constables: American and British Fictional Policemen*. Bowling Green, OH: Bowling Green Popular Press.

Downes, D. (1998). 'Toughing It Out: From Labour Opposition to Labour Government'. *Policy Studies*, 19/3–4: 191–8.

Downes, D., and Morgan, R. (2007). 'No Turning Back: The Politics of Law and Order into the Millennium', in M. Maguire, R. Morgan, and R. Reiner (eds), *The Oxford Handbook of Criminology* (4th edn). Oxford: Oxford University Press.

Downes, D., and Ward, T. (1986). *Democratic Policing*. London: Labour Campaign for Criminal Justice.

Draca, M., Machin, S., and Witt, R. (2008). *Panic on the Streets of London: Police, Crime and the July 2005 Terror Attacks*. London: LSE Centre for Economic Performance.

Dubber, M. (2005). *The Police Power*. New York: Columbia University Press.

Dubber, M., and Valverde, M. (eds) (2006). *The New Police Science*. Stanford, CA: Stanford University Press.

Duffy, B., Wake, R., Burrows, T., and Bremner, P. (2008). 'Closing the Gaps—Crime and Public Perceptions'. *International Review of Law, Computers and Technology*, 22/1: 17–44.

Dummett, M. (1980a). *Southall 23 April 1979*. London: National Council for Civil Liberties.

Dummett, M. (1980b). *The Death of Blair Peach*. London: National Council for Civil Liberties.

Dunhill, C. (ed.) (1989). *The Boys in Blue: Women's Challenge to Policing*. London: Virago.

Dunnighan, C., and Norris, C. (1999). 'The Detective, the Snout and the Audit Commission: The Real Cost of Using Informants'. *Howard Journal of Criminal Justice*, 38/1: 67–86.

Eaton, M. (1995). 'A Fair Cop—Viewing the Effects of the Canteen Culture in *Prime Suspect* and *Between the Lines*', in D. Kidd-Hewitt and R. Osborne (eds), *Crime and the Media: The Post-Modern Spectacle*. London: Pluto Press.

Eck, J., and Maguire, E. (2005). 'Have Changes in Policing Reduced Violent Crime?', in A. Bloomstein and J. Wallman (eds), *The Crime Drop in America* (2nd edn). Cambridge: Cambridge University Press.

Edwards, A. (2008). 'The Role of Defence Lawyers in a "Re-balanced" System', in E. Cape and R. Young (eds), *Regulating Policing*. Oxford: Hart.

Edwards, C. J. (2005). *Changing Policing Theories for 21st Century Societies* (2nd edn). Leichhardt, NSW: Federation Press.

Edwards, S. (1989). *Policing 'Domestic' Violence*. London: Sage.

Ehrlich, S. (1980). *Breaking and Entering: Police Women on Patrol*. Berkeley, CA: University of California Press.

Eisner, M. (2001). 'Modernisation, Self-control and Lethal Violence: The Long-term Dynamics of European Homicide Rates in Theoretical Perspective'. *British Journal of Criminology*, 41: 618–38.

Ekblom, P., and Heal, K. (1982). *The Police Response to Calls from the Public*. London: Home Office. Research and Planning Unit Paper 9.

Emsley, C. (1983). *Policing and Its Context 1750–1870*. London: Macmillan.

Emsley, C. (1996). *The English Police: A Political and Social History* (2nd edn). London: Longman.

Emsley, C. (2007). 'Historical Perspectives on Crime', in M. Maguire, R. Morgan, and R. Reiner (eds), *The Oxford Handbook of Criminology* (4th edn). Oxford: Oxford University Press.

Emsley, C. (2008). 'The Birth and Development of the Police', in T. Newburn (ed.), *Handbook of Policing* (2nd edn). Cullompton: Willan.

Emsley, C. (2009). *The Great British Bobby*. London: Quercus.

Ericson, R. (1982). *Reproducing Order: A Study of Police Patrol Work*. Toronto: University of Toronto Press.

Ericson, R. (1993). *Making Crime: A Study of Detective Work* (2nd edn). Toronto: University of Toronto Press.

Ericson, R., and Haggerty, K. (1997). *Policing Risk Society*. Oxford: Oxford University Press.

Ericson, R., and Haggerty, K. (2002). 'The Policing of Risk', in T. Baker and J. Simon (eds), *Embracing Risk*. Chicago, IL: Chicago University Press.

Ericson, R., Baranek, P., and Chan, J. (1987). *Visualising Deviance: A Study of News Organisation*. Milton Keynes: Open University Press.

Ericson, R., Baranek, P., and Chan, J. (1989). *Negotiating Control: A Study of News Sources*. Milton Keynes: Open University Press.

Ericson, R., Baranek, P., and Chan, J. (1991). *Representing Crime: Crime, Law and Justice in the News Media*. Milton Keynes: Open University Press.

Everson, W. (1972). *The Detective in Film*. New York: Citadel.

FARRALL, S., and LEE, M. (eds) (2008). *Fear of Crime: Critical Voices in an Age of Anxiety.* London: Routledge.

FARRALL, S., JACKSON, J., and GRAY, E. (2009). *Social Order and the Fear of Crime in Contemporary Times.* Oxford: Oxford University Press.

FARRELL, A. (1992). *Crime, Class and Corruption: The Politics of the Police.* London: Bookmarks.

FARRINGTON, D., and DOWDS, E. (1985). 'Disentangling Criminal Behaviour and Police Reaction', in D. Farrington and J. Gunn (eds), *Reactions to Crime: The Public, the Police, Courts and Prisons.* Winchester: Wiley.

FEELEY, M., and SIMON, J. (1994). 'Actuarial Justice: The Emerging New Criminal Law', in D. Nelken (ed.), *The Futures of Criminology.* London: Sage.

FELDMAN, D. (1990). 'Regulating Treatment of Suspects in Police Stations: Judicial Interpretations of Detention Provisions in the Police and Criminal Evidence Act 1984'. *Criminal Law Review*, 452–71.

FIELD, J. (1981). 'Police, Power and Community in a Provincial English Town: Portsmouth 1815–75', in V. Bailey (ed.), *Policing and Punishment in 19th Century Britain.* London: Croom Helm.

FIELD, S. (1990). *Trends in Crime and Their Interpretation: A Study of Recorded Crime in Post-War England and Wales.* London: HMSO. Home Office Research Study 119.

FIELD, S. (1999). *Trends in Crime Revisited.* London: Home Office. Home Office Research Study 195.

FIELDING, N. (1988). *Joining Forces.* London: Routledge.

FIELDING, N. (1989). 'Police Culture and Police Practice', in M. Weatheritt (ed.), *Police Research: Some Future Prospects.* Aldershot: Avebury.

FIELDING, N. (1994). 'Cop Canteen Culture', in T. Newburn and E. A. Stanko (eds), *Just Boys Doing Business: Men, Masculinity and Crime.* London: Routledge.

FIELDING, N. (1995). *Community Policing.* Oxford: Oxford University Press.

FIELDING, N. (2002). 'Theorising Community Policing'. *British Journal of Criminology*, 42/1: 147–63.

FIELDING, N. (2005). *The Police and Social Conflict* (2nd edn). London: Glasshouse.

FIELDING, N. (2009). *Getting the Best Out of Community Policing.* London: Police Foundation.

FIELDING, N., and FIELDING, J. (1992). 'A Comparative Minority: Female Recruits to a British Constabulary Force'. *Policing and Society*, 2/3: 205–18.

FIJNAUT, C., and MARX, G. (eds) (1996). *Undercover: Police Surveillance in Comparative Perspective.* The Hague: Kluwer.

FINE, B., and MILLAR, R. (eds) (1985). *Policing the Miners' Strike.* London: Lawrence & Wishart.

FINNANE, M. (2002). *When Police Unionise: The Politics of Law and Order in Australia.* Annandale, NSW: Federation Press.

FISHER, C., and MAWBY, R. (1982). 'Juvenile Delinquency and Police Discretion in an Inner-City Area'. *British Journal of Criminology*, 22/1 (January): 141–63.

FISHER, SIR H. (1977). *The Confait Case: Report.* London: HMSO.

FISHMAN, M. (1978). 'Crime Waves as Ideology'. *Social Problems*, 25/4: 531–43.

FISHMAN, M., and CAVENDER, G. (1998). *Entertaining Crime: Television Reality Programmes.* Hawthorne, NY: Aldine de Gruyter.

FITZGERALD, M. (1993). *Ethnic Minorities and the Criminal Justice System.* London: HMSO. Royal Commission on Criminal Justice Research Study 20.

FITZGERALD, M. (1999). *Report into Stop and Search*. London: Metropolitan Police.

FITZGERALD, M. (2001). 'Ethnic Minorities and Community Safety', in R. Matthews and J. Pitts (eds), *Crime, Disorder and Community Safety*. London: Routledge.

FITZGERALD, M. (2009). '"Race", Ethnicity and Crime', in C. Hale, K. Hayward, A. Wahidin, and E. Wincup (eds), *Criminology* (2nd edn). Oxford: Oxford University Press.

FITZGERALD, M., and HALE, C. (1996). *Ethnic Minorities: Victimisation and Racial Harassment: Findings from the 1988 and 1992 British Crime Surveys*. London: Home Office. Home Office Research Study 154.

FITZGERALD, M., HOUGH, M., JOSEPH, I., and QURESHI, T. (2002). *Policing For London*. Cullompton: Willan.

FOGELSON, R. (1977). *Big-City Police*. Cambridge, MA: Harvard University Press.

FORRESTER, D., CHATTERTON, M., and PEASE, K. (1988). *The Kirkholt Burglary Prevention Project*. London: Home Office. Crime Prevention Unit Paper 13.

FORST, B., and MANNING, P. (1999). *The Privatization of Policing*. Washington, DC: Georgetown University Press.

FOSTER, John. (1974). *Class Struggle in the Industrial Revolution*. London: Methuen.

FOSTER, J. (1989). 'Two Stations: An Ethnographic Study of Policing in the Inner City', in D. Downes (ed.), *Crime and the City*. London: Macmillan.

FOSTER, J. (2003). 'Police Cultures', in T. Newburn (ed.), *Handbook of Policing*. Cullompton: Willan.

FOSTER, J. (2008). '"It Might Have Been Incompetent, But It Wasn't Racist": Murder Detectives' Perceptions of the Lawrence Inquiry and its Impact on Homicide Investigation in London'. *Policing and Society*, 89–112.

FOSTER, J., NEWBURN, T., and SOUHAMI, A. (2005). *Assessing the Impact of the Stephen Lawrence Enquiry*. London: Home Office.

FOUCAULT, M. (1977). *Discipline and Punish*. Harmondsworth: Penguin/New York: Pantheon.

FRANCIS, P., DAVIES, P., and JUPP, V. (eds) (1997). *Policing Futures: The Police, Law Enforcement and the Twenty-First Century*. London: Macmillan.

FREEMAN, M. (1984). 'Law and Order in 1984'. *Current Legal Problems*, 1984.

FRIEDMANN, R. (1992). *Community Policing: Comparative Perspectives and Prospects*. Hemel Hempstead: Harvester Wheatsheaf.

FYFE, J. (1981). 'Race and Extreme Police–Citizen Violence', in R. McNeely and C. Pope (eds), *Race, Crime and Criminal Justice*. Beverly Hills, CA: Sage.

FYFE, J. (2002). 'Too Many Missing Cases: Holes in Our Knowledge About Police Use of Deadly Force'. *Justice Research and Policy*, 4/1: 87–102.

FYFE, N. (1992). 'Towards Locally Sensitive Policing—Politics, Participation and Power in Community/Police Consultation', in D. J. Evans, N. R. Fyfe, and D. T. Herbert (eds), *Crime, Policing and Place: Essays in Environmental Criminology*. London: Routledge.

GALBRAITH, J. K. (1992). *The Culture of Contentment*. London: Sinclair-Stevenson.

GAMBLE, A. (1994). *The Free Economy and the Strong State*. London: Macmillan.

GARLAND, D. (1996). 'The Limits of the Sovereign State: Strategies of Crime Control in Contemporary Societies'. *British Journal of Criminology*, 36/4: 1–27.

GARLAND, D. (1997). '"Governmentality" and the Problem of Crime: Foucault, Criminology, and Sociology'. *Theoretical Criminology*, 1/2: 173–214.

GARLAND, D. (2001). *The Culture of Control.* Oxford: Oxford University Press.

GASH, N. (1961). *Mr Secretary Peel.* London: Longman.

GATES, H. L. (1995). 'Thirteen Ways of Looking At a Black Man'. *New Yorker,* 23 October: 59.

GATRELL, V. (1980). 'The Decline of Theft and Violence in Victorian and Edwardian England', in V. Gatrell, B. Lenman, and G. Parker (eds), *Crime and the Law.* London: Europa.

GATRELL, V. (1988). 'Crime, Authority and the Policeman-State 1750–1950', in F. M. Thompson (ed.), *The Cambridge Social History of Britain.* Cambridge: Cambridge University Press.

GATRELL, V. (1994). *The Hanging Tree.* Oxford: Oxford University Press.

GEARY, R. (1985). *Policing Industrial Disputes.* Cambridge: Cambridge University Press.

GEHERIN, D. (1980). *Sons of Sam Spade.* New York: Ungar.

GELLER, W., and TOCH, H. (eds) (1996). *Police Violence: Understanding and Controlling Police Abuse of Force.* New Haven, CT: Yale University Press.

GIDDENS, A. (1990). *The Consequences of Modernity.* Cambridge: Polity Press.

GIDDENS, A. (2002). *Runaway World.* Cambridge: Polity Press.

GIFFORD, LORD (1986). *The Broadwater Farm Inquiry.* London: Broadwater Farm Inquiry.

GILL, M., and MAWBY, R. I. (1990). *A Special Constable.* Aldershot: Avebury.

GILL, P. (1987). 'Clearing Up Crime: The Big "Con"'. *Journal of Law and Society,* 14/2: 254–65.

GILL, P. (1994). *Policing Politics: Security Intelligence and the Liberal Democratic State.* London: Frank Cass.

GILL, P. (2000). *Rounding Up the Usual Suspects? Developments in Contemporary Law Enforcement Intelligence.* Aldershot: Ashgate.

GILLING, D. (1997). *Crime Prevention: Theory, Practice and Politics.* London: UCL Press.

GILLING, D. (2007). *Crime Reduction and Community Safety: Labour and the Politics of Local Crime Control.* Cullompton: Willan.

GILROY, P. (1982). 'The Myth of Black Criminality', in *Socialist Register 1982.* London: Merlin.

GILROY, P. (1983). 'Police and Thieves', in Centre for Research on Contemporary Cultural Studies, *The Empire Strikes Back.* London: Hutchinson.

GIRLING, E., LOADER, I., and SPARKS, R. (2000). *Crime and Social Change in Middle England.* London: Routledge.

GLEESON, E., and GRACE, K. (2008). *Police Complaints: Statistics for England and Wales 2007–8.* London: IPCC.

GLYN, A. (2006). *Capitalism Unleashed.* Oxford: Oxford University Press.

GODFREY, B., and LAWRENCE, P. (2005). *Crime and Justice, 1750–1950.* Cullompton: Willan.

GOLDING, B., and SAVAGE, S.(2008). 'Leadership and Performance Management', in T. Newburn (ed.), *Handbook of Policing* (2nd edn). Cullompton: Willan.

GOLDSMITH, A. (1990). 'Taking Police Culture Seriously: Police Discretion and the Limits of Law'. *Policing and Society,* 1/2: 91–114. (Reprinted in Reiner 1996a: ii.)

GOLDSMITH, A. (ed.) (1991). *Complaints against the Police: The Trend to External Review.* Oxford: Oxford University Press.

GOLDSMITH, A. (2003). 'Policing Weak States: Citizen Safety and State

Responsibility'. *Policing and Society* 13/1: 3–21.

GOLDSMITH, A., and LEWIS, C. (eds) (2000). *Civilian Oversight of Policing.* Oxford: Hart.

GOLDSMITH, A., and SHEPTYCKI, J. (eds) (2007). *Crafting Transnational Policing.* Oxford: Hart.

GOLDSTEIN, H. (1977). *Policing a Free Society.* Cambridge, MA: Ballinger.

GOLDSTEIN, H. (1979). 'Policing: A Problem-Oriented Approach'. *Crime and Delinquency,* 25/2: 236–58.

GOLDSTEIN, H. (1990). *Problem-Oriented Policing.* New York: McGraw-Hill.

GOLDSTEIN, J. (1960). 'Police Discretion not to Invoke the Criminal Process: Low Visibility Decisions in the Administration of Justice'. *Yale Law Journal,* 69: 543–94.

GOOLD, B. (2004). *CCTV and Policing.* Oxford: Oxford University Press.

GOOLD, B. (2009). *Surveillance.* London: Routledge.

GORDON, P. (1984). 'Community Policing: Towards the Local Police State'. *Critical Social Policy,* 10 (summer): 39–58.

GORDON, T. (2006). *Cops, Crime and Capitalism.* Halifax: Fernwood.

GORER, G. (1955). *Exploring English Character.* London: Cresset.

GOSSELIN, P. (2008). *High Wire: The Precarious Financial Lives of American Families.* New York: Basic Books.

GOULDNER, A. (1968). 'The Sociologist as Partisan'. *American Sociologist,* May.

GRAEF, R. (1989). *Talking Blues.* London: Collins.

GREEN, D. (2008). *When Children Kill Children: Penal Populism and Political Culture.* Oxford: Oxford University Press.

GREEN, D., GROVE, E., and MARTIN, N. (2005). *Crime and Civil Society.* London: Civitas.

GREEN, P. (1991). *The Enemy Without: Policing and Class Consciousness in the Miners' Strike.* Milton Keynes: Open University Press.

GREENWOOD, P., CHAIKEN, J., and PETERSILIA, J. (1977). *The Criminal Investigation Process.* Lexington, MA: D. C. Heath.

GREER, C. (2003). *Sex Crime and the Media.* Cullompton: Willan.

GREER, C. (2009a). 'Crime and Media: Understanding the Connections', in C. Hale, K. Hayward, A. Wahidin, and E. Wincup (eds), *Criminology* (2nd edn). Oxford: Oxford University Press.

GREER, C. (2009b). *Crime and Media: A Reader.* London: Routledge.

GREER, S. (1995). *Supergrasses: A Study in Anti-Terrorist Law Enforcement in Northern Ireland.* Oxford: Oxford University Press.

GREGORY, J., and LEES, S. (1999). *Policing Sexual Assault.* London: Routledge.

GRELLA, G. (1970). 'Murder and Manners: The Formal Detective Story'. *Novel,* 4/1.

GRIFFITH, J. (1997). *The Politics of the Judiciary* (5th edn). London: Fontana.

GRIGG, M. (1965). *The Challenor Case.* Harmondsworth: Penguin.

GRIMSHAW, R., and JEFFERSON, T. (1987). *Interpreting Policework.* London: Unwin.

GUDJONNSON, G. (2007). 'Investigative Interviewing', in T. Newburn, T. Williamson, and A. Wright (eds), *Handbook of Criminal Investigation.* Cullompton: Willan.

HACKER, J. (2006). *The Great Risk Shift: The Assault on American Jobs, Families, Health Care and Retirement And How You Can Fight Back.* New York: Oxford University Press.

HAIN, P. (ed.) (1979). *Policing the Police.* London: Calder.

HAIN, P. (ed.) (1980). *Policing the Police 2.* London: Calder.

HAIN, P. (1984). *Political Trials In Britain.* Harmondsworth: Penguin.

HALE, C. (2009). 'Economic Marginalisation, Social Exclusion and Crime', in C. Hale, K. Hayward, A. Wahidin, and E. Wincup (eds), *Criminology* (2nd edn). Oxford: Oxford University Press.

HALE, C., and FITZGERALD, M. (2009). 'The Politics of Law and Order', in C. Hale, K. Hayward, A. Wahidin, and E. Wincup (eds), *Criminology* (2nd edn). Oxford: Oxford University Press.

HALFORD, A. (1993). *No Way Up the Greasy Pole.* London: Constable.

HALL, N. (2005). *Hate Crime.* Cullompton: Willan.

HALL, P. T. (1998). 'Policing Order: Assessments of Effectiveness and Efficiency'. *Policing and Society,* 8/3: 225–52.

HALL, S. (1973). 'The Determination of News Photographs', in S. Cohen and Y. Young (eds), *The Manufacture of News.* London: Constable.

HALL, S. (1979). *Drifting into a Law and Order Society.* London: Cobden Trust.

HALL, S., CRITCHER, C., JEFFERSON, T., CLARKE, J., and ROBERTS, B. (1978). *Policing the Crisis.* London, Macmillan.

HALL, Steve, and MACLEAN, C.(2009). 'A Tale of Two Capitalisms: Preliminary Spatial and Historical Comparisons of Homicide'. *Theoretical Criminology,* 13/3: 313–39.

HALL, Steve, and WINLOW, S. (2003). 'Rehabilitating Leviathan: Reflections on the State, Economic Regulation and Violence Reduction'. *Theoretical Criminology,* 7/2: 139–62.

HALL, Steve, WINLOW, S., and ANCRUM, C. (2008). *Criminal Identities and Consumer Culture.* Cullompton: Willan.

HALLORAN, J., ELLIOTT, P., and MURDOCK, G. (1970). *Demonstrations and Communication.* Harmondsworth: Penguin.

HANMER, J., RADFORD, R., and STANKO, E. A. (eds) (1989). *Women, Policing and Male Violence.* London: Routledge.

HARCOURT, B. (2001). *Illusion of Order: The False Promise of Broken Windows Policing.* Cambridge, MA: Harvard University Press.

HARFIELD, C. (2006). 'SOCA: A Paradigm Shift in British Policing'. *British Journal of Criminology,* 46/4: 743–61.

HARRING, S. (1983). *Policing a Class Society.* New Brunswick, NJ: Rutgers University Press.

HARRIS, A. T. (2004). *Policing the City: Crime and Legal Authority in London, 1780–1840.* Columbus, OH: Ohio University Press.

HARRIS, D. (2002). *Profiles in Injustice.* New York: New Press.

HART, J. (1955). 'Reform of the Borough Police'. *English Historical Review,* 70: 411–27.

HART, J. (1956). 'The County and Borough Police Act 1835–56'. *Public Administration,* 34: 405–17.

HART, J. (1978). 'Police', in W. Cornish (ed.), *Crime and Law.* Dublin: Irish University Press.

HARVEY, D. (1989). *The Condition of Postmodernity.* Oxford: Blackwell.

HARVEY, D. (2005). *A Brief History of Neo-liberalism.* Oxford: Oxford University Press.

HAUGE, R. (1965). 'Crime and the Press', in N. Christie (ed.), *Scandinavian Studies in Criminology 1.* London: Tavistock.

HAY, D. (ed.) (1975). *Albion's Fatal Tree.* Harmondsworth: Penguin.

HAY, D., and SNYDER, F. (eds) (1989). *Policing and Prosecution in Britain 1750–1850.* Oxford: Oxford University Press.

HAYCRAFT, H. (1941). *Murder for Pleasure.* New York: Appleton, Century.

HAYCRAFT, H. (ed.) (1946). *The Art of the Mystery Story.* New York: Grosset & Dunlap.

HEAL, K., TARLING, R., and BURROWS, J. (eds) (1985). *Policing Today.* London: HMSO.

HEATON, R. (2000). 'The Prospects for Intelligence-Led Policing: Some Historical and Quantitative Considerations'. *Policing and Society*, 9/4: 337–56.

HEDDERMAN, C. (2008). *Building on Sand: Why Expanding the Prison Estate is Not the Way to 'Secure the Future'.* Kings College, London: Centre for Crime and Justice Studies.

HEIDENSOHN, F. (1992). *Women in Control—The Role of Women in Law Enforcement.* Oxford: Oxford University Press.

HEIDENSOHN, F. (1994). '"We Can Handle It Out Here". Women Police Officers in Britain and the USA and the Policing of Public Order'. *Policing and Society*, 4/4: 293–303.

HEIDENSOHN, F. (2008). 'Gender and Policing', in T. Newburn (ed.), *Handbook of Policing.* Cullompton: Willan.

HEIDENSOHN, F., and GELSTHORPE, L. (2007). 'Gender and Crime', in M. Maguire, R. Morgan, and R. Reiner (eds), *The Oxford Handbook of Criminology* (4th edn). Oxford: Oxford University Press.

HELD, D., and MCGREW, A. (2007). *Globalization/Anti-Globalization: Beyond the Great Divide.* Cambridge: Polity.

HENRY, A. (2007). 'Policing and Ethnic Minorities', in A. Henry and D. J. Smith (eds), *Transformations of Policing.* Aldershot: Ashgate.

HERBERT, S. (2000). 'Reassessing Police and Police Studies'. *Theoretical Criminology*, 4/1: 113–19.

HERBERT, S. (2001). 'Policing the Contemporary City: Fixing Broken Windows or Shoring Up Neo-liberalism?'. *Theoretical Criminology*, 5/4: 445–66.

HERBERT, S. (2006). *Citizens, Cops and Power.* Chicago, IL: Chicago University Press.

HEWITT, P. (1982). *The Abuse of Power.* Oxford: Martin Robertson.

HILL, A. (2000). 'Crime and Crisis: British Reality Television in Action', in E. Buscombe (ed.), *British Television.* Oxford: Oxford University Press.

HINTON, M. (2006). *The State in the Streets: Police and Politics in Argentina and Brazil.* Boulder, CO: Rienner.

HINTON, M., and NEWBURN, T. (eds) (2008). *Policing Developing Democracies.* London: Routledge.

HIRST, P. Q. (1975). 'Marx and Engels on Law, Crime and Morality', in I. Taylor, P. Walton, and J. Young (eds), *Critical Criminology.* London: Routledge.

HIRST, P., THOMPSON, G., and BROMLEY, S. (2009). *Globalisation in Question* (3rd edn). Cambridge: Polity Press.

HITCHENS, P. (2003). *A Brief History of Crime.* London: Atlantic Books.

HMIC (2009). *Adapting to Protest.* London: HM Inspectorate of Constabulary.

HOBBS, D. (1988). *Doing the Business: Entrepreneurship, the Working Class and Detectives in the East End of London.* Oxford: Oxford University Press.

HOBBS, D. (1995). *Bad Business.* Oxford: Oxford University Press.

HOBSBAWM, E. (1959). *Primitive Rebels.* Manchester: Manchester University Press.

HOBSBAWM, E. (1968). *Industry and Empire.* London: Penguin.

HOBSBAWM, E. (1969). *Bandits.* London: Penguin.

HOBSBAWM, E. (1994). 'Barbarism: A User's Guide'. *New Left Review,* 206/1: 44–54.

HOBSBAWM, E. (1995). *The Age of Extremes.* London: Abacus.

HOBSBAWM, E., and RUDE, G. (1969). *Captain Swing.* London: Penguin.

HOFSTRA, B., and SHAPLAND, J. (1997). 'Who is in Control?'. *Policing and Society,* 6/4: 265–82.

HOLDAWAY, S. (1977). 'Changes in Urban Policing'. *British Journal of Sociology,* 28/2: 119–37.

HOLDAWAY, S. (ed.) (1979). *The British Police.* London: Edward Arnold.

HOLDAWAY, S. (1983). *Inside the British Police.* Oxford: Basil Blackwell.

HOLDAWAY, S. (1989). 'Discovering Structure: Studies of the British Police Occupational Culture', in M. Weatheritt (ed.), *Police Research: Some Future Prospects.* Aldershot: Avebury.

HOLDAWAY, S. (1996). *The Racialisation of British Policing.* London: Macmillan.

HOLDAWAY, S. (2009). *Black Police Associations.* Oxford: Oxford University Press.

HOLDAWAY, S., SPENCER, C., and WILSON, D. (1984). 'Black Police in the UK'. *Policing,* 1/1: 20–30.

HOLLAND, B. (2007). 'View From the Inside: The Realities of Promoting Race and Diversity Inside the Police Service', in M. Rowe (ed.), *Policing Beyond Macpherson.* Cullompton: Willan.

HOLLWAY, W., and JEFFERSON, T. (1997). 'The Risk Society in an Age of Anxiety: Situating the Fear of Crime'. *British Journal of Sociology,* 48/2: 255–65.

HOME OFFICE (1981). *Racial Attacks: Report of a Home Office Study.* London: Home Office.

HOME OFFICE (1993). *Police Reform: A Police Service for the Twenty-First Century.* London: HMSO. White Paper Cm. 2281.

HOOGENBOOM, B. (1991). 'Grey Policing: A Theoretical Framework'. *Policing and Society,* 2/1: 17–30.

HOPE, T. (2000). 'Inequality and the Clubbing of Private Security', in T. Hope and R. Sparks (eds), *Crime, Risk and Insecurity.* London: Routledge.

HOPE, T. (2004). 'Pretend It Works: Evidence and Governance in the Evaluation of the Reducing Burglary Initiative'. *Criminal Justice,* 4/3: 287–308.

HORSLEY, L. (2005). *Twentieth-Century Crime Fiction.* Oxford: Oxford University Press.

HORTON, C. (1989). 'Good Practice and Evaluative Policing', in R. Morgan and D. Smith (eds), *Coming to Terms with Policing.* London: Routledge.

HOUGH, M. (1987). 'Thinking About Effectiveness'. *British Journal of Criminology,* 27/1: 70–9.

HOUGH, M. (1989). 'Demand for Policing and Police Performance: Progress and Pitfalls in Public Surveys', in M. Weatheritt (ed.), *Police Research: Some Future Prospects.* Aldershot: Avebury.

HOUGH, M. (2003). 'Modernization and Public Opinion: Some Criminal Justice Paradoxes'. *Contemporary Politics,* 9: 143–55.

HOUGH, M. (ed.) (2004). 'Evaluating the Crime Reduction Programme in England and Wales'. *Criminal Justice,* 4/3.

HOUGH, M. (2007a). 'Policing London, Twenty Years On', in A. Henry and

D. J. Smith (eds), *Transformations of Policing.* Aldershot: Avebury.

HOUGH, M. (2007b). 'Policing, New Public Management and Legitimacy in Britain', in T. Tyler (ed.), *Legitimacy and Criminal Justice.* New York: Russell Sage Foundation Press.

HOYLE, C. (1998). *Negotiating Domestic Violence: Police, Criminal Justice and Victims.* Oxford: Oxford University Press.

HOYLE, C., and ZEDNER, L. (2007). 'Victims, Victimisation and Criminal Justice', in M. Maguire, R. Morgan, and R. Reiner (eds), *The Oxford Handbook of Criminology* (4th edn). Oxford: Oxford University Press.

HUGGINS, M. (1998). *Political Policing.* Durham, NC: Duke University Press.

HUGHES, E. C. (1961). 'Good People and Dirty Work'. *Social Problems,* 10/1.

HUGHES, G. (1994). 'Talking Cop Shop— A Case-Study of Police Community Consultative Groups in Transition'. *Policing and Society,* 4: 253–70.

HUGHES, G. (1998). *Understanding Crime Prevention: Social Control, Risk and Late Modernity.* Buckingham: Open University Press.

HUGHES, G. (2006). *The Politics of Crime and Community.* Basingstoke: Macmillan.

HUGHES, G., and EDWARDS, A. (eds) (2002). *Crime Control and Community: The New Politics of Public Safety.* Cullompton: Willan.

HURD, G. (1979). 'The Television Presentation of the Police', in S. Holdaway (ed.), *The British Police.* London: Edward Arnold.

IANNI, E. R., and IANNI, R. (1983). 'Street Cops and Management Cops: The Two Cultures of Policing', in M. Punch (ed.), *Control in the Police Organization.* Cambridge, MA: MIT Press.

IGNATIEFF, M. (1979). 'Police and People: The Birth of Mr. Peel's Blue Locusts'. *New Society,* 49.

INCIARDI, J., and DEE, J. L. (1987). 'From the Keystone Cops to Miami Vice: Images of Policing in American Popular Culture'. *Journal of Popular Culture,* 21/2: 84–102.

INGLIS, G. (2009). *Confidence in the Police Complaints System.* London: IPCC.

INNES, M. (1999a). '"An Iron Fist in an Iron Glove?" The Zero Tolerance Policing Debate'. *Howard Journal of Criminal Justice,* 38/4: 397–410.

INNES, M. (1999b). 'The Media as an Investigative Response in Murder Enquiries'. *British Journal of Criminology,* 39/2: 268–85.

INNES, M. (2003a). *Investigating Murder: Detective Work and the Police Response to Criminal Homicide.* Oxford: Oxford University Press.

INNES, M. (2003b). '"Signal Crimes": Detective Work, Mass Media and Constructing Collective Memory', in P. Mason (ed.), *Criminal Visions.* Cullompton: Willan.

INNES, M. (2003c). *Understanding Social Control.* Maidenhead: Open University Press.

INNES, M. (ed.) (2006). 'Reassurance and the "New" Community Policing', Special Issue of *Policing and Society,* 16/2.

INNES, M. (2007). 'Investigation and Major Crime Enquiries', in T. Newburn, T. Williamson, and A. Wright (eds), *Handbook of Criminal Investigation.* Cullompton: Willan.

INNES, M., and FIELDING, N. (2002). 'From Community to Communicative Policing: "Signal Crimes" and the Problem of Public Reassurance'. *Sociological Research Online,* 7/2, www.socresonline.org.uk.

IPCC (2007). *Stockwell One.* London: IPCC.

IRVING, B., and MCKENZIE, I. (1989). *Police Interrogation.* London: Police Foundation.

JACKSON, JOHN (2008). 'Police and Prosecutors After PACE: The Road from Case Construction to Case Disposal', in E. Cape and R. Young (eds), *Regulating Policing.* Oxford: Hart.

JACKSON, J. (2004). 'An Analysis of a Construct and Debate: The Fear of Crime', in H.-J. Albrecht, T. Serassis, and H. Kania (eds), *Images of Crime II.* Freiburg: Max Planck Institute.

JACKSON, J., and SUNSHINE, J. (2007). 'Public Confidence in Policing: A Neo-Durkheimian Perspective'. *British Journal of Criminology,* 47/2: 214–33.

JACKSON, J., BRADFORD, B., HOHL, K., and FARRALL, S. (2009). 'Does the Fear of Crime Erode Public Confidence in Policing?'. *Policing: A Journal of Policy and Practice,* 3/1: 100–11.

JACOB, H., and RICH, M. (1980). 'The Effects of the Police on Crime: A Second Look'. *Law and Society Review,* 15/1: 109–22.

JACOBS, L., and SKOCPOL, T. (eds) (2005). *Inequality and American Democracy.* New York: Russell Sage.

JEFFERSON, T. (1987). 'Beyond Paramilitarism'. *British Journal of Criminology,* 27/1.

JEFFERSON, T. (1990). *The Case against Paramilitary Policing.* Milton Keynes: Open University Press.

JEFFERSON, T. (1993). 'The Racism of Criminalisation: Policing and the Reproduction of the Criminal Other', in L. Gelsthorpe and W. McWilliams (eds), *Minority Ethnic Groups and the Criminal Justice System.* Cambridge: University of Cambridge, Institute of Criminology.

JEFFERSON, T., and GRIMSHAW, R. (1984). *Controlling the Constable: Police Accountability in England and Wales.* London: Muller.

JEFFERSON, T., MCLAUGHLIN, E., and ROBERTSON, L. (1988). 'Monitoring the Monitors: Accountability, Democracy and Police Watching in Britain'. *Contemporary Crises,* 12/2.

JEFFERSON, T., WALKER, M. A., and SENEVIRATNE, M. (1992). 'Ethnic Minorities, Crime and Criminal Justice: A Study in a Provincial City', in D. Downes (ed.), *Unravelling Criminal Justice.* London: Macmillan.

JEFFERY, K., and HENNESSY, P. (1983). *States of Emergency.* London: Routledge.

JEWKES, Y. (2004). *Media and Crime.* London: Sage.

JOHN, T., and MAGUIRE, M. (2003). 'Rolling Out the National Intelligence Model: Key Challenges', in K. Bullock and N. Tilley (eds), *Essays in Problem-Oriented Policing.* Cullompton: Willan.

JOHN, T., and MAGUIRE, M. (2007). 'Criminal Intelligence and the National Intelligence Model', in T. Newburn, T. Williamson, and A. Wright (eds), *Handbook of Criminal Investigation.* Cullompton: Willan.

JOHNSON, B. (1976). 'Taking Care of Labour'. *Theory and Society,* 3/1.

JOHNSTON, L. (1991). 'Privatisation and the Police Function: From "New Police" to "New Policing"', in R. Reiner and M. Cross (eds), *Beyond Law and Order: Criminal Justice Policy and Politics into the 1990s.* London: Macmillan.

JOHNSTON, L. (1992). *The Rebirth of Private Policing.* London: Routledge.

JOHNSTON, L. (1996). 'What Is Vigilantism?' *British Journal of Criminology,* 36/2: 220–36.

JOHNSTON, L. (2000). *Policing Britain: Risk, Security and Governance.* London: Longman.

JOHNSTON, L. (2006). 'Transnational Security Governance', in J. Wood and B. Dupont (eds), *Democracy, Society and the Governance of Security*. Cambridge: Cambridge University Press.

JOHNSTON, L. (2007a). 'The Trajectory of "Private Policing"', in A. Henry and D. J. Smith (eds), *Transformations of Policing*. Aldershot: Ashgate.

JOHNSTON, L. (2007b). '"Keeping the Family Together". Police Community Support Officers and the "Police Extended Family" in London'. *Policing and Society*, 17/2: 119–40.

JOHNSTON, L., and SHEARING, C. (2003). *Governing Security*. London: Routledge.

JONES, D. (1982). *Crime, Protest, Community and Police in Nineteenth-Century Britain*. London: Routledge.

JONES, D. (1996). *Crime and Policing in the Twentieth Century*. Cardiff: University of Wales Press.

JONES, F. (2008). *Increase in Income Inequality*. Newport: Office for National Statistics.

JONES, R. (2007). 'The Architecture of Policing: Towards a New Theoretical Model of the Role of Constraint-Based Compliance in Policing', in A. Henry and D. J. Smith (eds), *Transformations of Policing*. Aldershot: Ashgate.

JONES, S. (1987). *Policewomen and Equality*. London: Macmillan.

JONES, S., and LEVI, M. (1983). 'The Police and the Majority: The Neglect of the Obvious'. *Police Journal*, 56/4: 351–64.

JONES, T. (2007). 'The Governance of Security', in M. Maguire, R. Morgan, and R. Reiner (eds), *The Oxford Handbook of Criminology* (4th edn). Oxford: Oxford University Press.

JONES, T. (2008). 'The Accountability of Policing', in T. Newburn (ed.), *Handbook of Policing*. Cullompton: Willan.

JONES, T., and NEWBURN, T. (1997). *Policing after the Act*. London: Policy Studies Institute.

JONES, T., and NEWBURN, T. (1998). *Private Security and Public Policing*. Oxford: Oxford University Press.

JONES, T., and NEWBURN, T. (2002). 'The Transformation of Policing? Understanding Current Trends in Policing Systems'. *British Journal of Criminology*, 42/1: 129–46.

JONES, T., and NEWBURN, T. (eds) (2006a). *Plural Policing: A Comparative Perspective*. London: Routledge.

JONES, T., and NEWBURN, T. (eds) (2006b). *Policy Transfer and Criminal Justice*. Maidenhead: Open University Press.

JONES, T., MCLEAN, B., and YOUNG, J. (1986). *The Islington Crime Survey*. Aldershot: Gower.

JONES, T., NEWBURN, T., and SMITH, D. (1994). *Democracy and Policing*. London: Policy Studies Institute.

JORDAN, J. (2004). 'Beyond Belief? Police, Rape and Women's Credibility'. *Criminal Justice*, 4/1: 29–59.

JORDAN, P. (1998). 'Effective Policing Strategies for Reducing Crime', in C. Nuttall, P. Goldblatt, and C. Lewis (eds), *Reducing Offending*. London: Home Office. Home Office Research Study 187.

JUDGE, A. (1972). *A Man Apart*. London: Barker.

JUDGE, A. (1994). *The Force of Persuasion*. Surbiton: Police Federation.

KARMEN, A. (2000). *New York Murder Mystery*. New York: New York University Press.

KARSTEDT, S., and FARRALL, S. (2006). 'The Moral Economy of Everyday Crime: Markets, Consumers and Citizens'. *British Journal of Criminology*, 46/6: 1011–36.

KELLING, G. *et al.* (1974). *The Kansas City Preventive Patrol Experiment*. Washington, DC: Police Foundation.

KELLING, G., and COLES, C. (1998). *Fixing Broken Windows: Restoring Order and Reducing Crime in Our Communities.* New York: Free Press.

KEMP, C., NORRIS, C., and FIELDING, N. (1992). *Negotiating Nothing: Police Decision-Making in Disputes.* Aldershot: Avebury.

KEMPA, M., STENNING, P., and WOOD, J. (2004). 'Policing Communal Spaces: A Reconfiguration of the "Mass Private Property" Hypothesis'. *British Journal of Criminology*, 44/4: 562–81.

KENT, J. (1986). *The English Village Constable 1580–1642.* Oxford: Oxford University Press.

KERR, P. (1981). 'Watching the Detectives'. *PrimeTime*, 1/1 (July).

KIDD-HEWITT, D., and OSBORNE, R. (1996). *Crime and the Media: The Post-Modern Spectacle.* London: Pluto Press.

KING, M., and BREARLEY, N. (1996). *Public Order Policing*, Leicester: Perpetuity Press.

KING, M., and WADDINGTON, D. (2004). 'Coping With Disorder?: The Changing Relationship between Police Public Order Strategy and Practice—a Critical Analysis of the Burnley Riot'. *Policing & Society*, 14/2: 118–37.

KING, N. (1999). *Heroes in Hard Times: Cop Action Movies in the US.* Philadelphia, PA: Temple University Press.

KING, P. (2000). *Crime, Justice and Discretion, Law and Social Relations in England 1740–1820.* Oxford: Oxford University Press.

KING, P. (2003). 'Moral Panics and Violent Street Crime 1750–2000: A Comparative Analysis', in B. Godfrey, C. Emsley, and G. Dunstall (eds), *Comparative Histories of Crime.* Cullompton: Willan.

KING, P. (2006). *Crime and Law in England 1750–1850. Remaking Justice from the Margins.* Cambridge: Cambridge University Press.

KING, P. (2007). 'Newspaper Reporting and Attitudes to Crime and Justice in Late-eighteenth- and Early-nineteenth-century London'. *Continuity and Change*, 22/1: 73–112.

KINSEY, R., and BALDWIN, R. (1982). *Police Powers and Politics.* London: Quartet.

KINSEY, R., LEA, J., and YOUNG, J. (1986). *Losing the Fight against Crime.* Oxford: Blackwell.

KLEIN, J. (2001). 'Blue-Collar Job, Blue Collar Career: Policemen's Perplexing Struggle for a Voice in Birmingham, Liverpool, and Manchester, 1900–1919'. *Crime, History and Societies*, 6/1: 5–29.

KLEINIG, J. (1996). *The Ethics of Policing.* Cambridge: Cambridge University Press.

KLICK, J., and TABARROCK, A. (2005). 'Using Terror Alert Levels to Estimate the Effect of Police on Crime'. *Journal of Law and Economics*, 48/2: 267–79.

KLINGER, D. A. (2004). 'Environment and Organisation: Reviving A Perspective on the Police'. *Annals*, 593: 119–36.

KLOCKARS, C. (1980). 'The Dirty Harry Problem'. *The Annals*, 452 (November): 33–47.

KLOCKARS, C. (1985). *The Idea of Police.* Beverly Hills, CA: Sage.

KLOCKARS, C. (1988). 'The Rhetoric of Community Policing', in J. R. Greene and S. D. Mastrofski (eds), *Community Policing: Rhetoric or Reality?* New York: Praeger.

KNIGHT, S. (2003). *Crime Fiction 1800-2000.* London: Macmillan.

LACEY, N. (2008). *The Prisoners' Dilemma: Political Economy and Punishment in Contemporary Democracies.* Cambridge: Cambridge University Press.

LACEY, N., and WELLS, C. (1998). *Reconstructing Criminal Law* (2nd edn). London: Butterworth.

LACEY, N., and ZEDNER, L. (1995). 'Discourse of Community in Criminal Justice'. *Journal of Law and Society*, 22/3: 301–25.

LA FAVE, W. (1962). 'The Police and Nonenforcement of the Law'. *Wisconsin Law Review*, January: 104–37, March: 179–239.

LAMBERT, J. (1970). *Crime, Police and Race Relations*. Oxford: Oxford University Press.

LANDAU, S. (1981). 'Juveniles and the Police'. *British Journal of Criminology*, 21/1 (January): 27–46.

LANDAU, S., and NATHAN, G. (1983). 'Selecting Delinquents for Cautioning in the London Metropolitan Area'. *British Journal of Criminology*, 23/2 (April): 128–49.

LANGBEIN, J. (1983). 'Albion's Fatal Flaws'. *Past and Present*, 98.

LARSON, R. (1976). 'What Happened to Patrol Operations in Kansas City?' *Journal of Criminal Justice*, 3/4: 267–97.

LASSMAN, P. (2000). 'The Rule of Man Over Man: Politics, Power and Legitimation', in S. Turner (ed.), *The Cambridge Companion to Weber*. Cambridge: Cambridge University Press.

LAURIE, P. (1970). *Scotland Yard*. London: Penguin.

LAWRENCE, P. (2000). 'Images of Poverty and Crime. Police Memoirs in England and France at the end of the Nineteenth Century'. *Crime, History and Societies*, 4/1: 63–82.

LAWRENCE, P. (2003). '"Scoundrels and Scallywags, and some honest men ..." Memoirs and the Self-Image of French and English Policemen, c.1870–1939', in C. Emsley, B. Godfrey, and G. Dunstall (eds), *Comparative Histories of Crime*. Cullompton: Willan.

LAWRENCE, R. (2000). *The Politics of Force: Media and the Construction of Police Brutality*. Berkeley, CA: University of California Press.

LEA, J. (1986). 'Police Racism: Some Theories and Their Policy Implications', in R. Matthews and J. Young (eds), *Confronting Crime*. London: Sage.

LEA, J. (2003). 'Institutional Racism in Policing: The Macpherson Report and its Consequences', in R. Matthews and J. Young (eds), *The New Politics of Crime and Justice*. Cullompton: Willan.

LEA, J., and YOUNG, J. (1984). *What Is To Be Done About Law and Order?* Harmondsworth: Penguin.

LEE, J. A. (1981). 'Some Structural Aspects of Police Deviance in Relations with Minority Groups', in C. Shearing (ed.), *Organizational Police Deviance*. Toronto: Butterworth.

LEE, M. (1901). *A History of Police in England*. London: Methuen.

LEE, M. (1998). *Youth, Crime and Police Work*. London: Macmillan.

LEE, M., and PUNCH, M. (2006). *Policing By Degrees*. Groningen: Hondsrug Pers.

LEE, M., and SOUTH, N. (2008). 'Drugs Policing', in T. Newburn (ed.), *Handbook of Policing* (2nd edn). Cullompton: Willan.

LEES, S. (2002). *Carnal Knowledge: Rape on Trial*. London: Women's Press.

LEIGH, A., READ, T., and TILLEY, N. (1996). *Problem-Oriented Policing: Brit Pop*. London: Home Office. Police Research Group Paper 75.

LEISHMAN, F., and MASON, P. (2003). *Policing and the Media: Facts, Fictions and Factions*. Cullompton: Willan.

LEON, C. (1989). 'The Special Constabulary'. *Policing*, 5/4: 265–86.

LEVI, M. (2006). 'The Media Construction of Financial White-Collar Crimes'. *British Journal of Criminology*, 46/6: 1037–57.

LEVI, M. (2007). 'Organised Crime and Terrorism', in M. Maguire, R. Morgan, and R. Reiner (eds), *The Oxford Handbook of Criminology* (4th edn). Oxford: Oxford University Press.

LEVI, M. (2008). 'Policing Fraud and Organised Crime', in T. Newburn (ed.), *Handbook of Policing* (2nd edn). Cullompton: Willan.

LEVITAS, R. (2005). *The Inclusive Society?* London: Macmillan.

LEVITT, S. (2004). 'Understanding Why Crime Fell in the 1990s: Four Factors That Explain the Decline and Six That Do Not'. *Journal of Economic Perspectives*, 18/1: 163–90.

LICHTER, R. S., LICHTER, L. S., and ROTHMAN, S. (1994). *Prime Time: How TV Portrays American Culture*. Washington, DC: Regnery Publishing.

LINEBAUGH, P. (2006). *The London Hanged: Crime and Civil Society in the Eighteenth Century* (2nd edn). London: Allen Lane.

LIPSET, S. M. (1969). 'Why Cops Hate Liberals, and Vice Versa'. *Atlantic Monthly*.

LLOYD, K., and FOSTER, J. (2009). *Citizen Focus and Community Engagement: A Review of the Literature*. London: Police Foundation.

LOADER, I. (1996). *Youth, Policing and Democracy*. London: Macmillan.

LOADER, I. (1997). 'Policing and the Social: Questions of Symbolic Power'. *British Journal of Sociology*, 48/1: 1–18.

LOADER, I. (2000). 'Plural Policing and Democratic Governance'. *Social and Legal Studies*, 9/3: 323–45.

LOADER, I., and MULCAHY, A. (2003). *Policing and the Condition of England*. Oxford: Oxford University Press.

LOADER, I. and WALKER, N. (2001). 'Policing as a Public Good'. *Theoretical Criminology*, 5/1: 9–35.

LOADER, I. and WALKER, N. (2006). 'Necessary Virtues: The Legitimate Place of the State in the Production of Security', in J. Wood and B. Dupont (eds), *Democracy, Society and the Governance of Security*. Cambridge: Cambridge University Press.

LOADER, I. and WALKER, N. (2007). *Civilising Security*. Cambridge: Cambridge University Press.

LOADER, I. and ZEDNER, L. (2007). 'Police Beyond Law?'. *New Criminal Law Review*, 10/1: 142–52.

LOADER, R., and SPARKS, R. (2007). 'Contemporary Landscapes of Crime, Order and Control: Governance, Risk, and Globalisation', in M. Maguire, R. Morgan, and R. Reiner (eds), *Oxford Handbook of Criminology* (4th edn). Oxford: Oxford University Press.

LOFTUS, B. (2007). 'Policing the "Irrelevant": Class, Diversity and Contemporary Police Culture', in M. O'Neill, M. Marks, and A.-M. Singh (eds), *Police Occupational Culture*. Oxford: JAI.

LOFTUS, B. (2008). 'Dominant Culture Interrupted: Recognition, Resentment and the Politics of Change in an English Police Force'. *British Journal of Criminology*, 48/6: 778–97.

LOFTUS, B. (2009). *Police Culture in a Changing World*. Oxford: Oxford University Press.

LOFTUS, B. (2010). 'Police Occupational Culture: Classic Themes, Altered Times'. *Policing and Society* [forthcoming].

LONG, M. (2003). 'Leadership and Performance Management', in T.

Newburn (ed.), *Handbook of Policing*. Cullompton: Willan.

LOVEDAY, B. (1985). *The Role and Effectiveness of the Merseyside Police Committee*. Liverpool: Merseyside Country Council.

LOVEDAY, B. (1991). 'The New Police Authorities'. *Policing and Society*, 1/3: 193–212.

LOVEDAY, B. (1997). 'Crime, Policing and the Provision of Service', in P. Francis, P. Davies, and V. Jupp (eds), *Policing Futures*. London: Macmillan.

LOVEDAY, B. (1999). 'Government and Accountability of the Police', in R. Mawby (ed.), *Policing across the World*. London: UCL Press.

LOVEDAY, B. (2000). 'Crime At the Core?', in F. Leishman, B. Loveday, and S. Savage (eds), *Core Issues in Policing* (2nd edn). London: Longman.

LOVEDAY, B. (2006). *Size Isn't Everything: Restructuring Policing in England and Wales*. London: Policy Exchange.

LOVEDAY, B., and REID, B. (2003). *Going Local. Who Should Run Britain's Police?* London: Policy Exchange.

LOVEDAY, B., MCCLORY, J., and LOCKHART, G. (2007). *Fitting the Bill*. London: Policy Exchange.

LUSTGARTEN, L. (1986). *The Governance of the Police*. London: Sweet & Maxwell.

McARA, L. and McVIE, S. (2005). 'The Usual Suspects? Street Life, Young People and the Police'. *Criminal Justice*, 5/1: 5–36.

McBARNET, D. (1978). 'The Police and the State', in G. Littlejohn, B. Smart, J. Wakeford, and N. Yuval-Davis (eds), *Power and the State*. London: Croom Helm.

McBARNET, D. (1979). 'Arrest: The Legal Context of Policing', in S. Holdaway

(ed.), *The British Police*. London: Edward Arnold.

McBARNET, D. (1981). *Conviction*. London: Macmillan.

McBARNET, D. (1982). 'Legal Form and Legal Mystification'. *International Journal of the Sociology of Law*, 10: 409–17.

McCABE, S., and SUTCLIFFE, F. (1978). *Defining Crime*. Oxford: Basil Blackwell.

McCABE, S., WALLINGTON, P., ALDERSON, J., GOSTIN, L., and MASON, C. (1988). *The Police, Public Order and Civil Liberties*. London: Routledge.

McCAHILL, M. (2002). *The Surveillance Web*. Cullompton: Willan.

McCARTHUR, C. (1972). *Underworld USA*. London: Secker & Warburg.

McCONVILLE, M., and SHEPHERD, D. (1992). *Watching Police, Watching Communities*. London: Routledge.

McCONVILLE, M., SANDERS, A., and LENG, R. (1991). *The Case for the Prosecution: Police Suspects and the Construction of Criminality*. London: Routledge.

McCONVILLE, M., HODGSON, J., BRIDGES, L., and PAVLOVIC, A. (1994). *Standing Accused*. Oxford: Oxford University Press.

MACDONALD, L. (1976). *The Sociology of Law and Order*. London: Faber & Faber.

MACK, J. (1976). 'Full-Time Major Criminals and the Courts'. *Modern Law Review*, 39.

McKENZIE, I. (1996). 'Violent Encounters: Force and Deadly Force in British Policing', in F. Leishman, B. Loveday, and S. Savage (eds), *Core Issues in Policing*. London: Longman.

McKENZIE, I., MORGAN, R., and REINER, R. (1990). 'Helping the Police with Their Inquiries: The Necessity Principle and Voluntary Attendance at the Police Station'. *Criminal Law Review*: 22–33.

McLaughlin, E. (1992). 'The Democratic Deficit: European Unity and the Accountability of the British Police'. *British Journal of Criminology*, 32/4: 473–87.

McLaughlin, E. (1994). *Community, Policing and Accountability*. Aldershot: Avebury.

McLaughlin, E. (2005a). 'From Reel to Ideal: *The Blue Lamp* and the Popular Construction of the English "Bobby"'. *Crime Media Culture*, 1/1: 11–30.

McLaughlin, E. (2005b). 'Forcing the Issue: New Labour, New Localism and the Democratic Renewal of Police Accountability'. *Howard Journal*, 44/5: 473–89.

McLaughlin, E. (2007). *The New Policing*. London: Sage.

McLaughlin, E., and Murji, K. (1997). 'The Future Lasts a Long Time: Public Policework and the Managerialist Paradox', in P. Francis, P. Davies, and V. Jupp (eds), *Policing Futures: The Police, Law Enforcement and the Twenty-First Century*. London: Macmillan.

McLaughlin, E., and Murji, K. (1998). 'Resistance Through Representation: "Storylines", Advertising and Police Federation Campaigns'. *Policing and Society*, 8/4, 367–99.

McLaughlin, E., and Murji, K. (1999). 'The Postmodern Condition of the Police'. *Liverpool Law Review*, 21: 217–40.

McLaughlin, E., and Murji, K. (2001). 'Lost Connections and New Directions: Neo-liberalism, New Public Managerialism and the Modernisation of the British Police', in K. Stenson and R. Sullivan (eds), *Crime, Risk and Justice*. Cullompton: Willan.

McMullan, J. (1996). 'The New Improved Monied Police: Reform, Crime Control, and the Commodification of Policing in London'. *British Journal of Criminology*, 36/1: 85–108.

McMullan, J. (1998). 'Social Surveillance and the Rise of the "Police Machine"'. *Theoretical Criminology*, 2/1: 93–117.

McNee, D. (1979). 'The Queen's Police Keepeth the Peace'. *Guardian*, 25 September: 25.

McNee, D. (1983). *McNee's Law*. London: Collins.

Macpherson, W. (1999). *The Stephen Lawrence Inquiry*. London: HMSO.

Maguire, M. (2000). 'Policing by Risks and Targets: Some Dimensions and Implications of Intelligence-Led Social Control'. *Policing and Society*, 9/4: 315–37.

Maguire, M. (2002). 'Regulating the Police Station: The Case of the Police and Criminal Evidence Act 1984', in M. McConville and G. Wilson (eds), *The Handbook of the Criminal Justice Process*. Oxford: Oxford University Press.

Maguire, M. (2004). 'The Crime Reduction Programme: Reflections on the Vision and the Reality'. *Criminal Justice*, 4/3: 213–38.

Maguire, M. (2007). 'Crime Data and Statistics', in M. Maguire, R. Morgan, and R. Reiner (eds), *The Oxford Handbook of Criminology* (4th edn). Oxford: Oxford University Press.

Maguire, M. (2008). 'Criminal Investigation and Crime Control', in T. Newburn (ed.), *Handbook of Policing* (2nd edn). Cullompton: Willan.

Maguire, M., and Corbett, C. (1991). *A Study of the Police Complaints System*. London: PACE.

Maguire, M., and John, T. (1996a). *Intelligence, Surveillance and Informants: Integrated Approaches*. London: Home Office. Crime Detection and Prevention Series Paper 64.

MAGUIRE, M., and JOHN, T. (1996b). 'Covert and Deceptive Policing in England and Wales: Issues in Regulation and Practice'. *European Journal of Crime, Criminal Law and Criminal Justice,* 4/3: 316–34.

MAGUIRE, M., and NORRIS, C. (1992). *The Conduct and Supervision of Criminal Investigations.* London: HMSO. Royal Commission on Criminal Justice Research Report 5.

MAITLAND, R. (1885). *Justice and Police.* London: Macmillan.

MANDEL, E. (1984). *Delightful Murder.* London: Pluto Press.

MANN, S., NOLAN, J., and WELLMAN, B. (2003). 'Sousveillance: Inventing and Using Wearable Computing Devices for Data Collection in Surveillance Environments'. *Surveillance & Society,*1/3: 331–55.

MANNING, P. (1979). 'The Social Control of Police Work', in S. Holdaway (ed.), *The British Police.* London: Edward Arnold.

MANNING, P. (1997a). *Police Work* (2nd edn). Prospect Heights, IL: Waveland Press.

MANNING, P. (1997b). 'Media Loops', in F. Bailey and D. Hale (eds), *Popular Culture, Crime & Justice.* Belmont, CA: Wadsworth.

MANNING, P. (2001). 'Theorising Policing: The Drama and Myth of Crime Control in the NYPD'. *Theoretical Criminology,* 5/3: 315–44.

MANNING, P. (2003). *Policing Contingencies.* Chicago, IL: Chicago University Press.

MANNING, P. (2007). 'A Dialectic of Organisational and Occupational Culture', in M. O'Neill, M. Marks, and A.-M. Singh (eds) *Police Occupational Culture.* Oxford: JAI.

MANNING, P., and REDLINGER, J. (1977). 'Invitational Edges of Corruption', in P. Rock (ed.), *Politics and Drugs.* Rutgers, NJ: Dutton.

MARENIN, O. (1983). 'Parking Tickets and Class Repression: The Concept of Policing in Critical Theories of Criminal Justice'. *Contemporary Crises,* 6/2: 241–66.

MARENIN, O. (ed.) (1996). *Policing Change, Changing Police: International Perspectives.* New York: Garland.

MARK, R. (1977). *Policing a Perplexed Society.* London: Allen & Unwin.

MARK, R. (1978). *In the Office of Constable.* London: Collins.

MARKHAM, G., and PUNCH, M. (2007). 'Embracing Accountability'. *Policing: Journal of Research and Practice,* 1/3: 300–8; 1/4: 485–94.

MARKS, M., and FLEMING, J. (2006a). 'The Right to Unionise, the Right to Bargain and the Right to Democratic Policing'. *The Annals,* 605/1: 178–99.

MARKS, M., and FLEMING, J. (2006b). 'The Untold Story: The Regulation of Police Labour Rights and the Quest for Police Democratisation'. *Police Practice and Research,* 7/4: 309–22.

MARKS, M. and GOLDSMITH, A. (2006). 'The State, the People and Democratic Policing: The Case of South Africa', in J. Wood and B. Dupont (eds), *Democracy, Society and the Governance of Security.* Cambridge: Cambridge University Press.

MARLOW, A. and LOVEDAY, B. (eds) (2000). *After Macpherson.* Lyme Regis: Russell House.

MARSHALL, G. (1965). *Police and Government.* London: Methuen.

MARSHALL, G. (1978). 'Police Accountability Revisited', in D. Butler and A. H. Halsey (eds), *Policy and Politics.* London: Macmillan.

MARSHALL, T. H. (1950). *Citizenship and Social Class.* Cambridge: Cambridge University Press.

MARTIN, C. (1996). 'The Impact of Equal Opportunities Policies on the Day-to-Day

Experiences of Women Police Constables'. *British Journal of Criminology*, 36/4: 510–28.

MARTIN, H.P., and SCHUMANN, H. (1997). *The Global Trap*. London: Zed Books.

MARTIN, J. P., and WILSON, G. (1969). *The Police: A Study in Manpower*. London: Heinemann.

MARX, G. (1988). *Undercover: Police Surveillance in America*. Berkeley, CA: University of California Press.

MARX, G. (1992). 'When the Guards Guard Themselves: Undercover Tactics Turned Inwards'. *Policing and Society*, 2/3: 151–72.

MASTROFSKI, S. D. (2004). 'Controlling Street-Level Police Discretion'. *The Annals* 593: 100–18.

MATHIESEN, T. (1997). 'The Viewer Society: Michel Foucault's "Panopticon" Revisited'. *Theoretical Criminology*, 1/2: 215–34.

MATZA, D. (1969). *Becoming Deviant*. New Jersey: Prentice Hall.

MAWBY, R. C. (1999). 'Visibility, Transparency, and Police–Media Relations'. *Policing and Society*, 9/3: 263–86.

MAWBY, R. C. (2002a). *Policing Images: Policing, Communication and Legitimacy*. Cullompton: Willan.

MAWBY, R. C. (2002b). 'Continuity and Change, Convergence and Divergence: The Policy and Practice of Police–Media Relations'. *Criminal Justice*, 2/3: 303–24.

MAWBY, R. C., and WRIGHT, A. (2008). 'The Police Organisation', in T. Newburn (ed.), *Handbook of Policing* (2nd edn). Cullompton: Willan.

MAWBY, R. I. (1991). *Comparative Policing Issues*. London: Unwin.

MAWBY, R. I. (ed.) (1999). *Policing across the World: Issues for the Twenty-First Century*. London: UCL Press.

MAWBY, R. I. (2008). 'Models of Policing', in T. Newburn (ed.), *Handbook of Policing* (2nd edn). Cullompton: Willan.

MAXWELL, C., GARNER, J., and FAGAN, J. (2002). 'The Preventive Effect of Arrest on Intimate Partner Violence: Research, Policy and Theory'. *Criminology and Public Policy*, 2/1: 51–80.

MAZOWER, M. (ed.) (1997). *The Policing of Politics in the Twentieth Century*. Providence, RI: Berghahn Books.

MEYER, M. (1980). 'Police Shootings at Minorities: The Case of Los Angeles'. *The Annals*, 452 (November).

MEYERS, R. (1981). *TV Detectives*. San Diego, CA: Barnes.

MEYERS, R. (1989). *Murder on the Air*. New York: The Mysterious Press.

MICHAEL, D. (1999). 'The Levels of Orientation Security Officers Have towards a Public Policing Function'. *Security Journal*, 12/4: 33–42.

MICHAEL, D. (2002). 'A Sense of Security? The Ideology and Accountability of Private Security Officers'. Ph.D. thesis, London School of Economics.

MILIBAND, R. (1978). 'A State of Desubordination'. *British Journal of Sociology*, 29/4.

MILLER, J., BLAND, N., and QUINTON, P. (2000). *The Impact of Stops and Searches on Crime and the Community*. London: Home Office.

MILLER, W. (1999). *Cops and Bobbies* (2nd edn). Columbus, OH: Ohio State University Press.

MILLIE, A. (2008). *Anti-Social Behaviour*. Maidenhead: Open University Press.

MILLIE, A., and HERRINGTON, V. (2005). 'Bridging the Gap: Understanding Reassurance Policing'. *Howard Journal*, 44/1: 41–56.

MILNE, S. (2004). *The Enemy Within: Thatcher's Secret War Against the Miners*. London: Verso.

MINTO, G. (1965). *The Thin Blue Line*. London: Hodder & Stoughton.

MIYAZAWA, S. (1992). *Policing in Japan: A Study in Making Crime*. Albany, NY: State University of New York Press.

MONKKONEN, E. (1981). *Police in Urban America 1860–1920*. Cambridge: Cambridge University Press.

MOORE, B., Jr. (1967). *The Social Origins of Dictatorship and Democracy*. London: Penguin/Boston, MA: Beacon.

MOORE, M. (2003). 'Sizing up Compstat: An Important Administrative Innovation in Policing'. *Criminology and Public Policy*, 2: 469–94.

MORGAN, J. (1987). *Conflict and Order: The Police and Labour Disputes in England and Wales 1900–1939*. Oxford: Oxford University Press.

MORGAN, R. (1989). 'Policing By Consent: Legitimating the Doctrine', in R. Morgan and D. Smith (eds), *Coming to Terms with Policing*. London: Routledge.

MORGAN, R. (1992). 'Talking About Policing', in D. Downes (ed.), *Unravelling Criminal Justice*. London: Macmillan.

MORGAN, R., and NEWBURN, T. (1997). *The Future of Policing*. Oxford: Oxford University Press.

MORGAN, R., REINER, R., and MCKENZIE, I. (1990). *Police Powers and Policy: A Study of Custody Officers*. Final Report to the Economic and Social Research Council.

MORRIS, P., and HEAL, K. (1981). *Crime Control and the Police*. London: Home Office Research Unit.

MORRIS, R. M. (2001). '"Lies, Damned Lies and Criminal Statistics": Reinterpreting the Criminal Statistics in England and Wales'. *Crime, History and Societies*, 5: 111–27.

MORRIS, T. (1985). 'The Case for a Riot Squad'. *New Society*, 29 November.

MORRISON, C. (1984). 'Why PC Plod Should Come off the Beat'. *Guardian*, 30 July: 8.

MOST, G., and STOWE, W. (eds) (1983). *The Poetics of Murder*. New York: Harcourt, Brace, Jovanovich.

MUIR, K. W., Jr. (1977). *Police: Streetcorner Politicians*. Chicago, IL: Chicago University Press.

MULCAHY, A. (2008). 'The Police Service of Northern Ireland', in T. Newburn (ed.), *Handbook of Policing* (2nd edn). Cullompton: Willan.

MULLIN, C. (1989). *Error of Judgement: The Truth about the Birmingham Bombings*. London: Chatto & Windus.

MURDOCK, G. (1982). 'Disorderly Images', in C. Sumner (ed.), *Crime, Justice and the Mass Media*. Cambridge: Institute of Criminology. Cropwood Papers 14.

MURJI, K. (1998). *Policing Drugs*. Aldershot: Ashgate.

MURJI, K. (2009). 'Enacting the Sacred: Nation and Difference in the Comparative Sociology of the Police'. *Journal of Transatlantic Studies*, 7/1: 23–37.

MVA and MILLER, J. (2000). *Profiling Populations Available for Stops and Searches*. London: Home Office.

MYHILL, A., and BEAK, K. (2008). *Public Confidence in the Police*. London: NPIA.

MYTHEN, G., and WALKLATE, S. (2006a). 'Criminology and Terrorism: Which Thesis? Risk Society or Governmentality?'. *British Journal of Criminology*, 46/3: 379–98.

MYTHEN, G., and WALKLATE, S. (2006b). 'Communicating the Terrorist Risk: Harnessing a Culture of Fear?'. *Crime, Media, Culture*, 2/2 123–42.

NAUGHTON, M. (2005). 'Redefining Miscarriages of Justice: A Revived

Human Rights Approach to Unearth Subjugated Discourses of Wrongful Criminal Conviction'. *British Journal of Criminology*, 45/2: 165–82.

NAUGHTON, M (2007). *Rethinking Miscarriages of Justice*. Basingstoke: Macmillan.

NELKEN, D. (2007). 'White-Collar and Corporate Crime', in M. Maguire, R. Morgan, and R. Reiner (eds), *The Oxford Handbook of Criminology* (4th edn). Oxford: Oxford University Press.

NEOCLEOUS, M. (1998). 'Policing and Pin-Making: Adam Smith, Police and the State of Prosperity'. *Policing and Society*, 8/4: 425–49.

NEOCLEOUS, M. (2000a). *The Fabrication of Social Order: A Critical Theory of Police Power*. London: Pluto Press.

NEOCLEOUS, M. (2000b). 'Social Police and the Mechanisms of Prevention'. *British Journal of Criminology*, 40/4: 710–26.

NEOCLEOUS, M. (2006). 'Theoretical Foundations of the "New Police Science"', in M. Dubber and M. Valverde (eds), *The New Police Science*. Stanford, CA: Stanford University Press.

NEWBURN, T. (1992). *Permissiveness and Regulation*. London: Routledge.

NEWBURN, T. (1999). *Understanding and Preventing Police Corruption: Lessons from the Literature*. London: Home Office Policing and Reducing Crime Unit.

NEWBURN, T. (ed.) (2005). *Policing—Key Readings*. Cullompton: Willan.

NEWBURN, T. (2007a). 'The Future of Policing in Britain', in A. Henry and D. J. Smith (eds), *Transformations of Policing*. Aldershot: Avebury.

NEWBURN, T. (2007b). 'Youth Crime and Youth Culture', in M. Maguire, R. Morgan, and R. Reiner (eds), *The Oxford Handbook of Criminology* (4th edn). Oxford: Oxford University Press.

NEWBURN, T. (2007c). '"Tough on Crime": Penal Policy in England and Wales', in M. Tonry and A. Doob (eds), *Crime and Justice 36*. Chicago, IL: University of Chicago Press.

NEWBURN, T., and HAYMAN, S. (2001). *Policing, CCTV and Social Control: Police Surveillance of Suspects in Custody*. Cullompton: Willan.

NEWBURN, T., and REINER, R. (2007a). 'Crime and Penal Policy', in A. Seldon (ed.), *Blair's Britain*. Cambridge: Cambridge University Press.

NEWBURN, T., WILLIAMSON, T., and WRIGHT, A. (eds) (2007). *Handbook of Criminal Investigation*. Cullompton: Willan.

NEWBURN, T., SHINER, M., and HAYMAN, S. (2004). 'Race, Crime and Injustice?: Strip Search and the Treatment of Suspects in Custody'. *British Journal of Criminology*, 44/5: 677–94.

NEWMAN, G. F. (1983). *Law and Order*. London: Granada.

NEYROUD, P. (2008). 'Policing and Ethics', in T. Newburn (ed.), *Handbook of Policing* (2nd edn). Cullompton: Willan.

NIEDERHOFFER, A. (1967). *Behind the Shield*. New York: Doubleday.

NOBLES, R., and SCHIFF, D. (2000). *Understanding Miscarriages of Justice*. Oxford: Oxford University Press.

NOBLES, R., and SCHIFF, D. (2004). 'A Story of Miscarriage: Law in the Media'. *Journal of Law and Society*, 31/2: 221–44.

NORRIS, C. (1989). 'Avoiding Trouble: The Police Officer's Perception of Encounters with the Public', in M. Weatheritt (ed.), *Police Research: Some Future Prospects*. Aldershot: Avebury.

NORRIS, C., and ARMSTRONG, G. (1999). *The Maximum Surveillance Society: The Rise of CCTV*. West Sussex: Berg.

NORRIS, C., and DUNNIGHAN, C. (2000). 'Subterranean Blues: Conflict as an Unintended Consequence of the Police Use of Informers'. *Policing and Society*, 9/4: 385–412.

NORRIS, C., and McCAHILL, M. (2006). 'CCTV: Beyond penal modernism?'. *British Journal of Criminology*, 46/1: 97–118.

NORRIS, C., and NORRIS, N. (1993). 'Defining Good Policing: The Instrumental and Moral in Approaches to Good Practice and Competence'. *Policing and Society*, 3/3: 205–22.

NUTTALL, C., GOLDBLATT, P., and LEWIS, C. (eds) (1998). *Reducing Offending*. London: Home Office. Home Office Research Study 187.

O'MALLEY, P. (1992). 'Risk, power and crime prevention'. *Economy and Society*, 21/3: 252–75.

O'MALLEY, P. (1997). 'Policing, Post-Modernism and Political Rationality'. *Social and Legal Studies*, 6/3: 363–81 [as reprinted in T. Newburn (ed.), *Policing—Key Readings*. Cullompton: Willan 2005].

O'MALLEY, P. (2004). *Risk, Uncertainty and Government*. London: Glasshouse.

O'MALLEY, P., and PALMER, D. (1996). 'Post-Keynesian Policing'. *Economy and Society*, 25/2: 137–55.

O'NEILL, M. and HOLDAWAY, S. (2007). 'Black Police Associations and the Police Occupational Culture', in M. O'Neill, M. Marks, and A.-M. Singh (eds), *Police Occupational Cultures*. Oxford: JAI.

OPERATIONAL POLICING REVIEW (1990). Joint Consultative Committee of the Police Staff Associations. Surbiton: Police Federation.

OSBORNE, D., and GAEBLER, T. (1992). *Reinventing Government*. New York: Addison-Wesley.

O'SULLIVAN, S. (2005). 'UK Policing and its Television Portrayal: "Law and Order"

Ideology or Modernising Agenda?'. *Howard Journal*, 44/5: 504–26.

OUSBY, I. (1976). *Bloodhounds of Heaven*. Cambridge, MA: Harvard University Press.

PACKER, H. (1968). *The Limits of the Criminal Sanction*. Stanford, CA: Stanford University Press and Oxford University Press.

PADDICK, B. (2008). *Line of Fire*. London: Simon & Schuster.

PALAST, G. (2004). *The Best Democracy Money Can Buy*. New York: Plume.

PALEY, R. (1989). 'An Imperfect, Inadequate and Wretched System'?: Policing London before Peel'. *Criminal Justice History*, 10: 95–130.

PALMER, J. (1978). *Thrillers*. London: Edward Arnold.

PALMER, S. H. (1988). *Police and Protest in England and Ireland 1780–1850*. Cambridge: Cambridge University Press.

PANDIANI, J. (1978). 'Crime Time TV: If All We Knew Is What We Saw'. *Contemporary Crises*, 2: 437–58.

PANEK, L. (2003). *The American Police Novel: A History*. Jefferson, NC: McFarland.

PANITCH, L., LEYS, C., ZUEGE, A., and KONINGS, M. (eds) (2004). *The Globalisation Decade*. London: Merlin.

PANTAZIS, C., and PEMBERTON, S. (2009). 'From the "Old" to the "New" Suspect Community: Examining the Impacts of Recent UK Counter-Terrorist Legislation'. *British Journal of Criminology*, 49/5: 646–66.

PAOLINE, E. (2003). *Rethinking Police Culture*. New York: LFB Scholarly.

PARISH, J. R., and PITTS, M. (1990a). *The Great Cop Pictures*. Metuchen, NJ: Scarecrow.

PARISH, J. R., and PITTS, M. (1990b). *The Great Detective Pictures*. Metuchen, NJ: Scarecrow.

PARK, W. (1978). 'The Police State'. *Journal of Popular Film*, 6/3: 229–38.

PASQUINO, P. (1991). 'Theatrum Politicum: The Genealogy of Capital—Police and the State of Prosperity', in G. Burchell, C. Gordon, and P. Miller (eds), *The Foucault Effect: Studies in Governmentality*. Hemel Hempstead: Harvester Wheatsheaf. [Originally in *Ideology and Consciousness*, 4/1 (1978): 41–54.]

PATTEN, C. (1999). *A New Beginning: Policing Northern Ireland*. The Report of the Independent Commission on Policing for Northern Ireland. Norwich: HMSO Copyright Unit.

PAWSON, R., and TILLEY, N. (1994). 'What Works in Evaluation Research?'. *British Journal of Criminology*, 34/2: 291–306.

PEARSON, G. (1983). *Hooligan*. London: Macmillan.

PHILIPS, D. (1977). *Crime and Authority in Victorian England*. London: Croom Helm.

PHILIPS, D. (1980). 'A New Engine of Power and Authority: The Institutionalisation of Law Enforcement in England 1780–1830', in V. Gatrell, B. Lenman, and G. Parker (eds), *Crime and the Law*. London: Europa.

PHILIPS, D. (1983). 'A Just Measure of Crime, Authority, Hunters and Blue Locusts: The "Revisionist" Social History of Crime and the Law in Britain 1780–1850', in S. Cohen and A. Scull (eds), *Social Control and the State*. Oxford: Martin Robertson.

PHILIPS, D., and STORCH, R. (1999). *Policing Provincial England, 1829–1856*. Leicester: Leicester University Press.

PHILLIPS, C., and BROWN, D. (1998). *Entry into the Criminal Justice System: A Survey of Police Arrests and Their Outcomes*. London: Home Office. Home Office Research Study 185.

PHILLIPS, C., and BOWLING, B. (2007). 'Ethnicities, Racism, Crime, and Criminal Justice', in M. Maguire, R. Morgan, and T. Newburn (eds), *The Oxford Handbook of Criminology* (4th edn). Oxford: Oxford University Press.

PILIAVIN, I., and BRIAR, S. (1964). 'Police Encounters with Juveniles'. *American Journal of Sociology*, 70: 206–14.

POLANYI, K. (1944). *The Great Transformation*. Boston, MA: Beacon.

POLICE FOUNDATION/POLICY STUDIES INSTITUTE (1996). *The Role and Responsibilities of the Police: Report of an Independent Inquiry*. London: Police Foundation/Policy Studies Institute.

POLICY STUDIES INSTITUTE (1983). *Police and People in London*; i, D. J. Smith, *A Survey of Londoners*; ii, S. Small, *A Group of Young Black People*; iii, D. J. Smith, *A Survey of Police Officers*; iv, D. J. Smith and J. Gray, *The Police in Action*. London: Policy Studies Institute.

PORTER, B. (1987). *The Origins of the Vigilante State*. London: Macmillan.

POTTER, C. B. (1998). *War on Crime: Bandits, G-Men, and the Politics of Mass Culture*. New Brunswick, NJ: Rutgers University Press.

POUNTAIN, D., and ROBINS, D. (2000). *Cool Rules*. London: Reaktion.

POWERS, R. G. (1983). *GMen: Hoover's FBI in American Popular Culture*. Carbondale, IL: Southern Illinois University Press.

POWERS, S. P., ROTHMAN, D. J., and ROTHMAN, S. (1996). *Hollywood's America: Social and Political Themes in Motion Pictures*. Boulder, CO: Westview.

POWIS, D. (1977). *The Signs of Crime*. London: McGraw-Hill.

PRIESTMAN, M. (2003). *The Cambridge Companion to Crime Fiction*. Cambridge: Cambridge University Press.

PUNCH, M. (1979a). *Policing the Inner City.* London: Macmillan.

PUNCH, M. (1979b). 'The Secret Social Service', in S. Holdaway (ed.), *The British Police.* London: Edward Arnold.

PUNCH, M. (ed.) (1983). *Control in the Police Organisation.* Cambridge, MA: MIT Press.

PUNCH, M. (1985). *Conduct Unbecoming: The Social Construction of Police Deviance and Control.* London: Tavistock.

PUNCH, M. (2003). 'Rotten Orchards: "Pestilence", Police Misconduct and System Failure'. *Policing and Society,* 13/2: 171–96.

PUNCH, M. (2007). *Zero Tolerance Policing.* Bristol: Policy Press.

PUNCH, M. (2009). *Police Corruption: Deviance, Accountability and Reform in Policing.* Cullompton: Willan.

PUNCH, M., and NAYLOR, T. (1973). 'The Police: A Social Service'. *New Society,* 24: 358–61.

QUINTON, P., BLAND, N., and MILLER, J. (2000). *Police Stops, Decision-Making and Practice.* London: Home Office.

RADZINOWICZ, L. (1948–86). *A History of the English Criminal Law and its Administration from 1750,* 5 vols. (v with Hood, R., *The Emergence of Penal Policy in Victorian and Edwardian England,* 1986). London: Stevens.

RAFTER, N. (2006). *Shots in the Mirror: Crime Films and Society* (2nd edn). New York: Oxford University Press.

RAMSAY, P. (2004). 'What is Anti-Social Behaviour?' *Criminal Law Review,* November: 908–25.

RAMSAY, P. (2006). 'The Responsible Subject as Citizen: Criminal Law, Democracy and the Welfare State'. *Modern Law Review,* 69/1: 29–58.

RAMSAY, P. (2008). 'Vulnerability, Sovereignty, and Police Power in the ASBO', in M. Dubber and M. Valverde (eds), *Police and the Liberal State.* Stanford, CA: Stanford University Press.

RATCLIFFE, J. (2008). *Intelligence-Led Policing.* Cullompton: Willan.

RAWLINGS, P. (1991). 'Creeping Privatisation? The Police, the Conservative Government and Policing in the Late 1980s', in R. Reiner and M. Cross (eds), *Beyond Law and Order: Criminal Justice Policy and Politics into the 1990s.* London: Macmillan.

RAWLINGS, P. (1995). 'The Idea of Policing: A History'. *Policing and Society,* 5/2: 129–49.

RAWLINGS, P. (1999). *Crime and Power: A History of Criminal Justice 1688–1998.* London: Longman.

RAWLINGS, P. (2002). *Policing: A Short History.* Cullompton: Willan.

RAWLINGS, P. (2008). 'Policing Before the Police', in T. Newburn (ed.), *Handbook of Policing* (2nd edn). Cullompton: Willan.

REIMAN, J. (2004). *The Rich Get Rich and the Poor Get Prison: Ideology, Class and Criminal Justice* (7th edn). Boston, MA: Allyn and Bacon.

REINER, R. (1978). *The Blue-Coated Worker.* Cambridge: Cambridge University Press.

REINER, R. (1980). 'Fuzzy Thoughts: The Police and Law and Order Politics'. *Sociological Review,* 28/2 (March): 377–413.

REINER, R. (1981a). 'The Politics of Police Power', in *Politics and Power 4: Law, Politics and Justice.* London: Routledge.

REINER, R. (1981b). 'Keystone to Kojak: The Hollywood Cop', in P. Davies and B. Neve (eds), *Politics, Society and Cinema in America.* Manchester: Manchester University Press.

REINER, R. (1984). 'Is Britain Turning into a Police State?'. *New Society,* 2 August.

REINER, R. (1988). 'British Criminology and the State'. *British Journal of Criminology,* 29/1: 138–58.

REINER, R. (1989a). 'Race and Criminal Justice'. *New Community*, 16/1: 5–22.

REINER, R. (1989b). 'The Politics of Police Research', in M. Weatheritt (ed.), *Police Research: Some Future Prospects*. Aldershot: Avebury.

REINER, R. (1991). *Chief Constables*. Oxford: Oxford University Press.

REINER, R. (1992a). 'Police Research in the United Kingdom: A Critical Review', in N. Morris and M. Tonry (eds), *Modern Policing*. Chicago, IL: Chicago University Press.

REINER, R. (1992b). 'Policing a Post-modern Society'. *Modern Law Review*, 55/6: 761–81.

REINER, R. (1993). 'Race, Crime and Justice: Models of Interpretation', in L. Gelsthorpe and W. McWilliams (eds), *Minority Ethnic Groups and the Criminal Justice System*. Cambridge: University of Cambridge Institute of Criminology.

REINER, R. (1994). 'The Dialectics of Dixon: The Changing Image of the TV Cop', in M. Stephens and S. Becker (eds), Police Force, Police Service'. London: Macmillan.

REINER, R. (ed.) (1996). *Policing*, i. *Cops, Crime and Control: Analysing the Police Function*; ii. *Controlling the Controllers: Police Discretion and Accountability*. Aldershot: Dartmouth.

REINER, R. (1998). 'Process or Product? Problems of Assessing Individual Police Performance', in J.-P. Brodeur (ed.), *How to Recognise Good Policing*. Thousand Oaks, CA: Sage.

REINER, R. (1999). 'Order and Discipline', in I. Holliday, A. Gamble, and G. Parry (eds), *Fundamentals in British Politics*. London: Macmillan.

REINER, R. (2006). 'Beyond Risk: A Lament for Social Democratic Criminology', in T. Newburn and P. Rock (eds), *The Politics of Crime Control*. Oxford: Oxford University Press.

REINER, R. (2007a). *Law and Order: An Honest Citizen's Guide to Crime and Control*. Cambridge: Polity Press.

REINER, R. (2007b). 'Political Economy, Crime and Criminal Justice', in M. Maguire, R. Morgan, and R. Reiner (eds), *The Oxford Handbook of Criminology* (4th edn). Oxford: Oxford University Press.

REINER, R. (2008). 'Policing and the Media', in T. Newburn (ed.), *Handbook of Policing* (2nd edn). Cullompton: Willan.

REINER, R., and CROSS, M. (eds) (1991). *Beyond Law and Order: Criminal Justice Policy and Politics into the 1990s*. London: Macmillan.

REINER, R., and LEIGH, L. (1992). 'Police Power', in G. Chambers and C. McCrudden (eds), *Individual Rights in the UK since 1945*. Oxford: Oxford University Press.

REINER, R., and NEWBURN, T. (2007). 'Police Research', in R. King and E. Wincup (eds), *Doing Research on Crime and Justice* (2nd edn). Oxford: Oxford University Press.

REINER, R., and SHAPLAND, J. (eds) (1987). 'Why Police? Special Issue on Policing in Britain'. *British Journal of Criminology*, 27/1.

REINER, R., and SPENCER, S. (eds) (1993). *Accountable Policing: Effectiveness, Empowerment and Equity*. London: Institute for Public Policy Research.

REINER, R., LIVINGSTONE, S., and ALLEN, J. (2000). 'No More Happy Endings? The Media and Popular Concern about Crime since the Second World War', in T. Hope and R. Sparks (eds), *Crime, Risk and Insecurity*. London: Routledge.

REINER, R., LIVINGSTONE, S., and ALLEN, J. (2001). 'Casino Culture: The Media and Crime in a Winner–Loser Society', in K. Stenson and R. Sullivan (eds), *Crime and Risk Society*. Cullompton: Willan.

REINER, R., LIVINGSTONE, S., and ALLEN, J. (2003). 'From Law and Order to Lynch Mobs: Crime News since the Second World War', in P. Mason (ed.), *Criminal Visions*. Cullompton: Willan.

REISS, A. J., Jr. (1971). *The Police and the Public*. New Haven, CT: Yale University Press.

REITH, C. (1938). *The Police Idea*. Oxford: Oxford University Press.

REITH, C. (1940). *Police Principles and the Problem of War*. Oxford: Oxford University Press.

REITH, C. (1943). *British Police and the Democratic Ideal*. Oxford: Oxford University Press.

REITH, C. (1948). *A Short History of the Police*. Oxford: Oxford University Press.

REITH, C. (1952). *The Blind Eye of History*. London: Faber & Faber.

REITH, C. (1956). *A New Study of Police History*. London: Oliver & Boyd.

REYNOLDS, E. A. (1998). *Before the Bobbies*. London: Macmillan.

REYNOLDS, G., and JUDGE, A. (1968). *The Night the Police Went on Strike*. London: Weidenfeld.

RIKAGOS, G. (2002). *Parapolice* Toronto: Toronto University Press.

ROBERTS, C., and INNES, M. (2009). 'The "Death" of Dixon? Policing Gun Crime and the End of the Generalist Police Constable in England and Wales'. *Criminology and Criminal Justice*, 9/3: 337–57.

ROBERTS, D. (1984). 'Tape-recording the Questioning of Suspects'. *Criminal Law Review*, September.

ROBERTS, R. (1973). *The Classic Slum*. London: Penguin.

ROBINSON, C. (1978). 'The Deradicalisation of the Policeman'. *Crime and Delinquency*, 24/2: 129–51.

ROBINSON, C. (1979). 'Ideology as History'. *Police Studies*, 2/2 (summer): 35–49.

ROBINSON, C., and SCAGLION, R. (1987). 'The Origins and Evolution of the Police Function in Society: Notes towards A Theory'. *Law and Society Review*, 21/1: 109–53.

ROBINSON, C., SCAGLION, R., and OLIVERO, J. M. (1994). *Police in Contradiction: The Evolution of the Police Function in Society*. Westport, CT: Greenwood.

ROCK, P. (1973). 'News as Eternal Recurrence', in S. Cohen and J. Young (eds), *The Manufacture of News*. London: Constable.

ROCK, P. (1977). 'Law, Order and Power in Late Seventeenth and Early Eighteenth-Century England'. *International Annals of Criminology*, 16. [Reprinted in S. Cohen and A. Scull (eds), *Social Control and the State*. Oxford: Martin Robertson, 1983.]

ROLPH, C. H. (ed.) (1962). *The Police and the Public*. London: Heinemann.

ROSE, D. (1992). *A Climate of Fear: The Murder of PC Blakelock and the Case of the Tottenham Three*. London: Bloomsbury.

ROSE, D. (1996). *In the Name of the Law: The Collapse of Criminal Justice*. London: Jonathan Cape.

ROSE, N. (1996). 'The Death of the Social? Refiguring the Territory of Government'. *Economy and Society*, 25/3: 321–56.

ROSE, N. (2000). 'Government and Control'. *British Journal of Criminology*, 40/2: 321–39.

ROSHIER, R. (1973). 'The Selection of Crime News by the Press', in S. Cohen and J. Young (eds), *The Manufacture of News*. London: Constable.

ROSOW, E. (1978). *Born to Lose*. New York: Oxford University Press.

ROWE, M. (2004). *Policing, Race and Racism*. Cullompton: Willan.

ROWE, M. (ed.) (2007). *Policing Beyond Macpherson*. Cullompton: Willan.

Rowe, M. (2008). *Introduction to Policing*. London: Sage.

Rowe, M., and Garland, J. (2003). 'Have You Been Diversified Yet? Developments in Police Community and Race Relations Training in England and Wales'. *Policing and Society*, 13/4: 399–411.

Rowe, M., and Garland, J. (2007). 'Police Diversity Training: A Silver Bullet Tarnished?', in M. Rowe (ed.), *Policing Beyond Macpherson*. Cullompton: Willan.

Royal Commission on Criminal Justice (1993). *Report*. London: HMSO. Cm. 2263.

Royal Commission on Criminal Procedure (1981). *Report and Law and Procedure*. London: HMSO. Cmnd 8092.

Royal Commission on Police Powers and Procedure (1929). *Report*. London: HMSO. Cmnd. 3297.

Royal Commission on the Police (1962). *Final Report*. London: HMSO. Cmnd 1728.

Rubinstein, J. (1973). *City Police*. New York: Ballantine.

Ruehlman, W. (1974). *Saint with a Gun*. New York: New York University Press.

St Johnston, E. (1978). *One Policeman's Story*. Chichester: Barry Rose.

Sampson, R. (2009). 'Disparity and Diversity in the Contemporary City: Social (Dis)order Revisited'. *British Journal of Sociology*, 60/1: 1–31.

Sampson, R., and Raudenbush, S. (1999). 'Systematic Social Observation of Public Spaces: A New Look at Disorder in Urban Neighborhoods'. *American Journal of Sociology*, 105/3: 603–51.

Sanders, A., and Young, R. (2007a). 'From Suspect to Trial', in M. Maguire, R. Morgan, and R. Reiner (eds), *The Oxford Handbook of Criminology* (4th edn). Oxford: Oxford University Press.

Sanders, A., and Young, R. (2007b). *Criminal Justice* (3rd edn). Oxford: Oxford University Press.

Sanders, A., and Young, R. (2008). 'Police Powers', in T. Newburn (ed.), *Handbook of Policing* (2nd edn). Cullompton: Willan.

Sanders, W. (1977). *Detective Work*. Glencoe, MN: Free Press.

Saulsbury, W., Mott, J., and Newburn, T. (eds) (1996). *Themes in Contemporary Policing*. London: Police Foundation/Policy Studies Institute.

Savage, S. (1984). 'Political Control or Community Liaison?'. *Political Quarterly*, 55/1 (January–March): 48–59.

Savage, S. (2007). *Police Reform*. Oxford: Oxford University Press.

Savage, S. and Milne, B. (2007). 'Miscarriages of Justice', in T. Newburn, T. Williamson, and A. Wright (eds), *Handbook of Criminal Investigation*. Cullompton: Willan.

Savage, S., and Wilson, C. (1987). 'Ask a Policeman: Community Consultations in Practice'. *Social Policy and Administration*, 21/3.

Savage, S., Charman, S., and Cope, S. (2000). *Policing and the Power of Persuasion*. London: Blackstone.

Sayers, D. L. (ed.) (1928). *Tales of Detection*. London: Everyman.

Scarman, Lord (1981). *The Scarman Report: The Brixton Disorders*. London: HMSO. Cmnd 8427.

Schlesinger, P., and Tumber, H. (1992). 'Crime and Criminal Justice in the Media', in D. Downes (ed.), *Unravelling Criminal Justice*. London: Macmillan.

Schlesinger, P., and Tumber, H. (1993). 'Fighting the War Against Crime: Television, Police and Audience'. *British Journal of Criminology*, 33/1: 19–32.

SCHLESINGER, P., and TUMBER, H. (1994). *Reporting Crime*. Oxford: Oxford University Press.

SCHLESINGER, P., TUMBER, H., and MURDOCK, G. (1991). 'The Media Politics of Crime and Criminal Justice'. *British Journal of Sociology*, 442/3: 397–420.

SCHWARTZ, R. D., and MILLER, J. C. (1964). 'Legal Evolution and Societal Complexity'. *American Journal of Sociology*, 70/1: 159–69.

SCRATON, P. (1985). *The State of the Police*. London: Pluto.

SCRATON, P. (ed.) (1987). *Law, Order and the Authoritarian State*. Milton Keynes: Open University Press.

SCRIPTURE, A. (1997). 'The Sources of Police Culture: Demographic or Environmental Variables?'. *Policing and Society*, 7/3: 163–76.

SENIOR, P., CROWTHER-DOWEY, C., and LONG, M. (2007). *Understanding the Modernisation of Criminal Justice*. Maidenhead: Open University Press.

SHADOIAN, J. (1977). *Dreams and Dead Ends*. Cambridge, MA: MIT Press.

SHAPLAND, J., and HOBBS, D. (1989). 'Policing on the Ground', in R. Morgan and D. Smith (eds), *Coming to Terms with Policing*. London: Routledge.

SHAPLAND, J., and VAGG, J. (1987). 'Using the Police'. *British Journal of Criminology* 27/1: 54–63.

SHAPLAND, J., and VAGG, J. (1988). *Policing by the Public*. London: Routledge.

SHARP, D., and ATHERTON, S. (2007). 'To Serve and Protect? The Experiences of Policing in the Community of Young People from Black and Other Ethnic Minority Groups'. *British Journal of Criminology*, 47/5: 746–63.

SHAW, M., and WILLIAMSON, W. (1972). 'Public Attitudes to the Police'. *Criminologist*, 7/26.

SHEARING, C. (1981a). 'Subterranean Processes in the Maintenance of Power'. *Canadian Review of Sociology and Anthropology*, 18/3: 283–98.

SHEARING, C. (ed.) (1981b). *Organisational Police Deviance*. Toronto: Butterworth.

SHEARING, C. (1984). *Dial-A-Cop: A Study of Police Mobilisation*. Toronto: University of Toronto Centre of Criminology.

SHEARING, C. (1992). 'The Relation between Public and Private Policing', in M. Tonry and N. Morris (eds), *Modern Policing*. Chicago, IL: Chicago University Press.

SHEARING, C. (1996). 'Reinventing Policing: Policing as Governance', in O. Marenin (ed.), *Policing Change, Changing Police*. New York: Garland.

SHEARING, C. (2006). 'Reflections on the Refusal to Acknowledge Private Governments', in J. Wood and B. Dupont (eds), *Democracy, Society and the Governance of Security*. Cambridge: Cambridge University Press.

SHEARING, C. (2007). 'Policing Our Future', in A. Henry and D. J. Smith (eds), *Transformations of Policing*. Aldershot: Ashgate.

SHEARING, C., and ERICSON, R. (1991). 'Culture as Figurative Action'. *British Journal of Sociology*, 42/4: 481–506.

SHEARING, C., and LEON, J. (1978). 'Reconsidering the Police Role: A Challenge to a Challenge of a Popular Conception'. *Canadian Journal of Criminology and Corrections*, 19.

SHEARING, C., and STENNING, P. (1983). Private Security: Implications for Social Control'. *Social Problems*, 30/5: 493–506.

SHEARING, C., and STENNING, P. (eds) (1987). *Private Policing*. Beverly Hills, CA: Sage.

SHEEHY, P. (1993). *Report of the Inquiry into Police Responsibilities and Rewards*, 2 vols. London: HMSO. Cm. 2280.

SHEPTYCKI, J. (1993). *Innovations in Policing Domestic Violence*. Aldershot: Avebury.

SHEPTYCKI, J. (1995). 'Transnational Policing and the Makings of a Postmodern State'. *British Journal of Criminology*, 35/4: 613–35.

SHEPTYCKI, J. (1997). 'Insecurity, Risk Suppression, and Segregation: Some Reflections on Policing in the Transnational Age'. *Theoretical Criminology*, 1/3: 303–15.

SHEPTYCKI, J. (1998a). 'Policing, Postmodernism and Transnationalisation'. *British Journal of Criminology*, 38/3: 485–503.

SHEPTYCKI, J. (1998b). 'The Global Cops Cometh'. *British Journal of Sociology*, 49/1: 57–74.

SHEPTYCKI, J. (ed.) (2000a). *Issues in Transnational Policing*. London: Routledge.

SHEPTYCKI, J. (2000b). 'Surveillance, Closed Circuit Television and Social Control'. *Policing and Society*, 9/4: 429–34.

SHEPTYCKI, J. (2000c). 'Policing and Human Rights: An Introduction'. *Policing and Society*, 10/1: 1–10.

SHEPTYCKI, J. (2002). *In Search of Transnational Policing*. Aldershot: Ashgate.

SHEPTYCKI, J. (2007). 'Police Ethnography in the House of Serious and Organised Crime', in A. Henry and D. J. Smith (eds), *Transformations of Policing*. Aldershot: Ashgate.

SHERMAN, L. (1978). *Scandal and Reform: Controlling Police Corruption*. Berkeley, CA: University of California Press.

SHERMAN, L. (1992a). 'Attacking Crime: Police and Crime Control', in M. Tonry and N. Morris (eds), *Modern Policing*. Chicago, IL: Chicago University Press.

SHERMAN, L. (1992b). *Policing Domestic Violence*. New York: Free Press.

SHERMAN, L. (1993). 'Why Crime Control Is Not Reactionary', in D. Weisburd,

C. Uchida, and L. Green (eds), *Police Innovation and Control of Police*. New York: Springer-Verlag.

SHERMAN, L. (2004). 'Research and Policing: The Infrastructure and Political Economy of Federal Spending'. *The Annals*, 593: 156–78.

SHERMAN, L., and BERK, R. (1984). 'The Specific Deterrent Effects of Arrest for Domestic Assault'. *American Sociological Review*, 49 (April): 261–72.

SHERMAN, L., FARRINGTON, D., WELSH, B., and MACKENZIE, D. (eds) (2002). *Evidence-Based Crime Prevention*. London: Routledge.

SHERMAN, L., GOTTFREDSON, D., ECK, J., REUTER, P., and BUSHWAY, S. (1997). *What Works? What Doesn't? What's Promising?* Washington, DC: Department of Justice.

SHINER, M. (2009). *Drug Use and Social Change: The Distortion of History*. Basingstoke: Macmillan.

SHPAYER-MAKOV, H. (2002). *The Making of a Policeman: A Social History of a Labour Force in Metropolitan London 1829–1914*. Aldershot: Ashgate.

SILVER, A. (1967). 'The Demand for Order in Civil Society', in D. Bordua (ed.), *The Police*. New York: Wiley.

SILVER, A. (1971). 'Social and Ideological Bases of British Elite Reactions to Domestic Crises 1829–1832'. *Politics and Society*, 1 (February).

SILVERMAN, E. (1999). *NYPD Battles Crime: Innovative Strategies in Policing*. Boston, MA: Northeastern University Press.

SILVESTRI, M. (2003). *Women in Charge: Policing, Gender and Leadership*. Cullompton: Willan.

SILVESTRI, M. (2007). '"Doing" Police Leadership: Enter the "New Smart Macho"'. *Policing and Society*, 17/1: 38–58.

SIM, J. (1982). 'Scarman: The Police Counterattack', in *Socialist Register 1982*. London: Merlin.

SINGH, G. (2000). 'The Concept and Context of Institutional Racism', in A. Marlow and B. Loveday (eds), *After Macpherson*. Lyme Regis: Russell House.

SKLANSKY, D. (2005). 'Police and Democracy'. *Michigan Law Review*, 103/7: 1699–830.

SKLANSKY, D. (2006). 'Not Your Father's Police Department: Making Sense of the New Demographics of Law Enforcement'. *Journal of Criminal Law and Criminology*, 96/3: 1209–43.

SKLANSKY, D. (2007). 'Police Reform, Occupational Culture, and Cognitive Burn-In', in M. O'Neill, M. Marks, and A.-M. Singh (eds), *Police Occupational Culture*. Oxford: JAI Press.

SKLANSKY, D. (2008). *Democracy and the Police*. Stanford, CA: Stanford University Press.

SKOGAN, W. (1990). *Disorder and Decline*. New York: Free Press.

SKOGAN, W. (2003). *Community Policing: Can It Work?* Belmont, CA: Wadsworth.

SKOGAN, W. (ed.) (2004). 'To Better Serve and Protect: Improving Police Practices'. Special Issue, *The Annals*, 593.

SKOGAN, W. (2006). *Police and Community in Chicago*. Oxford: Oxford University Press.

SKOGAN, W., and FRYDL, K. (eds) (2004). *Fairness and Effectiveness in Policing: The Evidence*. Washington, DC: National Research Council: National Academies Press.

SKOGAN, W., and HARTNETT, S. (1997). *Community Policing, Chicago Style*. New York: Oxford University Press.

SKOGAN, W., and MEARES, T. (2004). 'Lawful Policing'. *The Annals*, 593: 66–83.

SKOLNICK, J. (1966). *Justice without Trial*. New York: Wiley.

SKOLNICK, J. (1969). *The Politics of Protest*. New York: Bantam.

SKOLNICK, J. (2008). 'Enduring Issues of Police Culture and Demographics'. *Policing and Society*, 18/1: 35–45.

SKOLNICK, J., and BAYLEY, D. B. (1986). *The New Blue Line*. New York: Free Press.

SKOLNICK, J., and BAYLEY, D. B. (1988). *Community Policing: Issues and Practices around the World*. Washington, DC: National Institute of Justice.

SKOLNICK, J., and FYFE, J. (1993). *Above the Law: Police and the Excessive Use of Force*. New York: Free Press.

SMITH, D. A., and VISHER, C. A. (1981). 'Streetlevel Justice: Situational Determinants of Police Arrest Decisions'. *Social Problems*, 29/2 (December).

SMITH, D. J. (2007a). 'New Challenges to Police Legitimacy', in A. Henry and D. Smith (eds), *Transformations of Policing*. Aldershot: Ashgate.

SMITH, D. J. (2007b). 'The Foundations of Legitimacy', in T. Tyler (ed.), *Legitimacy and Criminal Justice*. New York: Russell Sage.

SMITH, G. (2001). 'Police Complaints and Criminal Prosecutions'. *Modern Law Review*, 64/3: 372–92.

SMITH, G. (2004a). 'Rethinking Police Complaints'. *British Journal of Criminology*, 44/1: 15–33.

SMITH, G. (2004b). 'What's Law Got To Do With It? Some Reflections on the Police in Light of Developments in New York City', in R. H. Burke (ed.), *Hard Cop/Soft Cop*. Cullompton: Willan.

SMITH, G. (2005). 'A Most Enduring Problem: Police Complaints Reform in England and Wales'. *Journal of Social Policy*, 35/1: 121–41.

SMITH, G. (2009). 'Why Don't More People Complain against the Police?'. *European Journal of Criminology*, 6/3: 249–66.

SMITH, N., and FLANAGAN, C. (2000). *The Effective Detective: Identifying the Skills of an Effective SIO.* London: Home Office.

SMITH, P. THURMOND (1985). *Policing Victorian London.* Westport, CT: Greenwood Press.

SOLOMON, E., EADES, C., and GARSIDE, R. (2007). *Ten Years of Criminal Justice under Labour: An Independent Audit.* Kings College, London: Centre for Crime and Justice Studies.

SOLOW, R. (2008). 'Trapped in the New "You're on Your Own" World'. *New York Review of Books*, 55/18: November 20.

SOUHAMI, A. (2007). 'Understanding Institutional Racism: The Stephen Lawrence Inquiry and the Police Service Reaction', in M. Rowe (ed.), *Policing Beyond Macpherson.* Cullompton: Willan.

SOUTH, N. (1988). *Policing for Profit.* London: Sage.

SOUTH, N. (2007). 'Drugs, Alcohol and Crime', in M. Maguire, R. Morgan, and R. Reiner (eds), *The Oxford Handbook of Criminology* (4th edn). Oxford: Oxford University Press.

SPARKS, R. (1992). *Television and the Drama of Crime.* Milton Keynes: Open University Press.

SPARKS, R. (1993). 'Inspector Morse', in G. Brandt (ed.), *British Television Drama in the 1980s.* Cambridge: Cambridge University Press.

SPITZER, S. (1987). 'Security and Control in Capitalist Societies: The Fetishism of Security and the Secret Thereof', in J. Lowman, R. J. Menzies, and T. S. Palys (eds), *Transcarceration: Essays in the Theory of Social Control.* Aldershot: Gower.

SPITZER, S., and SCULL, A. (1977). 'Privatisation and Social Control'. *Social Problems*, 25.

SQUIRES, P. (1998). 'Cops and Customers?: Consumerism and the Demand for Police Services'. *Policing and Society*, 8/2: 169–88.

SQUIRES, P. (2000). *Gun Culture or Gun Control? Firearms, Violence and Social Order*, London: Routledge.

SQUIRES, P. (ed.) (2008). *ASBO Nation: The Criminalisation of Nuisance.* Bristol: Policy Press.

SQUIRES, P., and KENNISON, P. (2010). *Shooting to Kill?: Policing, Firearms and Armed Response.* Oxford: WileyBlackwell.

SQUIRES, P., and STEPHEN, D. (2005). *Rougher Justice: Anti-social Behaviour and Young People.* Cullompton: Willan.

STEAD, P. (ed.) (1977). *Pioneers in Policing.* Montclair, NJ: Patterson Smith.

STEAD, P. (1985). *The Police of Britain.* New York: Macmillan.

STEEDMAN, C. (1984). *Policing the Victorian Community.* London: Routledge.

STEER, D. (1980). *Uncovering Crime.* London: HMSO. Royal Commission on Criminal Procedure Research Study 7.

STENNING, P. (ed.) (1995). *Accountability in Criminal Justice.* Toronto: University of Toronto Press.

STENNING, P. (2000). 'Powers and Accountability of the Private Police'. *European Journal of of Criminal Policy and Research*, 8/3: 325–52.

STENSON, K. (1993). 'Community Policing as a Governmental Technology'. *Economy and Society*, 22/3: 373–89.

STENSON, K. (2001). 'Someday Our Prince Will Come: Zero Tolerance Policing and Liberal Government', in T. Hope and R. Sparks (eds), *Crime, Risk and Insecurity.* London: Routledge.

STENSON, K., and SULLIVAN, R. (eds) (2001). *Crime in Risk Society*. Cullompton: Willan.

STENSON, K., and WADDINGTON, P. A. J. (2007). 'Macpherson, Police Stops and Institutionalised Racism', in M. Rowe (ed.) *Policing Beyond Macpherson*. Cullompton: Willan.

STEPHENS, M., and BECKER, S. (1994). *Police Force, Police Service*. London: Macmillan.

STEVENS, P., and WILLIS, C. (1979). *Race, Crime and Arrests*. London: Home Office Research Unit.

STEVENS, P., and WILLIS, C. (1981). *Ethnic Minorities and Complaints against the Police*. London: Home Office Research Unit.

STEVENSON, J. (1977). 'Social Control and the Prevention of Riots in England 1789–1829', in A. P. Donajgrodski (ed.), *Social Control in Nineteenth-Century Britain*. London: Croom Helm.

STEVENSON, J., and COOK, C. (1977). *The Slump*. London: Jonathan Cape.

STINCHCOMBE, A. (1963). 'Institutions of Privacy in the Determination of Police Administrative Practice'. *American Journal of Sociology*, 69/2: 150–60.

STORCH, R. (1975). 'The Plague of Blue Locusts: Police Reform and Popular Resistance in Northern England 1840–57'. *International Review of Social History*, 20: 61–90.

STORCH, R. (1976). 'The Policeman as Domestic Missionary'. *Journal of Social History*, 9/4 (summer): 481–509.

STORCH, R. (1989). 'Policing Rural Southern England before the Police: Opinion and Practice 1830–1856', in D. Hay and F. Snyder (eds), *Policing and Prosecution in Britain 1750–1850*. Oxford: Oxford University Press.

STYLES, J. (1977). 'Criminal Records'. *Historical Journal*, 20/4.

STYLES, J. (1982). 'An 18th Century Magistrate as Detective'. *Bradford Antiquary*, new series, 47.

STYLES, J. (1983). 'Sir John Fielding and the Problem of Criminal Investigation in 18th-century England'. *Transactions of the Royal Historical Society*, 33.

STYLES, J. (1987). 'The Emergence of the Police: Explaining Police Reform in Eighteenth- and Nineteenth-Century England'. *British Journal of Criminology*, 27/1: 15–22.

SUMNER, C. (1982). '"Political Hooliganism" and "Rampaging Rioters": The National Press Coverage of the Toxteth "Riots"', in C. Sumner (ed.), *Crime, Justice and the Mass Media*. Cambridge: Institute of Criminology. Cropwood Papers 14.

SUMNER, C. (1997). 'Social Control: The History and Politics of a Central Concept in Anglo-American Sociology', in R. Bergalli and C. Sumner (eds), *Social Control and Political Order*. London: Sage.

SUMSER, J. (1996). *Morality and Social Order in Television Crime Drama*. Jefferson, NC: McFarland.

SURETTE, R. (2007). *Media, Crime and Criminal Justice* (3rd edn). Belmont, CA: Wadsworth.

SYMONS, J. (1972). *Bloody Murder*. London: Penguin.

TARLING, R., and BURROWS, J. (1985). 'The Work of Detectives', in K. Heal, R. Tarling, and J. Burrows (eds), *Policing Today*. London: HMSO.

TAWNEY, R. H. (1931). *Equality*. London: Unwin [1964 reprint].

TAWNEY, R. H. (1935/1981). *The Attack and Other Papers*. Nottingham: Spokesman.

TAYLOR, D. (1997). *The New Police in Nineteenth-Century England: Crime, Conflict and Control*. Manchester: Manchester University Press.

TAYLOR, D. (1998). *Crime, Policing and Punishment in England, 1750–1914*. London: Macmillan.

TAYLOR, H. (1998a). 'The Politics of the Rising Crime Statistics of England and Wales 1914–1960'. *Crime, History and Societies*, 2/1: 5–28.

TAYLOR, H. (1998b). 'Rising Crime: The Political Economy of Criminal Statistics since the 1850s'. *Economic History Review*, 51: 569–90.

TAYLOR, H. (1999). 'Forging the Job: A Crisis of 'Modernisation' or Redundancy for the Police in England and Wales 1900–39'. *British Journal of Criminology*, 39/1: 113–35.

TAYLOR, I. (1981). *Law and Order: Arguments for Socialism*. London: Macmillan.

TAYLOR, I. (1997). 'Crime, Anxiety and Locality: Responding to the "Condition of England" Question at the End of the Century'. *Theoretical Criminology*, 1/1: 53–76.

TAYLOR, I. (1998a). 'Crime, Market-Liberalism and the European Idea', in V. Ruggiero, N. South, and I. Taylor (eds), *The New European Criminology*. London: Routledge.

TAYLOR, I. (1998b). 'Free Markets and the Cost of Crime: An Audit for England and Wales', in P. Walton and J. Young (eds), *The New Criminology Revisited*. London: Macmillan.

TAYLOR, I. (1999). *Crime in Context: A Critical Criminology of Market Societies*. Cambridge: Polity Press.

TAYLOR, R. (2001). *Breaking Away from Broken Windows* Boulder, CO: Westview.

TEMKIN, J. (2002). *Rape and the Legal Process* (2nd edn). Oxford: Oxford University Press.

TEMKIN, J., and KRAHE, B. (2008). *Sexual Assault and the Justice Gap: A Question of Attitude*. Oxford: Hart.

TERRILL, W., PAOLINE, E., and MANNING, P. (2003). 'Police Culture and Coercion'. *Criminology*, 41/4: 1003–34.

THIEL, D. (2009). *Policing Terrorism: A Review of the Evidence*. London: Police Foundation.

THOMPSON, E. P. (1968). *The Making of the English Working Class*. London: Penguin.

THOMPSON, E. P. (1971). 'The Moral Economy of the English Crowd'. *Past and Present*, 50.

THOMPSON, E. P. (1975). *Whigs and Hunters*. London: Penguin.

THOMPSON, E. P. (1980). *Writing by Candlelight*. London: Merlin.

THOMPSON, E. P. (1992). *Customs in Common*. London: Merlin.

TILLEY, N. (2008). 'Modern Approaches to Policing: Community, Problem-Oriented and Intelligence-Led', in T. Newburn (ed.), *Handbook of Policing* (2nd edn). Cullompton: Willan.

TOBIAS, J. (1967). *Crime and Society in the Nineteenth Century*. London: Penguin.

TUCK, M. (1989). *Drinking and Disorder: A Study of Non-Metropolitan Violence*. London: HMSO. Home Office Research and Planning Unit Study 108.

TULLETT, T. (1981). *Murder Squad*. London: Granada.

TUMBER, H. (1982). *Television and the Riots*. London: British Film Institute.

TURK, A. (1982). 'Policing in Political Context', in R. Donelan (ed.), *The Maintenance of Order in Society*. Ottawa: Canadian Police College.

TURNER, A. (2009). 'How to Tame Global Finance'. *Prospect*, August: 162.

TUSKA, J. (1978). *The Detective in Hollywood*. New York: Doubleday.

TYLER, T. (2004). 'Enhancing Police Legitimacy'. *The Annals*, 593: 84–99.

TYLER, T. (ed.) (2007). *Legitimacy and Criminal Justice*. New York: Russell Sage.

VALIER, C. (2004). *Crime and Punishment in Contemporary Culture*. London: Routledge.

VALVERDE, M. (2006). *Law and Order: Images, Meanings, Myths*. London: Routledge.

VAN MAANEN, J. (1978). 'Watching the Watchers', in P. K. Manning and J. Van Maanen (eds), *Policing*. Santa Monica, CA: Goodyear.

VICK, C. (1981). 'Police Pessimism', in D. Pope and N. Weiner (eds), *Modern Policing*. London: Croom Helm.

VOGLER, R. (1991). *Reading the Riot Act*. Milton Keynes: Open University Press.

VON HIRSCH, A., and SIMESTER, A. (eds) (2006). *Incivilities: Regulating Offensive Behaviour*. Oxford: Hart.

WACQUANT, L. (1992). 'Towards a Social Praxeology: The Structure and Logic of Bourdieu's Sociology', in P. Bourdieu and L. Wacquant, *An Invitation to Reflexive Sociology*. Cambridge: Polity.

WADDINGTON, D. (2007). *Policing Public Disorder*. Cullompton: Willan.

WADDINGTON, D., JOBARD, F., and KING, M. (eds) (2009). *Rioting in the UK and France: A Comparative Analysis*. Cullompton: Willan.

WADDINGTON, D., JONES, K., and CRITCHER, C. (1989). *Flashpoints: Studies in Public Disorder*. London: Routledge.

WADDINGTON, P. A. J. (1982a). 'Why the "Opinion Makers" No Longer Support the Police'. *Police*, December.

WADDINGTON, P. A. J. (1982b). 'Conservatism, Dogmatism and Authoritarianism in the Police: A Comment'. *Sociology*, November: 592–4.

WADDINGTON, P. A. J. (1983). 'Beware the Community Trap'. *Police*, March: 34.

WADDINGTON, P. A. J. (1987). 'Towards Paramilitarism: Dilemmas in Policing Civil Disorder'. *British Journal of Criminology*, 27/1: 37–46.

WADDINGTON, P. A. J. (1991). *The Strong Arm of the Law*. Oxford: Oxford University Press.

WADDINGTON, P. A. J. (1993a). *Calling the Police*. Aldershot: Avebury.

WADDINGTON, P. A. J. (1993b). '"The Case against Paramilitary Policing" Considered'. *British Journal of Criminology*, 33/3: 14–16.

WADDINGTON, P. A. J. (1994). *Liberty and Order: Public Order Policing in a Capital City*. London: UCL Press.

WADDINGTON, P. A. J. (1999a). *Policing Citizens*. London: UCL Press.

WADDINGTON, P. A. J. (1999b). 'Police (Canteen). Sub-Culture: An Appreciation'. *British Journal of Criminology*, 39/2: 286–308.

WADDINGTON, P. A. J., and WRIGHT, M. (2008). 'Police Use of Force, Firearms and Riot-Control', in T. Newburn (ed.), *Handbook of Policing* (2nd edn). Cullompton: Willan.

WADDINGTON, P. A. J., STENSON, K., and DON, D. (2004). 'In Proportion: Race and Police Stop and Search'. *British Journal of Criminology*, 44/6: 889–914.

WAKEFIELD, A. (2003). *Selling Security: The Private Policing of Public Space*. Cullompton: Willan.

WAKEFIELD, A. (2006). *The Value of Foot Patrol: A Review of Research*. London: Police Foundation.

WALBY, S., and ALLEN, J. (2004). *Domestic Violence, Sexual Assault and Stalking: Findings from the British Crime Survey*. London: Home Office.

WALDEN, J. (1982). *Visions of Order*. Toronto: Butterworth.

WALKER, A., FLATLEY, J., KERSHAW, C., and MOON, D. (2009). *Crime in England and Wales 2008/09*. London: Home Office.

WALKER, C. (2002). 'Miscarriages of Justice and the Correction of Error', in M. McConville and G. Wilson (eds.), *Handbook of Criminal Justice Process*. Oxford: Oxford University Press.

WALKER, C., and STARMER, K. (eds) (1999). *Miscarriages of Justice* (2nd edn). London: Blackstone.

WALKER, N. (1996). 'Defining Core Police Tasks: The Neglect of the Symbolic Dimension'. *Policing and Society*, 6/1: 53–71.

WALKER, N. (2000). *Policing in a Changing Constitutional Order*. London: Sweet & Maxwell.

WALKER, N. (2008). 'The Pattern of Transnational Policing', in T. Newburn (ed.), *Handbook of Policing* (2nd edn). Cullompton: Willan.

WALKER, S. (1993). *Taming the System: The Control of Discretion in Criminal Justice 1950–1990*. New York: Oxford University Press.

WALKER, S. (2004). 'Science and Politics in Police Research: Reflections on Their Tangled Relationship'. *The Annals*, 593: 137–55.

WALKLATE, S., and EVANS, K. (1999). *Zero Tolerance or Community Tolerance? Managing Crime in High Crime Areas*. Aldershot: Ashgate.

WALL, D. (1998). *The Chief Constables of England and Wales*. Aldershot: Avebury.

WALSH, J. L. (1977). 'Career Styles and Police Behaviour', in D. H. Bayley (ed.), *Police and Society*. Beverly Hills, CA: Sage.

WAMBAUGH, J. (1971). *The New Centurions*. London: Sphere/New York: Dell.

WAMBAUGH, J. (1973a). *The Blue Knight*. London: Sphere/New York: Dell.

WAMBAUGH, J. (1973b). *The Onion Field*. London: Sphere/New York: Dell.

WAMBAUGH, J. (1976). *The Choir-Boys*. London: Futura/New York: Dell.

WARD, T. (1986). *Death and Disorder*. London: Inquest.

WATERS, I. (1996). 'Quality of Service: Politics or Paradigm Shift?', in F. Leishman, B. Loveday, and S. Savage (eds), *Core Issues in Policing*. London: Longman.

WATERS, I. (2007). 'Policing, Modernity and Postmodernity'. *Policing and Society*, 17/3: 257–78.

WATSON, C. (1971). *Snobbery with Violence*. London: Eyre & Spottiswoode.

WATTS-MILLER, W. (1987). 'Party Politics, Class Interest and Reform of the Police 1829–56'. *Police Studies*, 10/1: 42–60.

WEATHERITT, M. (1986). *Innovations in Policing*. London: Croom Helm.

WEATHERITT, M. (ed.) (1989). *Police Research: Some Future Prospects*. Aldershot: Avebury.

WEATHERITT, M. (1993). 'Measuring Police Performance: Accounting or Accountability?', in R. Reiner and S. Spencer (eds), *Accountable Policing: Empowerment, Effectiveness and Equity*. London: Institute for Public Policy Research.

WEATHERITT, M. (ed.) (1998). *Zero Tolerance*. London: Police Foundation.

WEAVER, M. (1994). 'The New Science of Policing: Crime and the Birmingham Police Force, 1839–1842'. *Albion*, 26: 289–308.

WEBB, J. (1959). *The Badge: The Inside Story of the Los Angeles Police Department*. London: W. H. Allen/New York: PrenticeHall.

WEBER, M. (1964). *The Theory of Social and Economic Organization*. Glencoe, IL: Free Press.

WEBSTER, C. (2007). *Understanding Race and Crime*. Maidenhead: Open University Press.

WEINBERGER, B. (1981). 'The Police and the Public in Mid-19th-century Warwickshire', in V. Bailey (ed.), *Policing and Punishment in 19th Century Britain*. London: Croom Helm.

WEINBERGER, B. (1991). *Keeping the Peace? Policing Strikes in Britain 1906–1926*. Oxford: Berg.

WEINBERGER, B. (1995). *The Best Police in the World*. London: Scolar Press.

WEISBURD, D., and ECK, J. (2004). 'What Can Police Do to Reduce Crime, Disorder, and Fear?'. *The Annals*, 593: 42–65.

WEISBURD, D., UCHIDA, C., and GREEN, L. (eds) (1993). *Police Innovation and Control of Police*. New York: Springer-Verlag.

WEISBURD, D., MASTROFSKI, S., MCNALLY, A., GREENSPAN, R., and WILLIS, J. (2003). 'Reforming to Preserve: Compstat and Strategic Problem Solving in American Policing'. *Criminology and Public Policy*, 2/3: 421–56.

WESTLEY, W. (1970). *Violence and the Police*. Cambridge, MA: MIT Press.

WESTMARLAND, L. (2001a). *Gender and Policing: Sex, Power and Police Culture*. Cullompton: Willan.

WESTMARLAND, L. (2001b). 'Blowing the Whistle on Police Violence: Gender, Ethnography and Ethics'. *British Journal of Criminology*, 41/3: 523–35.

WHITAKER, B. (1964). *The Police*. London: Penguin.

WHITAKER, B. (1979). *The Police in Society*. London: Eyre Methuen.

WHITE, J. (1986). *The Worst Street in North London*. London: Routledge.

WHITE, J. (2007). *London in the Nineteenth Century: A Human Awful Wonder of God*. London: Cape.

WHITE, J. (2008). *London in the Twentieth Century: A City and Its People*. London: Vintage.

WHITFIELD, J. (2004). *Unhappy Dialogue: The Metropolitan Police and Black Londoners in Post-War Britain*. Cullompton: Willan.

WHITFIELD, J. (2007). 'The Historical Context: Policing and Black People in Post-War Britain', in M. Rowe (ed.), *Policing Beyond Macpherson*. Cullompton: Willan.

WILBANKS, W. (1987). *The Myth of a Racist Criminal Justice System*. Monterey, CA: Brooks/Cole.

WILKINSON, R., and PICKETT, K. (2009). *The Spirit Level: Why More Equal Societies Almost Always Do Better*. London: Allen Lane.

WILLIAMS, C. A. (2000). 'Counting Crimes or Counting People: Some Implications of Mid-Nineteenth Century British Police Returns'. *Crime, History and Societies*, 4/2: 77–93.

WILLIAMS, G. (2009). *Shafted: The Media, the Miners' Strike and the Aftermath*. London: Campaign for Press and Broadcasting Freedom.

WILLIAMS, M., and ROBINSON, A. (2004). 'Problems and Prospects with Policing the Lesbian, Gay and Bisexual Community in Wales'. *Policing and Society*, 14/3: 213–32.

WILLIAMS, P., and DICKINSON, J. (1993). 'Fear of Crime: Read All About It? The Relationship between Newspaper Crime Reporting and Fear of Crime'. *British Journal of Criminology*, 33/1: 33–56.

WILLIAMSON, T. (ed.) (2006). *Investigative Interviewing*. Cullompton: Willan.

WILLIAMSON, T. (ed.) (2008). *The Handbook of Knowledge-Based Policing*. Chichester: Wiley.

WILLIAMSON, T., and MOSTON, S. (1990). 'The Extent of Silence in Police Interviews', in S. Greer and R. Morgan (eds), *The Right to Silence Debate*. Bristol: Bristol University Centre for Criminal Justice.

WILLIS, C. (1983). *The Use, Effectiveness and Impact of Police Stop and Search Powers*. London: Home Office Research Unit.

WILLIS, C., MACLEOD, J., and NAISH, P. (1988). *The TapeRecording of Police Interviews with Suspects*. London: HMSO. Home Office Research Study 97.

WILSON, C. P. (2000). *Cop Knowledge: Police Power and Cultural Narrative in Twentieth Century America*. Chicago, IL: Chicago University Press.

WILSON, J. Q. (1968). *Varieties of Police Behavior*. Cambridge, MA: Harvard University Press.

WILSON, J. Q. (1975). *Thinking about Crime*. New York: Vintage.

WILSON, J. Q., and BOLAND, B. (1978). 'The Effects of the Police on Crime'. *Law and Society Review*, 12/3: 367–90.

WILSON, J. Q., and BOLAND, B. (1981). 'The Effects of the Police on Crime: A Response to Jacob and Rich'. *Law and Society Review*, 16/1.

WILSON, J. Q., and KELLING, G. (1982). 'Broken Windows'. *Atlantic Monthly*, March: 29–38.

WOFFINDEN, B. (1989). *Miscarriages of Justice*. London: Coronet.

WOOD, J., and DUPONT, B. (eds) (2006). *Democracy, Society and the Governance of Security*. Cambridge: Cambridge University Press.

WOOD, J., and SHEARING, C. (2007). *Imagining Security*. Cullompton: Willan.

WOODCOCK, J. (1991). 'Overturning Police Culture'. *Policing*, 7/3: 172–82.

WREN-LEWIS, J. (1981–2). 'TV Coverage of the Riots'. *Screen Education*, 40 (autumn–winter): 15–33.

WRIGHT, A. (2002). *Policing: An Introduction to Concepts and Practice*. Cullompton: Willan.

YOUNG, J. (1971). 'The Role of the Police as Amplifiers of Deviancy', in S. Cohen (ed.), *Images of Deviance*. London: Penguin.

YOUNG, J. (1999). *The Exclusive Society*. London: Sage.

YOUNG, M. (1991). *An Inside Job: Policing and Police Culture in Britain*. Oxford: Oxford University Press.

YOUNG, M. (1993). *In the Sticks: An Anthropologist in a Shire Force*. Oxford: Oxford University Press.

YOUNG, M. (1995). 'Black Humour—Making Light of Death'. *Policing and Society*, 5/2: 151–68.

YOUNG, R. (2008). 'Street Policing After PACE: The Drift to Summary Justice', in E. Cape and R. Young (eds), *Regulating Policing*. Oxford: Hart.

ZANDER, M. (2006). *The Police and Criminal Evidence Act 1984* (3rd edn). London: Sweet & Maxwell.

ZANDER, M. (2007). *Response to Home Office Consultation on the Future of PACE*. London: LSE.

ZEDNER, L. (2003). 'Too Much Security?'. *International Journal of the Sociology of Law*, 31/1: 155–84.

ZEDNER, L. (2006). 'Policing Before the Police'. *British Journal of Criminology*, 46/1: 78–96.

ZEDNER, L. (2009). *Security*. London: Routledge.

ZIMRING, F. (2007). *The Great American Crime Decline*. New York: Oxford University Press.

INDEX